Not the Other Avant-Garde

THEATER: THEORY/TEXT/PERFORMANCE
Enoch Brater, Series Editor

Recent Titles:

NOT THE OTHER AVANT-GARDE

The Transnational Foundations of
Avant-Garde Performance

Edited by James M. Harding and John Rouse

The University of Michigan Press
Ann Arbor

Copyright © by the University of Michigan 2006
All rights reserved
Published in the United States of America by
The University of Michigan Press
Manufactured in the United States of America
⊚ Printed on acid-free paper

2009   2008   2007   2006   4   3   2   1

A CIP catalog record for this book is available from the British Library.

Library of Congress Cataloging-in-Publication Data

Not the other avant-garde : the transnational foundations of avant-
    garde performance / edited by James M. Harding and John Rouse.
        p.   cm. — (Theater—theory/text/performance)
    Includes index.
    ISBN-13: 978-0-472-09931-3 (cloth : alk. paper)
    ISBN-10: 0-472-09931-0 (cloth : alk. paper)
    ISBN-13: 978-0-472-06931-6 (pbk. : alk. paper)
    ISBN-10: 0-472-06931-4 (pbk. : alk. paper)
    1. Experimental theater—History—20th century.   2. Experimental drama—
20th century—History and criticism.   I. Harding, James Martin, 1958–
II. Rouse, John.   III. Series.
PN2193.E86N68   2006
792.02'23—dc22   2005033818

Acknowledgments

First and foremost, we want to thank our contributors for the work that they put into making this anthology a reality. Working with them has been an immensely rewarding experience, one that has challenged us and transformed our thinking. We also want to thank LeAnn Fields for the support that she has shown for this project from beginning to end. We are grateful to her for her general advice and for her numerous insightful suggestions. LeAnn is an amazingly positive force in our profession, and working with her is a genuine privilege. Special thanks also go to Rebecca Mostov and the rest of the staff at University of Michigan Press for navigating this book through the production process. The preparation of this book would have been impossible without the help of Taylor Ball who worked long into numerous nights helping us complete the last round of editing. One could not ask for a better editorial assistant.

Several of the fundamental ideas John brought to our editorial discussions were first developed in conversation with colleagues in the University of California system. These conversations continue now under the aegis of the Multicampus Research Group in International Performance and Culture. We hope this anthology will provide a useful contribution to the group's research.

Finally, James would like to thank his family, Friederike Eigler, Lukas Eigler-Harding, and Daniel Eigler-Harding, for giving him the time, space and support to complete this project.

Contents

Introduction

James M. Harding and John Rouse

> The attempt to say what avant-garde criticism is *not,* but ought to be, tends to show indirectly (indeed, *ad absurdum*) what avant-garde art *is* in the minds of certain individuals or groups.
> —Renato Poggioli, *Theory of the Avant-Garde*

Theory, Avant-Garde Gestures, and Performance

For well over two decades, studies of the theatrical avant-garde have hovered amid a repetition of theoretical tropes drawn loosely from the influential arguments of scholars like Renato Poggioli, Matei Calinescu, and Peter Bürger—scholars whose theorizing of the avant-garde has overlooked performance as a *pivotal* category for defining the avant-garde itself. This project began as a response to this antiperformative bias in the theorizing of the avant-garde. It questions whether our understanding of avant-garde performance is compromised by being filtered through theories that fail to recognize, let alone conceptualize, the avant-garde gesture as first and foremost a performative act. Ultimately, however, this anthology pushes well beyond the simple conclusion that understanding avant-garde *performance* necessitates understanding the avant-garde as performative. The theoretical paradigms that emerge in this collection have much broader implications. They strike at the heart of avant-garde studies across the disciplines and are of relevance to all scholars of the avant-garde because they recognize the vital role that performance has to play in the theoretical definition of the avant-garde more generally.

In this regard, the very title of the anthology, *Not the Other Avant-Garde,* vies against the notion of a separate theory of avant-garde performance. It proposes a rethinking of the avant-garde that gives central prominence to the innovative and radical performative practices of experimental artists. At the same time, this title suggests new cultural directions and invites a consideration of the work of experimental artists from around the globe. Playing upon the notion of "the Other," it suggests that we reconsider the cultural boundaries that have historically demarcated scholarly conceptions of the avant-garde, for in doing so we can lay the foundation for a substantially retheorized notion of the avant-garde.

This retheorizing is the product of a conscious editorial strategy that draws critically upon recent trends in performance studies, and nowhere is our debt to performance studies more evident than in how we as editors conceptualized the opportunity presented by a performance-based approach to the avant-garde. We assumed that focusing on the performative foundations of avant-garde gestures could precipitate a retheorizing of the avant-garde in large part because that focus could move avant-garde studies in a direction that, in many respects, already serves as a point of departure for performance studies—in a direction, that is, that embraces a broad cultural understanding of performance and that recognizes the relevance to the conceptual paradigms that shape the avant-garde itself. The assumption here is that a culturally diverse understanding of performance can ultimately shift away from the Eurocentrism that has dominated avant-garde studies almost since its inception. Our aim is to move from a Eurocentric to a transnational conception of the avant-garde—one which recognizes that the sites of artistic innovation associated with the avant-garde tend to be sites of unacknowledged cultural hybridity and negotiation. We grounded our anthology in this recognition, hoping that its culturally diverse notions of performance will initiate a larger rethinking of the avant-garde than we have been able to accomplish within the limited scope of this single anthology.

We realize that a focus on performance in studies of the avant-garde is its own provocation, and that, as with any scholarship that takes aim at long-established theoretical and cultural paradigms, this anthology will likely encounter a measure of resistance. But if this extension proves to be controversial, we welcome the ensuing debate because it may generate a critical discussion about the avant-garde that is long overdue. Indeed, if there are those who suggest that conceptualizing the avant-garde (as this anthology does) along transnational lines is a vexed enterprise, we would note that the term *avant-garde* has always been vexed. This very point, in fact, is the central thesis of Paul Mann's important *Theory-Death of the Avant-Garde*. To be sure, Mann neither looks to performance nor beyond a Eurocentric frame. But he does conceptualize the avant-garde within a dynamic, evident at both practical and theoretical levels, of constantly evolving resistance and contestation—a dynamic that lends itself well to the course of inquiry this anthology pursues.

As a site of experimentation, contestation, and indeed as a mark of hybridity, the term *avant-garde* is less fixed than in flux, and its contested status invites a discussion about whether the avant-garde is fundamentally and ideologically tied to a Eurocentric cultural sensibility or whether the existing histories of the avant-garde have privileged a Eurocentric framing of practices that were always already present in a variety of unacknowledged forms across the spectrum of world cultures. This anthology embraces the latter position. But that embrace is at once an invitation and a challenge. If it demands a response, it does so from a conceptual terrain that necessitates a fundamental shift even in the terms with which we debate the avant-garde. The implications of that shift are manifold. Beyond the historiographical particulars of constructing fresh accounts of the avant-garde, changing the very terms with which it is conceptualized will be of significance to many scholars who are actively rethinking the aesthetics and histories of modernism.

Shifting the terms with which we debate the avant-garde suggests the need for a comparable shift in how we think about twentieth-century theater more generally. Ironically, it also bears on the conceptual grounding of performance studies. Indebted though we may be to the cultural definition of performance offered in works like Richard Schechner's *Performance Studies: An Introduction,* our focus on the avant-garde sets one of the more dominant definitions of performance into a critical dialogue with its own foundational assumptions. For while our primary aim in this book has been to make it increasingly problematic for scholars to situate Europe at the center of either performative innovation or politically charged experimental performance, that strategy's debt to performance studies is paid dialectically, returning in refracted form the definitions emanating from scholars like Barbara Kirshenblatt-Gimblett and Richard Schechner, who have argued not only that performance studies takes its "lead from the historical avant-garde" (Kirshenblatt-Gimblett) but, more importantly, that "if performance studies were an art, it would be avant-garde" (Schechner).[1]

Although such rhetoric may have more to do with positioning performance studies at the forefront of disciplinary innovation than with provoking new paradigms for the avant-garde itself, we single out these scholars' linking of performance studies to the avant-garde because that gesture is haunted by a Eurocentric specter that, we believe, can be exorcised if called out critically into the light of day. Indeed, this haunting underscores the stakes in the rethinking of the avant-garde that our anthology would provoke. If, on the one hand, we continue to conceptualize the avant-garde primarily as an expansive and globally influential European cultural commodity, then linking performance studies to the avant-garde as Kirshenblatt-Gimblett and Schechner do may not be all that desirable. For at a conceptual level, such linkage tends to establish disturbing parallels between performance studies' interest in global/intercultural performance and the kind of western cultural chauvinism that permeated the European avant-garde's interest in what it appropriated under the guise of primitivism, to cite only one example. If, on the other hand, we illuminate—as the essays collected in this volume do—a broad cultural and transnational diversity that, despite the existing historiography of the avant-garde, has always flourished beyond the Eurocentric short-sightedness of existing conceptions of the avant-garde gesture, then the linkage between the avant-garde and performance studies takes on a transformative resonance. Reinforcing, while drawing forcefully upon, the culturally diverse conceptions of performance embraced by performance studies theorists and scholars, a performance-based theory of the avant-garde can thus reorient our theoretical understanding of the avant-garde as cultural historical phenomenon.

Like any other reorientation, the one advocated by this anthology necessitates some critical awareness of how Anglo-European theories of the avant-garde have developed before the larger significance of a culturally diverse performance-based theory of the avant-garde becomes evident. Obtaining that awareness is not a particularly daunting task. With regard to history or theory, for example, we need only look back to the latter half of the twentieth century to discover the scholarly models that have largely shaped current conceptions of the avant-garde. Although one might look further back—at least as far as Ortega y Gasset's *Dehumanization of Art* (1925) or Walter Benjamin's "On Surrealism" (1929)—for critical assessments of the avant-garde as an already existing cultural phenomenon, much of the current scholarly discourse on the avant-garde still bears the stamp of work produced during the 1970s by scholars like Matei Calinescu and Peter Bürger in the wake of Renato Poggioli's *Theory of the Avant-Garde* (1962). Calinescu and Bürger are particularly important in this regard because at one level the competing notions of the avant-garde that they posit establish the larger working parameters against which the collective arguments of this anthology are positioned.

Implicit in our critical focus on Calinescu and Bürger is a tacit—

although, we would emphasize, highly qualified—acceptance of the characterizations of avant-garde tendencies that their predecessor, Renato Poggioli, articulated in his *Theory of the Avant-Garde*. We have little disagreement, for example, with Poggioli's now widely accepted description of the avant-garde as being consistently marked by an "activistic moment," in which art is deployed "to agitate *against* something or someone." Nor do we disagree with Poggioli's argument that this activism tends to be accompanied by antagonistic postures that, ranging from hostility "toward the public" to irreverence "toward tradition," are nonetheless almost always grounded in a critical "opposition to the historical and social order."[2] Such arguments echo across decades as well as across disciplines and have found resonance among scholars of the theatrical avant-garde like Christopher Innes, who bases the introductory paragraph of his *Avant-Garde Theater, 1892–1992* on Poggioli, or even like Richard Schechner, who in the introduction to *The Future of Ritual* not only echoes Poggioli with his argument that "the historical avant-garde was characterized by the twin tendency to make something new that was also in opposition to prevailing values," but also adopts Poggioli's own sense of history by finding a precedent in the Romantic poets.[3]

As we will see momentarily, it is precisely with regard to the unproblematic construction of such linkage that we must qualify how the work in this anthology concurs with the conceptual trajectory that runs from Poggioli through Calinescu and Bürger to Innes and Schechner. If, in principle, the essays in this anthology acknowledge the avant-garde's opposition to "the historical and social order," that is because Poggioli initially conceptualizes those arguments broadly and, consequently, because the very concepts of "opposition," "history," and the "social order" are pliable. In Poggioli's argument these concepts accommodate an exceptionally wide array of avant-garde activities but, more importantly, also accommodate a critical understanding of the avant-garde that runs against the grain of the Western cultural assumptions that surface later in his work and that intensify in the work of subsequent scholars. With regard to the intensification of those assumptions, Bürger provides a particularly important example, especially since this intensification indicates a central continuity in two works (Bürger's and Calinescu's) that offer substantially different notions of the avant-garde.

As is well known, Peter Bürger's own *Theory of the Avant-Garde* (1974) marked a radical departure from Poggioli's work. Arguing that the avant-garde is characterized first by a critical attitude toward art as an institution and second by an urge to bring art back into the sphere of quotidian experience where it can become an effective agent of change, Bürger's thesis is noteworthy in two respects. It provoked a controversial but generative shift in how we think about the avant-garde. But it also further tailored our understanding of the avant-garde to a specific historical and highly specialized European sensibility, one that situated the avant-garde urge to blur art and life against the backdrop of art's increasing autonomy (that separation of art from the social sphere which coincided with the aestheticism of *l'art pour l'art*).[4] Indeed, Bürger's intense focus on this distinctly European context is one of the important ways that his work differs from Calinescu's since that focus ultimately does not even allow for the viable American avant-garde that Calinescu recognizes.

Although it is important to understand how Calinescu and Bürger differ, the complement to that understanding is a critical awareness of the privileged assumptions they share, which have ultimately produced a narrow and culturally biased historiography of the avant-garde. So while the contrasting work of Calinescu and Bürger merits examination because it is typical of the divergent paths—which would initially appear to separate historians from theorists—that studies have taken since Poggioli's *Theory of the Avant-Garde,* those paths traverse a common conceptual typology. At the center of that typology, their notions of the avant-garde converge in at least three significant ways. They converge in a hierarchical ordering of aesthetic categories, in a reinforcement of European cultural prerogatives, and in a uniform linear conception of history.

Aesthetic Categories, Models of Literary Criticism, and Cultural Chauvinism

With regard to aesthetic categories, scholars as divergently inclined as Calinescu and Bürger unite in an antiperformance bias manifested in the use of paradigms drawn from literary history and criticism. Indeed, both scholars echo Poggioli's focus on literary culture as a point of departure for reflections on avant-garde proclivities across (and between) the disciplines. This focus might not be alarming were it not that, for all intents and purposes, even dramatic literature is precluded both from that point of departure and from what lies beyond it. Poggioli looks back to seminal figures among the symbolist poets, Rimbaud and Verlaine, for example, whom he positions on a continuum that goes back to the Romantics.[5] In a comparable focus, Calinescu pushes this discussion well back into the Renaissance and into published critical accounts of Renaissance poets, which he bridges to the literary objectives of radical Romantic poets who, he and Poggioli argue, set the stage for an emerging nineteenth-century cultural avant-garde. Bürger also draws connections between the avant-garde and the Romantics—Friedrich Schiller in particular, whose problematic theoretical attempts to assign a "social function" to art, Bürger suggests, was a catalyst for the subsequent, more radical attempts by the avant-garde to reunite art with "the praxis of life."[6]

It is worth noting that Bürger never mentions Schiller's work as a dramatist and perceives no correlation between his own conception of "praxis" and the spheres of the performative that the dramatic works of Schiller invites. Rather, his interest in Schiller remains abstract and theoretical, focusing entirely on Schiller's inability to adequately conceptualize the role of art in everyday life because his bourgeois sensibility limited the aesthetic questions he was able to ask. Here Bürger's disregard of the performative is particularly important. For while it is true that Schiller's dramatic works lend themselves well to the bourgeois theater that the European performative avant-garde rejected, that rejection involved gestures to radicalize audiences by wedging performance into the space of their bourgeois complacency. These gestures were a combination of both performance and praxis, a combination that repeatedly touches upon the quotidian and that unfortunately doesn't register in Bürger's discussion.

What is interesting about Bürger's critical account of Schiller—especially given Bürger's disregard of performance—is how he frames his discussion of Schiller with the literary-critical paradigms of hermeneutics developed by Hans-Georg Gadamer in *Truth and Method*. With regard to questions of the performative, there is a certain irony in this embrace of Gadamer, particularly because Bürger uses Gadamer's arguments to highlight how the insights of a paradigm are premised upon assumptions that precalibrate knowledge by limiting the types of questions one asks. We would argue that Bürger's theories of the avant-garde are shaped, indeed limited, by the questions he does not ask regarding performance but also regarding cultural specificity as well. While Bürger may effectively use Gadamer to make a critical transition into what he posits as the conceptual innovations of the (post-Romantic) avant-garde, his embrace of Gadamer's hermeneutics ultimately comes back to haunt him.

Drawing direct parallels with the scientific community's rigorous assessment of the traditional categories of the hard sciences, Bürger advocates the need to assess literary categories, not according to some absolute truth value, but rather according to their historical value. This means assessing them, first of all, according to the "questions they permit one to ask" and, second, according to the questions they "already" exclude.[7] Ironically, within the models of the avant-garde that he and Calinescu provide, performance is a casualty in both respects. Given the European avant-garde's pronounced hostility toward established literary culture, one might expect Bürger to use the parallel he draws with the scientific method as an opportunity to explore performance as a potential, indeed even a defining, site of the avant-garde's critical resistance to literature as an established cultural institution. But in this respect, Bürger implicitly concurs with Poggioli, as does Calinescu as well: with the exception of a few instances when performance is positioned in a subordinate relation to literary precedent and authority, all of these critics overlook performance as a viable category for understanding the avant-garde as a mode of artistic expression. In short, performance is already excluded from the questions they have allowed themselves to ask. In response, we echo Elin Diamond, who has suggested that comparable exclusions within modernist aesthetics betray an anxious recognition of performance as a "messy, *historicizing* moment that interrupts the integrity of the written document."[8] But if performance is messy, it is messy not only because it is far more ephemeral, nebulous, and unstructured as a cultural phenomenon than literature but also because historically it has proven to be more difficult to limit to a specific nationalistic agenda.

It is not a matter of coincidence that cultural historians speak of national literatures as if they are a given while at the same time speaking of national performances only in some specialized sense. The ideological underpinnings of national conceptions of literature are still evident today. The study of literature is so closely associated with the construction of national identities that it is worth asking whether the Eurocentric framing of the avant-garde which accompanies the focus on literature by critics like Poggioli, Calinescu, and Bürger is not in fact a product of conceptual habits that have long characterized Western literary criticism as an institution—habits, we might add, that arguably disparage performance from the perspective of many of the same assumptions of cultural superiority that characterized the privileging of print culture over oral traditions in the eighteenth century.

There are important echoes across the centuries in these two ideologically charged moments of cultural bias and privilege. An earlier and more equitable assessment of oral traditions vis-à-vis print culture might have diluted the cultural chauvinism that fueled the concept of individual European national literatures and ultimately helped drive colonial expansion. Similarly, a less invidious view of performance vis-à-vis literary culture (such as the type of assessment advocated in this anthology) can help dispel the conception of the avant-garde as an exportable European cultural commodity. If the literary paradigms endorsed by Poggioli, Calinescu, and Bürger are a kind of hegemonic center of authority in our conceptions of the avant-garde, a more equitable assessment of performance would disrupt, in an echo of Derrida, the literary text's colonialist-like ability "to govern . . . from a distance" and thus acknowledge the avant-garde's intercultural and transcultural groundings.[9]

Although performance, as a critical aesthetic category, may not carry the same burdensome nationalistic baggage that literature does and may not govern from a distance, the goal of this anthology is not a simple inversion that privileges performance at the expense of literature. That would merely repeat what is perhaps the most problematic truism to have found its way into popular scholarly conceptions of the theatrical avant-garde: the common assumption (based in large part on a simplistic reading of Artaud) that the theatrical avant-garde was fundamentally at odds with text-based theater. Even when we limit our focus to the Western tradition, it is important to recognize that theater historians have been arguing for some time *against* a conception of avant-garde theater that is based upon a simple dichotomy between text and performance.[10] Indeed, this dichotomy would sever expressionism, futurism, Dada, and even surrealism from the traditions of the European avant-garde theater, and exclude important figures like Gertrude Stein, whose literary dramatic works have long served as a crucial point of reference for American avant-gardists like the Living Theatre, Richard Foreman, and Robert Wilson.[11] We mention Stein in particular, not merely because of the prominent position she finally has been granted in studies such as Arnold Aronson's *American Avant-Garde Theatre* (New York: Routledge, 2000) but also because her work reminds us of the opportunities for rethinking the avant-garde that lie beyond an unjustified disregard of performance and beyond a concomitant simplistic dichotomy between text-based theater and unscripted performance. In simplest terms, we see in the reception of Stein's work among experimental artists as diversely inclined as the Living Theatre and Robert Wilson an example of coexisting but distinct trajectories within the American avant-garde. Scholars tend to see little problem in the fact that while the political *engagement* of the Living Theatre is legendary, so too is Wilson's almost exclusive focus on aesthetic form. At the same

time, scholars tend not to recognize that the contrasting trajectories
which the Living and Wilson exemplify are hardly unique to the American context. If Stein's dramatic literature has been a meeting point of
both the overtly political and the primarily aesthetic trajectories, it is
not their source. It merely highlights a divergence that scholars can find
in other cultural contexts as well. If there is ample room for both the
overtly political and the primarily aesthetic in the history of the American avant-garde, then we would be hard pressed to come up with a
justification for not extending a similar flexibility to other cultures as
we begin to assess the generative role that they have played in an emergent transnational avant-garde.

If our notions of the Western avant-garde have often simultaneously
embraced both radical politics and radical aesthetics, then the door has
long been open for the kind of parallel explorations included in this
volume, explorations whose divergent trajectories we feel little need to
reconcile. There is thus ample room in our conceptions of the avant-
garde for studies like John Conteh-Morgan's essay, which emphasizes
the strong political focus of African theater, as well as Joachim Fiebach's
essay, which, while rich in political implication, focuses on the aesthetic
forms of African performative expression—forms that have their own
evolutionary trajectory before, after, and even in response to the Europeans' appropriation of them for their own experimental theatrical
practices. Indeed, Fiebach's arguments make it increasingly difficult to
see in those forms the radical break with history that is typically
identified with the experimental performative practices of the Western
avant-garde.

At the very least, Fiebach's study of traditional African performance
practices highlights how selectively that break has been conceptualized
by Western scholars, and one of the larger implications emerging from
his piece is the constructed nature not only of the history of the avant-
garde itself but of the history from which it ostensibly broke. In fact,
Marvin Carlson makes a very similar point in his essay on avant-garde
drama in the Middle East, particularly in his discussion of the work of
Egyptian artists like Tawfiq al-Hakim, who was very much aware of,
and indeed impressed by, European experimental theater and who, having discovered the work of Ionesco, Vautier, and Adamov, quickly recognized that their supposed theatrical innovations could be found in the
artistic traditions of Egyptian performance culture. Fiebach's emphasis
on form in sub-Saharan performance, Carlson's on theatrical innovation
in Egypt, and Conteh-Morgan's on the development of an experimen-

tal political theater in Francophone Africa, join in concert with the other essays in this volume to counter the undynamic universalizing conception of history that existing narratives of the avant-garde presume. In short, what emerges from the essays collected here is a decentered and nonlinear notion of the histories of the avant-garde(s).

More about these historiographical questions momentarily, but first one further aspect of the relation of the avant-garde to literary culture warrants comment. If even within the European conceptual paradigm of the avant-garde the dichotomy between text and performance is more complex than is often assumed, it is even harder to maintain this dichotomy outside of Europe. Essays in this anthology demonstrate that Indian, Middle Eastern, Mexican, Argentinean, Japanese, and African cultures have co-opted European text and performance traditions not in moments of deference to or affirmation of those traditions, nor in moments of subordination to a literary culture that "govern[s] . . . from a distance," but rather in gestures that have taken great and irreverent liberties with those traditions, that subvert their governing authority, and that have radically modified and adapted them to their own cultural and political ends. Indeed, this propensity for adaptation is, in one form or another, identified by all the authors in this book whose essays discuss postcolonial performance. Their discussions point to a productive tension amid the uneven currents of history, a tension between indigenous and European forms and ideas. Sudipto Chatterjee's study of progressive, postindependence Bengali theater is particularly noteworthy in this regard, especially his discussions of performance and "colonial hybridity."

The conscious contrast with European drama marked by these moments of hybridity indicates a tendency cited not only by Chatterjee and Carlson but also by Adam Versényi and Jean Graham-Jones. They remind us that in their experimental practices, non-Western avant-gardes frequently felt little need to define themselves in opposition to the dramatic literary text. In this regard, it is worth mentioning Harry Elam's essay on the Black Arts Movement, a movement, as Elam reminds us, that was propelled as much by the production of dramatic literature as it was by experimental performance practices because of a long history of being excluded from the canon of drama literature. Similar tendencies are identifiable well beyond the African-American context. Repeatedly, this emphasis on dramatic literature contributed to a burgeoning or renewed sense of cultural identity that served as a locus of opposition vis-á-vis a history of repression. For artists like those mentioned by Elam or for those responding to the cultural legacies of colonialism, a break with the past coincided with the emergence of a postcolonial identity and a fundamental rethinking of the historical narratives produced and maintained by Western cultural assumptions.

Against the backdrop of disparate historical trajectories, these breaks with the past constitute primary instances of negotiated hybridity in the defining moments of a global avant-garde. David Goodman and Peter Eckersall identify similar instances in Japan. In this anthology, such hybrid gestures surface time and again, independent of one another. It is a rather astonishing discovery. These gestures mark a fundamental dimension of the very different historiography of avant-garde performance that this anthology advocates.

Origins, Historiography, and Breaks with History

In turning now to the underlying historiographical assumptions that have dominated European and U.S. studies of the avant-garde, we take up a more focused critique of Matei Calinescu's work. If Bürger has had a profound impact on theoretical conceptualizations of the avant-garde, then Calinescu has had a comparable impact on historical narratives of the avant-garde. His *Faces of Modernity* (1977),[12] while in many respects critical of Poggioli, nonetheless echoed Poggioli's own interest in the question of the avant-garde's "origins" and thus reaffirmed his linear conceptual history of the avant-garde. That echo and its reaffirmation of Poggioli's linear conception of history play off what has amounted to an oddly tolerated conceptual inconsistency in scholarship on the avant-garde, an inconsistency that has positioned the history of the avant-garde within a posited temporal linearity even as it has repeatedly emphasized the avant-garde's ruptures with history. In this regard, the question of origins, which has produced a fixed set of answers that scholars tend to rehearse as a matter of course, is indicative of a problematic conception of history itself.[13] In simplest terms, that linear conception of history has skewed our understanding of the avant-garde because it tends to fashion history after a Hegelian model—that is, as a uniform and universal force. The problem with this model is that it cannot take the avant-garde's break with history seriously because it ultimately privileges history (or Hegel's *Geist*) above all else.

After more than two decades of postmodern thinkers admonishing us not to think of history without always also thinking about historiography, there is a certain irony in discovering avant-garde studies to be one of the last refuges for conceptions of history grounded in philosophical idealism. If we are to take seriously the avant-garde's breaks with history, we must see in them a philosophy of history fundamentally different from that which has governed studies of the avant-garde heretofore. We must recognize in those breaks a profound awareness of the inseparability of historiography and history. With each of these ruptures, we must ask: Which history? Constructed at whose expense and based upon whose exclusion? In almost any other scholarly context, these questions would seem obvious. But bringing them to bear in this context finally opens the door to a consideration of avant-garde gestures emanating from cultural contexts beyond the borders of a conventional Eurocentric history of the avant-garde and beyond the suggestion of their European origins.

Unfortunately, that suggestion has been a mainstay of avant-garde studies for four decades and is thus prevalent enough to merit some individual attention—if only to highlight the radically different course in scholarship that this anthology advocates. Probably the most influential discussion of origins unfolded in the mid-1970s when Calinescu took issue with the historian Donald Drew Egbert, who a half-decade earlier in his near encyclopedic *Social Radicalism and the Arts* (1970) had similarly challenged the influential genealogy that Renato Poggioli had posited in *Theory of the Avant-Garde*. Neither Calinescu nor Egbert questioned the general etymology suggested by Poggioli. All three generally acknowledged that the term *avant-garde* is a gallicism initially used by the military as a characterization of elite, front-guard "shock troops." All agreed that, following the late Romantics, an emerging radical Left picked up the term in the nineteenth century as a metaphor for the front line of revolutionary political activism, and all generally agreed that sometime in the middle to late nineteenth century this metaphorical usage began circulating within the discourses of cultural criticism as a general characterization of politically oriented experimental art, a characterization that gained widespread currency in the twentieth century. The issue for Egbert and Calinescu was thus not so much the chronology that Poggioli mapped out, but rather a debate about when the term "avant-garde" actually surfaced within the discourses of cultural criticism.

The point of contention in this discussion centered on the first appearance of the term *avant-garde* as a description of cultural activity. Whereas Poggioli had attributed the term to Gabriel-Désiré Laverdant in a political tract from 1845,[14] Egbert found it in the radical political philosopher Henri de Saint-Simon in 1825.[15] In a historian's game of one-upmanship, Calinescu located a much earlier use by the sixteenth-century French humanist lawyer and historian Etienne Pasquier.[16] But as

Antoine Compagnon noted not long after the second edition of Calinescu's study (now titled *Five Faces of Modernity*) appeared, Pasquier's use
of the term had virtually nothing in common with the kind of "socially
committed art" that Saint-Simonians assumed when they characterize
the artists who, working together with scholars, scientists, and industri-
alists, would serve as the radical frontrunners of a new political and cultural order.[17] Like Donald Egbert before him, Compagnon pointed to
Saint-Simon's *Opinions* as the most likely initial source of the now pervasive association of the avant-garde with politically oriented artistic
expression. But this did not put the debate to rest.

After having taken issue with Egbert over who first used the term in
cultural criticism, Calinescu returned to Egbert's interest in Saint-
Simon's *Opinions, littéraires, philosophiques et industrielles* and in particular
to the chapter "L'Artiste, le savant et l'industriel," where, Calinescu
readily acknowledged, for the first time "the Romantic use of avant-
garde in a literary-artistic context was directly derived from the language
of revolutionary politics."[18] Noting that, though "generally attributed to
Saint-Simon," *Opinions* was in fact a collaborative volume, Calinescu
expressed dismay that Egbert had attributed "the use of the term avant-
garde to Saint-Simon" rather than to Saint-Simon's close friend and
associate, Olinde Rodrigues, who actually wrote the dialogue
("L'Artiste, le savant et l'industriel") where the term "avant-garde"
appears—a mistake that, oddly enough, Compagnon repeated in his
implicit critique of Calinescu[19] Given the avant-garde's own playful history with categories of authorship (both literary and artistic), there is
perhaps a certain irony in Calinescu's fixation on this instance of misattribution. Beyond that irony, however, we might ask whether this
fixation on authorship and originality actually enhances our understanding of the avant-garde.

The operative assumption in Calinescu's work is that the better we
understand where the term *avant-garde* originated, the better we will also
understand the avant-garde as a cultural phenomenon. Calinescu is certainly not unique in making this type of assumption; nor are we opposing it. In the late 1960s, for example, Theodor Adorno argued that "in
aesthetics the attempt to get at the essence of art through an inquiry into
its origins inevitably leads to disappointing results."[20] The disappointment here, however, strikes at the very heart of what this anthology
would offer as an alternative. In fixating on the origins of the term
avant-garde, Calinescu cast his lot with the linguistic and with the liter-

ary, opting for the letter rather than for the performative gesture. Our point of departure has been a recognition that the avant-garde gesture, indeed, the avant-garde urge is culturally diffuse.

A Note on Structure

For this anthology we have selected essays that illustrate two specific arguments: that the first- and second-wave avant-gardes (pre- and post-World War II) were always already a transnational phenomenon; and that the performative gestures of these avant-gardes were culturally hybrid forms that emanated simultaneously from a wide diversity of sources rather than from a European center. Advocating a progressive global perspective, we of course face the problem of inclusiveness. Strive as we might to provide a broad spectrum of cultural traditions, we have inevitably included some at the expense of others. Perhaps it is enough to say that our concern is to provide studies that exemplify, rather than exhaust, a global notion of the avant-garde. It is certainly our hope that the models provided by these essays will provoke an examination of comparable trends in performative traditions not explored in this anthology.

Acknowledging these gaps in coverage, we have elected not to spread the scope of our studies too widely and have frequently paired essays in an effort to provide a sense of the different issues that emerged within specific cultures before and after the last World War. A good example is the two essays on Japanese performance by Peter Eckersall and by David Goodman. While Japan does not stand for all of Asia (nor Argentina or Mexico for all of Latin America), we see advantages in providing considerations of developments within particular cultures over a period of decades, and we have weighed such concentration against the benefit of providing a wide array of perspectives on the avant-garde in vastly different cultural contexts.

This latter concern led to the inclusion of two of the five unpaired essays in this volume, Sudipto Chatterjee's study of postindependence Bengali theater and Marvin Carlson's of Egyptian theater. At one level, the same rationale applies to Harry Elam's "The *TDR* Black Theatre Issue: Refiguring the Avant-Garde." But in this case our decision to include the essay also derived from a desire to highlight our own subject position as Western scholars. Elam's detailed analysis of Schechner's role in the publication of *TDR*'s 1968 "Black Theatre Issue" raises critical questions that may be extended to our own problematic agency as Western editors who purport to give discursive space to marginalized voices. We hope those voices nonetheless emerge in this collection, and that they have as profound an effect on the readers' understanding of the avant-garde as they have had on ours.

We close by mentioning the two remaining unpaired essays in the anthology, which literally bookend the project. Hannah Higgins's essay presents a convincing case for considering the Fluxus movement as a more transparent model of tendencies that, in many respects, have always characterized the dynamics of avant-garde performance. As Higgins suggests, the highly creative transgression of borders (physical and cultural) that was a part of this postwar aesthetic contributed to a larger rethinking of the avant-garde within the international circle of artists who were associated with the Fluxus movement. While there may be limitations as to how far one can use Fluxus as a model for reconceptualizing avant-garde performance along transnational lines, Higgins's essay is certainly a step in the right direction. Indeed, her essay sets an example for rethinking a wide variety of movements that have long been framed within Western aesthetic models. James Harding's essay, coming as it does from one of the editors of this anthology, consciously lays out the theoretical strategies for such an undertaking, with the immediate objective of providing the conceptual paradigms with which readers can link the other essays in the anthology and see their collective significance.

It is our sincere hope that the essays in this volume will provoke other scholars to use studies of performance as a strategy for reconceptualizing the avant-garde in periods, regions, and cultures we have had to leave unaddressed. There is much more to discover about the transnational character of avant-garde movements than we have been able to examine, and at the very least we hope that the work herein will cultivate a critical reassessment of the place that studies of performance hold in enlarging our understanding of the histories of the avant-gardes in a global context.

Notes

1. Both passages come from Richard Schechner's *Performance Studies: An Introduction* (New York: Routledge, 2002), 3.

2. Poggioli, *Theory of the Avant-Garde,* 25–26. Gerald Fitzgerald's English translation of Poggioli's *Teoria dell'arte d'avantguardia* (Bologna: Societàeditrice il Mulino, 1962) was published in 1968 by Harvard University Press. All references are to the translation.

3. Richard Schechner, *The Future of Ritual* (New York: Routledge, 1993), 7. Christopher Innes's book *Avant-Garde Theatre, 1892–1992* was also published by Routledge in 1993.

4. See chapter 3 of Peter Bürger, *Theory of the Avant-Garde,* trans. Michael Shaw (Minneapolis: University of Minnesota Press, 1984). Bürger's book was originally published as *Theorie der Avantgarde* (Frankfurt am Main: Suhrkamp, 1974).

5. Poggioli, *Theory of the Avant-Garde,* 11.

6. Bürger, *Theory of the Avant-Garde,* 46, 49.

7. Bürger, *Theory of the Avant-Garde,* 4.

8. Elin Diamond, "Modern Drama/Modernity's Drama," *Modern Drama* 44 (2001): 4.

9. Jacques Derrida, *Writing and Difference,* trans. Alan Bass (Chicago: University of Chicago Press, 1978), 235.

10. See, for example, *Contours of the Theatrical Avant-Garde,* ed. James Harding (Ann Arbor: University of Michigan Press, 2000), which is devoted to the question of performance and textuality. In particular, see the essays by Christopher Innes, Michael Vanden Heuvel, and Erika Fischer-Lichte.

11. One need only look at the collection of plays in Bert Cardullo and Robert Knopf's anthology *Theatre of the Avant-Garde, 1890–1950* (New Haven: Yale University Press, 2001) to see how grounded in text-based theater is the European avant-garde tradition.

12. Calinescu's *Faces of Modernity* was first published by Indiana University Press in 1977. A second, revised edition entitled *Five Faces of Modernity* was published in 1987 by Duke University Press, three years after the English translation of Bürger's *Theory of the Avant-Garde.*

13. Although one might select a number of different examples, the opening chapter of David Graver's *Aesthetics of Disturbance: Anti-Art in Avant-Garde Drama* (Ann Arbor: University of Michigan Press, 1995) comes to mind.

14. For Poggioli's discussion of Laverdant, see *Theory of the Avant-Garde,* 9.

15. Donald Drew Egbert, *Social Radicalism and the Arts* (New York: Knopf, 1970), 121.

16. Calinescu, *Five Faces of Modernity,* 97–98.

17. Antoine Compagnon, *The 5 Paradoxes of Modernity* (New York: Columbia University Press, 1990), 34.

18. Calinescu, *Five Faces of Modernity,* 101.

19. Calinescu, *Five Faces of Modernity,* 101. Compagnon repeated the mistake in his implicit critique of Calinescu (*The 5 Paradoxes of Modernity,* 34); more recently, Bert Cardullo did so again in the introduction to the anthology *Theater of the Avant-Garde,* coedited with Robert Knopf. The misattribution in Cardullo's introduction is a particularly odd occurrence given the clear debt that Cardullo owes Calinescu's work. For Cardullo's discussion of Rodrigues and Saint-Simon, see "En Garde! The Theatrical Avant-Garde in Historical, Intellectual, and Cultural Context," in *Theater of the Avant-Garde,* 12.

20. Theodor Adorno, *Aesthetic Theory,* trans. C. Lenhardt (New York: Routledge and Kegan Paul, 1984), 447.

From Cutting Edge to Rough Edges
On the Transnational Foundations of
Avant-Garde Performance

James M. Harding

> Assume therefore that, as a result of specific historical circumstances, a
> theory or idea pertaining to those circumstances arises. What happens to
> it when, in different circumstances and for new reasons, it is used again
> and, in still more different circumstances again? What can this tell us
> about theory itself, its limits, its possibilities, its inherent problems and
> what can it suggest to us about the relationship between theory and
> criticism, on the one hand, and society and culture on the other?
> —Edward Said, "Traveling Theory"

"In Advance Of": An Introduction

From its very inception the Western theatrical avant-garde has found
itself entangled in the cultural politics of colonialism. Examples of this
entanglement are not difficult to find since they are often scantly masked
beneath aesthetic categories like primitivism or negritude, to name only
the most obvious, or even beneath a patronizing embrace of Asian performance traditions, as occurred in Russia, Germany, and France. In
Ubu Roi, for example, Alfred Jarry provocatively embraced a fashioned
savage primitivism that not only shocked William Butler Yeats but that
theater historians have also consistently cited as "the beginning of the
performative avant-garde."[1] In Zurich, the Dadaists displayed similar
proclivities. Hugo Ball costumed himself in a facsimile of a witch doctor's headdress before reciting his *Lautegedichte* at the Cabaret Voltaire.[2]
His friend and cofounder of the cabaret, Richard Huelsenbeck, followed
the reading of his own fabricated "Negro poems" with a debate on their
authenticity, and when Jan Ephriam, the owner of the cabaret, gave
Huelsenbeck examples of genuine African poems that he had collected
as a sailor, Huelsenbeck recited them at the cabaret but decided that they
would be better (perhaps even more authentic) if, as in his fabricated

poems, he added the sound "Umba" to the end of each line.[3] Even Antonin Artaud's intense fascination with Balinese dance theater was mediated, as is well known, by the colonial fair where he first encountered Balinese dancers.[4] While these and similar moments in the history of avant-garde performance indicate the extent to which experimental artists were anxious to find alternatives to bourgeois cultural expression, they also remind us that the Western avant-garde sustained European cultural prerogatives even amid its most vociferous assaults on bourgeois culture. The legacies of such entanglement have left historians of the avant-garde confronting a grossly *underplayed* dilemma. Either we argue that the whole of the avant-garde is not contained within the particulars of its colonialist attitudes and thus circumvent the entanglement, or we cite it as an example of the pervasive ideological corruption wrought by Western imperialism and begin the hard search for models of artistic expression uncontaminated by colonialist presumptions.

Granted, my construction of this dilemma is polemical, but the stakes are higher than they might first appear. For the choice one makes here has a major impact on how we understand the legacies of the avant-garde, especially with regard to its influence (beyond the borders of Europe and) on the world stage. A profoundly neglected uncertainty looms over the question of whether the expanding influence of the avant-garde indicates an escape from its colonialist birthing or is another example of imported Western cultural hegemony. With this latter concern in mind, the limits of our current theories of the avant-garde and the need to revisit the colonialist underpinnings of avant-garde performance become evident. Indeed, there is a special appropriateness to this return now. At a time when we hear calls for a radical reassessment of the very concept "avant-garde" and its concomitant histories, a return to the avant-garde's subtle entanglement in the politics of colonialism offers the possibility not only of fundamentally retheorizing the avant-garde but of shifting its basic terrain. The argument here is very simple: if we turn a blind apologetic eye to that entanglement or if we see only it and dismiss the idea of the avant-garde as another ideological conduit for European cultural hegemony, then we have failed to recognize that the colonialist underpinnings of avant-garde performance mark it not as a European but as a fundamentally global cultural phenomenon.

The arguments that follow do not downplay the contested intercultural exchanges and vexed negotiations that have shaped this phenomenon. Indeed, the shortest summary of this essay's main assertion is that nothing more aptly characterizes the avant-garde than the moments of

contested intercultural exchange at its colonialist birthing. Those
exchanges mark not only the avant-garde, but culture itself, and in an
effort to maintain the critical integrity of those contested moments, I
have chosen to characterize the avant-garde as a transnational phenomenon, first because the term highlights the global dimensions of the
avant-garde, and second because the term *transnationalism* is itself contested, signifying both the processes of global hegemony and the practice
of counterhegemonic resistance.

Center to Edge/Edge to Center

Important opportunities for rethinking the history, indeed the very concept, of the avant-garde can be found by considering whether the notion
of an edge (in this case, the cutting edge) presupposes a center or, at the
very least, a point of origin from which one might plot a rectilinear
course to the edge itself. With respect to the avant-garde, the question
of whether we can have an edge without a center is another way of asking whether we can have an advanced guard without some anchored
sense of what is at its rear. Historically, scholars have presumed that the
former necessitates the latter and have characterized this edge-to-center
relationship dialectically, positioning the avant-garde at margins hostile
to the bourgeois center of society. While this critical paradigm is evident
at least as far back as Renato Poggioli's *Theory of the Avant-Garde* (1962),
some of the most important theoretical work along this line emerged in
the early 1990s when Paul Mann rejected the notion that the avant-
garde occupies a stable site of resistance vis-à-vis society at large. Moving from a static to a more dynamic understanding of avant-garde gestures, Mann places the trajectory of the avant-garde within an enduring
continuum of negation and affirmation, or what he calls the "anti and its
recuperation."[5] Recuperation, he argues, "is not simply the defeat of
negation; rather both are functions of the same dialectal apparatus."[6] The
avant-garde, following Mann, is thus propelled forward in an ever
expanding process of innovation that is dogged by an inescapable and
equally expanding process of appropriation. Indeed, according to this
argument, the two processes are one. Hostile though it may be to bourgeois culture, the avant-garde thus not only reaffirms the social mainstream in the authority its rebelliousness tacitly acknowledges; it also
revitalizes the center of that exceptionally resilient mainstream by feeding it with fresh cultural expression.

    Yet for all the significance of Mann's problematizing of the avant-garde's anticultural or negating gestures, his argument still falls well within the established paradigm of conceptualizing the avant-garde as an edge undulating outward from a center taken for granted. Indeed, Mann's argument meshes quite well with Michael Kirby's classic definition of the avant-garde in *The Art of Time* (1969): "'avant-garde' refers specifically to a concern with the historical *directionality* of art. An advanced guard implies a rear guard or at least the main body of troops following behind."[7] There is a lot to be learned from the reaffirmation of this paradigm in Mann's argument, especially since the dialectic of "the anti and its recuperation," like the militaristic origins of the term *avant-garde* itself, bears a striking resemblance to the structures of Western bourgeois expansionism. This resemblance, while overlooked in Mann's arguments, touches upon what is perhaps the most disturbingly familiar and resoundingly conservative note within the seemingly dissonant and radical cords of avant-garde expression. Indeed the very notion of a front guard feeding the vital center presents us with a discomforting reminder that the term *avant-garde* first emerged as a characterization of artistic practice in the heyday of nineteenth-century European colonial enterprise, when edge-to-center/center-to-edge relationships structured the hegemonic mechanisms of empire. The subtle affirmation of empire in Artaud's interest in Balinese dance theater (which he encountered at the Paris Colonial Exhibition in 1931) is but one example of the myriad ways that colonialist attitudes and European avant-garde proclivities could circulate with relative ease within the same conceptual economy. Indeed, they often converged. Certainly this was the case with Western modernism's fascination with what it appropriated from other cultures under the conceptual rubric of primitivism, an appropriation that provided what subsequently became staple contours of European avant-garde expression.

The European construction of primitivism has far-reaching implications not merely for modernism in general but for the avant-garde in particular. Any serious rethinking of the avant-garde thus must grapple with this latter example from the contested edges of empire, where an assumption of European cultural superiority and its ability to civilize "savage" cultures after its own Western image provided ideological cover for the appropriation, on physical, intellectual, and aesthetic levels, of non-Western cultural artifacts. Significant steps toward precisely such a reassessment of the avant-garde play an important role in the latter chapters of Rebecca Schneider's book *The Explicit Body in Performance,* where, in the preface to an eloquent exploration of the blurred notions of the primitive and the feminine in the Western modernist imaginary, she argues that the European avant-garde positioned itself within racist and contradictory constructions of the primitive. While assuming, on the one hand, that the "'primitive' practices and artifacts of 'other' cultures . . . [were] less evolutionarily developed" than European culture,[8] the avant-garde simultaneously embraced, on the other hand, "the savage primitive" as a mode of "confrontation [with] the tenets of high modernism."[9] The context for these disparate inclinations, Schneider argues, was a nostalgia for the prelapsarian, which the Western avant-garde first projected onto African and Oceanic cultures and then embraced in a gesture of reestablishing "connectedness to all that modernity had 'lost.'"[10] Whatever opposition such gestures mounted against the modern institutions of Western bourgeois society, the characterizations of non-Western cultures as prelapsarian or as less developed were but two sides of a single coin purchasing European cultural prerogatives at the expense of a richer and more dynamic intercultural exchange between different peoples. Predictably, it was an expense paid for by non-Western cultures.

While nostalgia for the prelapsarian is a signature trope of modernist aesthetics, the flip side of this nostalgia has played a far more enduring role in the history and historiography of the avant-garde. Indeed, there is a pressing need for scholars to rethink their understanding of the avant-garde in such a way as to disentangle the idea of an art that is "in advance of" from a simultaneous reaffirmation of the hierarchical assumption that non-Western cultures were less sophisticated or less developed than their European counterparts. This is no easy task, especially since the idea of an art that is "cutting edge" or that is "in advance of" tends to imply, by its very definition, a hierarchy of evolution. So if we are to break from the Western cultural chauvinism of movements like primitivism, we need to disabuse ourselves of Eurocentric truisms about the cutting edge of art that have found their way into works as important as Richard Schechner's *The Future of Ritual*. When in the early pages of that work Schechner mentions in passing that the "historical avant-garde took shape in Europe during the last decades of the nineteenth century. . . . [and] soon spread to many places around the world,"[11] the chronology he endorses reminds us that the center-to-edge/edge-to-center framing of the avant-garde in scholarship is as much a model for constructing an ideologically loaded and biased history of European artistic influence as it is a model for characterizing the forward and most advanced positions of artistic expression. Ironically, it is a model that places Europe simultaneously at both center and edge: privileging it as the center of innovation while positioning it at the cultural frontiers as the harbinger of the new. Yet this truism propagates a myth, placing European expression at the cutting edge because European artists supposedly understood what non-Western artists were presumably incapable of comprehending about their own work. It is to erase the moments of exchange between European and non-European (e.g., African, Asian, Oceanic) cultures and to perpetuate the injustices that historically marked those exchanges by positing their consequence as a point of origin rather than as a product of an earlier moment of appropriation, subordination, and conquest. In short, the model assumed by Schechner (and he is certainly not alone in this assumption) tacitly elides the contested exchange between cultures and privileges a representation that posits the repackaged return of looted intellectual and aesthetic property "to many places around the world" as European originality, innovation, and enlightenment. The center-to-edge model underlying Schechner's chronology assumes a uniform, rectilinear historiography of aesthetic innovation that provides ideological cover for erasing a dubious and circular path of return.

From the "Cutting Edge" to "Rough Edges"

The one redeeming quality of this selective chronology of the avant-garde is that it is merely a matter of scholarly convention to locate the foundations of avant-garde expression subsequent to the moments of intercultural exchange rather than in the exchanges themselves. Since colonial history reminds us that these exchanges were far from equitable, one can speculate that this historiographic convention is another example supporting Walter Benjamin's contention that history is seldom written by the vanquished. But there is much more to be gained by breaking with convention and shifting our focus back to this earlier contested and largely erased moment. The issue here is not merely to offer some record of that moment, as does Christopher Innes's chapter "The Politics of Primitivism" in *Avant-Garde Theatre, 1892–1992*. It is rather to finally see the aporia beneath the apology in Innes's recognition, on the one hand, that "the whole artistic enterprise of interculturalism remains inherently problematic" because of its links to "nineteenth-century imperialism" while, on the other, he glosses over the implications of that recognition with the claim that "the attempt to reproduce the effects of 'primitive' or ritual theatre helps to explain avant-garde elements that might otherwise seem puzzling."[12] For not only does that moment of problematic intercultural exchange belong to the history of the avant-garde, which, as Innes recognizes, is reason in itself for including it, but highlighting that moment of contested exchange provides us with a vantage point from which we might begin to retheorize the avant-garde as a whole—something that Innes does not do. To some extent, that vantage point sets three distinct theoretical areas into critical relief. Roughly speaking, those areas can be characterized as contested edges, simultaneous articulations, and apostate adaptations. But the individual titular categories are less important than the theorizing they facilitate.

Above all, a return to the site of cultural exchange and contestation between cultures gives us a very different vision of the center-to-edge/edge-to-center relationship than that which heretofore has served as a paradigm for conceptualizing the avant-garde. The most crucial revision of that paradigm, gained in the step back to the site of cultural contestations, is the recognition of a plurality of edges devoid of an identifiable center, a plurality that the rectilinear center-to-edge/edge-to-center convention in scholarship on the avant-garde has obscured. Here, a rethinking of the avant-garde can fruitfully begin with a move from a singular to plural notion of the edge. In simplest terms, that move necessitates that we reconceptualize our notion of the vanguard within a theory of borders, and that we supplant *the cutting edge* with *the rough edges* of contestation, "struggle," and "negotiation," which as Michal Kobialka has noted, are implied in the "palimpsest quality" of borders "and the multifocal aspect of representational systems or practices used to narrate" them.[13] Some justification for this turn to border theory as a segue into a reconceptualized vision of the avant-garde can be found in the fact that, while two-sided, the border is, like the cutting edge, "a site of resistance or compliance."[14] It is, to echo once again Paul Mann's theory of the avant-garde, a site of "the anti and its recuperation." But more important still is the multisided nature of the border that moves us beyond the universalized notions of history and aesthetics implicit in the linear undercurrents of terms like *cutting edge*. For if nothing else, border theory reminds us that in culture(s) there is no such thing as a jagged edge protruding into an empty space. *The cutting edge* always cuts into its other, one edge not only going against another but also assuming the authority to define or erase the other in the act of expansion. How little is this sense of expansion to be found in the existing theories of the avant-garde! As of yet, scholarship has provided us with a notion of the avant-garde that is conceptualized in relation to its "rear guard" (Kirby) and characterized as "forward look-ing" (Schechner). Yet, conveniently, scholars have neglected to con-sider what the conventional conception of the avant-garde displaces in its forward march and what those displacements say about the paucity of our existing theories of the avant-garde.

Arguably, these displacements are a product of a conceptual framing that has radically limited our ability to see the friction between conflicted edges that provided one of the more important igniting sparks of avant-garde activity—important because it is a spark ignited from a variety of cultural sources spreading simultaneously in a variety of cul-tural directions. Border theory can go a long way toward illuminating those conflicted edges beneath the *cutting edge*. Moreover, moving from the singular notion of the cutting edge to a notion of *borders* where each edge is always already (at least) two-sided, we encounter a profound reminder of the extent to which the implied singular in the notion of a cutting edge maintains an artificially constructed center that is forcefully imposed and that ironically seeks to dull the potential influence of its other not by outpacing it but by exclusion and by casting out that which, though positioned with the vanguard, is heterogeneous to the ideological order whose borders the cutting edge, as a concept, marks and regulates, no matter how cutting that edge might be. If, as Kobialka argues, the border can also be understood as "a wound,"[15] the cutting edge is not only conceptually a perpetrator of that wound; it also buries its victims beneath a historiography that has both elided the defining moments of cultural contestation at the founding of avant-garde practice and erected a European center in their stead.

It is in critical opposition to that fabricated European center that we can look to border theory for a decentered conception of the avant-garde. In this respect, drawing upon the theory of the border in order to decenter the Eurocentric has not only conceptual but also widespread territorial implications for locating and (re)formulating the history of avant-garde expression. In a very literal sense, to decenter the avant-garde is to reconceive its territorial domain and to look beyond the con-ventionally conceived borders of Europe for the convergence of artistic innovation and oppositional politics that so frequently has characterized avant-garde expression. Here the issue is as much how we conceptualize cultural borders as it is how we conceptualize the cutting edge. Indeed, how we conceptualize the former largely determines how we ultimately conceptualize the latter. For it is only possible to use the cutting edge as an arm of Eurocentric exclusions if one adheres to what border theorists have recognized to be an antiquated nineteenth-century definition of culture. Some of the more helpful thinking along this line has come from Alejando Lugo, who, in an important essay entitled "Reflections on Border Theory," argues that "the border region . . . can erode the hegemony of the privileged center" by a process of "deterritorializing" our notions of culture.[16] A pivotal aspect of Lugo's argument that has direct bearing on how we conceptualize avant-garde culture is his recasting of "the border region" beyond the nineteenth-century notions of culture and the nation that enjoyed wide uncritical currency well into the late twentieth century and that established borders by conceptualizing culture around notions of "harmony" and "shared patterns of belief"[17] as well as around notions of homogeneity, "fraternity," and "imagined community."[18] By contrast, Lugo embraces more recent theoretical arguments that have advocated "the transformation of the nature of *the cultural* (from homogeneity to heterogeneity)."[19] Drawing upon the work of scholars like Renato Rosaldo and James Clifford, he posits a notion of culture not as that which is the "harmony" within borders but rather as that which never emerges from the borderlands of contingency, fragmentation, and contestation; as that which is at both center and edge a borderland of ever emergent, competing, and oppositional interests; or, to translate Lugo's ideas into terms relevant to our own discussion, as that which, while potentially positing an ideological notion of the cutting edge, is nonetheless constituted by a multiplicity of emergent, conflicted edges. Following this line of argument, to speak of the cutting edge of culture is not to address the farthest points from the cultural center; it is, when pluralized, to speak of culture as such.

For our immediate purposes, the point of rehearsing Lugo's arguments is that if we move beyond an antiquated notion of a homogenous European culture (i.e., homogenous vis-à-vis the rest of the world) toward a notion of culture as that which is ever emergent, contingent, and contested, we confront a definition of culture that is not only profoundly exemplified in the contested moments of intercultural exchanges of primitivism but also suggests that the clashing heterogeneous traditions of those moments indicate avant-garde culture more generally. In the specific example of primitivism, we discover an instance of avant-garde expression that is conceptually constituted within a global constellation and that only as a result of the most blatant acts of erasure can be characterized as European. In the specifics of border theory we discover a definition of culture that recommends the example of primitivism as a segue into what we can posit as the global dynamics that, although having largely gone unacknowledged in scholarship, have nevertheless always characterized the avant-garde as a whole. The contrast here is between a definition of the avant-garde that, on the one hand, is centered around an imagined European cultural homogeneity that expanded in influence, or a definition, on the other hand, whose territorial coordinates were always already heterogeneous, dispersed, and diversely located in moments of contestation. More about these competing definitions will come momentarily.

Beyond Linear Historiographies: Simultaneity

If border theory helps us to deconstruct and thus regulate the unchecked slippage between a notion of the cutting edge that signifies aesthetic innovation and a notion of the cutting edge that promotes a linear model of European cultural dominance and influence, it also leaves us with the subsequent task of theorizing the avant-garde beyond the Eurocentric moorings that have substantially limited the parameters within which scholars have charted both the scope of and the conceptual structure governing the history of experimental aesthetics. One course beyond those limitations involves some reflection on the fundamental role that the related notions of simultaneity and transnationalism can play in reframing the historiography of the avant-garde. While the latter of these two notions is the more crucial and in fact is the one that helps us to negotiate between the two competing definitions mentioned above, the notion of simultaneity can serve as an important primer for our discussion of transnationalism because it helps clarify the avant-garde as a deterritorialized phenomenon. To this end, we can certainly get some bearing from the lessons of primitivism, which cannot be identified as either wholly European or wholly African because, even amid its problematic colonial undercurrents, it was a product of the borderlands and resulted in the kind of hybrid transcultural phenomenon that Diana Taylor has characterized in another context as that in which "both the dominant and the dominated are modified through their contact with another culture."[20] But the point here is not so much primitivism's hybrid expression as it is the simultaneity of the traditions that converge in its forms.

That simultaneity not only gives primitivism ambiguous territorial boundaries; it also suggests the need to look for a comparable territorial ambiguity in a wide range of avant-garde expressions regardless of whether those expressions emerge in distinct instances of (inter)cultural hybridity. Indeed, even in areas where the aesthetic practices of the European avant-garde were either not related to or, in fact, ran counter to the colonial appropriations that mark primitivism, those practices have enjoyed a historiographic privilege that has eclipsed a register of the independent significance of often commensurate performative practices emerging outside of Europe. One case in point is the vociferous anti-colonial attitudes of the Parisian surrealists who denounced the 1931 Colonial Exhibition in Paris as "colonial piracy" and "with the help of the Communist Party" staged "a counter-exhibition entitled 'The Truth about the Colonies.'"[21] This well-known avant-garde provocation effectively coalesced aesthetic and radical political expression. But we still have yet to fully appreciate the implications that a comparable coalescence in the anticolonial work of, say, Haitian artists (who were among the victims of colonialism) has for the historiography of the avant-garde, and this despite the fact that within the ranks of the surrealist avant-garde, we even come across clear acknowledgments not of *derivative* but of *independent* parallels between the politically engaged aesthetics of the surrealists and that of their Haitian contemporaries.

Those acknowledgments can hardly be dismissed as a variation on the nostalgia for the prelapsarian that characterizes primitivism. Breton himself, in a 1946 visit to Haiti, paid homage to the Haitian "enthusiasm for liberty and its affirmation of dignity," both of which, according to Breton, were manifested in a "lyrical element . . . [that] emerges from the aspirations of the entire people."[22] These were political aspirations, and combined with the traditions associated with voodoo, the politically charged Haitian lyricism to which Breton refers produced a volatile aesthetic cocktail that could compete with almost anything the surrealists had served up in their efforts to place their experiments with dreams, trance, and automatic writing "in service of the revolution." The point behind this short digression is less about precedent than it is about the presumption of European influence in the historiography of the avant-garde. It is about techniques traditionally associated with the innovations of the European avant-garde not only surfacing either earlier, simultaneously or even later in cultures outside of Europe but doing so as significant moments of innovation from within non-European traditions. In short, the convergence of aesthetics and politics in Haiti, a convergence that, in fact, was in service of an actual revolution, is but one small example of a vanguard beyond the pale of a scholarly reluctance to look past conventionally conceived European borders to find the narrative material for constructing the history of the avant-garde, a reluctance evident even when that vanguard can be located in simultaneous temporal proximity to its European counterparts.

In light of such an example, it is tempting to conclude this rethinking of the avant-garde with an overdue call for scholars to break from their Eurocentric fixation and to finally acknowledge the global simultaneity of the basic forms of avant-garde expression. But there is the potential for the overly simplistic and reductive in such a call—that is, the potential for succumbing to a critical compromise that, while recognizing a global simultaneity in the emergence and forms of avant-garde expression, still inadvertently elides the crucial moments of contestation in the borderlands of the cutting edge. To conclude with a notion of simultaneity would thus leave us with an important deterritorialized conception of the avant-garde, but, by the same token, the conclusion would never adequately grapple with the competing definitions of the avant-garde mentioned earlier, and this would substantially diminish our understanding of the complex dynamics governing avant-garde culture more generally. Far from merely presenting us with an either/or proposition, the competition between those two definitions arguably reflects a crucial irreconcilable antinomy within the avant-garde itself, that is, an enduring moment of contestation that constitutes avant-garde culture as such and that offers us an important variation on Paul Mann's argument that the avant-garde always already contains "the anti and its recuperation." The issue thus is not whether one chooses a heterogeneous and dispersed notion of the avant-garde over and above one centered around an imagined European cultural homogeneity, or, more simply put, whether one embraces the idea of global simultaneity over Eurocentrism, but rather whether one recognizes that in characterizing the avant-garde, the two definitions cannot entirely be distinguished.

Toward a Theory of the Transnational Avant-Garde

To conceptualize the avant-garde around a notion of global simultaneity does not in and of itself dispose of the problematic Eurocentric undercurrents of the "avant-garde" as a concept. Here we are not talking about specific modes of artistic practice that are identifiably international and comparable but rather about an abstract category of cultural criticism that first emerged in discussions of cultural politics among European intellectuals in the late nineteenth century and that, when applied internationally, provides us with a lens through which to perceive and assign (not an exhaustive but rather) a specific type of significance and worth to performance practices on a global scale. For better or worse, that lens casts a European conceptual hue across an amazing diversity of cultural traditions, and, to put it bluntly, the danger that this European lens presents is that it potentially distorts and filters as much as it magnifies and illuminates. This is not to say that the European origins of the avant-garde *as a category of cultural criticism* automatically disqualify it as a tool for understanding the significance of experimental performance beyond the borders of Europe. Indeed, to reject a category of criticism solely because of its European ties would be as problematic as pretending that those ties are irrelevant. But if the extension of this category is to circumnavigate the currents feeding a subtle perpetuation of European cultural hegemony, then the study of avant-garde practices as a global phenomenon must take conscious critical account of the European conceptual heritage structuring the avant-garde as an idea and as a conceptual tool for assigning cultural and political value. Otherwise, embracing the unacknowledged global simultaneity of avant-garde expression may ironically replicate the very Eurocentrism it seeks to avoid and devolve into something that, as Masao Miyoshi argues is the case with a poorly conceived multiculturalism, tends to look "suspiciously like another alibi to conceal the actuality of [repressive] global politics."[23]

Although there are conceivably other possibilities for avoiding this potential devolution, one important answer to the question of how to use the idea of an avant-garde as a lens that illuminates both the blindness and insight it brings to our understanding of global performance practices is to supplement, in the definition of the avant-garde, the concept of simultaneity with what we here would argue are the *transnational* foundations of avant-garde practice. Partly this argument pivots on the logic of analogy and capitalizes on a structural parallel between the perennially contested status of the avant-garde and the contested status of the term *transnational* itself. More important, however, is the manner in which the conflicted historical referents of the term *transnationalism* set in critical relief the contextual historical dynamics governing the avant-garde as a global phenomenon. Understanding the nature of that dynamic thus arguably necessitates brief scrutiny of how the term *transnationalism* has reshaped our understanding of the political legacies of colonialism and European cultural hegemony.

As is frequently the case with terms that gain wide currency in scholarly discourse, the term *transnational* and its variants are marked by often simultaneous and contradictory trajectories. These disparate trajectories are pronounced enough in the study of literature, for example, that prominent scholars like John Carlos Rowe have begun to consider a citation of both as a requisite part of defining the terms. Indeed, Rowe begins his recent *PMLA* article "Nineteenth-Century United States Literary Culture and Transnationality" by noting that the term *transnationalism* not only characterizes "a critical view of historically specific late modern or postmodern practices of globalizing production, marketing, distribution, and consumption for neocolonial ends" but that it also "is used to suggest counterhegemonic practices" that are comparable to "Homi Bhabha's privileging of 'cultural hybridity' as a way to resist global homogenization."[24] Arguably, these concurrent contradictory trajectories also mark a crucial dynamic that characterize the avant-garde as a global phenomenon. If, on a geographical level, we finally acknowledge that the forms of avant-garde expression were always dispersed and global, then, on a conceptual level, the contradictory trajectories of the term *transnationalism* help us to remain critically conscious of the extent to which we, in defining these expressions as avant-garde, always skirt the fence (that precarious balancing act on the border) between the neocolonial and the counterhegemonic.

Of these two trajectories, Rowe's characterization of the former is clearly indebted to the seminal work of theorists like Miyoshi, who in such essays from the early 1990s as "A Borderless World? From Colonialism to Transnationalism and the Decline of the Nation-State" offered powerful arguments connecting the practices of eighteenth- and nineteenth-century colonialism with the repressive dynamics of late-twentieth-century global capitalism (in the form of "multinational enterprises" and "transnational corporations").[25] The importance of this connection and especially of Miyoshi's concomitant discussion of the discursive ideology that, under the guise of "cultural studies and multiculturalism," easily masks a naive complicity with contemporary neocolonialist attitudes is that the path from colonialism to a neocolonial transnationalism that Miyoshi maps out in his argument provides an important arc for understanding the enduring legacies of the avant-garde's cultural imbrications in the politics of colonialism.[26] The earliest manifestations of those imbrications are easy to recall. In our discussion of primitivism, we have already noted the colonialist birthing of the avant-garde. But in this discussion it is easy to overlook the larger significance of the fact that throughout the twentieth century the European wing of the avant-garde never severed its ties to the political and cultural interests that had spearheaded colonial expansionism in the first

place. As far back as the early 1960s, relatively traditional theorists like
Renato Poggioli argued that, for all its seemingly radical sentiments, the
avant-garde (the reference here is a presumed European avant-garde)
could not "help paying involuntary homage to democratic and liberal-
bourgeois society."[27] In other words, it could not help paying homage
to the very society that was at the vanguard of colonial expansion and
that, as Miyoshi so persuasively argues, rather undemocratically gave rise
to (and indeed provided tacit if not explicit ideological sanction of) the
later displacements and homogenizations of transnational global capitalism. While Poggioli's linking of the avant-garde to bourgeois society
arguably presages Paul Mann's characterization of the avant-garde as
always already containing its own moment of recuperation, there is a
much more important historical insight to be gained from recognizing
that the bond cited by Poggioli was ultimately a bond to the social currents that laid the foundation for what Miyoshi characterizes as the neocolonialism of late-twentieth-century global capitalism.

That insight hinges on an adaptation of Miyoshi's primary concern in
tracing the origins of transnationalism back to colonialism and empire.
The central argument to emerge from the connection that Miyoshi
establishes between these two stages of global capitalism echoes the
Marxist critique of postmodernity: the legacy of colonialism is not constituted in the move from colonialism to postcolonialism, but rather in
an evolution from colonialism to the (far more elusive and ultimately
more repressive) neocolonialism of transnational capitalism. Although
this summary does a disservice to the richness of Miyoshi's arguments,
his more general questioning of the assumption that we have broken
with colonialism and entered into an era of postcolonialism is, in its simplest expression, particularly important to our concerns here because of
the avant-garde's early conceptual entanglements in the cultural politics
of colonialism. If, as Miyoshi claims, we have never truly departed from
colonialism, then it behooves us to consider whether the colonialist
birthing of the avant-garde was a mere aberration, i.e., a singular point
of departure for a history quite distinct from its beginning (a history
divorced from its colonialist beginnings), or whether—following in
what Miyoshi sees as the historical development of Western neocolonialism in the geopolitical sphere—that birthing was the beginning of a
global dynamic that, though evolving, has always been a crucial aspect of
the avant-garde as a phenomenon.

This latter possibility is intriguing on a number of different levels.
First and foremost, it offers a political historical context for our earlier

assertion that *the rough edges of contestation,* that is, the problematic moments of contested intercultural exchange that marked the beginning of the avant-garde as a cultural phenomenon, are characteristic of avant-garde expression throughout the twentieth century. More important, however, are the subtle ways that Miyoshi's arguments clarify the shape of these contested exchanges. Perhaps the most significant of these clarifications only emerges from the admonishment with which Miyoshi closes his essay. Not only does he caution against "allowing ourselves to get absorbed into the discourse on 'postcoloniality'" because, doing so, we may collaborate "with the hegemonic ideology" of neocolonialism, but he also argues that the same endorsement of neocolonialism results from allowing ourselves to be absorbed into the discourse on "post-Marxism."[28] It thus should come as no surprise that in linking the discourses of postcoloniality and post-Marxism, Miyoshi implicitly suggests that Marxism's historical role in the resistance to colonialism has continued relevance for maintaining sites of resistance to the processes of neocolonialism. But that relevance is particularly important to us, in part because of the avant-garde's long (if somewhat strained) historical affiliation with the Marxist Left and in part because almost from its inception Marxism has functioned as an international movement. At one level, then, Marxism has provided an international political and structural link that has cut across cultural lines and that in an amazing variety of forms has captivated the attention of experimental artists on a global scale. Amid these historical currents, at least one strand of the transnational avant-garde takes shape as a by-product of the international politics of Marxism rather than as a global extension of a European category of cultural criticism.

Marxism's impact upon the experimental arts, that is, the specific forms of artistic expression it has precipitated, has varied widely from culture to culture, and that variation, along with its Marxist underpinnings, is a good example of the way that we might conceptualize the transnational foundations of the avant-garde more generally. There is much to be learned from the example provided by the diverse appeal of the political discourses of Marxism, especially because that appeal underscores not only a wide and simultaneous critical consciousness of global politics among artists internationally but also because the application of that consciousness to experimental artistic expression frequently has taken the form of artists addressing specific and local concerns vis-à-vis the impact of colonial and neocolonial processes of globalization and homogenization. While these adaptations may be evidence of the amazing flexibility of Marxist thought, the proclivity demonstrated by an artistic tailoring of Marxist political sensibilities to local cultural concerns is by no means unique to experimental arts informed by the discourses of Marxism. The international response of experimental artists to Marxism indicates a transnational consciousness that has consistently marked the attitudes of experimental artists across the globe.

Recognizing that Marxism created an international context to which experimental artists responded on a global scale is merely a reminder that theater practitioners and experimental performance artists, regardless of their geographical location, have seldom practiced their craft in a vacuum. Indeed, one of the central arguments for a transnational conception of the avant-garde is that within the experimental arts, there are countless examples of significant figures outside of Europe who not only transformed the shape of theatrical expression and focus within their own cultures but who also had an intense awareness of and interest in the experimental work of their European counterparts. While this interest certainly affected their aesthetics, it did so on their own terms. As the essays in this anthology demonstrate, African, Asian, and Latin American experimental artists have been far from provincial in their aesthetic views and have displayed cosmopolitan sensibilities that demonstrated familiarity with European theatrical innovations. The problem is not with their interest in Western experimental practices. It is rather with the one-dimensional representation that Western scholars of the avant-garde have offered of that interest.

The tendency has been to see that interest through an overly simplistic notion of influence. Scholars thus have confused interest with mere imitation rather than recognizing that the general interest in Western experimental forms by non-European artists not only possesses numerous dynamic moments of profoundly creative, independent, and, above all, experimental adaptation but, more importantly, has repeatedly led to *apostate adaptations,* that is, to adaptations that owe no allegiance to the integrity of their European origins and that become experimental precisely because of that lack of allegiance. Diana Taylor has argued a very similar point in her discussion of how deceptively recognizable Latin American theater has seemed to be to theater historians versed in European theatrical traditions:

> The deceptive *familiarity* of Latin American theatre . . . has led to errors in criticism. As no indigenous theatre survived intact after the century following the conquest, it goes without saying that all the

dramatic forms currently used in Latin America are derived *in some degree* from Western drama. While certain dramatic forms were force-fully imposed during the colonial period, since then Latin American dramatists have tended to "borrow" models. . . . Nonetheless, they do not borrow indiscriminately. Given a choice, people tend to take what they need.[29]

Certainly, Latin American theater is not unique in its selective borrow-ing of theatrical models. Indeed, to place this and similar practices in a larger international context is one way to tease out the avant-garde propensities in the strategies mentioned by Taylor. First of all, the type of borrowing she refers to is, as a technique, a crucial aspect of theatrical experimentation and innovation. Thus it is hardly a leap to see in this strategy the nascent aesthetic practices that we deem avant-garde, and there is nothing particularly European about experimental borrowing. This point is only strengthened if one considers the implications of Tay-lor's statement, "Given a choice, people tend to take what they need." If the needs cited by Taylor are not intended to coincide with or repli-cate European norms—and that is certainly what she suggests—there is a kind of random appropriation and adaptation to the practice of bor-rowing that also coincides with the aesthetics of the avant-garde, in par-ticular the techniques associated with the *objet trouvé*. Here we discover a rather innovative, if not subversive, inversion of those very techniques. Rather than looking to Europe for models of experimental theatrical expression, experimental artists in areas as diverse as Latin America, Japan, and Francophone Africa have treated European experimental forms as *found objects* that could be appropriated and adapted to meet par-ticular local needs.

Consistently, this phenomenon of experimental appropriation and adaptation has positioned global avant-garde expression in close prox-imity to what Rowe characterizes as the second dominant trajectory suggested by the term *transnationalism:* namely, the "counterhege-monic practices" that he likens to Homi Bhabha's notion of "cultural hybridity."[30] With regard to the avant-garde, much of the significance of this comparison derives from the fact that Bhabha posits hybridity as a mode of subversion that stands in direct contrast to "theorists who engage in the battle for 'power' but do so only as the purists of differ-ence."[31] Not only does Bhabha question whether such pure cultural difference exists (either as a site of opposition and resistance or even as a site of absolute hegemonic authority); he also argues that hybridity is

hardly tantamount to a capitulation to (European) cultural hegemony.
On the contrary:

> If the effect of colonial power is seen to be the *production* of hybridiza-
> tion rather than the noisy command of colonialist authority or the
> silent repression of native traditions, then an important change of per-
> spective occurs. The ambivalence at the source of traditional dis-
> courses on authority enables a form of subversion, founded on the
> undecidability that turns the discursive conditions of dominance into
> the grounds of intervention.[32]

By positing a notion of hybridity, the subversive qualities of which are
the direct result of an "undecidability" or a slippage in the signs of colonial authority, Bhabha offers us a conceptual dynamic whereby the symbols of cultural hegemony signify the hegemony even as they are simultaneously vulnerable to a "strategic reversal of the process of
domination," that is, even as they potentially and simultaneously signify
their contrary and opposite.

There is a clear echo of Paul de Man in Bhabha's notion of hybridity,
an echo that not only suggests a relevant cultural application for de Man's
poststructuralist characterization of textuality but that also provides a crucial passageway for Bhabha's notion of hybridity to enter into the discourses of the avant-garde. "The paradigm for all texts," de Man argues,
"consists of a figure (or a system of figures) and its deconstruction. But
since this model cannot be closed off by a final reading, it engenders, in
its turn, a supplementary figural superposition which narrates the unreadability of the prior narration."[33] Of particular relevance to our project of
rethinking the avant-garde is de Man's concept of unreadability, which
we might productively extend to the discourse of the avant-garde
specifically because de Man uses this concept as shorthand for what he
otherwise describes as a "model [that] cannot be closed off by a final
reading." Presuming that de Man is correct in the paradigm that he offers
"for all texts," extending his concept of "unreadability" to the discourses
of the avant-garde (and particularly to the narrative history of the avant-
garde) acknowledges that only a matter of rhetorical convention keeps
the conceptual parameters of the avant-garde within Eurocentric boundaries, and if those parameters cannot be closed off, then the lack of closure offers an important opportunity for expanding our understanding of
the conceptual dynamics of the avant-garde itself. The extension of de
Man's concept to the avant-garde thus takes a critical step toward open-

ing up its discourses to new readings both in the sphere of the textual and, via Bhabha, ultimately in the sphere of the cultural. Indeed, as we will see momentarily, the significance of this extension for our understanding of the avant-garde emerges in the intersection of the underlying notions governing de Man's concept of "unreadability" and those governing Bhabha's concept of "undecidability."

The parallel first between de Man's notion of "unreadability" and Bhabha's notion of "undecidability," and second between de Man's concept of "a supplementary figural superposition" and Bhabha's concept of "hybridity," is underscored by Bhabha's contention that the slippage between the symbols of colonial authority and their subversion never resolves the contestation between cultures. Like the discursive model that "cannot be closed off by a final reading," the slippage in the symbols of colonial authority leaves the symbols deconstructed and unreadable because of their contradictory trajectories, and the irreconcilable cultural contestation underlying that deconstruction marks the hybrid itself. Hybridity, Bhabha argues, "is not a third term that resolves the tension between two cultures . . . in a dialectical play of 'recognition.'" It is rather a term that denotes the entrance of "other 'denied' knowledges . . . upon the dominant discourse," an entrance that "estrange[s] the basis of its authority its rules of recognition."[34] Arguably, it is those "other 'denied' knowledges" that fill the space of de Man's "unreadability" and that culturally and subversively diversify the discourses of the avant-garde. If de Man's concept of "unreadability" is shorthand for discursive models that "cannot be closed off by a final reading," then Bhabha's argument here suggests that his concept of "undecidability," which serves as the backdrop for his concept of hybridity, refers to "other 'denied' knowledges" or to those cultural expressions that would at first appear to be elided by a dominant discourse. In that subversive act of inversion, which gives voice to those "other 'denied' knowledges" and which emerges from the margins of discursive models like those of the avant-garde that cannot be closed off, Bhabha's concept of hybridity emerges as a crucial concept for understanding the transnational avant-garde.

In many respects, Bhabha's notion of hybridity returns us precisely to the colonialist moments of cultural contestation that mark the earliest phases of avant-garde expression, that is, to the site where the Eurocentric narrative authority of conventional histories of avant-garde can be challenged if we recognize how *the rough edges* of that contestation mark a fundamental hybridity in the avant-garde, a hybridity that changes the

established "rules of recognition" for characterizing avant-garde performance. With Bhabha's concept of hybridity, we thus segue into a
definition of transnationalism and of a transnational avant-garde that
rebuts the assumption that extending the conceptual lens of the avant-
garde internationally compromises our understanding of particular performance practices. Indeed, the idea of an avant-garde that is characterized first by strategies of adaptation and appropriation for local ends and
second by strategies of subversion that change "the rules of recognition"
(by reversing the processes of domination and hegemony) stands in
marked contrast to the arguments of critics who, for example, would
categorically reject the relevance of extending the idea of an avant-garde
guard beyond Western theatrical traditions.

The immediate consequence of this shift in focus is to force a critical
reassessment of the historical functions of the term *avant-garde* itself, and
if as a consequence of this shift we have rendered the avant-garde an
example of what Edward Said has called "traveling theory," we can offer
in conclusion some response to his open question, "whether by virtue of
having moved from one place and time to another an idea or a theory
gains or loses in strength, and whether a theory in one historical period
and national culture becomes altogether different for another period or
situation."[35] If nothing else the critical movement toward a notion of a
transnational avant-garde suggests that linking the term *avant-garde* with
a specific historical lineage conceptualizes it as an unproblematic signifier
of a particular history of European theatrical practice. By conceptualizing the term this way, scholars have bound themselves to argue that any
discussion of a non-European theatrical avant-garde, first of all, necessitates a severing of the term *avant-garde* from what implicitly amounts to
an assumed "true" signified (i.e., the European experimental theatrical
tradition of the early and middle twentieth century). Any effort to maintain such a secure connection between signifier and signified is problematic, to say the least. More importantly, it misses the pivotal argument of this anthology: namely, that the connection between the term
avant-garde and the European experimental theatrical tradition is an ideological construct rather than a historically unified moment of authentic
signification. This ideological construct lays claim to, and gives Europe
credit for, a whole range of political and stylistic theatrical practices and
elides the originality and often simultaneous existence of comparable
political and stylistic innovations in the theater and performance practices of other cultures.

Notes

1. Rebecca Schneider, *The Explicit Body in Performance* (New York: Routledge, 1997), 139.

2. Hugo Ball, *Flight Out of Time: A Dada Diary,* trans. Ann Raimes, ed. John Elderfield (Berkeley: University of California Press, 1996), 70.

3. Richard Huelsenbeck, *Memoirs of a Dada Drummer,* trans. Joachim Neugroschel, ed. Hans J. Kleinschmidt (Berkeley: University of California Press, 1991), 9.

4. Antonin Artaud, *The Theatre and its Double,* trans. Mary Caroline Richards (New York: Grove, 1958).

5. Paul Mann, *The Theory-Death of the Avant-Garde* (Bloomington: Indiana University Press, 1991), 81.

6. Ibid.

7. Michael Kirby, *The Art of Time* (New York: Dutton, 1969), 18.

8. Schneider, *Explicit Body in Performance,* 129.

9. Ibid., 134.

10. Ibid., 129.

11. Richard Schechner, *The Future of Ritual: Writings on Culture and Performance* (New York: Routledge, 1993), 6.

12. Christopher Innes, *Avant-Garde Theatre, 1892–1992* (New York: Routledge, 1993), 18.

13. Michal Kobialka, "Introduction," *Of Borders and Thresholds* (Minneapolis: University of Minnesota Press, 1999), 3.

14. Ibid.

15. Ibid.

16. Alejandro Lugo, "Reflections on Border Theory," in *Border Theory: The Limits of Cultural Politics,* ed. Scott Michaelsen and David E. Johnson (Minneapolis: University of Minnesota Press, 1997), 45.

17. Ibid., 49.

18. Ibid., 54.

19. Ibid., 50.

20. Diana Taylor, "Transculturating Transculturation," in *Interculturalism and Performance,* ed. Bonnie Marranca and Gautam Dasgupta (New York: PAJ, 1991), 63.

21. Michael Richardson, introduction to *Refusal of the Shadow: Surrealism and the Caribbean,* ed. Michael Richardson, trans. Krzysztof Fijalkowski and Michael Richardson (London: Verso, 1996), 4.

22. Paul Laraque, "Andre Breton in Haiti," in Richardson, *Refusal of the Shadow,* 212.

23. Masao Miyoshi, "A Borderless World? From Colonialism to Transnationalism and the Decline of the Nation-State," *Critical Inquiry* 19 (1993): 728.

24. John Carlos Rowe, "Nineteenth-Century United States Literary Culture and Transnationality," *PMLA* 118.1 (2003): 78.

25. Miyoshi, "A Borderless World," 734.

26. Ibid., 751.

27. Renato Poggioli, *Theory of the Avant-Garde* (1962), trans. Gerald Fitzgerald (Cambridge: Harvard University Press, 1968), 106–7.

28. Miyoshi, "A Borderless World," 751.

29. Taylor, "Transculturating Transculturation," 67.

30. Rowe, "Nineteenth-Century Literary Culture," 78.

31. Homi Bhabha, *The Location of Culture* (New York: Routledge, 1994), 111.

32. Ibid., 112.

33. Paul de Man, *Allegories of Reading* (New Haven: Yale University Press, 1982), 205.

34. Ibid., 113–14.

35. Edward Said, "Traveling Theory," in *The World, The Text and the Critic* (Cambridge: Harvard University Press, 1983), 226.

The *TDR* Black Theatre Issue
Refiguring the Avant-Garde

Harry J. Elam, Jr.

In May 1968, the *Drama Review (TDR)* published its "Black Theatre Issue," edited by playwright Ed Bullins, marking a seminal moment in American theater history and heralding black theater's arrival as a radical intervention into the conventional practices and policies of American theater. Immediately after its publication, the Black Theatre Issue became a critical "collective manifesto" for the Black Theater Movement (BTM) of the late 1960s and early 1970s. And yet, devoting an issue of *TDR*—the journal at the vanguard of the study and critique of contemporary performance trends and practices—solely to the texts and theorizations of black theater needs examination, for it is rife with symbolic import, ideological contradictions, and cultural politics. On the one hand, the issue symbolically incorporated black theatrical experimentation as an emerging force to be recognized in the American avant-garde. On the other hand, the racialized editorial policies and promotional strategies for this, and only this, issue emphasized its distinctness, its separation from this same avant-garde.

The racial politics and complex interrelationships between the notion of an American avant-garde and the BTM as embodied in the *TDR* Black Theatre Issue require serious unpacking. Black theater practitioners such as Bullins and Amiri Baraka, whose Black Arts rhetoric vehemently opposed the dearth of social efficacy in white theatrical experimentation of the times, now found themselves courted, promoted, and published by a journal that championed these same white avant-garde aesthetics. Despite serving on the editorial board of *TDR*, the voice of the American avant-garde, Ed Bullins, in an article entitled "The So-called Western Avant-garde Drama," rejected Western experimentation and proclaimed, "It is a post-American form of Black theater we Black Artists should be seeking. It is Black Art that like a dagger pointed at the vitals of America, and through the rips 'we' (US) can enter the New Epoch."[1] Bullins calls for white cultural death concurrently with the affirmation of new black artistic life. His call is interestingly consistent with the manifestos of avant-garde movements such as Dada, futurism, the Theater of Cruelty, and the Living Theatre, which are replete with proclamations of mainstream artistic death and decay interrupted by the birth of new aesthetic paradigms. Such declarations are articulated throughout the Black Theatre Issue and the BTM. And yet, despite these vehement repudiations of Western aesthetics, black artists were knowledgeable about, trained in, and influenced by avant-garde traditions. As Mike Sell observes,

> Bullins along with such Black Arts luminaries as Amiri Baraka, Larry Neal, Don Lee, Sonia Sanchez, Nikki Giovanni, Gwendolyn Brooks, and Etheridge Knight had absorbed the lessons of twentieth-century political and philosophical thought, including the linguistic, phenomenological and existential trends. Likewise, they knew about Dada, Surrealism, Pound, Eliot, Hughes and Hurston and DuBois. In short, many of the black artists were fully cognizant of the modernist critique of language and the avant-garde's century-long exploration of the boundaries of text, performance and activism.[2]

Sell notes the impact that Western artistic experimentation had on the black arts and points out that non-Western African philosophical and aesthetic practices also informed the movement. What I want to call attention to here is the dyadic flow of artistic influence: that the BTM affected American experimental practices even as it was affected by them. Too often this synergy is ignored, and the interplay between radical politics and radical performance strategies goes unexplored. As Richard Schechner, the executive editor of *TDR,* offers, "using English, living in America they [black playwrights] cannot easily avoid the wide sweep of theatrical tradition."[3] I take it that they did not, and ask how we should place them in relation to such a tradition. Closely reading the Black Theatre Issue on and through the presuppositions and definitions of a historical Western avant-garde not only sheds light on the impact of this collective manifesto, but also refigures the meanings of "avant-garde" and the racializations that this phrase so often implies.

Despite, or perhaps because of, attempts to ignore race or to profess color blindness, definitions of the Western historic avant-garde have been embedded in racial categories. Avant-garde scholars from Peter Bürger to Paul Mann, Hal Foster, and James Harding point out that definitions of the avant-garde are always contested and contestatory, conflictual and even contradictory.[4] Yet they share assumptions. From Bürger, echoed in the work of Paul Mann, comes the argument that roots of the historical avant-garde date to the nineteenth-century European middle class and the desire of certain artists to reject bourgeois ideals.[5] Bürger believes that with this avant-garde thrust, art became self-critical and rebelled against the aestheticism of artistic practice: "In bourgeois society, it is only with aestheticism that the full unfolding of the phenomenon of art became a fact, and it is to aestheticism that the historical avant-garde respond."[6] Bürger's discussion obscures any non-Western artistic practice in which a different sense of artistic functionality is in operation. Moreover, his designation of avant-garde origins, even as it locates resistance as critical to any avant-garde practice, posits whiteness and European ideals as a normative, unmarked presence behind any definition of the historic avant-garde. Mann argues in *Theory-Death of the Avant-Garde* that the avant-garde's demand for artistic and social change places it in a dialectically marginalized relationship to the mainstream. "The avant-garde is outside of the inside, the leading edge of the mainstream, and thus marginal in both senses: excluded and salient."[7] Mann sees an inherent doubleness in the avant-garde, in that its practices include the mainstream by rejecting it.

In a parallel notation of doubleness, Larry Neal, a leading theorist of the Black Arts Movement, places the articulation of a new black aesthetic in dialectical relation with the eradication of the old mainstream white order. In his seminal essay "The Black Arts Movement," originally published in the Black Theatre Issue, Neal states, "The motive behind the Black aesthetic is the destruction of the white thing, the destruction of white ideas and white ways of looking at the world."[8] Clearly remarked in Neal but unremarked in Mann is the way in which the mainstream and the margin are racialized. Mann maintains that the avant-garde functions as a "centralized margin," "the leading edge" of the mainstream that not only pushes the mainstream forward and outward but also inheres within it. Yet, I would suggest that experimental movements emerging from the already marginalized and racialized other, such as the BTM, have never had the luxury of such insider status; centralized marginality implies a privilege associated with whiteness. Notions of transgression, of sexual license, of edginess and social resistance—all of which were particularly associated with the racial other at the turn of the nineteenth century—became co-opted and fetishized within the "centralized margin" of the white avant-garde. Thus, the resistance of the historical avant-garde owes a cultural debt to the already marginalized racial other.

Christopher Innes in his comprehensive study *Avant Garde Theatre, 1892–1992* develops the theory that the avant-garde is always a return to the primitive. Perhaps paradoxically, what defines this avant-garde movement is not overtly modern qualities, such as the 1920s romance of technology—George Antheil's *Airplane Sonata,* Corrado Govani's *poésie elettriche,* or Enrico Prampolin's "theater of mechanics"—but primitivism. The latter has two complementary facets: the exploration of dream states or the instinctive and subconscious levels of the psyche; and the quasi-religious focus on myth and magic, which in the theater leads to experiments with ritual and the ritualistic patterning of performance.[9]

Implicit in Innes's invocation of the primitive is the racialization of the avant-garde as white Western artists who turned to the exotic other as a source for their experiments. Innes does speak to the inherent dangers and overt racism of such projects, yet he repeatedly notes a dissatisfaction with Western artistic norms that led modern and contemporary white Western artists to search for a functional aesthetic that would facilitate a ritualized and spiritual artistic experience of deeper cross-cultural or intercultural meaning. In an attempt to capture an energy outside of their cultural experience, Western artists appropriated practices from the racial other—Artaud from the Balinese, Picasso from African art. In a discussion of the processes of racialization in the history of the avant-garde, Holland Cotter astutely comments, "Picasso invented modern European art with the help of Africa. [Nigerian artist Aina] Onabolu [in 1903] invented modern African art with the help of Europe. Which of the two made the more revolutionary move? In most accounts, Picasso gets the nod by default, because Onabolu doesn't exist for Western art history, nor does the modern African art that followed him."[10] The artistic valorization of Picasso's primitivism comes at the expense of Onabolu's achievement because Picasso's rebellion is within the system, on "the leading edge" of the white mainstream, while Onabolu is not. Historically, Western avant-garde art has celebrated and appropriated the "avant" energy of the racial other even as it excluded the work of the racial other. Thus, it has included race by excluding it.

Quite similarly, the desire of white experimentalist groups in the 1960s and early 1970s to expand the boundaries of theater can be read as racialized. Their antiestablishment stances inevitably placed them in relation to the already marginalized and increasingly disgruntled black masses and the radical theatrical paradigms of the BTM. And yet Arnold Aronson in *American Avant-Garde: A History* does not include the work of the BTM, nor does he note the significance of race even as he defines the American avant-garde as "oppositional" to "established culture" and positions it as constantly in negotiation with ideas of "the real"—concepts that were fundamental to the work of the BTM.[11] Such critical blinders not only demean black artistic achievement but limit any examination of the racial politics of the avant-garde. Consequently, the question with the BTM and the Black Theatre Issue is not so much whether it fits into an American avant-garde, but how the avant-garde fits into it.

Editorial Comment: "The King is Dead"

Ed Bullins's editorial comment "The King is Dead," which opens the Black Theatre Issue, is itself an avant-garde document, eschewing the conventional form of editorial foreword, stepping outside of the traditional editorial expectations to offer a metacommentary on the state of the arts. Provocatively, "The King is Dead" does not provide an overview of the articles and plays contained in the issue but instead reviews the social context in which these works and the BTM operate by riffing on the notion of dead kings. Bullins's editorial comment discusses what transpired when he, along with Amiri Baraka and a group from his Newark-based black revolutionary theater project Spirit House, attended a production of the play *Kongi's Harvest* by Nigerian playwright and Nobel Prize winner Wole Soyinka on April 4, 1968, the day that Martin Luther King, Jr. was assassinated. Consequently, the title of Bullins's commentary explicitly refers to the death of the civil rights leader. Yet, as evidenced by the epigraph by Floyd McKissick that precedes the Bullins piece, King's death is not observed with the reverence that now greets him as a national icon. McKissick writes, "Dr. Martin Luther King was the last prince of nonviolence. He was a symbol of nonviolence, the epitome of nonviolence. Nonviolence is a dead philosophy and it was not the black people that killed it."[12] According to McKissick, Martin Luther, the "last" King, is dead, as is his philosophy of nonviolence. McKissick implies that the violent actions of whites not only have assassinated the last King, but terminated the ideology of nonviolent black response. He warns that blacks will now respond with a different timbre and fervor. McKissick's epigraph, in concert with Bullins's article, implies that King's murder and the symbolic death of nonviolence hold artistic as well as cultural and social consequences. The death of this king fundamentally alters the environment for black theater.

Significantly, Bullins relates that he and his entourage learned of King's assassination in a theater, the lobby of the New Lafayette Theater, underscoring the connections that the Black Theatre Issue draws between black art and politics. Emphasizing the import of theater in times of crises, Bullins, Baraka, and their entourage still attended the play's "long" first act, even though they heard word of King's passing prior to the performance. At intermission, they watched the news reports of the assassination on the television set in the Negro Ensemble Company's front offices, as the theater literally became the space in which to respond to critical social events. Positing this space for witnessing the emerging social upheaval inside a theater confirmed for Bullins the necessary interrelationship between black theater and the outside social conditions of black life. And so he "wondered at that moment about those Black theatre people who profess not to be concerned about politics, or 'just let their Blackness speak for itself.'"[13] For Bullins the death of the King heightened the need for a socially committed black art. In these urgent times, black art could not afford apolitical complacency. The cover of the Black Theatre Issue, designed by Maxine and Roberta Raysor, foregrounds these connections, featuring a poster announcing a benefit performance by the Black Arts Alliance for the Black Panther Party for Self-Defense.

Soon to be cultural minister of the Black Panther Party in Oakland, California, intensely conscious of the current conditions and the urgent demand for a new black arts practice, Bullins in these introductory pages of *TDR* steps outside of conventional spheres and normative codes of conduct and commentary, calling for the death and destruction of past systems. Bullins reports that he, Baraka, and the others walked out on *Kongi's Harvest,* staged by the Negro Ensemble Company (NEC), symbolically rejecting Old World traditions and nonrevolutionary black art. Although it was written by an African playwright working within a non-Western tradition, *Kongi's Harvest* did not move Bullins and his posse. With its nuanced tale of a dictator who deposes an African king and attempts to unite tribal factionalism with Western modernity, *Kongi's Harvest* lacked explicitly radical reflection on the social conditions of African-American life. At the end of the first act, Bullins reports that, as he and Baraka determined not to return for the second act, Baraka "said something about the play having some sparks of life but coming out of a dead order"[14]—again this theme of death, a reference to deceased or dying black cultural practices and an implicit cry for a new artistic order. In articulating the paradigms of the Black Revolutionary Theatre Movement, Bullins, Baraka, and others distanced themselves from the more integrationist philosophies of the NEC and disparaged it for not promoting social activism in its art. While the NEC in its early seasons presented several works by non–African–American and non-Western playwrights such as Soyinka, the documents published in the *TDR* Black Theatre Issue represent new work of strictly African-American practitioners, determined to etch out a distinctly African-American aesthetic practice. The death of these black kings, as proclaimed in Bullins's opening, provided impetus for a new art to emerge.

Bullins goes on to describe the apocalyptic explosion in the streets in the aftermath of Martin Luther King's death. As he made a phone call on Second Avenue, a passerby informed Bullins that riots had started in Harlem. A member of Baraka's troupe told the group that "officials of Newark, the New Jersey State government and the Mafia were vowing to 'kill' Amiri."[15] As suggested by the vivid history Bullins paints, the artists of the BTM operated within these contrasting urgencies. With the real threat of death coming from the white power structure and with the tumultuous sparks of dissatisfaction rising from black urban enclaves following King's passing, black arts practitioners sought to create a new artistic life. Recalling James Baldwin's 1964 racial jeremiad, *The Fire Next Time,* but also situating revolutionary theatrical production at a flaming nexus of black unrest, Bullins hoped that his own "new theatre building had been missed by the fire this time."[16] The uncertainty of the times and the passionate faith that an old regime was dying out were critical factors in the emergence of the Black Theater Movement.

The title of Bullins's introduction, "The King is Dead," also signifies on Schechner's role in the editing of this issue of *TDR*. In unprecedented fashion, Schechner ceded total editorial control to Bullins and announced this decision in his own editorial comment, tellingly entitled "White on Black." Paradoxically, by proclaiming his power to dispense with authority in this way, Schechner reminds his audience that he still has power. At the same time he waves editorial control, Schechner reserves the prerogative to write an opening critique, opining that the issue is "long on plays and short on articles" and mentioning that "he didn't like some of the plays."[17] In speaking from this vantage point of white critical authority, he maintains power over the issue even as he discusses giving up editorial command. Schechner himself notes the contradictory politics in his relinquishing of power:

> There is a danger in that [vacating editorial control]. It is the old danger of patronization. By liquidating my editorial authority, I renounced my editorial responsibilities. In treating Bullins unlike I treat other invited editors, I was perhaps, "making allowances" for his blackness. The nuances of black-white relationships in this country are complicated. Not only is there no guarantee of a non-racial judgment in racial matters, there is possibly no way of avoiding racial judgments.[18]

Schechner's comments reflect what William Sonnega refers to as "white liberal compensatory difference."[19] In wanting to honor black aesthetic autonomy, Schechner potentially overcompensates in ways he would not for white guest editors. Such white compensatory racial strategies, Sonnega argues, do not produce social change, but rather reinforce white liberal privilege and "the traditional liberal tenet of toleration."[20] As Schechner himself recognizes, his position is complex, subject to racialized readings that he cannot avoid and is complicit in producing. Symbolically providing the space for black voices to spew forth in the pages of *TDR* without his editorial constraint, Schechner willingly participates in his own death. He writes, "If this issue was to be subjective, whose subjectivity should it reflect? I chose Bullins's over my own."[21] Thus, for this issue Bullins becomes "king" because the previous king is dead. This kingly passing also predicts the death of white Western aesthetic practices and oppressive white political regimes that the movement imagined in both the articles and the performance pieces contained within the journal. The death of this white king allows for a new black creative and political space.

Yet, even in death, Schechner criticizes the Black Theatre Issue plays for not embracing avant-garde traditions. In dismissing these works, Schechner voices a dangerous double standard. Schechner faults their artistic merits, yet he had championed the works of the historic European avant-garde—such as *Ubu Roi* by Alfred Jarry (1896) and Tristin Tzara's Dada drama *Le Coeur à gaz* (1921)—and happenings and environmental theater of the 1960s that could be labeled dramatically uninteresting. What Schechner credits in these works but not in the plays in the Black Theatre Issue is an avant-garde notion of what constitutes theater and the relationship between audience and performers. When Fermin Germier stepped onto the stage of the Théâtre de l'Oeuvre in 1896 as King Ubu and uttered the now famous first word of the play, "merdre," it caused an uproar. The anarchist Dada events organized by Tzara, André Breton, and Francis Picabia in Paris in the 1920s, featuring poetry, abstract art, readings, and even the ringing of electric bells, led to vehement audience response, even anger. At the Dada Festival held at the Salle Gaveau on 26 May 1920, the players insulted the audience, and the spectators responded by pelting them with "pieces of raw meat, vegetables, eggs, and tomatoes, which the Dadas flung back."[22] What has become significant about these theatrical occasions is not their conventional artistic merit but their attack on theatrical conventions. They disrupted the traditional alignment of audience and spectators in the theater space and demanded of the audience a response other than complacency.

Although unacknowledged by Schechner, the plays in the Black Theatre Issue similarly challenged audience expectations and reoriented the separation between spectators and stage performers. In Baraka's *Home on the Range,* a character he calls the Black Criminal shoots a gun over the heads of the audiences as he shouts, "This is the tone of America. My country 'tis of thee. This is the scene of the Fall."[23] At the end of Ronald Milner's play *The Monster,* the dean of a fictitious black college turns to the black audience and pleads with them, "Be for your own!! The others have already done for theirs!! They cannot and will not respect you until you have done for your own!!"[24] Both these plays shatter the fourth wall in order to shake the audience's complacency and propel their black spectators to think about, and potentially to act toward, social change. Joseph White in *Ole Judge Mose is Dead* subverts his audience's expectations by presenting a satirical vision of two presumably subservient Negro janitorial workers. Left by the white undertaker to clean the floor of a mortuary, these seeming "Uncle Toms" voice a latent revolutionary fervor and gleefully beat the corpse of white Judge Mose, who in life "hated all colored folks, ain't no doubt about it."[25] Their irreverence has symbolic resonance. Defiling the corpse, they figuratively confront the power of white hegemony and emblematically assault white aesthetic and political values.

This symbolic indictment has much in common with "The Indictment and Trial of M. Maurice Barrès by Dada," which the Dadaists, led by André Breton, staged at the Salle des Sociétés Savantes on 13 May 1921. The ridicule of both of these figures, the real Barrès and fictional Judge Mose, holds metaphorical significance, as through ritualized

scapegoating they become representative of a vehemently opposed ideology. Barrès, a progressive-turned-conservative and major literary
figure, "put his talent at the service of the ideals of property, country and
religion—values condemned by Breton, who feared the malicious
influence of Barrès on French youth."[26] The Dada performance, like
White's play, treated Barrès with a rebellious, carnivalesque irreverence.

One significant difference between the Dadaists' "Indictment" and
White's *Ole Judge Mose* is the latter's explicit violence, and the inherent
and real danger lurking just below its surface. It expresses a smoldering
desire for racial revolution. This signal difference of racial threat is representative of how the BTM and the plays in the Black Theatre Issue
refigured European avant-garde means of shocking the audience. The
works in the Black Theatre Issue conjoin their attack on white aesthetic
standards with an assault on white political power and with a call for
white death. In *Ole Judge Mose,* to paraphrase Walter Benjamin, even the
dead are not safe.[27] If the historic avant-garde turned to the racial other
as a benign, exotic, romanticized artistic source that could be co-opted,
appropriated, the BTM and the Black Theatre Issue posited the black
other as a threat ready, willing, and able to destroy whiteness. These
plays shocked their audiences, disrupting stage conventions through the
palpable terror of racial violence. Certainly this antiwhite theatrical prejudice rubbed against the sentiments of *TDR*'s white liberal audience.
And despite attempts by Bullins and Schechner to widen it, the audience
base for the Black Theatre Issue remained overwhelmingly white.
Schechner explains that with this issue they "wanted to reach a black
readership. Beyond the usual commercial considerations—larger circu-
lation and so on—we wished to stimulate debate about theatre within
black communities." And so Schechner provided Bullins "with a large
number of issues for free distribution to theatres and schools that would
not normally purchase *TDR*."[28] Yet even the advertisements in this
issue—a full-page announcement for *Modern Spanish Theatre* from E. P.
Dutton, half-page from Random House for *The Complete Plays of Jean
Racine*—"overwhelmingly reaffirm the very Western European traditions that the issue ostensibly questions."[29] Schechner's introductory
commentary, then, speaks directly to this white clientele. His critique of
the black plays contained within the issue becomes a strategy of temper-
ing or even controlling the black menace.

Schechner finds the black plays contained in the issue "too conventional." He points out what he deems a paradox: "While rejecting the

white avant-garde, the black writers had, perhaps inadvertently, accepted white Odets."[30] Schechner connects the practices of the Black Theater Movement to the tradition of agit-prop, *Waiting for Lefty,* the plays of Clifford Odets and the Workers' Theater Movement of the 1930s. Such a conjunction affirms that both movements used theater as means to an end, seeking to effect social change through the artistic medium. Both movements responded to social urgencies—cries for workers' rights during the depression, black social dissatisfaction and demands for Black Power in the late 1960s and early 1970s—and demanded in their form and content a functional expression of art. Schechner's critique suggests that social functionalism is antithetical to avant-garde expression, that the avant-garde is simply an art-for-art's-sake movement, and that contemporary avant-garde expression is foreign to black theater practices.

> As I read over the material for this issue it became clear to me that the aesthetics most commonly debated in *TDR*—happenings, environmental theatre, new kinds of criticism, regional theatre, actor training—are most lively in the context of a certain segment of white American society. Most of these movements are irrelevant to black theatre.[31]

This binary that Schechner establishes and that is further informed by the Black Theater Movement's rhetoric of difference elides the connections of black theatrical experimentation to the concurrent practices of white theater groups. Frustrated with traditional theatrical conventions and inspired by the same atmosphere of the urgency, counterculture theater groups in the 1960s and 1970s altered the definitions of theatrical practice. As evidenced by Schechner's own determination to publish the Black Theatre Issue, the work of the Black Theater Movement influenced and was in turn influenced by these experiments. Moreover, Schechner's assessments of conventionality and of the avant-garde are strictly based on traditional white normative standards and comparative models. Even in noting the relation of the Black Theater Movement to social protest theater, the measure is the white Odets. In the Black Theatre Issue promoter Woodie King writes:

> It is sad when a black writer is compared to Albee, Miller, Williams, Odets or O'Neill. (Can you dig a black writer being compared to

Beaumont and Fletcher?) It is sad because the black writer is caught in
the white "comparison bag." And that is usually a "form bag" that has
no relation at all to black experience.[32]

Such a reliance on white as normative keeps the meanings of avant-
garde within a white Western paradigm. It fails to consider not only how
BTM practices might constitute an avant-garde but also how these practices demand a different criterion of measurement. Different practices
may expand and inform previous definitions of the avant-garde.

Revolutionary Mimesis and Desire

The focus of the Black Theatre Issue on play texts, which Schechner disparaged and Bullins embraced, evidences the revision that the BTM
advances on the antitext, performance-based aesthetics of the U.S.
avant-garde. The production of happenings, the counterculture rebel-
lions of the Open Theatre, the collective rituals of groups such as the
Living Theater and Schechner's own Performance Group de-empha-
sized the traditional power of the playwright and script-oriented theater
pieces and expanded the definitions of theater by relying on spontaneity,
improvisation, and actor-based ensemble experimentation. The Black
Theatre Issue's emphasis on texts stood in stark contrast to these initiatives but must not be read as a return to the traditional. Rather, the valorization of texts in the Black Theatre Issue equally broadened
definitions of what constituted theatrical practice by providing black
audiences and practitioners with an alternative body of work. The volume facilitated production, including plays by fourteen authors, two
plays by Amiri Baraka, *Home on the Range* and *Police,*[33] and one by
Bullins, *Clara's Ole Man*. Needing scripts that reflected their social and
artistic ideologies, black theaters emerging around the country produced
these plays and thus developed a common aesthetic vocabulary and artistic repertoire. These works became part of a new canon, as the production of black theater moved from localized insularity to national prominence. The Black Theatre Issue preceded the publication of *Black Fire*
(1968), edited by Amiri Baraka and Larry Neal,[34] *A Black Quartet* (1968),
edited by Ben Caldwell,[35] Ed Bullins's *New Plays for a Black Theatre*
(1969),[36] and Woodie King's *Black Drama Anthology* (1972). Bullins
would go on to edit a short-lived journal entitled simply *Black Theatre*.
Thus the Black Theatre Issue anticipated the flowering in black arts publishing that followed. The volume represents, then, a seminal moment in

the Black Theater Movement and its dissemination. Accordingly Bullins's two subheadings for the two sections of the issue, "Black Revolutionary Theatre" and "Theatre of Black Experience," testify not only to the import of these emerging categories in black theater, but to their distinctiveness from white Western traditions.

Schechner's description of the BTM plays as "too conventional" places them within a schema of white Western normativity that fails to recognize an avant-garde practice that both embraces and transcends conventional social realism. In form and content these works identify a social reality, yet their social realism is not limited to mimetic representation but also incorporates the passion, vision, and imagined reality of revolutionary desire. Accordingly, Sonia Sanchez's *The Bronx is Next* figures a riot in Harlem where black revolutionaries systematically remove the black property owners and their belongings before setting fire to the buildings.[37] Ben Caldwell's *Riot Sale* similarly focuses on the dramatic tensions of urban unrest. As angry black crowds gather in the streets, threatening to explode, the white police quell their rebellious fervor by firing off cannons filled with money. Rather than staying true to their demand for actual, lasting social change, the black masses succumb to the immediate and ephemeral gratification of free money lying in the streets. No longer collective and unified, individuals push each other, struggling to collect the discharged dollar bills.[38] If this play warns of the revolution derailed and unrealized, Caldwell's *The Job* realizes violent social upheaval, featuring a black revolutionary who strikes back at the inherent racism of a welfare-based jobs program by beating to death the white job interviewer.[39] Jimmy Garrett's *And We Own the Night,* Amiri Baraka's *Police,* and Sanchez's play all refer to or feature the death of policemen at the hands of blacks. Such scenes of riots and confrontations with the police clearly represent the social reality of the times: the riots that broke out in black enclaves throughout the country in the late 1960s were invariably sparked by confrontations with police or instances of police abuse. In each of these plays, the onstage irreverence and violence not only negotiates with the existent urgencies but imagines the fulfillment of revolutionary insurgency, the achievement of the violent, oppositional objectives expressed within the rhetoric of black nationalism. This imagining of the future certainly constitutes an "avant" practice, an alternative "coming before" in terms of content, predicting and perhaps even inciting revolutionary actions.

The union, then, of "mimesis and desire" characterizes what we may term the BTM's avant-garde praxis. Writing in *Performing Black-*

ness: Enactments of African-American Modernism, Kimberly Benston terms
this praxis a "moral mimesis" because of the emphasis within the content on affecting existent moral codes and social behavior in audiences.[40] "[B]y destroying complacent dependence on current ideas of
dramatic structure," Benston writes, "and by thus opening up a vast
new field of subject matter, these advocates of what we might call
'moral mimesis' open up the floodgates for a spate of new formal, as
well as thematic possibilities."[41] The plays of the Black Theater Movement, Benston suggests, mediate between a "potentially pacifying naturalism" and a "putatively activating inspiration."[42] This activating
inspiration directs the spectators toward a desired, agitational blackness, an emerging revolutionary psyche. Accordingly, to inculcate this
new blackness, the plays revise the normative organization of the family traditionally found in American domestic realism. Garrett's *And We
Own the Night* culminates with the execution of the mother figure by
the black revolutionary protagonist, Johnny, because she serves as a
retarding influence, disrupting the advance of change through her love
of the white man. "I trust them [white people]," the mother says.
"Ain't' no nigger never been right." Johnny responds by firing into
her back as she turns to exit. He retorts, "We're . . . new men, Mama,
. . . Not niggers. Black men."[43] The son asserts his manhood through
the murder of his mother. Reversing the stereotypical hierarchy of
black matriarchy, severing the allegiance of black mother and son in
Lorraine Hansberry's *Raisin in the Sun,* the play pronounces that the
foremost alliance for black men must be to the collective struggle for
black liberation.

Ed Bullins's *Clara's Ole Man,* the final play in the Black Theatre Issue,
also presents an articulation of family decidedly different from that traditionally realized in American family drama.[44] At the end of the play the
gathered characters reveal to Clara's erstwhile suitor, Jack, that "Clara's
ole man," whose return Jack had been anticipating, is not only already
present, but not a man at all but a woman, Big Girl. Rather than the het-
eronormative nuclear family unit, Big Girl and Clara represent an alternative family, a lesbian couple. Earlier in the play Big Girl reveals that she
has rescued Clara from a traditional Christian upbringing in which her
parents taught her nothing about herself and allowed her to become
pregnant with a baby later lost in childbirth. Thus, lesbianism represents
not only a radical reordering of the social status quo but a more "healthy"
existence for Clara. The play pushes further to construct an equally alternative extended family unit that includes Big Girl's mentally retarded sis-

ter, Baby Girl, her sickly, alcoholic Aunt Toohey, and the three young gang members that have stepped in off the street to avoid the police after a robbery. By positing Big Girl as the focal power figure, by revealing her authority and her story, Bullins's play works to undermine the structural linkages that feminist critics such as Jill Dolan and Elin Diamond charge operate in conventional domestic realism, constricting gender roles and perpetuating patriarchal hegemony.[45] Kimberly Benston argues that the dénouement of homosexuality in *Clara's Ole Man* sabotages "the imbrication of family, patriarchy, and narrative enshrined by classic realist theater."[46] The content of this play and the works of the BTM more generally, as represented in the Black Theatre Issue, question what is normal and normative as they assert a new social order.

Clara's Ole Man ends with Clara and Big Girl exiting to attend a club while the gang, following the will of Big Girl, beats Jack, the transgressor. This communal beating ritualistically punishes Jack's offense but, more importantly, restores the stability of the community, Big Girl's extended family. Similarly, the majority of the plays in the Black Theatre Issue culminate with collective affirmations. Their demands for a new agitational blackness require such unity. Thus, Johnny in *We Own the Night* speaks of "We" even as he singularly kills his mother. He does it for the good of all black men. Herbert Stokes's *The Uncle Toms* forges a new image of black brotherhood as two revolutionaries convince two former young "Uncle Toms" to forego their accommodationist attitudes and to fight together for black liberation.[47] These plays transform mimetic realism through symbolic demonstrations of communality, through theatrical representations of identity politics that violently disciplines those who would dare to oppose this desired vision of a communal revolutionary blackness.

Ritual and Methexis

The structure of these plays in performance evolves toward a collective, ritualized representation, toward what Benston terms *methexis*, "a communal helping out":

> Spiritually and technically, this movement is from mimesis, or representation of an action to methexis or "communal helping out" of the action by all assembled. It is a shift from drama—the spectacle observed—to ritual, the event which dissolves traditional divisions between actor and spectator, between self and other.[48]

The move away from mimesis to methexis represented a shift from conventional dramatic processes to a more flexible form that invited spectators and performers to interact as equal participants. Aware of the events' direct correlation to their own social reality, engulfed by the intensity of the proceedings, black spectators often responded vociferously and actively participated. In his seminal article on black theater audiences, Thomas Pawley notes the cultural propensity of black audiences to vocally respond—often inappropriately—in the theater.[49] Yet the participatory black response at BTM performances testified not simply to cultural experiences, but to the interaction of mimesis and desire within the performance, to the immediacy of the plays' messages in conjunction with the imagined victory over white oppression that the black spectators could participate in vicariously. Geneviève Fabre argues in *Drumbeats, Mask and Metaphor* that black drama "calls to question the principles of theatrical catharsis, desperate pity or complicity. It puts the audience in a position where it cannot escape the representation (it should feel involved) or participation in it (it is not entertainment)."[50] Rather than catharsis, these plays worked toward methexis. More than entertainment, the moral mimesis of the BTM sought to achieve social efficacy through ritualistic communion with the audience—ritualistic in that it operated as a signifying practice commenting on existing social circumstance as well as a symbolic mediation linking the gathered community to the greater social cause beyond.

In *Taking It to the Streets: The Social Protest Theatre of Luis Valdez and Amiri Baraka,* I discuss this notion of the ritual of black revolutionary theater in great detail.[51] What I want to foreground here is that as they approached methexis, the performances of the BTM radically reoriented the relation between spectator and performer, pointing back to the ritualistic origins of theater but also achieving the transformative strategies advocated by white experimental groups such as the Living Theatre and Open Theatre. Discussing the communion of spectators and performers advocated by the latter theaters, Arnold Aronson observes, "If in fact some transformation of the spectators' consciousness were to occur, then it was essential that the audience become part of the performance, if not on a physical level then at least on a spiritual."[52] Clearly such a goal directly related to the aims of the BTM. In these ritualistic performances, the spiritual and symbolic informed the social organization of the gathered community of spectators and performances. Performances often became infectious communal celebrations, symbolic acts that united audience and performers with the greater social protest movement for black rights. Those gathered at the ritual ceremony acted as a congregation and implicitly or explicitly participated in the proceedings.[53] The BTM intended its performances to be transformative and regenerative, like ritual. As methexis, they affirmed cultural unity while demonstrating that the spectators' own oppressive social circumstances were ultimately transformable. The ritualistic action of these social protest performances revitalized the oppositional struggles of blacks and confirmed for those in attendance the righteousness of their cause. Within the social and cultural upheaval of the late 1960s and early 1970s, the performances of BTM created a reiterative rather than an imitative context. And the spectators, much like the ritual congregation, communed with the actors and participated in the proceedings.

The revolutionary rhetoric of the BTM stressed that black theater should not only create a communion with black spectators but also function as a vital force within the life of the black community. In his seminal document "The Black Arts Movement"—which follows Bullins's and Schechner's commentaries in the Black Theatre Issue and soon became a crucial manifesto of the movement, repeatedly cited and often republished—Larry Neal states, "These plays are directed at problems within black America. They begin with the premise that there is a well-defined Afro-American audience. An audience that must see itself and the world in terms of its own interests."[54] Neal imagines a black community of shared political and cultural interests and believes that the theater can play a critical role in directing that community towards self-determination. Evident in such a theatrical practice is the desire not only to affirm the collective energy of the gathered black spectators but to "link [the theater] itself concretely to the struggles of that community, to become its voice and its spirit." Radically refiguring what Neal derides as the "decadent attitude toward art—ramified throughout most of Western society," the BTM envisioned the theater as a significant, functioning institution within the marginalized black community that could help to supplant and undermine the legitimacy of the dominant culture.[55] They enlarged their perception of what constituted a theater and what theater could be and do. Accordingly, when Amiri Baraka moved from Harlem to Newark in 1966, he established not only a theater but a community cultural center, Spirit House. There he initiated a range of programs, including the African Free School for youth. He named the new cultural center Spirit House and its acting troupe the Spirit House Movers because he hoped to move people's spirits and to be as integral to the life of the community "as a grocery store."[56]

One means by which the troupe accomplished this goal was by emphasizing the integration of spirit and culture in performances as well as their inherent connection to the cause of black liberation. Neal termed the Black Arts Movement "the aesthetic and spiritual sister of the Black Power concept."[57] This notion of spirit and spirituality is a revolutionary one. Beyond mere religious assignations, this designation of spirituality locates it in the sacro-secular realm, generating communal empowerment, emotional engagement, and ultimately social change. Neal differentiates this new spirituality from an older model.

> The Old Spirituality is generalized. It seeks to recognize Universal Humanity. The New Spirituality is specific. It begins by seeing the world from the concise point-of-view of the colonized, where the Old Spirituality would live with the oppression while ascribing to the oppressors an innate goodness, the New Spirituality demands a radical shift in point-of-view.[57]

Such a radical spirituality found representation in the content of BTM plays, but such representation also necessitated structural innovations, "moral mimesis," that integrated the symbolic and the actual, the productive and the celebratory, the political and the cultural within theatrical performances.

Through generating collective affirmation of values and objectives, the BTM sought to construct "a distinctively black expressive resistance." Famously, Amiri Baraka charges in "The Revolutionary Theatre," his own profoundly influential Black Arts manifesto—Neal quotes it in his "Black Arts Movement"—that "the Revolutionary Theatre should force change, it should be change."[59] He demands a theatrical practice that is conducted and constituted in activating difference. It performs and is performative, or, as Benston argues, it is a "cause that would be always its own effect."[60] Critics have pointed out the parallels in the imagery presented Antonin Artaud's seminal document of the historical avant-garde, "The Theatre of Cruelty," to Baraka's vivid, horrific images and his violent language in "The Revolutionary Theatre."[61] Like Artaud, Baraka bombards his reader with violent, cruel images. He too seeks to purge our cultural order through rites of purification. "What we show must cause the blood to rush, so that pre-revolutionary temperaments will be bathed in this blood, and it will cause the deepest soul to move."[62]

While Artaud writes metaphorically about a theater of plague that is "victorious and vengeful,"[63] Baraka and BTM sought actual social victories by employing theater as a means to produce real social change. Christopher Innes writes that the "attempt to merge theatrical performance and reality is characteristic of the avant garde approach" and that the Living Theater took this practice "to extremes."[64] The Living Theater, following the dictums of Artaud's Theater of Cruelty, attempted to create a theater in which audience and spectators functioned "like victims burnt at the stake signaling through the flames."[65] They subjected their ensemble to a real atmosphere of "hostility, persecution and isolation" as they prepared for a production of Jack Gelber's *The Connection* in 1959.[66] For Baraka and the BTM the merging of the real and theatrical came though the direct relation the theater had to the violence and outrage of contemporary African American life. Thus, Bullins's introductory commentary to the Black Theatre Issue, where he discusses the fires that engulfed Harlem after the murder of Martin Luther King, Jr., represents a take on Artaud's metaphor of "signaling from the flames" different from that of the Living Theater. In Bullins's detail, the events themselves constitute a form of social drama as black unrest signals through the flames for change. Whereas the Living Theater sought to generate heat onstage, the BTM sought to harness the sparks, the dangerous, rebellious fervor rising in the black urban enclaves of America. Sonia Sanchez's play in the collection, *The Bronx is Next,* connects the immediacy of these real flames to the social urgency of change within her play as she imagines the forces of black revolutionary change setting fire to the city. In Artaud's imagery, cruelty pushes the audiences and spectators out of complacency. Even as they burn at the stake they exhibit a determination and agency. He points to a deep-seated spirit of anarchy and atavistic desire present in the world, and this is what Baraka and BTM sought to tap into as well. Artaud discusses the theater of plague as a "spiritual force," as "a revelation."[67] Larry Neal proclaims, as we noted previously, that "Black Arts is the aesthetic and spiritual sister of the black power concept. As such it envisions an art that speaks directly to the needs and aspirations of Black America. The Black Arts Movement believes that your ethic and your aesthetics are one."[68] Yet we must note a critical difference in Artaud and Baraka, one that reflects the distance of the BTM from the white historical avant-garde more generally. Although Baraka and Artaud both vehemently call for the destruction of the Western social order, only Baraka seeks also to "reshape this world" through a dynamic social practice, and thus, as Benston argues, he "departs from the 'disinterested' rigors of Artaudian gesture."[69]

A New World Order

While the Black Theatre Issue and the BTM's theoretical paradigms proudly proclaim the death of the Western aesthetic and demand the overthrow of white oppressive regimes, their cultural politics are not simply nihilistic. Neal vehemently declares that the "motive behind the new Black aesthetic is the destruction of the white thing, the destruction of white ideas, and white ways of looking at the world."[70] Mike Sell effectively argues that "the 'white thing' often cited by Black Arts critics and artists was quite literally that—a menagerie of commodities. But it was also a cultural *ethos,* which justified alienation in terms of the financial profit to be gained by the buying and selling of people-as things."[71] Consequently, combating the white thing meant not only fighting the polices of commodification and materialism endorsed by the white American power structure but also articulating policies of black cultural, economic, and political autonomy. Destruction of the white thing needed to be joined with the construction of a new "black thing" that only blacks could understand, a black cultural nationalism. Neal defined for black artists a "meaningful role in the transformation of society" and maintained that the black arts was an "ethical movement" "consistent with the demands for a more spiritual world."[72]

In articulating a black aesthetic theory, Neal and other black artists and critics in the 1960s and early 1970s not only diametrically opposed white Western cultural orientations, they sought a distinctly black way of creating, strictly reflective of "African American cultural tradition." Here then is a seeming paradox: The BTM advocated separatism and black cultural nationalism, yet the inclusion of BTM plays in *TDR,* even in an issue edited by Ed Bullins, points toward an assimilation and an incorporation of the movement into white aesthetic practices. The publishing of the Black Theatre Issue could be seen as signifying the acceptance of the new black drama into the American avant-garde by bestowing on it the *TDR* seal of approval. And yet the paradigms of black cultural nationalism, rather than assimilating white Western cultural traditions, asserted black difference, championed a black way of creating, and articulated a distinctly black cultural system. Black cultural nationalism as expressed by Neal and others reaffirmed the ties of the black artist to the black collective and structured the relation between that artistic practice and the black community. The publication of the Black Theatre Issue in the very white *TDR,* then, would seem to contradict this black radical ideology.

Yet I would suggest that this issue embodies a dynamic "insider/outsider" subversiveness that repeatedly characterized the BTM's cultural nationalism: the movement opposed existent political structures even as it used them to its advantage. Accordingly, Amiri Baraka and Larry Neal's black revolutionary theater, the Black Arts Repertory Theater School (BARTS), founded in Harlem in 1965, received funding from the federal government through a Harlem Youth Opportunities Unlimited (HARYOU) grant. Still BARTS refused to allow whites, including Sargent Shriver, the director of the Office of Economic Opportunity, the government agency that provided their funding, to attend performances.[73] Accepting grant money from the government represented a conscious scheme for BARTS's economic survival that was rife with ideological tensions. Taking the money while preventing white spectatorship enacted a dualistic strategy of "getting over" or capitalizing on the system while at the same time mocking and challenging the very principles of white authority.

Similarly, the Black Theatre Issue both accepts and resists Schechner and *TDR*'s largesse. The heavy reliance on play texts and the positioning and content of Bullins's introduction work against the journal's established conventions. Bullins, whose service on the editorial board of *TDR* qualified him as the prototypical insider/outsider, calculatingly constructed this issue to provoke both the journal's traditional white subscriber base and its new black clientele. Mike Sell notes that Bullins's "editorial strategy is structured by a polemical position and the strategic needs of revolutionary subjectivity."[74] Bullins purposefully makes whites uncomfortable—the same whites who asked him to edit the issue—while at the same time attempting to unify diverse voices with the BTM. In an article entitled "Must I Side with Blacks or Whites," white critic Eric Bentley rhetorically asks, "What is the white theatregoer [at a black revolutionary performance] to do? . . . Play at being Black? That surely is an effort at identification with the victim which soon becomes ludicrous."[75] The white readers/viewers were implicitly and explicitly included and excluded as representatives of the white Western political and aesthetic power structure from participation in the new black theater. As a consequence, they potentially experienced a dis-ease and dissonance with the materials of the Black Theatre Issue.

For black readers, the issue sought to provoke their racial awareness and radical consciousness. Thus, the Black Theatre Issue reflects a condition that Philip Bryan Harper believes is emblematic of Black Arts poetry, which was intended to be heard by whites and overheard by blacks. For according to this fantasy, not only would to be heard be to annihilate one's oppressors, but to be overheard would be to indicate to one's peers just how righteous, how nationalistic, how potently black one is, in contradistinction to those very peers, who figured as the direct address of the Black Arts works.[76]

Harper argues that Black Arts poetry calls black nationalist consciousness into being by defining it against black integrationist ideology as well as white hegemony. The "very peers" figured "in direct address" are those "Negroes" who identify with the Euro-American social order "against which the speaking I" of Black Arts poetry is "implicitly contrasted."[77] Correspondingly, the accommodationist black mother who is killed by her son Johnny in Garrett's *And We Own the Night* represents those reactionary Negroes who must "hear" the assault that is directed at them, while Johnny's actions call into being the revolutionary black "We" of the title that "overhears." In Harper's terms the BTM constructs this "We," this collective black radical subject, by naming it, and moves Black Arts nationalism beyond mere rhetoric. This is an "avant" step preceding and predicting the movement's realization of an activist black community, motivating its spectators, creating its own authority. The Black Theatre Issue of *TDR* constitutes what Sell terms a "highly self-conscious performance of textual Blackness," which in its strategic deployment of black expressive resistance mocks and models avant-garde assaults on the audience.[78] The Black Theatre Issue not only resists assimilation into the standard notions of the American avant-garde but necessitates a call for a radical redefinition of the term.

The Black Theatre Issue presents and represents a collective manifesto: of a movement determined to create a radical alternative to the sterility of the American theatre, an alternative vision of an American avant-garde.[79] Sell argues that despite the emergence of an "avant-garde culture of unprecedented acuity," the reason for invisibility of the BTM in the traditional history of the American avant-garde lie with the very policies of the BTM—its concern for the immediacy of the moment, its disdain for commodification or for "notions of value, permanence, and significance":

The paradox of their attack on text and objects is that, while Black theorists, poets, playwrights and performers generated an avant-garde culture of unprecedented acuity and popularity, the very success of their project has in many ways guaranteed their invisibility within a fundamental textual and theater history.[80]

My sense is that failure to recognize the theatrical experimentations of the BTM within previous studies of the avant-garde more fundamentally testifies to the ways in which definitions and theories of the avant-garde have been inherently racialized. Here is a movement that artistically and critically established alternatives to mainstream theater, that forged in practice a functional aesthetic and ritualistic commune of performers and spectators. What needs to be acknowledged is the innovative, "forward-thinking" methods by which black artists attempted to wed theory and practice, ethic and aesthetic, culture and politics to the particular circumstances of African American life. In times of contingency and urgency, black arts sought a new social order and new control.[81] And yet, critics—including Schechner—have only recognized the BTM within limited racial paradigm and have used its social objectives and racial focus to demean its innovative artistic achievements. Perhaps, then, returning to this Black Theatre Issue will enable us to problematize further definitions of the avant-garde and to recognize the new possibilities, as well as existing limitations, of its use.

Notes

I thank James Harding for his excellent notes on this essay. I also must acknowledge Michele Birnbaum for her helpful criticism and revealing insights into the argument.

1. Ed Bullins, "The So-Called Western Avant-Garde Drama," *Liberator* 7.12 (1967): 17.

2. Mike Sell, "[Ed.] Bullins as Editorial Performer: Textual Power and the Limits of Performance in the Black Arts Movement," *Theatre Journal,* 53 (2001): 413.

3. Richard Schechner, "White on Black," *Drama Review* 12.4 (1968): 27.

4. See Peter Bürger, *Theory of the Avant-Garde,* trans. Michael Shaw (Minneapolis: University of Minnesota Press, 1984), xlix; Hal Foster, *Return of the Real: The Avant-Garde at the End of the Century* (Cambridge: MIT Press, 1996), 5; Paul Mann, *The Theory-Death of the Avant-Garde* (Bloomington: Indiana University Press, 1991), 8; James M. Harding, introduction to *Contours of the Theatrical Avant-Garde,* ed. James M. Harding (Ann Arbor: University of Michigan Press, 2000), 5.

5. Mann, *Theory-Death,* 10.

6. Bürger, *Theory of the Avant-Garde,* 17.

7. Mann, *Theory-Death,* 13.

8. Larry Neal, "The Black Arts Movement," *Drama Review* 12.4 (1968): 33.

9. Christopher Innes, *Avant Garde Theatre, 1892–1992* (New York: Routledge, 1993), 3.

10. Holland Cotter, "A Revolution in African Art," *New York Times,* February 17, 2002, sec. 2.1.

11. See Arnold Aronson, *American Avant-Garde: A History* (New York: Routledge, 2000).

12. Floyd McKissick, quoted by Ed Bullins, "The King is Dead," *Drama Review* 12.4 (1968): 23.

13. Bullins, "The King is Dead," 24.

14. Ibid., 25.

15. Ibid., 25.

16. Ibid., 26.

17. Schechner, "White on Black," 26–27.

18. Ibid., 25.

19. William Sonnega, "Beyond a Liberal Audience," in *African American Performance and Theater History: A Critical Reader,* ed. Harry J Elam, Jr. and David Krasner (New York: Oxford University Press, 2001), 84–85.

20. Ibid., 84.

21. Schechner, "White on Black," 26.

22. John D. Erickson, *Dada: Performance, Poetry and Art* (Boston: Twayne, 1984), 57.

23. Amiri Baraka, *Home on the Range,* in *Drama Review* 12.4 (1968): 110.

24. Ron Milner, *The Monster,* in *Drama Review* 12.4 (1968): 104.

25. Joseph White, *Ole Judge Mose is Dead,* in *Drama Review* 12.4 (1968): 153.

26. Erickson, *Dada,* 58.

27. Walter Benjamin in "Ten Theses on the Philosophy of History," in *Illuminations,* trans. Harry Zohn (New York Schocken Books, 1978), 255, states, "Only that historian will have the gift of fanning the spark of hope in the past who is firmly convinced that *even the dead* will not be safe from the enemy if he wins."

28. Schechner, "White on Black," 26.

29. I thank James Harding for bringing this point to my attention.

30. Schechner, "White on Black," 26.

31. Ibid., 25.

32. Woodie King, "Black Theatre Present Condition," *Drama Review* 12.4 (1968): 118.

33. Amiri Baraka, *Police,* in *Drama Review* 12.4 (1968): 112–16.

34. Amiri Baraka and Larry Neal, *Black Fire* (New York: Morrow, 1968).

35. Ben Caldwell, *A Black Quartet* (New York: New American Library, 1970).

36. Ed Bullins, *New Plays for a Black Theatre* (New York: Bantam, 1969).

37. Sonia Sanchez, *The Bronx is Next,* in *Drama Review* 12.4 (1968): 78–84.

38. Ben Caldwell, *Riot Sale,* in *Drama Review* 12.4 (1968): 41–42.

39. Ben Caldwell, *The Job,* in *Drama Review* 12.4 (1968): 43–46.

40. Kimberly Benston, *Performing Blackness: Enactments of African-American Modernism* (New York: Routledge, 2000), 37.

41. Ibid.

42. Ibid., 36.

43. Jimmy Garrett, *And We Own the Night,* in *Drama Review* 12.4 (1968): 69.

44. Ed Bullins, *Clara's Ole Man,* in *Drama Review* 12.4 (1968): 159–71.

45. See Jill Dolan, *The Feminist Spectator as Critic* (Ann Arbor: University of Michigan Press, 1988), 108; Elin Diamond, "Realism's Hysteria," in *Unmaking Mimesis* (New York: Routledge, 1997), 5–7.

46. Kimberly Benston, "The Aesthetic of Modern Black Drama: From Mimesis to Methexis," in *The Theatre of Black Americans,* ed. Errol Hill (Englewood Cliffs: Prentice-Hall, 1980), 1:61.

47. Herbert Stokes, *The Uncle Toms,* in *Drama Review* 12.4 (1968): 58–60.

48. Ibid., 62.

49. Thomas Pawley, "The Black Theatre Audience," in Hill, *Theatre of Black Americans,* 2:109–20.

50. Geneviève Fabre, *Drumbeats, Mask and Metaphor* (Cambridge: Harvard University Press, 1983), 104.

51. Harry J. Elam, Jr., *Taking It to the Streets: The Social Protest Theater of Luis Valdez and Amiri Baraka* (Ann Arbor: University of Michigan Press, 1996).

52. Arnold Aronson, *American Avant-Garde: A History* (New York: Routledge, 2000), 85.

53. More recent ritual theorists such as Ranjini Obeyeskere do not agree with Turner that those gathered at ritual ceremonies uniformly act as a congregation. Obeyeskere differentiates between audience members who act as *spectators* and those who act as *participants* in the ritual enactment. See "The Significance of Performance for its Audience: an Analysis of Three Sri Lankan Rituals," in *By Means of Performance,* ed. Richard Schechner (Cambridge: Cambridge University Press, 1990), 118–30.

54. Neal, "The Black Arts Movement," 39.

55. Ibid., 36, 39.

56. Amiri Baraka, quoted by Saul Gottlieb, "They think you're an airplane and you're really a bird," *Evergreen Review,* December 1967, 51.

57. Neal, "The Black Arts Movement," 29.

58. Ibid., 39.

59. Amiri Baraka, "The Revolutionary Theatre," in *Home: Social Essays* (New York: Morrow, 1966), 210.

60. Benston, *Performing Blackness,* 32.

61. For a discussion of the relationship between Amiri Baraka's practice and theory and the theater of Antonin Artaud, see Mance Williams, *Black Theatre in the 1960s and 1970s* (Westport: Greenwood, 1985), 21–23; Leslie Sanders, *The Development of Black Theater in America* (Baton Rouge: Louisiana State University Press, 1988), 126–30; and Benston, *Performing Blackness,* 31–33.

62. Baraka, "The Revolutionary Theater," 213.

63. Antonin Artaud, *The Theatre and Its Double,* trans. Mary Caroline Richards (New York: Grove, 1958), 27.

64. Innes, *Avant Garde Theatre,* 184.

65. Artaud, *Theatre and Its Double,* 13.

66. Innes, *Avant Garde Theatre,* 184.

67. Artaud, *Theatre and Its Double,* 25, 30.

68. Neal, "The Black Arts Movement," 29.

69. Benston, *Performing Blackness,* 32.

70. Neal, "The Black Arts Movement," 47.

71. Mike Sell, "The Black Arts Movement: Performance, Neo-Orality, and the Destruction of the 'White Thing,'" in Elam and Krasner, *African American Performance,* 57.

72. Neal, "The Black Arts Movement," 30.

73. For a fuller discussion of BARTS and HARYOU see Elam, *Taking It to the Streets,* 43–44.

74. Sell, "Bullins as Editorial Performer," 419.

75. Eric Bentley, "Must I Side with Blacks or Whites," in *Theatre of Black Americans,* 138–42.

76. Philip Brian Harper, "Nationalism and Social Division in Black Arts Poetry of the 1960s," in *African American Literary Theory: A Reader,* ed. Winston Napier (New York: New York University Press, 2000), 472.

77. Ibid., 468.

78. Sell, "Bullins as Editorial Performer," 420.

79. Neal, "The Black Arts Movement," 33.

80. Sell, "The Black Arts Movement," 58.

81. Benston, *Performing Blackness,* 51.

Avant-Garde and Performance Cultures in Africa

Joachim Fiebach

Beyond the Borders of Western Innovation

The Western transformative and avant-garde arts are, on the one hand, a new and unique phenomenon in the histories of world cultures. They emerged in European and North American societies at the end of the nineteenth century, engendered and conditioned by the histories of their originating cultures, and *primarily* geared to play a major role in shaping *their own* specific societal contexts. On the other hand, some essential characteristics of the aesthetics and practices of this avant-garde were neither new nor a uniquely Western innovation.

There are, of course, substantive differences between twentieth-century transformative arts, originating within complex industrialized and fully fledged capitalist societies, and those performance cultures that have been shaped by basically preindustrial, precapitalist contexts. The Western avant-garde has been a highly creative, innovative, and historically specific phenomenon in the histories of cultural production on this planet; indeed, it is this very specificity that has had a deep and broad impact on the arts the world over. Since futurism and the Bauhaus, cutting-edge communicative technologies have not only provided inspiration and structural models, but often also *the* thematic core of many transformative and avant-garde artworks. The montage and collage formats so frequently employed by the Western avant-garde correspond with the communication revolution's historically new definition of space and time (simultaneity) in Western societies. They reflect the entirely new possibilities of shrinking space and the exponentially accelerating new speed of essential societal processes that advancements in communicative and transportation technologies facilitated. Indeed, the accelerating speed of innovation, in both form and attitude, became the hallmark of Western avant-garde aesthetics.

That Western aesthetic was positioned in fundamental contrast to the slow pace in which pre-twentieth-century dancing and miming bodies could move and construct their performances as constitutive components of the public sphere, especially in premodern, predominantly oral societies such as those in Africa. This contrast needs to be kept in mind. While contending that essential components of the avant-garde arts are also visible as defining characteristics of performance cultures prior to the historical Western avant-garde, I do not mean to imply that developments in these cultures should be considered "avant-garde" in the "Western" sense. In most instances, particularly in Africa, even the contemporary performance landscape should not be looked at through a Western-conditioned lens searching for rigid divides between "avant-garde" and "non-avant-garde." One seldom, if at all, encounters the notion of an avant-garde in the sub-Saharan discourse on performance and theater. Therefore, when investigating relationships between the Western avant-garde and African performance traditions, one must not look for identities but rather try to explore significant affinities and similarities.

Nonnaturalism and Collage Technique in Premodern Societies

Nonnaturalism and the collage format have been dominant characteristics of cultural production in premodern, and in particular, African, societies for ages—long before African carvings and Asian theater forms became major models for forward-looking European artists in the twentieth century. Traditional African theatrical activities were a constitutive factor in the societal processes in which they were embedded. Hence, they could provide examples for the Western avant-garde's efforts to make artworks integral to "real life."

Premodern and especially non-Western performance cultures offered formidable models that influenced the formation and development of the avant-garde and forward-looking Western arts in the twentieth century. Theatrical practices in Asia and the European Middle Ages played a major role in Craig's arguments for a theater art that could overcome the illusionist and naturalist inclinations of hegemonic European theater since the Renaissance. Meyerhold considered the Balagan, an offshoot of the commedia dell'arte tradition, and the Japanese Kabuki to be models for the new, antinaturalist theater he was striving to create. And Artaud's vision of a "theater of cruelty," which many artists and theoreticians read as an entirely new Western approach to theater, was essentially informed by Asian and Mexican performance cultures.

In many respects, Western avant-garde arts have recuperated cultural practices, in particular artistic techniques and forms, that had been forgotten, abandoned, or decried in the specific history of European cultures since the Renaissance. These acts of recuperation have often built on significant similarities between premodern practices in non-Western cultures and transformative cultural practices developed since the early twentieth century. For instance, the collage format, often regarded as *the* invention of the Western avant-garde movement, has been a fundamental component of "traditional" African cultures for centuries.

Sub-Saharan "traditional" arts and performance cultures share a strict antinaturalism with contemporary forward-looking theater and the Western avant-garde in particular. Seen on a certain level of abstraction, both converge in the fundamentally *flexible* attitude toward doing performances and in the readiness and willingness to alter received types of performance. Moreover, they converge in the openness to employ all means and techniques historically available and at the artists' disposal[1] to incorporate other or new, diverse components into long-cherished performance structures, and thus to adapt artistic creation to changing spatial and temporal circumstances. Both treat performances as "open artworks." The epitome of this treatment is the collage or montage format, championed by the avant-garde in order to combat the "organic artwork" that was canonized as the only possible standard of "civilized" artistic production, as the ideal of a high culture since the Renaissance.

Therefore, African sculptures, carvings, and masks, which had been massively plundered and brought to Europe in the wake of the thoroughgoing colonization of Africa after the Berlin conference in 1884–85, became significant objects of reference for the renewal (revolution) of the European cultural landscape, from Picasso and cubism in the first decade of the new century to Dada and surrealism in the second. The distinctly "antinaturalistic" outlook of African artworks inspired European artists and critics fighting to undo the hegemonic European classical and realist tradition based on the conception that the fine and performing arts should approximate a true-to-life reproduction of external reality, producing faithful representations of the normal appearance of things and activities. Apart from the Yoruba bronzes, and, to a certain

extent Benin relief sculptures, African artifacts presented strange, per-
turbing, and at the same time fascinatingly disproportionate, entirely
untruthful spatial relationships, illogically arranged, irrational, and inde-
cipherable clusters of strangely shaped beings, and grotesquely deformed
human bodies or human body parts that had no affinity whatsoever with
bodies perceivable in "real life." Carvings featured huge orifices and
menacingly protruding eyeballs, superhuman-sized arms twisted wildly
around miniscule bodies, and the mingling of apparently supernatural
beings and human beings. Masks blended all sorts of materials—for
example, strings of human or animal hair and vegetable fibers glued onto
wood; this collage of materials often rendered them into terrifying
objects. As for the "legitimate birth of cubist collage," Eddie Wolfram
has claimed that the "vogue for primitivism, particularly for African
sculpture," contributed to the creation of a favorable climate for the new
art movement.[2]

Concealed behind the Western orientalist label *primitivism* there
appears to be, to a certain extent, an affinity between ways of seeing and
understanding the world. Since the early avant-garde's interest in
African artistic production, the carvings and masks often have been
interpreted as the expression of societies not yet contaminated by rigorous reasoning and a logocentric worldview, societies still governed by
"pristine prerationalist" thought and nonstifling irrational praxis facilitat-
ing unfettered artistic creativity, unbounded social behavior, and free-
roaming imagination. Recuperating elements of such "pristine" thought
patterns and ways of seeing, avant-garde movements hoped to overcome
the logocentrism and bourgeois morality dominating European cultures.
Thus, African artworks seemed to provide perfect models for the
Dadaist's violent rejection of Western life and the surrealists' search for
the liberation of the unconscious and its unfettered (spontaneous, "automatic") artistic expression. Silke Greulich highlights the role the orientalist construction of the "Negro model" and the "myth of primitivism"
played in attempts at creating a specific Dadaist and surrealist theater.[3]
Richard Huelsenbeck and Tristan Tzara referred explicitly to African
culture in their fierce attacks on the type of rationalism that dominated
European culture. One had, as they put it, to abandon any kind of intel-
lectuality. Dealing with "Negro sculpture, Negro literature, and Negro
Music," one could get a sense of primitivism.[4]

Most premodern and modern sub-Saharan performance cultures are
inseparably intertwined with other societal realities, as were most premodern European ones. The avant-garde could use them as frames of

reference in its endeavor to overcome the deep rift between the realm of "autonomous arts" and other societal realities that had opened since the late Middle Ages, but only by ignoring their specific networks of social connection. More exploration is needed to determine the extent to which the relationship between art and society in premodern and most non-Western performance cultures preceded the avant-garde's desire to make the arts a vital, constitutive component of its own societal processes. The following brief look at instances of African performance cultures shows that the avant-garde's effort to interweave the arts and "real life" has been *in a sense only* a move to *restore a relationship* that existed prior to and—for Africa—parallel to and entirely independent from the rise of transformative twentieth-century European performance culture.

Flexibility and Spontaneity in *Bwami* Performance

The *Bwami* of the Lega, a form of "traditional" African cultural production, is based on "avant-garde-like" principles and artistic techniques such as flexibility, openness to change, and a strict "nonnaturalism." As ritual ceremonies, Bwami performances have been essential constituents of Lega societal mechanisms, in a way setting a precedent for the historical avant-gardes' bid to merge art with real life.

Bwami is an association that enacted the profusely ritualistic performances of the Lega, an originally stateless and oral society in the Congo. Bwami as an institution survived many decades of onslaughts by slave raiders, missionaries, and the colonial administration of the Belgian Congo. Daniel Biebuyck notes that Bwami is many things in one. Like a big corporation or a religion without gods, it has been instrumental in reinforcing ties of kinship, lineages, and clans. It has been at the same time a sophisticated aesthetic practice displaying fine art, literary performance, dances, and dramatic performance.[5] "Despite regional variations in number, sequence, duration, . . . the ritual cycles are structured around aphorisms that are sung, interpreted, danced, and acted out, while certain objects (natural artifacts, art objects) are displayed, manipulated, carried, and moved around in dramatic performances by groups of initiates."[6] But only *basic structural principles are constant, with many variations* in the number and the sequences of rites performed.[7] "It is almost impossible for an alien like myself," writes Biebuyck, "to detect any *internal coherence in the sequences* the Lega choose to follow. That they tend to emphasize and visualize the totality of events in a sequence, the totality of sequences in a rite, and the totality of rites in an initiation rather than each individual happening or component, is unquestionable. It is the total impact that matters." The individual style, preference, and taste of each leading practitioner (preceptor) are cultivated, and *improvisation* and "new ways of doing things are constantly sought."[8] "At the center of the proceedings are dramatic performances including music, dancing, singing, . . . gestures, light and sounds. . . . Performances are accompanied by the revelation, display, manipulation and interpretation of artworks, used jointly with manufactured and natural objects."[9]

> Even for the Lega the *striking and unexpected interpretations along with the element of surprise,* the festive mood, and the poetic style, transforms every dance and song, every display of objects, every rite and initiation, into a fascinating and entertaining experience. Although the basic themes are well known in advance, the atmosphere that is created on each occasion keeps the ceremonies from being tedious and redundant. Thus each rite seems to be unique and original.[10]

> Masks play a part in all forms of presentation. They may be worn on the face, the temples, or the top or the back of the head; they may be fastened to other parts of the body such as the knees or the arms; they are sometimes dragged over the ground, swirled around by their beards, or attached to a fence. In some rites masked dancers emerge from the initiation house; in others they remove the masks from their shoulder bags or baskets during the rite and do with them whatever the ritual prescribes.[11]

The Lega Bwami is only one instance of the many diverse modes of performance or theatrically communicative events that have remained major constituents of sub-Saharan realities until today. They are symbolic practices with clear-cut societal purposes. As *symbolic actions,* they are also "instrumental acts," geared to achieve social, political, and ideological ends, to effect something other than aesthetic entertainment.

Tradition and Improvisation in Oral Performance

There is an astounding abundance of diverse, aesthetically dominated modes of performance, or "theater proper," in sub-Saharan Africa. Storytelling and praise-singing are the most widespread and, perhaps, most interesting forms. Storytelling treats its received and to a large extent well-known "contents" (stories) quite flexibly, casually, and innovatively. The presentation is open to all sorts of interjections, to responses from the spectators, and to being modified with regard to changing spatial and temporal circumstances such as changes in performance locale or audience. Each presentation tends to be the composition of a new artwork. Interested in enhancing their status as great *creative* artists, the performers often add special (individual) episodes to inherited narratives, throw minor details of the plots into relief, and leave out more important events of well-known stories. Thus, the traditional staging of stories and in particular praise-songs could be considered "work in progress" or a version of the avant-garde's cherished "nonorganic," open artwork.

Biebuyck's and Matene's comments on the Mwindo epic of the small Nanya ethnicity in the Congo give an idea of typical structural and functional features. The Mwindo epic is not a text performed only on esoteric ceremonial occasions. There is nothing secret about it. Normally a chief or the senior of a local descent group invites a bard and supporting artists to perform a few episodes of the epic in the evening, around the men's hut in the middle of the village. "Large crowds of people, male and females, young and old, . . . come to listen or rather to be participant auditors."[12] During the performance the artists receive

> not only from the host, but also from many auditors, *masabo* gifts consisting mainly of small amounts of *butéd*-money, beads, and armlets. They would also receive . . . the praises of the crowd, praises expressed in words and gestures (symbolic drying of the sweat, adjusting of the clothing, pulling of the fingers, and straightening of the back of the dancing narrator). . . . If excitement ran high and beer and food were plentiful, the narrator would be invited to continue parts of the narration on the following evening. The interesting point is that the narrator would never recite the entire story in immediate sequence, but would intermittently perform various select passages of it.[13]

The editors note that "the epic is first sung, then narrated" episode by episode:

> While singing and narrating, the bard dances, mimes, and dramatically represents the main peripeties of the story. In this dramatic representation, the bard takes the role of the hero. The normal musical accompaniment consists of a percussion stick . . . which, resting on a

few little sticks so as to have better resonance, is beaten with drum-
sticks by three young men. . . . These men . . . are recruited among
the members of the bard's own descent groups and/or his close affines
. . . or blood friends. They know large fragments of the epic, and,
whenever necessary, help the bard to remember and to find the
thread of his story. . . . The percussionists and members of the audience sing the refrains of the songs or repeat a whole sentence during
each short pause made by the bard. In this capacity, they are called
. . . those who agree with. . . , those who say yes. Members of the
audience also encourage the reciter with short exclamations (including onomatopoeia) and handclapping or whooping.[14]

How the African collage- or montage-like approach translates into
handling details of oral presentations is best observed in the audiotaped
documentation of the performance of the Ozidi saga, the traditional great
epic of the Ijo of the Niger delta, which took place over seven nights in
a place in Ibadan, 1963. On night six the performer mentioned that the
mytho-legendary epic hero Ozidi "had had his bed already made." A
spectator immediately corrected him, "had had his mat already laid out."
The performer responded to the intervention: "There, is it wrong to call
that a bed? *(Laughter)* / All right, mat it is then!"[15] In former times, the
Ijo did not sleep on bedsteads but on mats. Using techniques reminiscent
of avant-garde collage or montage, the performer interwove the imaging
of a contemporary habit with the presentation of an entirely different
custom of everyday life. Giving details of a fight between two people, he
dramatized the clash by narrating how they drove each other to "the
market on the beach" and then further, "as far as this market inland,
Mokola market. *(Laughter).*"[16] The Mokola market was a modern place,
located in the city of Ibadan. It had nothing to do with an ancient market in the Niger delta where the fighting scene was set. In order to convey the intensity and the fierceness of the fight, the performer casually
inserted the reference to an actual, well-known place in the presentation
of a supposedly ancient event like a sudden cut in a modern montage,
entirely uninhibited by any normative demand for sticking to a canonized organic artwork and to true-to-life representation.

In contrast to the avant-garde's overriding objective, to constantly
create something entirely new, African ritualistic actors and the performers of great epics are expected to render (repeat) handed-down
forms and contents as faithfully to tradition as possible. They themselves
insist on continuing truthfully only what was set as standard by (timeless)

cultural ancestry. Although any oral performance at least slightly modifies the received tradition, the performers claim that they fully represent the revered story or epic that has been an inherent component of their culture since its (legendary-historical or mythical) origin.

In order to destroy familiarized ways of seeing, to violently jolt audiences out of their bourgeois smugness, avant-garde performances were often designed to work aggressively on spectators, to "surprise" spectators, to virtually hammer their newness and "uniqueness" into the spectators' perception. In contrast, African artists try hard to please audiences, and they entice them to join in the performative activity. They see themselves as one with their audiences, committed to faithfully serving their community's common interests. Therefore, the performance formats are based on the spectators' participation. An excellent example of this participation is the diversity of formulas with which an audience demands the continuation of a storytelling session. These formulas are essential to almost all forms of storytelling, all over the continent. They include the "paukwa" of Swahili tale telling or the Ijo "O Story" uttered by a "caller" and underscored by the "yes" with which the group of spectators responds.[17]

On second look, some of the differences between avant-garde and traditional African performances appear to be less extreme. Biebuyck stressed the interest, even the eagerness of the "preceptors" to show something new, something different in any new Bwami performance. And the Bwami is not the only example. Traditional storytellers, praise-singers, and theater companies vie for specific excellence. They wish to stand out among other performers and troupes, and they crave to be conspicuously rewarded for their distinct abilities and accomplishments by gifts (money) given to them during the performance itself.

Oral performance, or "oral literature" for that matter, encapsulates by its very structure a dialectical pragmatism. A new composition, altering at least some details of the work presented, is often rendered as *the* faithful delivery of a well-known story handed down across the centuries, as the *immutable* narration of a creation myth and the biography of past heroes. On the other hand, while asserting that they convey truthfully what is received from the past, the performers nevertheless stress their creative power. The performer of a version of the Sundiata (the most famous epic of West Africa, perhaps of the whole of sub-Saharan Africa) who was recorded by D. T. Niane in Guinea in the early 1960s started his composition with a praise-song-like self-representation:

I am a griot. It is I, Djeli Mamoudoi Kóuyaté, son of Bintou Kóuyaté, master in the art of eloquence. . . . The art of eloquence has no secrets for us; without us the names of kings would vanish into oblivion, we are the memory of mankind. . . . My word is pure and free of all untruth; it is the word of my father's father. I will give you my father's words just as I received them; royal griots do not know what lying is. . . . Listen to my word, you who want to know; by my mouth you will learn the history of Mali.[18]

Other performers state openly that there are very different versions of the supposed "immutable story," indicating that they offer a variation of, if not even a deliberately innovative approach to, handed-down materials.[19] Singers may demand that audiences receive their performance in "deferential" silence.[20] Storytellers often suggest that *they* are the creators of the performed stories and epics whose narrative contours at least are well-known, handed-down by the audiences' cultural tradition. Voicing their claim to individual achievement, they underscore that their composition is the greatest, the most truthful, and at the same time the most original one. Okabou, the performer of the Ozidi saga, presented himself as *the* great artist telling the story of his fatherland:

Okabou is my name . . .
Now it's the story of my fatherland that I have undertaken to tell.
So it isn't any story of some other town that I am telling.
And Okabou, I repeat, Okabou is my name.[21]

Collage, Revue, and Masquerade in Yoruban Performance

Aesthetically dominant activities long have been integral practices of "premodern" African societies. A significant feature of this relationship is the fluid boundaries between efficacy-oriented theatricality such as the Bwami initiation rite and theater that is separated out from other societal practices and whose chief objective is to render entertainment and aesthetic pleasure. The collage format appears to be best suited to negotiating the complex and historically changing relations between the different types of performance and between performance culture and society in general. Thus, African "traditional" cultural productions developed, in historically specific forms and contexts, attitudes and artistic practices often regarded as *the* fundamental innovations of the "hypermodern" avant-garde.

Perhaps the most important complex of Yoruba performances is historically based on and related to the appearance of *egungun,* the masked representatives of the (spirits) of the dead and (ancient) ancestors. Tracing the history of the traditional Yoruba professional, itinerant theater, some troupes of which operated at least until the early 1980s, Joel Adedeji came to the conclusion that dancing egungun originated as early as the fifteenth or sixteenth centuries as essential agents of funeral rituals at the ancient courts of Yoruba kings. The professional traveling theater, named *alarinjo, agbegijo,* or *apidan,* emerged from these ritual practices no later than the end of the eighteenth century. Performances resemble the loosely ordered "avant-garde" collage-structured theater. Organized as sets of causally unconnected "numbers" or feats, they might remind us of the revue-like form that Eisenstein practiced in the early 1920s as the presentational structure of a "montage of attractions." Most importantly, however, as specifically *artistic (entertaining) phenomena* they are in essence inseparably intertwined with *their societal realities* or, alluding to the prime avant-garde desire, with "real life."[22]

In the 1820s, Clapperton and Landers, two British visitors, saw the accomplished enactment of a python snake by an apidan troupe.[23] Apidan collage productions in the 1970s still contained "numbers" with the basic contours and symbolic essence of that snake presentation. As Joel Adedeji put it, the program for every performance is that of a variety show:

> The theatre operates on a form of repertory system. A company or troupe could have several productions from a stock-pile of masks. The masque-dramaturgist is free to base his masque on a satirical motive or on his conception of certain live or vital forces in society. Sometimes there is no sharp dividing line between the serious and the comic; it is therefore pointless to divide the masques into the two basic classical dramatic types of tragedy and comedy. Performances take place in . . . open-space; no scenery is necessary, except that, occasionally, the genius of a masque-dramaturgist manifests itself in the use of "symbolic scenery." Generally, the objective in staging is not the simulation of a locality but the creation of an atmosphere.[24]

In a later discussion he added, "The sketches were mainly improvisational and *capable of infinite changes.* . . . Lack of pre-meditation and any carefully worked out 'scenario' affected the shape of the masques as, sometimes, the enthusiasm of both the actor and spectator resulted in unrestrained indulgence in farce."[25]

Kacke Götrick has described how troupes in the 1970s altered constantly and casually, at short notice, the ordering of the sequences of the feats they were presenting in response to the estimated or clearly stated interests of varying audiences. She provides ample evidence of the interaction between performers and spectators during a performance. Götrick's detailed description of a performance in 1976 gives an idea of the collage format and, perhaps, of the aesthetics and the philosophy on which this type of theater was predicated. The area of the stage was the court of the compound of a *balogun,* one of the traditional leaders in Ibadan. The balogun, who had invited and entertained the troupe, sat elevated in a special place. The opening number involved praise-singing and dancing for the patron. Then child players danced and did tricks with their clothes. After a while an adult performer joined them and asked the audience of roughly three hundred people to be quiet—which they never were—and to watch the performance. Then he tried to turn his garment inside out. Ayelabola, the troupe's leader, entered and greeted the patron, dancing and singing, recounting (in a praise-song) his great deeds. An actor was ordered by Ayelabola to prostrate himself before the balogun and do some acrobatic feats (somersaulting, etc.). After that, the actor walked into the audience to collect gifts (money). Two mime attractions followed. Performers, accompanied by chorus singing, moved a large mat in a pattern symbolizing ruffled water. This was followed by acting out the movements of several leopards, a scene with apparently mythical symbolical connotations. One leopard dashed from a roof, rushed to a child in the audience, and carried it away, accompanied by the spectators' laughter. The next two numbers showed the Cocotte, a stereotype figure satirizing "loose" women, and the Hunter.

> In the meantime, the following sketch was prepared by two adult actors in the middle of the stage, covering two of the older children with their *ago* to enable them to change. As soon as the Hunter was covered by an *ago,* another actor started to chant about smallpox. Somewhat later the two children were uncovered, now visible as two bundles, one light red, the other lilac. The bundles acted the part of persons struck by smallpox. . . . Spectators, mostly women and children, went up to them to offer one-kobo-coins, the chanting actor

praying for them and particularly for Balogun that they might be spared from the disease. Finally he thanked the audience for the money.

One of the following attractions was a dramatic skit featuring violent clashes between a boy, a father, and an old man. The audience intervened, imploring the old man to do something for the boy, who acted as if he were dead. In the middle of the drama a quarrel arose among some spectators. Others tried to put a stop to further commotion. The audience was as much interested in the quarrel as in the drama.[26] Following numbers were about a Hausa tradesman and a crocodile, the latter probably substituting for, or resembling, the old python number and, perhaps, carrying a handed-down mythical meaning. The appearance of the Beautiful Woman, dressed in green and played by the troupe's leader, was the last attraction. Played by Ayelabola, she danced up to the balogun and as a favor showed him the strings of beards tied around her waist under the skirt. She kept dancing for a while and then collected money from the spectators, signaling the end of the show.

Even as professional practitioners of a separate theater art, the apidan or alarinjo players were always attached to their roots, to ritualistic masquerading. They had a close relationship with egungun masqueraders who were not members of the troupes dancing at special social occasions, festivals, and funerals. As Adedeji noted, "The masque-dramaturgs still go by their original descriptive name, *egungun apidan.*"[27] They were obliged to be members of the powerful Ogboni Society, which venerated the god Obatala, a society whose members claimed ownership of the earth on which the Yoruba lived, which Obatala was believed to have created.

> The substance of what the masque-dramaturgist wishes to communicate or share with his audience is revealed in the material of his creation which also underlines his main preoccupations, namely religion and human situations. His themes depict first his faith in the ancestor and the emotional influence that the supernatural exercises on his life; they also indicate some vagueness in his own conceptualization of the ancestor and the deities, and this may qualify the reason why he operates within the realm of allegory and symbolism.[28]

The masque dramaturg used the masques of his "repertoire" to demonstrate "two main aspects of his own skill, the use of the serious masques to assert his supernatural attainments, and the use of the comic masques to satirize."[29]

Receptivity, Innovation, and the Intercultural in African Performance

African performance cultures have been open to assimilating new materials and theatrical techniques, but also in adopting "other" (foreign) perspectives on the world. "Restless," sometimes even eager to modify and refurbish received structures in response to changing historical contexts, they remind us of the avant-garde's obsession with constantly renewing its aesthetics and artistic practices. Discussing views on the multifunctional features of the African epic with regard to *nanga* performances in Tanzania, Mugyabu Mulokozi claimed that "the multifunctional features of the *nanga* are a manifestation of the epos' responsiveness to changing socio-historical-performance contexts and needs."[30]

A brief look at the intricate, discrete history of the *beni ngoma* (*beni* dances or theatrical festivals) in eastern Africa since the late nineteenth century gives an idea of the fundamental alterability of a "traditional" type of cultural production. Constantly changing their multilayered structures, their practitioners, and the different interests and social strata they were serving, Beni ngoma persisted as a great form of cultural performance well into the late 1960s.

Although the "beni" history began entirely independent from any European transformative cultural practice, it was heavily influenced by European political, economic, and cultural imperialism, developing significant anticolonial features in the 1930s. Beni ngoma proper emerged in Swahili cities along the East-African coast (Tanzania, Kenya) in the late 1890s. *Beni* is the swahilicized word for band, originally the European military brass band. The new instruments (horns, trumpets) and tunes were played by rival associations that gave themselves primarily British names. The first one established in Mombasa was called Kingi Beni (the King's Band).[31] The competing groups were internally organized along the lines of European naval ranks—admiral, captain, and so on. They displayed characteristic costumes and acted out salient habits and attitudes of the colonizing powers (Britain, Germany), which had demonstrated their overwhelming might by laying waste to rebellious areas along the coast, maintaining a firm imperialist grip on their African territories. Mombasa beni ngoma, for instance, paraded through the streets of the city before World War I with floats depicting, as an observer described it, "natives dressed as admirals and other officers sitting on the bridge, drinking whisky and sodas, and puffing cigarettes, going through a pantomime all the while of receiving reports from orderlies."[32] The competing associations tried to outdo each other not only by staging the most embellished replica of European life but by lavishly consuming food and drink and by performing contests of satiric poetry. They were very expensive enterprises, carried out and financed by members of wealthy and aristocratic social groups. At first glance, it appears as if the competitions originated primarily from the drive to most efficiently adopt, and thus succumb to, the new, powerful colonizer's way of life. Beni ngoma, however, were a new form in a long tradition of urban performance contests along the East African coast. The costumes and attitudes they portrayed were new, signifying the rapid speed with which Swahili and Arab youth in particular responded adaptively and creatively to the new world with which they had to cope.[33] But potlatch-like performance contests between different moieties and household groupings, which are at the core of the beni festivals or parades, had been a major characteristic of East-African coastal city life long before the British and German imperialist subjugation, traceable to the early nineteenth century. In 1903, the German Carl Velten, who collected material on African ways of life shortly before the turn of the century, presented a wealth of *ngoma ya mashindano* (performance contests) that were entirely geared to deal with conflicts, tensions, and the struggle for sociocultural prestige between different quarters and different groups of coastal cities, performances that depicted typical features of coastal African life without any marked European influence.[34]

Thus, before World War I beni ngoma's prime objective and "content" was to show off and negotiate urban Africans' social positions, social roles, and power relations among *themselves.* The performances acted out and asserted their *African* identities under the given circumstances, at a certain point of time in *their* history. It is small wonder that the British were quite uneasy about performances that, while obviously "imitating" European behavior, seemed on the surface just to underscore the colonizers' superiority and full ideological control over the colonized.

After World War I, other social strata, for instance groups of high-school-educated clerks working in the colonial administration, took over beni activities on a much more modest level, probably as a practice deemed to foreground and assert *their* creativeness, their cultural potential vis-à-vis their dull, routine-governed life in a subordinate social stratum. It was in that new context that literacy and the rigid division between work and leisure time, which had spread to the peoples of the interior, began to play a role in appraising the time-consuming performances, often lasting several days. In the late 1920s, the African newspaper *Mambo Leo (Things of Today)* admonished those who still foolishly wasted their time, their energies, their bodies, and their money on useless, non-money-making activities to come to their senses and terminate all merely "consumptive" dance performances.[35]

In the 1930s, prime elements of beni had spread westwards into rural areas of what was then Tanganyika, and south and southwest into industrial areas of central Africa. In some cases those associations that staged performance contests still used the name *beni;* other dance societies presented their variants of dance activities under the name *mganda.* They competed, and to a certain degree blended with dance forms, such as *kalela,* which apparently sprang from cultures different from the coastal ones.[36] Beni dancing teams played a role in the most significant of central African industrial protests in the mid-1930s—the Copperbelt upheavals. According to Henderson's analysis of the Copperbelt disturbances, the Mbeni society "was genuinely a dance society. . . . But it was also an organization which . . . was run by men of prestige and standing. . . . Their ranking members like the 'King,' the 'Governor,' or the 'Doctor' were chosen from among powerful men in the towns . . . who had earned the respect of their fellow workers."[37]

In 1969–70, the community of the recently established University College Dar es Salaam, part of what was then the University of Eastern Africa, could still watch primarily domestic servants dance mganda on campus, sometimes as performance contests between several groups. It was, especially for me, a puzzling experience. The dancers looked like devoted colonial clerks: they wore shorts, thick white woolen socks, and impeccable white, short-sleeved shirts, and they danced in drill-like, orderly lines. However, the music (drumming) and the dance movements were similar to those of traditional dance performances staged by groups from the interior of Tanzania. And the handling of the fly whisk, the sign of respected persons in received African cultures, was an integral component of the mganda shows. I became even more bewildered watching dramas that young workers in the mganda performers' outfit danced in the African, nondrilled, rather individualized, "loose" fashion, dramas that, in accord with the prevailing Tanzanian nationalist agenda, satirized young workers who put on the airs of important, entirely westernized elite persons, carrying Western-style briefcases, wearing big sunglasses, and fancy Western hats. It was those experiences that led Ranger, who then was professor of history at University College Dar es Salaam, to investigate the complex, discrete history of beni.[38]

Dialectical Pragmatism: Linking African Worldviews and Avant-Garde Philosophies

The holistic understanding of societal structures and mechanisms and of the relationship between nature and culture, perceived by early avant-garde artists and theorists as a "primitive" worldview predicated on irrationality, is in fact a dimension of a distinct, sophisticated rationality and of a dialectical pragmatism. The flexibility and openness of the performance structures derive from that pragmatism and speak of a dialectical ("holistic") thought pattern. Human life, societal structures—indeed, all things—are conceived as essentially multilayered, multifaceted, complex, and in a sense paradoxical. Social mechanisms, the relationship between culture and nature, the earthly world and the supernatural, man and deities are considered to be in a state of harmonious, mutually benefiting coexistence and, at the same time, to be troublesome, dangerous, contradictory, destructive processes. A flexible, pragmatic approach to any new situation, to changing historical circumstances, appears to be the appropriate way to survive and master the complex, difficult-to-sustain world. The "earthly," all-encompassing pragmatic worldview and attitude are the opposite to one-dimensional thinking and a dogmatic pursuit of allegedly immutable principles.[39]

Spending almost twenty years with Zulu people, Axel-Ivor Berglund emphasized the complexity and productivity of their pragmatic thought-patterns and symbolism. Zulu regard oppositions as different sides of one and the same coin, and they handle the practical problems of everyday life accordingly. Berglund avoided the term *ancestor* in his book, using instead the word *shade* because the former term invites thinking in Western dichotomies that treat the dead as if they are totally separated from the living. There are no such rigid demarcation lines among the Zulu. Berglund quotes an informant: "Father is departed, but he is," the idea being that the father is present and active although he is no longer living as the speaker is. Symbols remain comparatively stable although the materials serving as their signifiers are often altered. "If at funerals stones are not available, sods of earth are used to replace the stones. In the Mapumulo area I saw chips from clay vessels used to replace the stones and informants made it clear that the corpse was like the hard clay of the vessel; this in turn was associated with stones."[40] Referring to a case in a customary court, Berglund pointed to the pragmatic flexibility of handling difficult-to-judge legal and other matters:

> Zulu thought-patterns do not have a fixed code of laws which stipulate boundaries between moral and immoral use of anger. Although, in theory, the divisions are clear, in practice there is room for manipulating the boundaries. Secondly, it is the circumstances related to a particular case of anger that will finally decide whether it was moral or not.[41]

Modifying Lévi-Strauss's characterization of the type of rationality and praxis developed by oral societies, African dialectical "bricolage" pragmatism is, in essence, the opposite to the rigidly dichotomizing Cartesian thought pattern of the Western tradition that spawned the canonizing of normative art forms. It has, on the other hand, much in common with the avant-garde's search for a new understanding of the world and a new aesthetics. Praise of "primitivism" encapsulated the orientalists' desire to regain or to find a holistic, uncompartmentalized perspective on the world that could accommodate paradoxes, contradictions, and the "discontinuous continuity" of historical processes. The collage-like format is the very epitome of a pragmatic, bricolage-type approach to performance and to art forms in general.

The egungun masquerading testifies to the complex relationship between the sophisticated perspectives on the world and "paradoxical" performance cultures. Dancing the egungun, a kind of spirit of the dead or of the ancestors, the performer's body is entirely disguised. Even the flesh of the hands is concealed. This is to present the egungun as a *deadly,* awe-inspiring force. It is, however, egungun masquerading out of which the professional comic apidan springs, a hilarious, fun-making, and most entertaining theater. This indexes a rather strange or perhaps paradoxical conception of death and the dead. Death is the Other, the very opposite to life, thus to the live body, but death has at the same time the characteristics of the live body. Death or the dancing spirit of the dead is a sensuous phenomenon, and a source of sensuous pleasure, too. Even those egungun who dance at funerals, awesome and dreadful guardians of the deceased, terrifying manifestations of death and the powerful ancestors, are fun-makers, often highly skilled in satirical and comic histrionics. It is this separated-out theater's inseparable links with dead-serious, efficacious instrumental practices, the realization of dominant social values, and the incumbent affiliation with ideologically and politically powerful institutions that led Margaret Drewal to conclude that the professional performers enjoy virtually the same societal ("ontological") status as egungun masqueraders who come out to dance at rituals and on seasonally ritualistic festive occasions only. Focusing on Yoruba rituals and especially on egungun/apidan performances, Drewal stressed that ritual spectacles were plays that at the same time operated "as another mode of being," which, as with other modes of being, people shifted into and out of. She claimed that spectacle dwells conceptually at the juncture of "two planes of existence—the world and the other world, at the nexus of the physical and the spiritual," and at the nexus of the "visible and invisible."[42]

Egungun are on the whole rather "lively" phenomena, much open to change. They are curious about new things, embracing fragments from foreign cultures rapidly and avidly. For example, around the turn of the century, at the first stage of colonial penetration of Yorubaland, Dennett met an egungun who had performed at the funeral of an important chief. The egungun

> presented himself before my tent, and told me that he was the father (deceased) come from heaven, and what was I going to give him. The men, they said, know that the Egun is a man dressed up, but they respect the dress. . . . This Egun wore top boots made by the Hausa. He also wore pants instead of the native cloth. His shirt and overcloth were of a rich texture, but no different from that worn by the well-to-do. But he wore a net-like mask in front of his face which gave him a weird appearance. Men and boys followed him, and seemed to be much impressed when the Egun cried out in a voice evidently his own: "I am from heaven, therefore you must respect me."[43]

Small wonder then, that in Nigeria's much-commodified cultural scene of the 1970s egungun carried calling cards, always ready to serve spectators as potential paying customers. As an American researcher noted, "a white plastic demon mask has been incorporated into a traditional masquerade costume. The horrific horned mask has been satirically juxtaposed with a fabric inset featuring the words 'African Beauty.'" This mask is "perfectly acceptable in the traditional funerary context." In a neighboring town the researcher saw an egungun who carried his calling cards reading, "For the play which is enjoyable, call: 'Egungung-who-does-kindness, does not cruelty,' with his players—L.

Ogunge, Manager." The egungun concluded his performance at a
funeral with a new hit by Sonny Ade delivered "in the rough, guttural"
voice meant to simulate that of the monkey with whom egungun have
been closely connected in Yoruba tradition. "Change has always been
present in Yoruba cultural systems, and those are just a few examples of
how the more contemporary aspects of Yoruba life have been merged
with the more traditional patterns in a mode consistent with Yoruba
values."[44]

The extent to which the collage-like performance of initiation rites
can act out complexity, ambivalence, contradictory social positions,
clashing interests and conceptions of the world may be best outlined by
a cursory glance at a main component of the Bambara initiation cycle—
the masks or performers *koré dugaw*. These are tricksters or clowns who
represent viciousness, destructiveness, highly attractive critical intelli-
gence, and creativity as inextricably intertwined characteristics of human
beings. Dominique Zahan describes in detail that koré dugaw have been
to village spectators the most appealing performers in initiation procedures that transform youth into adults, with considerable claim to political and religious (ideological) leadership. Koré has been the last or highest stage of the initiation cycle in which the initiated are to gain insight
into the core values of the community, and into secrets of the world. It
is just at this most important level that the clowns play a major role. Koré
dugaw parody, satirize, mock, ridicule everybody and everything held in
highest esteem by the community.[45] On the other hand, the clowns
appear to embody the real, wise, human being, the owner of deepest
knowledge.[46] In addition, their costumes, their speech, and their bodily
movements seem to openly criticize ruling aristocratic attitudes and ideologies. Apparently "taking sides" with the dominated peasants, they
scathingly ridicule in particular dominant values and the deeds that other
types of performers (royal griots) affirmatively praise. The clowns fight
the dreadful hyena-masks signifying the king's agents for brutally controlling the peasants. Engaging the dangerous, much feared hyenas, the
clowns apparently perform the underdog's critical attitude toward an
oppressive power structure and its hegemonic value system. Koré dugaw
wear a wooden sword, a parody of the iron swords of the warriors and
their policing guard (the hyenas). Grotesquely inverting the political and
cultural hegemony of the warriors as a ruling social stratum, they call
themselves "war chiefs." They claim to possess an artillery called "tuck-
ing-in-the-cake." Their soldiers would only know one distance—that
between "la coude" (elbow) and the mouth, alluding to the principal

interests and needs of the peasants and inferior strata to produce and consume, to eat and drink, thereby leading a peaceful life instead of waging
destructive wars.[47]

The *oriki,* the traditional praise-singing performances of the Yoruba,
provide another example. They show, in addition, the extent to which
premodern African worldviews are similar to aspects of thought patterns
underlying the aesthetics of modern transformative artists and avant-garde
practitioners. In her authoritative book, *I Could Speak Until Tomorrow,*
Karin Barber emphasizes the praise-song's "disjunctiveness" and "dis-
parateness of its constituent units" or, as I would like to reword it, its collage-like structure corresponding with a "bricolage" worldview.[48] "An
oriki text . . . is not narrative like a chronicle or consecutively ordered
like a king-list. There is no necessary or permanent relationship between
one item in an oriki chant and the next: each may refer to a different
topic."[49] With regard to Bakhtin's notion of the dialogic, Barber claims
that oriki "could be seen as the living embodiment of the dialogic."
Bakhtin's language, originally used to describe the Western novel's exhibition of "indeterminacy, a certain semantic open-endedness, a living
contact with unfinished, still-evolving contemporary reality," seems "to
be made for oriki."[50] Analyzing the significance of facial marks in an
oriki, she concludes, "Difference is what the oriki celebrate."[51]

The praise of difference is inseparably linked to the affirmation of a
socially divided, hierarchically structured world, in which, however, the
Other as the Different is negatively valued.[52] Barber begins her chapter
on "Disjunction and Transition" with statements on the oriki's contradictory, almost paradoxical stance:

> Oriki mark difference. They are imprinted with signs of idiosyncrasy
> through which they evoke and recall the differences between entities.
> But at the same time they are the means by which boundaries
> between entities are crossed. . . . Through it, power flows. . . . It is
> the disjunctiveness of the discourse of oriki that makes it possible for
> them to assert identities and at the same time to cross boundaries
> between individuals and groups.

All oriki mark individuality, "but all have a tendency to float, to be
shared by more than one subject. An individual's 'own' oriki are a tissue
of quotations, a collection of borrowings from diverse sources."[53]

The modifications of "sacrosanct" received performance formats in
always slightly different versions, the manifestation of "discontinuous

continuity," of "discrete sameness"—these manifestations give evidence to the complexity of premodern cultures, their sophisticated approach to the contradiction-fraught, paradoxical, difficult-to-cope-with relationship between the individual and society, and with the world in general.

Pondering specific qualities and essential features of African religion(s), Wole Soyinka and Ulli Beier emphasize the openness and thus creativeness of handed-down cultures. Beier claims that both Christianity and Islam are conservative forces that actually "retarded Nigeria's ability to cope with the modern world, whereas traditional religions—Yoruba religion, at least—were much more open, and much capable of adaptation." Soyinka adds succinctly: "Yes, and for that very reason liberating!"[54]

Conclusion

Although the Western transformative and avant-garde arts are, as I noted in my introduction, a new and unique phenomenon in the histories of world cultures, essential components and characteristics of their aesthetics and artworks are neither new nor a uniquely Western innovation. Nonnaturalism and the collage format had been dominant characteristics of cultural production in premodern societies, African societies in particular, for centuries. Small wonder, then, that African carvings and Asian theater forms became major models for forward-looking European artists in the twentieth century.

The Bwami of the Lega, a "traditional" African cultural production, is based on avant-garde-like principles and techniques such as flexibility, openness to change, and a strict "nonnaturalism." As ritual ceremonies, Bwami performances have been essential constituents of Lega societal mechanisms, in a way setting a precedent for the historical avant-gardes' bid to merge art with "real life."

Africa boasts a variety of separated-out, aesthetically dominated types of performance with avant-garde-like features. Storytelling and praise-singing are the most widespread forms of African traditional theater. Each "staging" of legends, epics, and other stories alters to a certain degree well-known plots or sequences of episodes, and performers often weave in, collage-like references to contemporary events, locales, and objects.

Traditional sub-Saharan collage-like performances are inseparably intertwined with other societal realities. The close interrelationship between ritualistic and aesthetic theatricality, fundamental to the history of Yoruba egungun masquerading, is a case in point. African performance cultures change in response to changing historical circumstances.

"Premodern" theatrical forms have been open, and often even eager to adopt new and foreign cultural components and to modify their performing techniques, objects, music styles, and performing spaces. In many instances, this practice can be compared to the avant-garde's obsession with permanent artistic innovation and the incorporation into artworks of any cultural and technological means at the artist's disposal. Traditional African performances are a manifestation of the dialectical pragmatism and specific rationality that govern dominant African worldviews and praxis. Premodern African perspectives on society and nature tend in many respects to be similar to the avant-garde's philosophies, and this is probably an important reason why European forward-looking artists of the early twentieth century took such an interest in "primitive," especially African, cultures.

Notes

1. Peter Bürger, *Theorie der Avantgarde* (Frankfurt am Main: Suhrkamp, 1974). Also see W. Martin Lüdke, ed., *Theorie der Avantgarde. Antworten auf Peter Bürgers Bestimmung von Kunst und bürgerlicher Gesellschaft* (Frankfurt am Main: Suhrkamp, 1976).

2. Eddie Wolfram, *History of Collage: An Anthology of Collage, Assemblage and Event Structures* (London: Studio Vista Macmillan, 1975), 15.

3. Silke Greulich, "Untersuchungen zur Rolle des Darstellerkörpers in ausgewählten Theatrekonzepten und Inszenierungen der europäischen Avantgarde zwischen 1916 und 1930," M.A. thesis, Seminar Theatrewissenschaft/Kulturelle Kommunikation, Humboldt-Universität zu Berlin, 2001.

4. Richard Huelsenbeck and Tristan Tzara, *Dada siegt! Blinaz und Erinnerung* (Hamburg: Nautilus/Nemo Press, 1985), 17f.

5. Daniel Biebuyck, *Lega Culture: Art, Initiation, and Moral Philosophy among a Central African People* (Berkeley: University of California Press, 1973), 66–67.

6. Ibid., 74.

7. Ibid., 84–85.

8. Ibid., 125; emphasis added.

9. Ibid., 142.

10. Ibid., 157, emphasis added.

11. Ibid., 167–68.

12. *The Mwindo Epic,* trans. and ed. Daniel Biebuyck and Kohombo C. Matene (Berkeley: University of California Press, 1971), 13.

13. Ibid., 13–14.

14. Ibid., 13.

15. *The Ozidi Saga,* trans. from the Ijo of Okabou Ojobolo by J. P. Clark (Ibadan: Ibadan University Press and Oxford University Press, 1977), 286–87.

16. Ibid., 299.

17. Ibid., 100.

18. Ebrahim Hussein, "Tale-Telling as a Performing Art" and following discussion, in *Theatre and Social Reality: International Colloquy for Theatre People from Countries of the Third World,* ed. Joachim Fiebach (Berlin: Henschel, 1977), 50–55.

19. See *Sunjata: Three Mandinka Versions,* ed. Gordon Innes (London: School of Oriental and African Studies, 1974), and *The Oral Performance in Africa,* ed. Isadore Okpewho (Ibadan: Spectrum Books in association with Safari Books, 1990).

20. See Henri A. Junod, *The Life of a South African Tribe,* 2d ed., vol. 2 (London: Macmillan, 1927), 89.

21. *The Ozidi Saga,* 272.

22. Joel A. Adedeji, "The Origin and Form of the Yoruba Masque Theatre," *Cahiers d'Etudes Africaines* 12 (1972): 254–63. See also Adedeji's "The Aldrinjo Theatre: The Study of a Yoruba Theatrical Art from its Earliest Beginnings to the Present Times," Ph.D. diss., Ibadan, 1969.

23. Hugh Clapperton, *Journal of a Second Expedition into the Interior of Africa from the Bight of Benin to Socctoo,* facsimile rpt. of 1829, 1st ed. (London: Cass, 1966), 53–56.

24. Adedeji, "Origin and Form," 254–63.

25. Joel A. Adedeji, "'Alarinjo': The Traditional Yoruba Travelling Theatre," in *Theatre in Africa,* ed. Oyin Ogunba and Abiola Irele (Ibadan: Ibadan University Press, 1978), 39.

26. Kacke Götrick, *Apidan Theatre and Modern Drama: A Study in a Traditional Yoruba Theatre and Its Influence on Modern Drama by Yoruba Playwrights* (Stockholm: Almquist and Wiksell, 1984), 51–52.

27. Adedeji, "Alarinjo," 34.

28. Adedeji, "Origin and Form," 262.

29. Adedeji, "Alarinjo," 49.

30. Mugyabusa Mlinzi Mulokozi, "The Nanga Epos of the Bahaya: A Case Study in African Epic Characteristics," doctoral thesis, University of Dar es Salaam, 1986, 92.

31. Terence O. Ranger, *Dance and Society in Eastern Africa, 1890–1970: The Beni Ngoma* (Berkeley: University of California Press, 1975), 22.

32. Quoted in ibid., 14.

33. Ranger, *Dance and Society,* 31f.

34. Carl Velten, *Sitten und Gebräuche der Suaheli* (Göttingen: Vandenhoeck and Ruprecht 1903), 148–71. See Joachim Fiebach, *Literatur der Befreiung in Afrika* (Munich: Damnitz, 1979), 35–39.

35. Ranger, *Dance and Society,* 97–98.

36. Ibid., 126f.

37. Henderson, cited in Ranger, *Dance,* 139f.

38. Ranger, *Dance,* preface. See also Leroy Vail and Landeg White, *Power and the Praise Poem: Southern African Voices in History* (Charlottesville: University Press of Virginia, 1991), who note: "Most descriptions of the region's oral poetry emphasize . . . extreme fragmentation." Yet despite the variety of genres and multiplicity of languages there is the "existence of a common aesthetic, an extremely adaptable but continuous poetic tradition extending over a long period of time and over a wide area" (41).

39. See Joachim Fiebach, *Die Toten als die Macht der Lebenden. Zur Theorie und Geschichte von Theatre in Afrika* (Berlin: Henschel, 1986), esp. 186–89. See also John Miller Chernoff, *African Rhythm and African Sensibilities* (Chicago: University of Chicago Press, 1979); Edmund R. Leach, ed., *Dialectic in Practical Religion* (Cambridge: Cambridge University Press, 1968); and Ulli Beier, *The Return of the Gods: The Sacred Art of Suzanne Wenger* (Cambridge: Cambridge University Press, 1975).

40. Axel-Ivor Berglund, *Zulu Thought-Patterns and Symbolism* (Bloomington: Indiana University Press, 1976), 29.

41. Ibid., 265.

42. Margaret Thompson Drewal, *Yoruba Ritual: Performers, Play, Agency* (Bloomington: Indiana University Press, 1992), 103–4.

43. R. E. Dennett, *Nigerian Studies* (London: Macmillan, 1910), 29–30.

44. Marilyn Hammersley Houlberg, "Egungun Masquerades of the Remo Yoruba," *African Arts* 11.3 (1978): 26–27. The history (or histories) of masks like the central Malawian *nyau,* which originally represented the dead, and praise-poems in eastern and southern Africa, reveal similar or pertinent features. They corroborate that African cultures are, so to speak, flexible, marked by openness, mobility, alterability, ready to respond to and try to master historical change by eagerly adopting new elements into structural elements and functions of cultural performances.

45. Dominique Zahan, *Sociétés d'initiation Bambara: Le N'domo, le Ko* (Paris: Mouton, 1960), 20–83.

46. Ibid., 138–94.

47. The villagers' perspectives on war and warriors appear to be the direct opposite of the presentations ("representative theatricality") of royal warriors and war in general in various versions of the Sunjata epic as, for instance, documented and interpreted by Gordon Innes in his introduction to *Sunjata: Three Mandinka Versions.*

48. Karin Barber, *I Could Speak Until Tomorrow: Oriki, Women and the Past in a Yoruba Town* (Edinburgh: Edinburgh University Press, 1991), 25.

49. Ibid., 26.

50. Ibid., 36–37

51. Ibid., 142.

52. Ibid., 144 and 189f.

53. Ibid., 248–49.

54. Wole Soyinka and Ulli Beier, *Orisha Liberates the Mind: Wole Soyinka in Conversation with Ulli Beier on Yoruba Religion* (Bayreuth: Iwalewa, 1992), 4. Regarding characteristics of precolonial or "traditional" Yoruba societies and culture, compare Sandra T. Barnes, ed., *Africa's Ogun: Old World and New* (Bloomington: Indiana University Press, 1989); and Andrew Apter, *Black Critics and Kings* (Chicago: University of Chicago Press, 1992).

The Other Avant-Garde
The Theater of Radical Aesthetics and the
Poetics and Politics of Performance in
Contemporary Africa

John Conteh-Morgan

> Perhaps somewhere in the Althusserian realms of uneven historical
> developments there are surviving or newly emerging contexts where
> radical art and revolutionary politics can yet converge into a vital
> contemporary avant-garde.
> —James M. Harding, Introd., *Contours of the Theatrical Avant-Garde*

> And it is becoming increasingly clear that our Western avant-garde is, in
> world perspective, nothing other than a return to the most traditional
> theatre.
> —Richard Schechner, *Public Domain*

To the scholar of postcolonial African theater, current debates in the
American academy on the avant-garde are somewhat bewildering, not
to say strangely self-absorbed. At a time when the "avant-garde urge," in
its theatrical manifestation at least, is finding vibrant, localized expression
in many societies, especially in the postcolonial world,[1] when some of
the stylistic features, radical ideological positions, and iconoclastic gestures associated with it are emerging or, better still (as shall be shown
later, and as the second epigraph acknowledges), *re*-emerging and flourishing in the modern theater within these societies—sometimes with
dangerous consequences to its practitioners from state authorities—it has
been pronounced dead in Euro-American theater by an influential body
of critical opinion.[2]

According to this opinion, and in accents reminiscent of the death-of-
tragedy debates of the late 1960s,[3] what currently passes for avant-garde
in American theater is nothing but the "decadent" variety of the real
thing—the historical, or as it is sometimes called, the modernist, avant-
garde—whose illustrious, if fractious and sectarian existence (in natural-

ism, Dadaism, surrealism, the Theater of the Absurd, and other movements, as well as in groups like the Living Theatre and the Performance Group) lasted from the mid-1890s to the late 1970s.[4] The successor experimental theater, sometimes called "neo-avant-garde,"[5] argue these critics, has lost the oppositionality characteristic of its historical predecessor. It has become part of the establishment on whose bodies it depends for sponsorship.[6] Institutionalized into educational programs, it has lost sight of the resistance functions of the historical avant-garde whose stylistic and technical features, in its hands, have degenerated into fads—"'mechanical' technique[s]," in Bürger's words,[7] a mere "cluster of alternatives."[8]

Its pursuit of newness and aestheticism, in other words, is detached from any socially transformative function. It no longer constitutes a force of negation against the commodification of art in society. If anything, it articulates in the theatrical sphere, according to Bürger[9] and Jameson,[10] the economic logic of "late capitalism" for new and constantly changing products to stimulate consumerist desire. In short, where the historical avant-garde struggled against what Bürger calls the "social ineffectuality" of the institution of art, and sought, albeit unsuccessfully, to reintegrate it into the "praxis of life," to transform art, that is, into a form of social action comparable to that of sacred ritual in pre- or nonindustrial societies, the neo-avant-garde joyously accepts the status of its products as "works of art"—in the sense of aesthetic products defined by an exchange rather than a use value—commodities, in other words, that are at once consumable (from a commercial and audience-reception point of view), and entertaining.[11]

Now, if the real or authentic theatrical avant-garde is indeed dead (some lone voices deny this), it seems to me that no useful purpose can be served by the endless bemoaning of this fact, or the continuous berating of the products and achievements of its neo-avant-garde successor because they do not conform to an aesthetic or, especially, ideological template. To the extent that the rebelliousness, the radical politics, and the "lost paradise of aesthetic insurrection,"[12] associated with the historical or modernist avant-garde have migrated and now gone transnational and more specifically postcolonial, a more fruitful approach, perhaps, might be to study the avant-garde *relationally,*[13] not only in its older, and now allegedly dead modernist Euro-American expressions—however rich and influential these may be in the global cultural and other economy—but also in its (chronologically more recent) postcolonial figurations. Such an approach will contribute, by providing spatial and temporal distance, to a fuller understanding of the *phenomenon* of the avant-garde in its diverse and incommensurate histories and contexts by uncoupling it from its Euro-American cultural expressions, with which it has tended to be conflated and become synonymous. That the modernist avant-garde movements, theatrical and artistic, derived, as has been often noted,[14] an important fund of their stylistic and formal techniques (rather like their postcolonial counterparts, incidentally), from the so-called primitive theatrical forms within postcolonial societies, makes such a relational approach even more interesting.

In this essay, I propose to focus on one specific example, from French-speaking Africa, of a postcolonial theater movement of the aesthetic avant-garde, itself only a subclass of the general class of "radical theater." The essay falls into two distinct parts. After a brief definition of the notion of radical theater, it successively addresses, in the two subsections of the first part, this theater's political, as distinct from its aesthetic, modes of expression and the vexed question of the relationship between the two. The second part of the essay concentrates exclusively on the theater of radical aesthetics, discussing first its historical and cultural conditions of possibility and its poetics, establishing parallels between it and the Euro-American avant-garde, and determining its originality with regard to the latter. It is my contention that while the postcolonial and modernist theatrical avant-gardes share many common formal features (no influence implied, however), the *project* or politics into whose service these features are pressed in the postcolonial avant-garde differs in significant ways from that of its modernist predecessor. But at this point, a few words on "radical theater" in Africa will be in place.

The term *radical theater,* as applied to Africa, refers to at least two interrelated but nonetheless distinguishable theatrical practices. The first, and the one most often associated with African theater, is *political.* It describes a use of the theater as an instrument of resistance to, or subversion of, the dominant political order. There is, however, another practice, more experimental or aestheticist, and certainly more recent at least in francophone Africa. It also refers to an act of subversion, this time, however, not of the political, order, at least not directly, but of the hegemonic *aesthetic* and cultural order. This is the type of practice advocated, for example, by the fictional character Grozi in *Elle sera de jaspe et de corail* (*It Shall Be of Jasper and Coral* [1983, 2000]),[15] the novel by the Cameroonian Werewere Liking, in his poetic outburst at the prevailing theater conventions in his artistically unimaginative and alienated fictional society, appropriately called Lunaï.

Grozi's antitextualist contempt for a word-based drama in which speech and gestures merely translate a preexistent reality, and his call for a theater in which the imagination is teased into contact with "other worlds" through the interplay of "scents," "[vowel] sounds," and "vibrations," are hallmarks of this practice:

> Au théâtre qu'on cesse d'aligner les mots doublés de gestes purement illustratifs . . . que d'autres vibrations entrent en jeu pour nous émouvoir jusqu'au fond . . . que des sons de voyelles nous frappent l'hypophyse et nous remettent en contact avec d'autres mondes. . . . Que des odeurs nous remettent de l'eau dans la bouche. . . . Que les silences nous permettent de méditer et d'élargir nos horizons. Qu'ils nous soit donné l'extase de l'explosion initiale qui créa des mondes.[16]

> [In the theater they should stop tempering words by adding purely illustrative gestures . . . Other vibrations should come into play and move us to the core. The sound of vowels should strike our pituitary gland and put us back in touch with other worlds. . . . Smells should make our mouths water. . . . And silences should allow us to meditate and to widen our horizons. May we receive the ecstasy of the original explosion that created worlds.][17]

But to fully grasp the nature and specificity of this aesthetically radical or avant-garde theater (and the focus of this essay), it will be useful to frame the discussion with a recall in broad strokes of the major stages of development of its nonidentical twin partner: the theater of radical politics.

The Theater of Radical Politics: From the Colony to the Postcolony

The tendency to conflate militant political theater with radical theater *tout court* in African dramatic criticism is not surprising. Not only has radical political theater had more practitioners in Africa, it also has had a longer history, which can be divided into two phases—an anticolonial nationalist or antiapartheid phase and a postnationalist one. The first goes back to the 1890s, at least in a country like Nigeria, where the then emerging Western-inspired theater, became, in its association with African separatist churches, a vehicle of anticolonial cultural and, by extension, political, assertion. But it was not until in the 1940s, with the

intensification of the movement for independence, that the radical political orientation in African theater became pronounced.[18] With its relative potential to reach a mass nonliterate audience, the theater became a
privileged site of critique of colonial rule and its cultural assumptions,
and of imagining a radically different political order.

A number of examples from different time frames (before and after
independence), and regions (western and southern Africa) will be given.
The first is that of the Nigerian playwright Hubert Ogunde. Between
1945 and 1950 he used the theater extensively to represent colonial rule
not only as exploitative (*Strike and Hunger,* 1945) and repressive (*Bread and
Bullets,* 1950), but also as usurpatory, in its use of deceptive treaties and
outright force to acquire power (*Tiger's Empire,* 1946).[19] Also in the 1940s
in the Ivory Coast, the "théâtre indigène" movement occasionally
departed from its staple of satirical plays directed against indigenous traditions to expose, in such work as Germain Coffi Gadeau's *Les recrutés de
Monsieur Maurice* (1942), the practice of forced labor in French territories.[20]

But not all drama of the colonial or immediate postcolonial periods
was so openly political and confrontational. Some of it functioned by
indirection, taking an ostensibly cultural turn in, for example, the history
plays of such writers as the Senegalese Amadou Cissé Dia or the Ivorian
Bernard Dadié. But even when it did, its objectives were no less political, and in the context of the period, even radically so. Re-visioning and
re-presenting the African past in a play like Dia's *Les derniers jours de Lat
Dior* (1965) or Dadié's *Beatrice du Congo* (1970) may not be an open act
of political insubordination in the Ogunde manner; but to the extent
that these plays challenged the cultural superstructure and, in their
specific case, the historical discourses of legitimation of colonial power,
they constituted an effective intervention in the struggle to dismantle
that power.[21]

But it was perhaps in the South Africa of the 1970s and 1980s, during
the struggle against apartheid, that the theater of radical politics, in such
plays as Mthuli Shezi's *Shanti* (1981), Maisha Maponya's *The Hungry
Earth* (1979), and *Survival* (1971) by the Workshop 71 group, took on a
frankly revolutionary character.[22] Using what Steadman calls a "presentational" style and the technique of direct address, this theater, whether
it be in the form of the "township musical," protest, or agitation and
propaganda play, went beyond the mere exposure of ills to urge insurrection and violent political action on its audiences.[23]

But the theater of direct political critique did not disappear with colonial rule. If anything, the severe crises of state and society in contempo-

rary Africa have given it a sharper, and even leftist, Marxist-inspired edge. Unlike Hubert Ogunde, whose theater figures a monolithic Nigerian nation (now represented by striking workers, now by King Onikoye of *Tiger's Empire*) engaged in struggle against an equally monolithic imperial nation, or Mthuli Shezi, whose *Shanti* is about an imagined, undifferentiated, and essentialized "black" nation against an equally undifferentiated "white" nation, the radical theater of the postcolonial era— revolutionary and socialist as distinct from nationalist and petit bourgeois like its predecessor— sees issues of power and domination in socioeconomic, class and gender, terms, rather than in racial or national.

The Manichaeanism remains, of course, but the parties to the conflict have changed. In such plays as *Once upon Four Robbers* (1991) by the Nigerian Femi Osofisan, *The Trial of Dedan Kimathi* (1977) by the Kenyans Ngugi Wa Thiongo and Micere Mugo, *L'Oeil* (1975) by the Ivorian Zadi Zaourou, and *Je soussigné cardiaque* (1981) by the Congolese Sony Labou Tansi, the African nationalist state and its elites, figured as predatory and brutal, and symbolized by stereotypical characters like the banker (in *Dedan Kimathi*), the district governor, Sogoma Sangui (in *L'Oeil*), and the businessman Perono and his accomplice in government Bala Ebara *(Je soussigné cardiaque),* have replaced the colonial state and its rulers. The armed robbers, peasants, students, and progressive intellectuals, on the other hand—"those not in the privileged position to steal government files, award contracts. . . , buy chieftaincy titles"[24]—have now taken the place of the monolithic and oppressed "Africans" or (in the case of South Africa) "blacks" of the radical theater of the anticolonial/apartheid eras.

Radical Politics and Radical Aesthetics: Disentangling a Relationship

Now, to say that the activist political orientation—nationalist and petit bourgeois or socialist and revolutionary—has come to define radical theater (a definition helped by the well-publicized cases of state harassment and imprisonment of many of its practitioners)[25] and to characterize this theater in terms of its contents is in no way to imply an indifference on its part to aesthetic values. On the contrary, Femi Osofisan, for example, explains how the pursuit of his political objectives—confronting the "terror of the state,"[26] stirring the "[Nigerian middle] class . . . into combat,"[27] and awakening the consciousness of the "members of the underprivileged class"[28]—have all gone hand in hand with a *search for a new and appropriate theatrical form*. He asks:

> How should these fine ideas express themselves on *stage?* By experi-
> ence I had learnt already the inadequacy, for our audience, of the
> form of conventional western drama. . . . The drama which our
> people savour is still one in the mould of "total theatre." . . . Hence,
> in search of an appropriate form, the wise thing to do was to turn
> back to our traditions.[29]

And to those "traditions" he does indeed turn, using[30] the devices of the folktale, for example, as a structuring principle in *Once upon Four Robbers,* or ancient Yoruba legend (but stripped of what he sees as its rul-ing-class conservatism) in *Morountodun* (1982). A similar concern to find a form that is derived from the culture of the rural folk, and that is acces-sible to a mass audience of peasants and workers, animates the well-known example of Ngugi's Kamiriithu theater,[31] or indeed Zadi Zaourou's *L'Oeil*.[32]

But if the theater of radical politics is not indifferent to formal inno-vation, in which sense does it differ from African experimental or avant-garde theater proper? The answer, it seems to me, lies in the *place* and *role,* in short in the *function* of the aesthetic in both practices. If, in spite of their undeniable formal innovation, the specific plays mentioned are perhaps best remembered for their angry, revolutionary politics, it is because the aesthetic dimension remains *subordinate to the political,* a mere handmaid to it, or, in Osofisan's revealing instrumentalist metaphors of the theater, a strategy of "ruse," "guile," or "masking."[33] When innova-tion is mobilized at all, it is for purely *pragmatic* reasons: to wrap and smuggle political goods across social boundaries policed by repressive but unintelligent state censors, or to coax popular audience participation by speaking its "language." On this practice of "radical theater," the the-ater itself is self-effacing in the process of sociopolitical transformation, a mere tool, a pure medium that would cease to be relevant, and probably to exist, once the "just" society is achieved. It enjoys no independent existence.

In aesthetically radical or avant-garde theater, on the other hand, the theater is grasped in its specificity as object and practice. The subversion of the dominant conventions of playmaking and theater organization, and the constant search for new ones, are the defining characteristics of this trend. To borrow Erika Fischer-Lichte's helpful distinction in another context, in the African theater of radical aesthetics, the conception of theater as "art form" takes precedence over the "relation of theater and life."[34] Werewere Liking, one of the most important practitioners of this new aesthetic, makes a similar distinction through her other fictional character, Babou, in *Elle sera de jaspe et de corail:*

> Et surtout, que l'on cesse de vociférer des discours électoraux sur scène. Que là au moins on nous permette d'entrevoir la beauté ou la laideur telles qu'elles sont en elles-mêmes et en nous.[35]

> [And above all, they must stop clamoring electoral speeches on stage. There at least may we have the pleasure of seeing beauty or ugliness as they are in themselves and in us.][36]

But this is not to suggest, conversely, that such a practice, considered as a signifying system, is *pure* modernist intransitivity and artistic self-consciousness, any more than the theater of radical politics is *pure* realist transitivity or referentiality. The theater of radical aesthetics does *imply* a politics and, given the context, even a radical politics, a point to which we shall return. But the latter (which is more than socioeconomic transformation) is a function of the theatrical, is constituted in the theatrical, and not exterior to it. To put it differently, in the aestheticist or avant-garde orientation of African "radical theater," the theater *is* the politics. It is the politics in the way it is practiced, organized, and conceived (often as a metaphor of creativity and renewal, both of self and community), in the way it enacts a vision of human relations, in the way, finally, that it functions as a model of culture and community. It is an art of living.[37]

The Example of Francophone Africa

Nowhere has this orientation been pursued with greater vigor and coherence in the past two and a half decades than in the work of such theater practitioners as the Cameroonian Werewere Liking, the Guinean Souleymane Koly (both based in Côte d'Ivoire), the later Zadi Zaourou (Cote d'Ivoire), Sony Labou Tansi and the later Tchicaya U'Tamsi (both of the Congo), and the Togolese Sénouvo Zinsou and Koffi Effoui, to name just these. And that they should all be French-speaking, incidentally, should not be surprising.[38] Unlike the British, the culturally prescriptive and assimilationist French tried more systematically to establish a "high" culture in their colonies,[39] an effort that explains the equally systematic and even doctrinaire moves over the last two decades, on the part of many francophone dramatists, to break away from that culture as it came to be embodied by the new African elite. France not only insisted that its colonial subjects speak what Damas called (1966) "le français de France/le français du Français/le français français," [The French of France/the Frenchman's French/French French],[40] but also that the budding dramatists among them write plays according to (some dehistoricized) "European" dramatic conventions: "au plus près du goût européen" [closest to European taste].[41]

But which dramatic conventions, which "European [theatrical] taste" exactly did France transmit to its African colonies and encourage in the budding dramatists in those territories? It was certainly not the modernist avant-garde practice of an Artaud, who, at about the same time as the French were introducing literary drama in Africa through the school system (in the 1930s), was himself engaged in repudiating what he saw as the "tyranny" of that very type of drama in France. While he was advocating the birth of a new theater infused with the energies of (Balinese-type) performance traditions from the "primitive" societies of the non-industrialized world (which also happened to be colonized societies), official and imperial France pursued the repression, ideological and physical, in its colonies, of those very traditions (and not, uncommonly, the looting[42] of the "art" objects connected with them). This was done on the grounds that these traditions were not "theater," but at best proto-theatrical practices that needed to be stripped of their magico-religious dimension (never mind that *some* of these traditions were secular, and had nothing religious about them), and developed into proper "theater."[43] There could be no more starkly contrasting contexts than that of European colonization, in which the modernist avant-garde developed (and of which Artaud and his followers may have been unaware),[44] and that of neocolonial conditions of struggle for cultural decolonization, from which the Francophone postcolonial avant-garde emerged half a century later.

But French colonial educators were not recommending the fairground, music hall, or vaudeville traditions in French theater, either. With their commedia dell'arte roots, these traditions (in many ways similar to African oral performances) must have been considered "popular" or "low" culture by France,[45] and therefore not worthy of export to its colonies, any more than were the musings on the theater of an Artaud, which official France could not but have disapproved of, as part of the primitivist temper, the "negrophilia"[46] afflicting French intellectuals, who were cosmopolitan, deracinated, antimodern. It was a temper that, in the name of reason, progress, and its *mission civilisatrice,* France would not allow into its colonies, busy as it already was stamping it out at its very source.[47]

But what then was the "European [theatrical] taste" that French educators sought to transmit in their African colonies? It was quite simply the one associated with the *literary* theater of French "high" culture—that of the French classical age.

Pointing to the influence of this "taste" in the making of his early plays, Zadi Zaourou, for example writes: "Elles sont à l'image du théâtre classique français, avec des grandes tirades cornéliennes" [They resemble French classical plays, with grand tirades in the manner of Corneille].[48] In his book of theater criticism and personal recollections, Bakary Traoré also writes about the efforts of students in the colonial Senegal of the 1930s to produce plays in French:

S'inspirant des maîtres du XVIIᵉ siècle, on s'efforce à lier les événements par des rapports de cause à effet, de façon à assurer à l'intrigue un commencement, un développement et un dénouement.

[Drawing our inspiration from the masters of the seventeenth century, we sought to link events in a relationship of cause and effect, so as to give the plot a beginning, a development, and an ending].[49]

Given the deliberateness and doctrinaire nature of the French approach, it is not surprising that when the revolt against that approach and the literary theatrical tradition it sought to teach exploded on the French-African stage (between the late 1970s and the present), it should also have taken, in typical French fashion, the self-conscious form of a theatrical movement or school. Liking writes: "Depuis 1980, plusieurs groupes animés par des universitaires ont lancé tout un *mouvement* vite baptisé 'Théâtre de Recherche'!" [By 1980 several groups led by academics had launched a *movement* that was quickly christened "Experimental Theater"].[50]

She defines the objective of her theater, in the context of these developments, as being "participer à un essor des arts africains contemporains . . . ça veut dire que nous essayons de vivre de manière vraie, sans copier les modèles" [to participate in the growth of contemporary African arts . . . which means striving to live authentically, without copying models].[51] The central African dramatist Vincent Mambachaka also displays a sense of being part of a larger movement in the francophone theatrical world: "notre génération entre dans la création effective. Ce qui m'importe, c'est de trouver ma propre écriture. De réinventer un langage" [Our generation is getting into the phase of real creativity; what matters to me is to develop an *écriture*, to reinvent a language].[52]

Of course, the movement of radical aesthetics is not a unitary project. Its practitioners may have the same aims—to renew African theater through the stage adaptation of African cultural performances—but they have resorted to a diverse range of styles and conventions to express these aims. This said, however, it remains equally true that most plays within this movement exhibit in various combinations certain features that mark them off from the drama of the relatively young, but hegemonic French-derived tradition that had come, through the westernized nationalist elites, to constitute a local "high" culture, a center within the global periphery. The rest of this essay will be devoted to a consideration of these features and their cultural significance, as they find expression especially in the theater of Werewere Liking and to a lesser extent that of Senouvo Zinsou.

The Poetics of Francophone Experimental Theater

The first of these features is the new theater's rejection of the textualist bias of the dominant theater tradition. One of the new movement's most popular practitioners, Souleymane Koly, puts the matter in these terms: "les spectacles qui 'passent' le mieux sont ceux ou le texte est très léger" [the shows that are best received are those that contain the least text].[53] Sony Labou Tansi explains more explicitly:

> C'est surtout une intention de casser le texte "classique," si j'ose dire. Un texte magnifique n'est pas toujours un bon prétexte de spectacle. . . . Durant les répétitions, le travail avec les comédiens peut faire évoluer le texte qui n'est plus un "canevas". Il s'agit d'entremêler la mise en scène à l'écrit. Le théâtre, ce n'est pas un travail d'écriture.

> [The intention, really, is to break up the "classical" text, if I can put it that way. A wonderful text is not necessarily a good pretext for a show. . . . During rehearsals, the work with the actors can lead to changes in the text, which is then no more than a "scenario." It is a question of mixing mise-en-scène with text. Theater is not about writing texts.][54]

So, unlike the French-inspired practice that highlights the textual (with its emphasis on plot construction, character depiction, rhetorical language), the new theater of radical aesthetics privileges the performative: spectacle, mise-en-scène, music—those elements that Aristotle and, after him, a long mainstreamWestern tradition have pejoratively characterized as "the least artistic," and as more dependent on "the art of the stage machinist than on that of the poet."[55]

The shift from text to performance in the theater of radical aesthetics accounts for this theater's systematic return, in an interesting example of theatrical intraculturalism, to indigenous African oral performances. Religious ritual (Liking's *Les mains veulent dire*, 1981, Zaourou's *Le secret des dieux*, 1999, or Labou Tansi's *La rue des mouches*, 1985); concert-party spectacles (Zinsou's *On joue la comédie*, 1984); epic or folktale narratives (Liking's *Un touareg s'est marié à une pygmée*, 1992, and Zinsou's *La tortue qui chante*, 1987, respectively); puppet and folk theater idioms (Liking's *Dieu Chose*, 1988, and Souleymane Koly's *Adama Champion*, 1979, respectively), to give just these examples, are among the many forms on which the theater of radical aesthetics draws. Once repressed by official colonial culture, as was earlier stated, these nonelite/nonwesternized idioms have been appropriated and celebrated by francophone dramatists since the late 1970s as the site of "authentic" African theatrical cultures; "authentic" because they are not dependent, like the establishment forms of the literary theatrical culture, on the traditions of the former imperial power.

This is not to suggest, of course, that these idioms are completely absent from plays of the French-inspired theater. One only need read works like Oyono-Mbia's *Trois prétendants, un mari* (1964), Jean Pliya's *Kondo le requin* (1966), or Cheikh Ndao's *L'exil d'Albouri* (1967) to be convinced of the contrary. The difference between the two sets of works, however, lies in the place of, and use to which are put, indigenous performances in each of them. In the French-derived tradition, it is elements, *lexical items* (to use an analogy from linguistics) that are extracted from the various performance "languages" (the figure of the oral narrative performer, healing scenes, dance sequences, and so on), and then embedded within a *theatrical syntax* that itself remains Western. These elements therefore do not affect the structure of the play; they are used mostly to create atmosphere, or lend a (spurious) cultural flavor to the work. In short, they can be dispensed with. In the plays of the aesthetically radical theater on the other hand, the syntax of the play reproduces that of the source performance "language." In other words, a play like *Les mains veulent dire* does not only use elements of a ritual of affliction, but *is,* in form, structure, performance style, and function, a ritual of healing.

A second important feature of many of the plays of the new aesthetic (especially those that are modeled on religious ceremonial) is their changed function. Their goal is no longer sociopolitical transformation or the heightening of political consciousness, as is the case with plays of the dominant French-inspired tradition, but cultural, spiritual, and psychological conversion. Theatrical performance becomes an act of worship or devotion during which a (culturally) alienated community of celebrants is reconnected, after a rigorous process of guided self-investigation, to a primordial, but obscured or repressed, source of selfhood (cultural, psychological, and spiritual). Theatrical performance, thus, becomes a form of ritual initiation into self-understanding, one on whose successful outcome the regeneration of both self and community depends. As Liking's one-time collaborator, Marie-José Hourantier—a theorist of the new movement—puts it in connection with one of the plays of the genre,

> En traquant le mal, en le décrivant, en le dénonçant . . . la Malade fait ses pas vers la lucidité et pourra danser sa guérison au rythme des incantations apaisantes. . . . *Les mains veulent dire* cherche à initier tous les participants en leur faisant découvrir le pourquoi et le comment d'un mal social.

> [By tracking down the malady, describing it, denouncing it . . . the Patient takes her first steps towards lucidity and, to the rhythms of soothing incantations, can dance her way to good health. . . . *Les mains veulent dire* seeks to initiate all the participants by making them discover the why and how of a social ill.][56]

So where the dominant theater makes social or political revolution a condition of communal health, the theater of radical aesthetics reverses the order, making cultural and spiritual well-being a prerequisite for social progress and self-directed development.

The focus on the spiritual and subconscious dimensions of human experience explains the preference by the spiritualist trend within the new radical theater movement for the nonrational techniques of trance, dreams, and fantasy, techniques that speak to, or even assault, the senses. It also explains its mobilization of an expanded range of "languages" that include the nonverbal: music, dance, costuming, symbolic gestures and objects. "Nos chansons sont aussi des prises de paroles" [Our songs are also acts of speaking], explains Liking.[57] In a play like *Les mains veulent dire,* for example, even musical instruments have a meaning beyond the purely utilitarian. They function as characters endowed with the power of speech. To the Grand Priestess's first question to the Patient, "Ma fille de quoi souffres-tu" [What ailment afflicts you, daughter],[58] a drum provides the elements of an answer, which, translated into speech, mean, "Tu souffres, elle souffre, la croix, la joie sans foi" [You suffer, she suffers, the cross, joy without faith].[59] But the use of paralinguistic forms is not limited to ceremonial plays. In the secular works of practitioners like Souleymane Koly, speech is used sparingly. The action, as in a *kotèba* performance—the model for such plays as *Adama Champion*—is narrated through dance, music, mime, and body movements, a technique he resorts to not merely for reasons of cultural authenticity, but also, as he explains, for ease of communication with his multiethnic audiences.[60]

To focus attention on the use of a plurality of languages by the practitioners of the theater of radical aesthetics is not to deny the use of such elements in the plays of the literary tradition. The difference here again lies in the use to which music, dance, gestures, and so on are put. In the French-inspired tradition, the burden of communication is carried by speech. When music and dance are used to communicate and not just to entertain, as they often are, they play a subordinate role to speech: as illustrators, in images and movement, of meanings that are encoded primarily in the verb. In the new, nonlogocentric, radical theater on the other hand, words are decentered. They no longer occupy place of pride in the communicative scheme, as they do in the literary theater, but become just one mode of communication among many. And even then they are valued more, especially in the ceremonial plays, for their euphonious and incantatory, rather than their communicative, function. This fact explains the textual slightness of the new plays. To attempt to extract their total meaning merely from reading them is to set oneself up for disappointment. Their full effect can only be experienced in performance.

It is not a coincidence in this regard that many of the aesthetically radical playwrights are also theater directors: Liking of the Ki-Yi Mbock Theatre, Koly of the Kotéba Ensemble, and the late Sony Labou Tansi of the Rocado Zulu Theatre. The theater for them, in a crucial departure from the literary tradition in francophone drama, is not so much about representing texts, but about (bodies in) performance. It is a physical activity. The dominant tradition for sure is also about performance, but with a crucial difference. Here, actors are not supposed to draw attention to themselves lest they distract the audience from the message that they are supposed to declaim and (the meaning of performance in this context) *illustrate* in gestures and body movement. As persons, they are transparent mediums representing characters, playing a role with which the actor becomes one. In the theater of radical aesthetics, on the other hand, actors are not self-effacing signs. They maintain a distance vis-à-vis the role they are playing (in *On joue,* for example, the actor grudgingly playing Chaka often slips out of role to remind the spectator of his real name,[61] and draws attention to himself as dancer, mime, musician, or even boxer,[62] and to his body in its material expressiveness).[63]

The focus on the body of the actor is particularly important in Liking's ceremonial theater, where acting is not the art of impersonating, but of interrogating, and expressing the innermost self, and helping the spectators do the same. The actor is an "éveilleur,"[64] an awakener of consciousness, a sacred figure who helps the spectator discover his or her creative potential, the God within, as Liking's fictional character, Grozi, puts it.[65] The actor is the individual who triggers

> un processus d'autorévélation chez le public. . . . Comme l'acteur s'est révélé à lui même, il cherchera à montrer comment se dépouiller des protections de la vie quotidienne et s'assumer seul. Il arrache les masques pour . . . aboutir à la révélation de l'être réel. . . . Il sait qu'il peut combler les vides en aidant l'autre, son frère, à s'accomplir, en rendant transparent ce qui est sombre.
>
> [a process of self-revelation in the audience. . . . Just as the actor revealed himself to himself, so he will try to show how one can rid oneself of the masks of daily life and take control of oneself. He tears off masks in order to reveal the real person. . . . He knows he can fill the void by helping the other, his brother, to realize himself by making transparent that which is murky.][66]

And such an activity is not conducted through words, as has been noted, but through the fingers, hand, feet, in short through the body, which, in its slightest twitches, gestures, and postures, signifies: "La répétition du geste, sa décomposition, ses rythmes sont autant de signes pour le spectateur, signes qui concurrencent le langage parlé" [The repetition of the gesture, its constitutive moments, various segments, and rhythm are that many signs for the spectator, signs that compete with speech].[67]

A site of knowledge and communication, the body in Liking's ritual theater is a sacred organ that, fully understood and utilized (in her mystical terms), keeps the individual attuned, like an antenna, to the nonmaterial, spiritual plane of existence. The need for actors to be aware of the potentialities of their bodies, in order to discharge their true function, explains the importance Liking attaches to yoga-like exercises in their training.[68]

Concomitant with the emphasis on the actor as the center of the theatrical event is the new theater's predilection for collective creation. Many of its plays are the product not of a solitary author whose text is handed over for execution to a director and thence to a passive group of actors, but of the collaborative effort of actors, directors, and sometimes spectators. Once a scenario (a "texte-chantier" [textual site]) has been agreed upon, explains Zaourou using an analogy from construction, it is "aux acteurs de s'en abreuver et d'organiser un spectacle" [up to the actors to familiarize themselves with it and organize the show].[69] To the practitioners of radical aesthetics, the actual process of playmaking is more important than the finished play itself. This approach does not only inform their practice, but is also the subject of some of their plays. One of these, Liking's *Quelque Chose-Afrique,* for example, stages a group of actors putting together a play two weeks before its scheduled, commissioned performance. In its disorder, the play's performance space is a true theatrical building site, to use Zaourou's metaphor. Because no architect/author has supplied them with a design, the performers themselves have to come up with one, which means not just determining subject and dialogue, a task made more complicated for them by the sensitive fictional context of censorship in which they work, but also gestures, costumes, set, and so on. Although the play contains an internal stage director, Sita, her role, like that of the aesthetically radical dramatist, is basically that of coordinator or midwife. She prods the performers to bring forth ever more daring and creative ideas and improvisations, and weaves their suggestions into a harmonious whole. She tells them:

Laissons alors libre cours aux élans sans trop nous interrompre. Je prends note des meilleures propositions. N'hésitons pas à introduire les anciennes danses et chorégraphies non encore exploitées dans d'autres spectacles.

[Let us give free rein to our passion with as few interruptions as possible. I'll note down the best suggestions. Let us not hesitate to introduce old dances that have not yet been used in other plays.][70]

An earlier work in this mold is *On joue la comédie,* in which the internal
producer's insistence in involving the audience in the making of the
play—the (planted) audience sneaks into what is in fact a rehearsal, and
is only "discovered" when the performers break up for the day—leads to
an outraged reaction from a spectator, Le Petit Monsieur: "Ce n'est pas
ça que j'appelle théâtre . . . Le théâtre doit être instructif, éducatif" [This
to me isn't theater . . . The theater has to instruct and educate].[71]

This reaction and the rejoinder that it elicits from the internal producer, "vous feriez mieux d'aller au cours du soir" [you'd be better off
going to evening school], illustrates an important feature, mentioned
earlier in this essay, of the theater of radical aesthetics: artistic self-consciousness. It is nonillusionistic, and uses a variety of strategies to obtain
this effect. These include the incorporation of popular art forms like
masking, dancing, puppetry; the cultivation of acting styles that draw
attention to the presence of the performer and discourage total
identification between him or her and the character portrayed; the dis-
ruption of the traditional idea of the linear plot, and hence the illusion of
reality, through a range of denarrativization techniques like fantasy,
trance, the grotesque; and the recourse to the device of the play within
a play. The aim of the new radical theater is not to repeat, in the realist
manner, socially and politically produced meanings. It is rather to reveal
the processes of constitution and naturalization of those meanings—and
to encourage actors and audience to join in the production of new ones.
It is the shock to his literary expectations constituted by this practice that
explains the fictional spectator's disruptive reaction in *On joue.* Nurtured
in the ways of the established theater, he had come to watch a play on
Chaka, a figure of the past, whose deeds are held up in conventional
francophone drama as a model of heroic conduct. What he gets instead
is an invitation to join in the making of a play, and perhaps worse, an
irreverent parody of his preferred drama.

Modernist and Postcolonial Avant–Gardes:
Overlapping Poetics, but . . .

It is difficult at this point not to be struck, in spite of the vast differences
in context, by the commonality of formal qualities mentioned earlier

between the postcolonial avant-garde in its contemporary francophone expression and its modernist predecessor. "Even if the context is different," observes Chantal Boiron, "statements [such as Sony Labou Tansi's, quoted above, on the need to "break up the 'classical' text"] bring to mind the avant-gardist experiments of a Craig or Appia . . . of the Living Theatre . . . of the famous 'performances' of the 1970s."[72]

A nonliterary, antitextualist orientation;[73] a spatial conception of theater as "a concrete physical space which asks to be filled, and to be given its own concrete language to speak"[74]—that is, the nonverbal language of mime, hieratic gestures, dance, music; a predilection for collective creation; a valorization of the director and the actor and a corresponding depriviledging of the playwright; a flexible use of theatrical space that aims to break down the barrier between actor and audience; an emphasis on the sensory and perceptual as opposed to the disembodied and the intellectual; a nonnaturalistic, self-reflexive conception of the theater, and, finally, a view of performance as sacred, an act of worship—these are among the many features common to both the postcolonial and the modernist avant-gardes.[75]

I highlight this similarity, however, not to imply that the modernist avant-garde, given its historical anteriority, influenced its francophone postcolonial successor in the specific sense of providing it with a set of techniques, acting styles, or conceptions of space. How could that be possible, when the modernist avant-garde derived, using an outsider cultural perspective, aspects of its own inspiration from the rituals and other performance practices of the "traditional," "primitive" cultures of the colonized world, rituals from which postcolonial theater practitioners—located within these same societies, and using an insider perspective—were later to draw their inspiration? It is one of the ironies in transnational cultural relations that what has been considered modernist or postmodernist, avant-garde, cutting edge, in the West and (more recently) in the westernized theater practices in postcolonial societies, is in fact quite simply "traditional" or "premodern," as Schechner acknowledges in one of the epigraphs to this essay, and as Suresh Awashi, Ola Rotimi, and Elaine Savory have shown in connection with Indian, Nigerian, and Anglophone Caribbean theater, respectively.[76]

If one is to speak appropriately of an influence of the modernist on the postcolonial avant-garde, it is more in the sense that the former, by bringing to, and celebrating in, the powerful and prestigious Western stage archaic idioms that had been devalued by colonial culture, legitimized the use of those idioms in the eyes of postcolonial theater practitioners. In short, the encounter with, or the detour through, the modernist avant-garde was the catalyst that strengthened postcolonial theater practitioners in their voyage of rediscovery of their repressed and devalued heritage.

. . . Differential Politics

If the embrace and celebration of the "primitive," in the vocabulary of one, or the "indigenous" in that of the other, is one of the shared and defining characteristics of both the modernist and the postcolonial avant-gardes, the *politics of this embrace* is significantly different between the movements. To the former, "primitive" dramatic spectacles provide the tools for a critique and radical subversion of modernity. In their masterful use of the wordless "language" of trance and hieratic gestures, and of a "poetry in space,"[77] these models have been interpreted, through the primitivist lenses of an Artaud for example, as constituting pathways to "an unknown, obscure and fabulous reality,"[78] or of what I have called elsewhere "a state of . . . prelapsarian . . . human wholeness . . . from which [modern Western humanity] has been severed with the advent of an impoverishing 'logos,' self consciousness and reflexivity."[79]

But the search for a spiritual Eden, a world of "Speech before words,"[80] is not the only plank in the politics of the modernist avant-garde. The struggle for psychological wholeness in modern societies governed by instrumental rationality, and seen as repressive of desire, is another. A longing, sometimes bordering on the anarchistic, for total freedom, for spontaneous behavior unrestrained by social norms, is a central feature of the movement. The Living Theatre's 1968 collective creation, *Paradise Now,* and *Dionysus in 69* by the Performance Group are perfect illustrations of this longing. In these play-ceremonies, actors, in defiance of social taboos, go naked, imitate copulation, and encourage the spectators to join them in doing the same. According to the commentary in the "Rite of Universal Intercourse" sequence of *Paradise Now,* for example, "the release of the Sexual Energy from her inactive dormant state leads to that fulfillment which is here called Perfect Bliss or Peace."[81] And this is not to mention the actors' complaint about not being able to "travel without a passport"[82] or "smoke marijuana."[83]

The search for "perfect bliss" and the quest for spiritual transcendence, the struggle to overthrow the "repressive machinery civilization constructs to keep itself intact"[84] by means of ceremonial theater—that "counterforce of great . . . sexual, and life-giving power"[85]—might constitute a worthy politics[86] for avant-garde theater practitioners operating in conditions of postmodernity (associated with advanced industrial societies) that they consider repressive and alienating. But these concerns, some would say luxuries, are far from those of their postcolonial francophone counterparts, who operate not in conditions of postmodernity, but of premodernity or at best peripheral modernity, and who therefore press "indigenous" performances to quite different ends: not the search for spirituality—their "traditional" societies have an abundance of it—but the creation of new, African-based (theatrical) cultures. In other words, theirs is a political project, and not the expression of existential angst. The postcolonial francophone avant-garde, if one were to provide contrasting definitions of it, is a movement of return to the local and the ethnic (the African), and a rejection of the foreign (Western) seen as a threat to its identity. The modernist avant-garde, on the other hand, is a flight from the (Western) local, seen as effete, and an embrace of the non-Western (foreign/primitive) seen as regenerating. One is narrowly nationalistic and in various degrees celebrates "roots" and cultural "authenticity." The other is rootlessly cosmopolitan and advocates what Vanden Heuvel calls the "undo[ing] of the closure of [social] textuality"[87] in favor of a world of social indeterminacy and liminality. In either case, the movements reflect the contrasting historical and sociological circumstances of their emergence and development: neocolonial cultural and economic domination in the case of one, hence the rejection of the culture of the victor (in its original form or its mimicked or reworked variant by the nationalist elites); imperial conquest in the case of the other, and hence, conversely, the tolerant, but distorting, embrace of the debris of defeated cultures, in what Smith calls the construction of "a new and universal [read: European] art."[88]

For the postcolonial avant-garde then, the reversion to indigenous forms, even when it adopts religious or mystical overtones as in Liking's theater, is nothing short of a *political* struggle for national self-retrieval and cultural reenfranchisement, seen as the precondition for any act of self-directed, national development, as the necessary foundation for the construction of an alternative modernity, *driven by African needs*. The pursuit of this goal takes several forms. And it is to them that we shall now turn.

The first and perhaps most straightforward form relates to the need felt by many of the francophone avant-garde dramatists to make their theater accessible to a wider audience. If the dominant literary drama inherited from France has remained, even at its most politically populist, an elite preoccupation, cultivated only by the tiny minority of Western-educated members of the population, it is not only because it is scripted and in French. It is also because of its formal procedures, which are foreign to a population that in the majority is nonliterate, and therefore only conversant with oral traditions of performance. The Spectator makes this point to the actor playing Chaka in the 1975 version of *On joue:*

> Vous me comprendriez si vous pensiez aux millions de nos conci-toyens qui dans les principes ont les mêmes droits que vous et moi mais qui, en fait, n'ont, par exemple, pas le privilège d'aller au théâtre parce qu'on ne leur a donné ni les moyens matériels, ni la formation intellectuelle, ni le temps d'accéder.
>
> [You would understand if you thought of our compatriots who in principle have the same rights as you and me, but who in reality do not enjoy the privilege of going to the theater because they lack the material or intellectual means, or the time.][89]

It is partly to restore to the theater a function equivalent to that enjoyed by performances in indigenous communities—a privileged medium of communication with a popular audience—that postcolonial dramatists of the francophone avant-garde opted for the textualization in their works of ancient performance idioms: "Je veux faire un travail," Souleymane Koly explains, "dans lequel tout africain puisse jouer et qui puisse être compris par tout africain quelle que soit . . . son niveau social" [I want to create a drama in which every African can participate and that can be understood by every African whatever their . . . social level].[90]

This objective is very different from that of the modernist avant-garde, which takes precisely the opposite position, and cultivates an elite, vanguard audience of devotees who stand out by their rejection of the commercialized and conventional theater of mass consumption. As Bürger has argued,[91] this theater's cultivation of a cult of the new, its recourse to the exotic, the nonconventional, and the obscure, is the formal expression of its resistance to mass appropriation.

If the need to communicate with popular African audiences by using their idioms is an important consideration for some practitioners of the postcolonial avant-garde, for others (Liking, Zaourou, and Zinsou, for example) the turn to performance transcends the pragmatic issue of communication. It is pregnant with political significance. To represent indigenous theatrical forms on the francophone stage—a stage on which they have been repressed or marginalized as the "native" Other of "civilized" (that is, French-based) drama—is to rescue these forms and the ordinary people whose cultural heritage they represent from the cultural and political margins of national life. It is to bring them literally to artistic, and metaphorically to political, center stage, and not just to use them, as does the modernist avant-garde, for artistic inspiration and spiritual renewal.[92] Implicated in the aesthetics of the new theater is a politics of contestation of the dominant notion of national culture seen as inauthentic because of its cultural imitativeness, and the struggle for a new conception of the nation and its identity that is rooted in, and does not merely gesture at, the practices of the "people."

But it is not just the playwrights' embrace of various indigenous cultural performances that is important; it is also the way in which the specific techniques characteristic of these performances have been vested with radical possibilities. Two examples will be given. The first is the technique of group participation and collective creation. In modernist drama, where it is also in widespread practice, it is not only used to create a festive atmosphere. It is also an attempt to promote a countervailing ideal of social existence, one based on communal structures of existence and not on the prevalent alienating individualism. Theorizing this sentiment in the period of rising modernity, a century earlier, Nietzsche wrote:

> Under the charm of the Dionysian [performance drama], not only is the union between man and man reaffirmed, but nature which has been alienated . . . or subjugated, celebrates once more her reconciliation with her lost son, man. . . . Now, with the gospel of universal harmony, each one feels himself not only united, reconciled and fused with his neighbor, but as one with him.[93]

The technique of collective creation in postcolonial avant-garde theater addresses a more pointedly political concern, that of democratic participation in politics. This theater sees the author-generated drama of the establishment tradition as the aesthetic analogue of the politics of anticolonial nationalism, which in the postindependence period has spawned so many undemocratic regimes. As I have observed elsewhere,[94] it is the politics of the vanguard elite embodied in the visionary and charismatic leader, of which Chaka is a powerful symbol in francophone drama. He formulates a political program that is then imposed on a passive population whose input counts for naught, that is, when it is at all solicited. It is a politics based on what Bakhtin would have called a "pedagogical" and not a "dialogical" relationship. It presupposes a custodian of the truth on the one hand (the leader/author), and a recipient of that truth (the subject/audience) on the other.

It is this leader-as-messiah/father model of politics, I argue, with its almost inevitable slide into paternalism and authoritarianism, that is rejected by the postcolonial avant-garde. Implicated in the latter's practice of collective creation is a democratic vision of politics as founded on a consensus between rulers and ruled. Just as the actors and the audience of the postcolonial theater of radical aesthetics participate in the creation of a play, so in political terms the population should be given the participatory rights of "citizen" and not just left with, as was the case in colonial times, and has been in the case in most of the postcolonial period, the burdensome duties of "subject." As the Third Spectator argues, again in the earlier version of *On joue,* that most paradigmatic of plays of the new aesthetic:

> Le théâtre restera toujours le pire des impérialismes si seulement une minorité d'individus disposent du droit de tout prévoir, de tout établir, de tout ordonner, de fixer de façon immuable un texte, des gestes, les moindres détails d'une illusion que l'on impose à un public passif.

> [The theater will remain the worst of imperialisms if only a minority of individuals has the right to work out all the details, organize everything, and definitively determine a text, gestures, and the smallest details of an illusion that is imposed on a passive audience.][95]

Reference by the Third Spectator to "the details of an illusion that is imposed on a passive audience" also raises the issue of the politics of the metadramatic techniques that we saw as characteristic of the postcolonial avant-garde theater. The sense of irony displayed by many of the works in this tradition, their metatheatrical playfulness and nonillusionism, does not signify entertainment or a lack of seriousness. Rather, these aesthetic features reflect an awareness of the *contingent* nature, the constructedness, of social and political "truths." It is an awareness that, while disconcerting for audiences in search of absolutes, grand narratives (national liberation, nation building, progress), or foundations, like the Petit Monsieur, could make for a more tolerant politics, a politics of the provisional and the negotiable, of the "petits récits," in the same way that the conviction by plays of the established tradition of possessing the "truth" could lead to intolerance of dissent.

A final aspect of the new postcolonial theater worth considering is the political significance of its corporealization of dramatic action. Performers, it was observed earlier, especially in connection with the theater of religious ceremonial, do not always illustrate a character. Theirs is not an act of mimesis, but of catharsis in the same way that celebrants in a Pentecostal revivalist meeting, for example, undergo a transformative experience, spiritual and psychological, through dance and song. But what is implied in this focus on the performing body and other perceptual values, and the corresponding deprivileging of speech or *logos*? It is a politics of resistance to the ideology of colonial modernity and by extension of its progenitor, Enlightenment rationality, which views the body as a source of obscurity, an impediment to true knowledge. A site of the sensual, the instinctive, and of appetites, the body, associated, in Cartesian thought, with the state of childhood, and in Enlightenment rationality with woman and the native/colonial subject (both viewed as the "Other" of Enlightenment rationality and, in the case of the native/colonial subject, as representing the childhood of humanity), is the obstacle to be transcended through an act of purification or (for the colonial subject) an embrace of colonial modernity, if true and certain knowledge, associated with cognition, is to be reached.[96] The devaluation by the French of the corporeal and sensory values of the theater they encountered in Africa, and the corresponding emphasis on the word, causality, psychological coherence, and observable reality in the theater they introduced into Africa, is the objective correlate of this rationalist vision. Now, by creating a modern theater that valorizes the senses and the body as a source of true and certain knowledge, the theater of radical aesthetics, in its religious mode at least, defiantly reasserts those values of the sensorium associated with Africa by a certain nationalist identitarian discourse. But such a reassertion, like other aspects of the new radical aesthetic project, is not without its problems. And it is with a consideration of some of these that I will conclude this essay.

Problems and Perspectives

The first problem raised by the shift to performance in the theater of radical aesthetics relates to accessibility. While the use on the modern stage of indigenous performance media is a worthy act of cultural reclamation, it does not necessarily guarantee access to the contents of postcolonial avant-garde theater by all Africans. Some of these forms are esoteric and, even in traditional communities, are available only to initiates or community elders. But because of their embeddedness in specific cultural communities, the secular forms are not necessarily any more intelligible to everyone; a problem made more acute by the fact that what little text exists in these plays is still in French. For Souleymane Koly to say, in light of this, that by using dance, body movements, and so on, he hopes to reach "every African whatever their ethnic background,"[97] or for Liking to write that "we privilege gestures and sounds; these are things that can appeal to everyone and can go across frontiers, cultural barriers,"[98] is, it seems to me, to engage in a facile pan-Africanism. Alternatively, it is to subscribe to what the Beninois philosopher Paulin Hountondji has described as a "unanimist" view of African societies, one that erases difference and erects a theory of undifferentiated sameness of Africans.[99]

But even if communication among African spectators was facilitated by the new drama's shift to performance, it is not clear that anything of interest will *necessarily* be communicated. Indeed there is a real danger that to reach the broadest audiences possible, the plays of the new theater will be emptied of all engaging content to become pure movement, sound, and color, thereby reinscribing the very idea of African theater as exotic, and of the African performer as nothing but a dancing body. This problem, as Boiron has pointed out, is intensified by the need faced by these dramatists to satisfy the tastes and expectations of the Western audiences of the international festival circuits where this theater is in demand:

> Un texte trop compliqué . . . peut être un handicap quand on a affaire à des acheteurs japonais ou américains. Un spectacle musical ou gestuel aura plus de chances de répondre aux exigencies du "marché."

> [A complicated text . . . can constitute a serious impediment to Japanese and American buyers. A musical or gestural show will have a better chance of responding to the needs of the "market."][100]

The evolution of some performance-based theater into mere signs without referents is already noticeable in Liking, who seems to have abandoned intellectually challenging drama, and who in such works as *Dieu chose* (1988), *Les Cloches* (1988), *Perçus Perçues* (1991), and *Quelque*

Chose-Afrique has to some increasingly veered to a feast of drumming, movement, and colors. Another example is Souleymane Koly, who after early and well-received efforts to create a new theatrical language based on the *kotéba* idiom, has taken, according to Hourantier,[101] the easy route of using song and dance purely for entertainment.

But the dangers of commodification of the new drama, its lurch to entertainment—rather like the "neo-avant-garde" referred to in the beginning of this essay—and thus its potential to reproduce stereotypes about African performances are not its only (potential) weaknesses. Certain aspects of its vision, as this is expressed in the serious plays, are also open to objection, notwithstanding the fact that this vision is rooted in African soil, which seems to be the new drama's claim to superiority over its Western-inspired rival. And the situation becomes even more complex when what passes for "indigenous" and "authentic," and therefore necessarily acceptable, is, on close inspection, of foreign provenance. Such is the case, for example, with the representation of the performing body as a locus of knowledge, a point of intersection between the physical and spiritual realms of human experience. As I have written elsewhere in connection with the negritudist vision of the Guinean writer Camara Laye,[102] this emphasis on, and mystical conception of, the body, especially in the drama of religious ceremony, ironically reproduces one of the most tenacious discourses by which the modern West both constructed and marginalized the colonized: that of the "rational" European on the one hand, and the "spiritual" African on the other; of the former who is all mind, and the latter who is all body. One of the weaknesses of vision of the new drama lies in the fact that it does not challenge and subvert this dualism on the grounds of its ahistoricity or the limits it sets to human self-definition, among other points. Rather, it reproduces its structure of invented identities, contenting itself with reversing the valences on them. The rational and the spiritual are human attributes and are not a function of skin color, and a truly radical drama is one that does not dance to imposed identities, but one that refuses to amputate important dimensions of human experience.

If I have drawn attention to some of the weaknesses of the theater of radical aesthetics, it is to show that the return to roots is not the panacea to the problems of francophone theater, as it is sometimes heralded. A play based on foreign models should not be automatically condemned as un-African and therefore unprogressive, any more than one inspired by indigenous African performance resources can necessarily be hailed as

liberating. While a certain rootedness of form and vision in the humus
of the local culture is important in establishing communication between
playwright and audience, it is not a sufficient criterion for a politically
progressive and radical theater.

Notes

Completion of this essay was made possible by a W. E. B. DuBois Fellowship at Harvard
University, where an earlier version of it was presented in May 2002. My thanks go to
the College of Humanities, Ohio State University, for partly sponsoring my Harvard
visit, and to Professor Henry Louis Gates and his staff at the DuBois Institute for a most
congenial and stimulating visit. My warm thanks also go to my colleague Dr. Eugene
Holland of the Department of French and Italian at OSU for his helpful comments on
this essay.

1. For examples of postcolonial avant-garde theater movements from Africa and
the Caribbean, for example, see Suresh Awashi, "Encounter with Tradition," *Tulane
Drama Review* 33.4 (1989): 48–69; and Elaine Savory, "Strategies for Survival: Anti-
Imperialist Theatrical Forms in the Anglophone Caribbean," in *Imperialism and Theatre:
Essays on World Theatre, Drama and Performance,* ed. J. Ellen Gainor (London: Routledge,
1995), 243–56, respectively. For examples of similar "root movement[s]," as Schechner
calls them, in various Asian countries, see Richard Schechner, introduction to *The Future
of Ritual: Writings on Culture and Performance* (London: Routledge, 1995), esp. 14–16.

2. For example, Peter Bürger, *Theory of the Avant-Garde,* trans. Michael Shaw (Min-
neapolis: University of Minnesota Press, 1984); Daryl Chin, "The Avant-Garde Industry,"
Performing Arts Journal 9.2–3 (1985): 17–75; Paul Mann, *The Theory-Death of the Avant-Garde*
(Bloomington: Indiana University Press, 1991); Schechner, *The Future of Ritual;* Arnold
Aronson, *American Avant-Garde Theatre: A History* (London: Routledge, 2002).

3. George Steiner, *The Death of Tragedy* (London: Faber and Faber, 1961); Jean-
Marie Domenach, *Le retour du tragique* (Paris: Seuil, 1967).

4. I am of course aware that this periodization is a subject of controversy among
specialists of the historical avant-garde. Thus, Schechner extends the life of this movement to the 1970s and, sometimes hesitatingly, to the 1980s; see Schechner, "An Interview," in *Contours of the Theatrical Avant-Garde: Performance and Textuality,* ed. James
Harding (Ann Arbor: University of Michigan Press, 2000, 207). But others place its
demise in the 1930s; see Raymond Williams, "The Linguistics of Writing Language and
the Avant-Garde," in *The Linguistics of Writing: Arguments between Language and Literature,*
ed. Nigel Fabb et al. (Manchester: Manchester University Press, 1987), 34; see also Erika
Fischer-Lichte, "The Avant-Garde and the Semiotics of the Antitextual Gesture," in
Harding, *Contours,* to take just these examples.

5. Miklós Szabolcsi, "Avant-garde, Neo-avant-garde, Modernism: Questions and
Suggestions," *New Literary History* 3 (1971): 49–70.

6. Aronson, *American Avant-Garde Theatre,* 198–201.

7. Bürger, *Theory of the Avant-Garde,* 60.

8. Schechner, *The Future of Ritual,* 8.

9. Bürger, *Theory of the Avant-Garde,* 59–63.

10. Frederic Jameson, "Postmodernism or the Cultural Logic of Late Capitalism,"
in *Postmodernism: A Reader,* ed. Thomas Docherty (New York: Columbia University
Press, 1993), 64–65.

11. Bürger, *Theory of the Avant-Garde,* 15–54.

12. Mann, *Theory-Death,* 14.

13. For a useful study of the relationships between the "historical avant-garde" and avant-garde movements contemporary to it in Latin America, see George Yudice, "Rethinking the Avant-garde from the Periphery," in *Modernity and its Margins: Reinscribing Cultural Modernity from Spain and its Margins,* ed. Anthony Geist and Jose Monleon (New York: Garland, 1999), 52–80. In *American Culture between the Wars* (New York: Columbia University Press, 1993), 59–104, Walter Kalaidjan also examines what he calls "the avant-garde wing of the Harlem Renaissance" (95) in the context of the "international avant-gardes" (87). For an interesting use of this approach in the area of modernism and the visual arts, see Bernard Smith, *Modernism and Post-Modernism: A Neo-Colonial Viewpoint* (London: London University Institute for Commonwealth Studies, 1992).

14. Christopher Innes, *Avant-Garde Theatre 1892–1992* (New York: Routledge, 1993), 6–18; Richard Schechner, *Public Domain: Essays on the Theatre* (Indianapolis: Bobbs-Merrill, 1969), 209–28; M. H. W. Steins, "L'influence de l'ethnologie sur l'avant-garde français et allemand du XXe siècle," *Actes du VIIe Congrès de l'Association Internationale de Littérature Comparée,* ed. Béla Köpeczi and György Vajda (Stuttgart: Kunst und Wissen/Erich Beiber, 1980), 1:725–33; Smith, *Modernism and Post-Modernism,* 1–13.

15. Werewere Liking, *Elle sera de jaspe et de corail* (Paris: Harmattan, 1983), trans. Marjolijn Jager in *It Shall be of Jasper and Coral and Love-across-a-Hundred-Lives* (Charlottesville: University Press of Virginia, 2000).

16. Liking, *Elle sera de jaspe,* 101.

17. Liking, *It Shall be of Jasper,* 73.

18. Joel Adedeji, "The Church and the Emergence of the Nigerian Theatre: 1866–1914," *Journal of the Historical Society of Nigeria* 6.1 (1971): 25–45; Ebun Clark, "The Nigerian Theatre and the Nationalist Movement," *Nigeria Magazine* 115–16 (1975): 24–33.

19. Clark, "Nigerian Theatre."

20. François Amon d'Aby, *Le théâtre en Côte d'Ivoire* (Abidjan: CEDA, 1988).

21. Gary Warner, "L'histoire dans le théâtre africain francophone," *Présence francophone* 11 (1975): 37–48; and Helen Gilbert and Joanne Tompkins, *Post-Colonial Drama: Theory, Practice, Politics* (London: Routledge, 1996).

22. David Kerr, *African Popular Theatre* (London: James Currey, 1995).

23. Ian Steadman, "Race Matters in South Africa," in *Theatre Matters: Performance and Culture on the World Stage,* ed. Richard Boon and Jane Plastow (London: Cambridge University Press, 1998), 64.

24. Femi Osofisan, *Once upon Four Robbers* (Ibadan: Heinemann, 1991), 24.

25. In 1975, for example, two South African theater groups—the People's Experimental Theatre and the Theatre Council of Natal—were among several organizations that were charged with sedition and banned, and their members imprisoned (see Steadman, "Race Matters in South Africa," 62–63). In the same year, police in the Ivory Coast interrupted the third performance of Zadi Zaourou's *L'Oeil* on the grounds that it was a threat to public order. In 1977, the Kenyan Ngugi Wa Thiong'o was detained for a year for his theater activities with the Kamiriithu Center, and more specifically for his coauthored play *I will Marry When I want,* deemed "a threat to public security" (Kerr, *African Popular Theatre,* 246). The relationship between theater radicals and the law was no better during colonial times. Ogunde was often harassed by the police, forbidden to

take his plays to the northern region of the country, and taken into custody for some of them (Clark, "Nigerian Theatre"), while the French governor of the Ivory Coast in 1942 banned Coffi Gadeau's piece on forced labor, *Les recrutés de Monsieur Maurice*.

26. Femi Osofisan, "'The Revolution as Muse': Drama as Surreptitious Insurrection in a Post-Colonial Military State," in Boon and Plastow, *Theatre Matters*, 11.

27. Ibid., 15.

28. Ibid., 24.

29. Ibid., 20.

30. See Sam Ukala, "Politics of Aesthetics," in *African Theatre: Playwrights and Politics*, ed. Martin Banham et al. (Oxford: James Currey, 2001), 29–41.

31. Ingrid Björkman, *Mother, Sing for Me: People's Theatre in Kenya* (London: Zed Books, 1989).

32. Louise Jefferson, "A Clash of Codes: *L'Oeil* by Bernard Zadi Zaourou," *French Review* 55.6 (1982): 824–34.

33. Osofisan, "The Revolution as Muse," 11.

34. Fischer-Lichte, "The Avant-Garde," 79.

35. Liking, *Elle sera de jaspe*, 101.

36. Liking, *It Shall be of Jasper*, 73.

37. It is important to remember that while useful, the distinctions that I have set up for the two types of radical theater do not refer to discrete entities, and are not meant to be rigidly understood. Just as the same dramatist might practice one or the other radical theater orientation from one play to the next, so the same play can satisfy criteria in both radical practices. Zadi Zaourou and Sony Labou Tansi offer good examples of these possibilities. After an early period during which the former wrote radical political drama (*Les Sofas, L'Oeil* 1975), he turned to theater experimentation with such works as *Les rebelles du bois sacré* (1982), *Le secret des dieux* (1984), and *L'homme au visage de mort* (1989). The plays of Sony Labou Tansi, on the other hand, unify aesthetic innovation and political radicalism with an inevitability that has made him one of the most acclaimed of contemporary dramatists.

38. Formal innovation, especially of the type that involved, say, indigenizing French, or using indigenous narrative or dramatic techniques, was not as well received and encouraged by French colonial cultural policy as it was by British policy. The result has been that English-speaking writers from Africa started experimenting much earlier than their francophone counterparts with indigenous idioms. Thus while Faber and Faber did not hesitate to publish a novel in indifferent English in 1952—Amos Tutuola's *The Palm Wine Drinkard*—French publishers rejected the first francophone novel to infuse its French with African speech patterns—Ahmadou Kourouma's *Les soleils des independences,* which first appeared in 1968 in Canada. Seuil in Paris subsequently published it in 1970 after it had won critical acclaim. Similarly, while English-speaking dramatists were seriously experimenting with African performance forms in their plays as far back as the early 1960s, it was a good two decades later that a similar activity gathered pace among francophone dramatists. Among the best-known and earliest theater experimentalists in English-speaking Africa are Wole Soyinka, Ola Rotimi, John Pepper Clark of Nigeria, Ama Ata Aidoo, Efua Sutherland of Ghana, and Mukotani Rugyendo of Uganda.

39. For a recent analysis of French colonial educational policies in Africa, see A. Y.

Yansane, "The Impact of France on Education in Africa," in *Double Impact: France and Africa in the Age of Imperialism,* ed. G. Wesley Johnson (Westport, Conn.: Greenwood Press, 1985).

40. Léon-Gontras Damas, *Névralgies* (Paris: Présence Africain, 1966). Unless otherwise stated, all translations from the original French are mine.

41. Bakary Traoré, *Le théâtre négro-africain et ses fonctions sociales* (Paris: Présence Africaine, 1958), 49.

42. On the looting of African art objects during the colonial period, see Elazar Barkan and Ronald Bush, introduction to *Prehistories of the Future: The Primitivist Project and the Culture of Modernism,* ed. Elazar Barkan and Ronald Bush (Stanford: Stanford University Press, 1995).

43. Charles Béart, *Recherche des éléments d'une sociologie des peuples africains à partir de leurs jeux* (Paris: Présence Africaine, 1960). For a study of French critical reception of African indigenous performances, including during the colonial period, see John Conteh-Morgan, "French Critics and African Theatre 1900–1999," *Oeuvres et Critiques* 26.1 (2001): 15–28.

44. On the reasons for the invisibility of what Jameson terms "the colonized other" and for "the structure of colonial appropriation" (50) in European modernist consciousness, a consciousness that they helped constitute, see Frederic Jameson, "Modernism and Imperialism," in *Nationalism, Colonialism and Literature,* ed. Terry Eagleton, Frederic Jameson, and Edward Said (Minneapolis: University of Minnesota Press, 1990), 43–66. One can also consult Raymond Williams's "Introduction: The Politics of the Avant-Garde," in *Visions and Blueprints: Avant-garde Culture and Radical Politics in Early Twentieth-Century Europe,* ed. Edward Timms and Peter Collier (Manchester: Manchester University Press, 1988), 1–15, where he mentions that the arts of Asia and Africa, "highly developed in their own places" (5), took on a primitivist aura in European modernist culture, whose cultural "unconscious" (5) they became.

45. It is important to note that long before official France, through its church and state authorities, was repressing popular traditions of performance in Africa during the colonial period—on the moral and sociopolitical grounds of their heathenism and threat to "civilized" order—it had visited a similar treatment on its own popular performance traditions as far back as in the seventeenth century. Thus, as Virginia Scott has shown, in *The Commedia Dell'Arte in Paris: 1644–1697* (Charlottesville: University Press of Virginia, 1990), in spite of the support and protection of Bourbon kings that a wildly popular idiom like the commedia dell'arte enjoyed in seventeenth-century France, it was constantly engaged in battle with church officials and state institutions like the Parlement de Paris, which accused it variously of being a school for scandal and disorder, of making "a sewer and house of Satan of the Hôtel de Bourgogne," and causing "the ruin of the families of some poor artisans . . . who for more than two hours before the play pass their time in . . . gambling, gluttony, and drunkenness" (Scott, 323). These accusations contributed to the commedia's final suppression in France in 1697. The art of the jugglers did not enjoy the favors of the period's legislators of artistic or moral taste any more than did the commedia. A famous criticism by Boileau of Molière's *Fourberies de Scapin* (1671), it will be remembered, is that the playwright dared associate high and low comedy in his play. In other words, the task of civilizing the "native" at home (in France) preceded that of civilizing the "native" abroad (in the colonies). The difference between the two

processes is one of degree, not of kind. For a study of the civilizing process at home and abroad undertaken by what Elias calls "the secular upper classes of the West," see Norbert Elias, *The Civilizing Process* (Oxford: Blackwell, 2000), esp. 382–87, 421–36.

46. Jean Laude, "La négrophilie et la critique de l'exotisme," in *La Peinture française et l'art nègre* (Paris: Klinckseick, 1968).

47. For an example of studies devoted to the African dimension in French modernist culture, see James Clifford, "An Ethnographic Surrealism," in *The Predicament of Culture: Twentieth Century Ethnography, Literature, and Art* (Cambridge: Harvard University Press, 1988); Marie-Denise Shelton, "Primitive Self: Colonial Impulses in Michel Leiris' *L'Afrique fantôme*," in Barkan and Bush, *Prehistories of the Future;* and Phyllis Taoua, *Forms of Protest: Anti-Colonialism and Avant-Gardes in Africa, the Caribbean, and France* (Portsmouth: Heinemann, 2002).

48. Barthélémy Kotchy, "New Trends in the Theatre of the Ivory Coast (1972–1983)," *Theatre Research International* 9.3 (1984): 239.

49. Traoré, *Le théâtre négro-africain,* 81.

50. Werewere Liking, "Théâtres de Recherche et professionalisme théâtral en Côte d'Ivoire. L'exemple du K-Yi Mbock Théâtre," in *On Stage: Proceedings of the Fifth International Janhienz Jahn Symposium on Theatre in Africa,* ed. Ulla Schild (Gottingen: Edition Re, 1992); emphasis added.

51. Christine Pillot, "Le 'Vivre vrai' de Werewere Liking," *Notre Librairie* 102 (1990): 58.

52. Chantal Boiron, "Limoges: L'atelier théâtral," *Notre Librairie,* spec. issue, "Créateurs africains à Limoges" (1993): 17.

53. Ibid.

54. Ibid., 19.

55. Aristotle, *Poetics* (New York: Dover, 1997), 13–14.

56. Marie-José Hourantier, "*Les mains veulent dire,* lecture du spectacle," in Werewere Liking and Marie-José Hourantier, *Spectacles rituels* (Abidjan: Les Nouvelles Editions Africaines, 1987), 82, 85.

57. Boiron, "Limoges," 17.

58. Werewere Liking, *Les mains veulent dire,* in Liking and Hourantier, *Spectacles rituels,* 23.

59. Ibid.

60. Boiron, "Limoges," 17.

61. Senouvo Zinsou, *On joue la comédie* (1975), rev. ed. (Lomé: Editions Haho; Haarlem: In de Knipscheer, 1987), 22.

62. Ibid., 38–40.

63. For a study of the various types of corporeal presence on the stage in general, see David Graver, "The Actor's Bodies," *Text & Performance Quarterly* 17.3 (1997): 221–34.

64. Hourantier, "Lecture du spectacle," 183.

65. Liking, *Elle sera de jaspe,* 105.

66. Hourantier, "Lecture du spectacle," 224.

67. Ibid., 181.

68. Ibid., 226–41.

69. Boiron, "Limoges," 17.

70. Werewere Liking, *Quelque Chose-Afrique* (unpublished), 90.

71. Zinsou, *On joue la comédie,* 16.

72. Boiron, "Limoges," 19.

73. Even if it was later combined with text drama, as Christopher Innes, "Text/Pre-Text/Pretext: The Language of Avant-Garde Experiment," in Harding, *Contours,* 62–69, points out, or abandoned by such groups as the Living Theatre, the Performance Group, and Peter Brook's International Center for Theatrical Research.

74. Antonin Artaud, *The Theatre and its Double,* trans. Mary Caroline Richards (New York: Grove Press, 1958), 37.

75. For a trenchant discussion of the features of the modernist avant-garde, see Innes, "Text/Pre-Text/Pretext."

76. Awashi, "Encounter with Tradition"; Ola Rotimi, "Much Ado about Brecht," in *The Dramatic Touch of Difference,* ed. Erika Fischer-Lichte, Josephine Riley, and Michael Gissenwehrer (Tubingen: Gunter Narr Verlag, 1990), 253–261; Savory, "Strategies for Survival."

77. Artaud, *Theatre and its Double,* 38.

78. Ibid., 61.

79. John Conteh-Morgan, *Theatre and Drama in Francophone Africa: A Critical Introduction* (London: Cambridge University Press, 1994), 32.

80. Artaud, *Theatre and its Double,* 60.

81. Judith Malina and Julian Beck, *Paradise Now* (New York: Random House, 1971), 84.

82. Ibid., 15.

83. Ibid., 17.

84. Schechner, *Public Domain,* 217.

85. Ibid.

86. For a scathing dismissal, from the activist political Left, of this "politics of ecstacy," as one of its practitioners, Schechner, called it (*Public Domain,* 209–28), see R. G. Davis, "The Radical Right in American Theatre," *Theatre Quarterly* 5.19 (1975): 67–72.

87. Michael Vanden Heuvel, *Performing Drama/Dramatizing Performance* (Ann Arbor: University of Michigan Press, 1991), 83.

88. Smith, *Modernism and Post-Modernism,* 9.

89. Zinsou, *On joue la comédie,* 109.

90. Boiron, "Limoges," 17.

91. Bürger, *Theory of the Avant-Garde,* 55–82.

92. For a trenchant analysis of what Taoua calls "the tension . . . between the ahistorical abstraction enabling vanguard primitivism and the historical circumstances of colonial exploitation," see *Forms of Protest,* 3–50.

93. Nietszche, *The Birth of Tragedy* (New York: Alfred Knopf and Random House, 1967), 37.

94. John Conteh-Morgan, "Theatre and the Performance of the Nation in Africa," in *The Short Century: Independence and Liberation Movements in Africa, 1945–1994,* ed. Okwui Enwezor (Munich: Prestel Verlag, 2001).

95. Zinsou, *On joue la comédie,* 109.

96. For a discussion of the ideology of what has been called the white "maleness" of reason, see Susan Bordo, *The Flight to Objectivity: Essays on Cartesianism and Culture* (Albany: State University of New York Press, 1987); and Linda M. Alcoff, *Epistemology: The Big Questions* (Cambridge, Mass.: Blackwell, 1998), 387–92.

97. Boiron, "Limoges," 17.

98. Chantal Boiron, "Une nouvelle exigence, Werewere Liking," *Notre Librairie,* spec. issue, "Créateurs africains à Limoges" (1993): 52.

99. Paulin Hountondji, *The Struggle for Meaning: Reflections on Philosophy, Culture and Democracy in Africa,* trans. John Conteh-Morgan (Athens: Ohio University Press, 2002), 107–8, 131–33.

100. Boiron, "Limoges," 17.

101. Hourantier, "Lecture du spectacle," 50.

102. John Conteh-Morgan, "Camara Laye," in *The Routledge Encyclopedia of African Literature,* ed. Simon Gikandi (London: Routledge, 2002), 284–86.

Avant-Garde Drama in the Middle East

Marvin Carlson

Western knowledge of the theater and drama of the Middle East has been traditionally hampered by two widespread and erroneous assumptions, each of which has in its own way prevented even generally well-informed students of theater from developing even the most basic understanding of the theatrical culture of this complex and fascinating part of the world.[1]

The first assumption is the more basic, and the more damaging one: it is that there never has been any significant drama in the Middle East due to the strong opposition to depictions of the human figure in Islamic fundamentalism. Like many widespread and popular beliefs about the cultures of other people, this assumption, is based on a generalized distortion of fact. Certainly within some parts of the traditions of Islamic fundamentalism (the Islamic faith, like the Christian, being composed of an almost infinite variety of sects and subsects with varying sets of observances) such a prohibition exists, and certainly this prohibition has supported a long-standing suspicion of theater within Islam. But to generalize from this to the widely held assumption that there has been little or no significant theater throughout the Arabic world as a result of religious prejudice would be rather like assuming that because of the almost universal condemnation of the drama among the fathers of the church and the long and tenacious suspicion of the theater within the Western church (most thoroughly documented in Jonas Barish's excellent work, *The Anti-Theatrical Prejudice*),[2] there would be little or no development of the drama within the Christian world of Europe and America. In fact, a long and complex theatrical tradition exists in many parts of the Islamic world. Court and public dramatic activities of various sorts have been traced back well into the

125

Middle Ages, and dramatic texts exist from tenth-century Cairo that are far more complex and sophisticated than anything that appeared in Europe for several centuries after this period. There is even, in Iran, a still-living tradition of Islamic religious drama, not unlike the European passion plays, about which I will speak more presently. During the twentieth century a number of Arabic countries have produced a body of dramatic literature that is as significant as that produced by almost any country in Europe, even though the European bias of most theater scholars has prevented it from being widely recognized.

This European bias is the ground for the second erroneous assumption, one that is widely held not only among the comparatively few theater students in the West who have some acquaintance with drama in the Arab world, but also, unfortunately, among many Arabic writers themselves who study the drama of their own countries. This is the assumption, based on the colonialist worldview, that whatever significant drama does exist or has existed in the Arab world resulted from that world's gradually becoming aware of and learning to imitate European models. M. M. Badawi's *Modern Arabic Drama in Egypt,* the standard English work on this subject, opens with the unqualified statement, "It is an established fact that modern Arabic drama was borrowed from the West independently by Marun al-Naqqash in the Lebanon in 1847 and by Ya'qub Sannu in Egypt in 1870."[3]

According to this model, the French occupation of what is now Lebanon, Syria, and Egypt and the subsequent and longer-lasting British occupation of Egypt provided the intellectual and cultural climate for the birth of dramatic tradition in those countries. There is some truth in this model, as there is in the misapprehension about the incompatibility of theater and Islam. Certainly it is true that there was no real literary tradition of drama in the Middle East before the middle of the nineteenth century, when a Beirut businessman, Marun al-Naqqash, became fascinated with European theater and began writing and producing plays based on French and Italian models. There is a direct line of descent from these early experiments of al-Naqqash and his family to translations, imitations, and productions of European, especially French, plays in Damascus, Alexandra, and Cairo in the 1870s. The major Egyptian pioneer in this tradition was Ya'qub Sannu, who worked in both Damascus and Cairo, wrote or translated some thirty plays, and founded the first "National" theater in Cairo in 1870. According to this genealogy, the Arabic drama begins with al-Naqqash's *al-Bakhil* in 1847, and when the Arabic theater is mentioned at all in encyclopedias of drama (and it is often omitted entirely), this drama is normally considered its grounding example. The folk and popular theater traditions of these countries, and especially the puppet-theater tradition, which has been well documented for centuries, since these fall outside the tradition of European literary theater and are essentially free of its influence, have been often ignored by theater historians, even in the Arabic countries themselves.

The search for equivalents of avant-garde theatricalism outside the normal parameters constructed by students of European theater history must therefore, in the case of the theater of the Middle East, confront at the outset both of these deeply entrenched biases: that which assumes that the Arab world in general has produced little or no theater; and, that somewhat more informed view which recognizes at least a modern theatrical tradition but which assumes that it amounts to little more than a pale imitation of European traditions.

The temptation of this second bias is particularly strong in considering such a phenomenon as avant-garde drama, not only because the concept of the avant-garde itself grows out of the European tradition, but also because the colonial and postcolonial dramatists and dramatic theorists of the Middle East, especially during the late nineteenth and early twentieth centuries, very consciously looked to Europe for their cultural models. If the modern Arabic drama began by looking to dramatists like Molière, as the first national theaters were established in the 1870s and 1880s the models became Ibsen and the early realists, and as new dramatic movements, from symbolism to the theater of the absurd, had a vogue in Europe, they were echoed by dramatists in the Middle East, especially in the traditional centers of drama, in Damascus, Cairo, and Beirut. Thus one can certainly find examples of Arabic drama all during the twentieth century that was thought by its authors and by Arabic critics alike to be avant-garde precisely in the European manner, looking to European sources and inspiration.

Under these circumstances, can any case be made for a Middle Eastern avant-garde theater that operates on its own terms and not simply as a colonial or postcolonial reflection of a European model? Indeed, such a case has already been made by at least a few significant theorists and dramatists, with arguments that I think worthy of serious attention.

Perhaps the most provocative and unexpected such claim was made in the late 1970s by Peter J. Chelkowski, a specialist in Iranian culture writing on the traditional Iranian passion play, the *Ta'ziyeh*. A series of articles by Chelkowski on the Ta'ziyeh appeared in a number of literary and performance journals between 1975 and 1979,[4] culminating in the

leading essay in a 1979 book devoted to this dramatic form[5] with a title
the author himself characterized as "deliberately controversial" but strikingly appropriate to our present concern: "Ta'ziyeh: Indigenous Avant-
Garde Theatre of Iran."[6] Clearly Chelkowski is making no claim that
the creative inspiration for this traditional religious theater had anything
in common with that of Western avant-garde drama. The Ta'ziyeh is a
popular communal form with its roots not in literature or high art but in
religious celebrations, in dramatic narrations of the lives and deaths of
religious heroes and martyrs, and in festival processions mourning their
loss dating back to the tenth century.

The argument that Chelkowski makes, however, is plainly relevant to
the inspiration behind the current volume, that theatrical activities very
similar to those claimed as their own by the European avant-garde in fact
can be found in many theatrical cultures, where they were generated and
developed with no thought of European artistic concerns. The "avant-
garde" features of the Ta'ziyeh that Chelkowski emphasizes are for the
most part those that arise from its mixing of materials from history, legend, popular culture, and everyday life, its casual use of found material
and space, its frank acknowledgment of the apparatus of production, and
its breaking down of the barrier between performance and audience.
Calling the rural Ta'ziyeh "the unconscious avant-garde of the 'poor
theatre,'" Chelkowski goes on to explain:

> It totally engages the participation of the audience and it has extraor-
> dinary dynamic flexibility. There are no barriers of time and space.
> For instance, Napoleon Bonaparte can appear on the stage along with
> Hussein, the Virgin Mary, Alexander the Great, and the Queen of
> Sheba. The text is not fixed; episodes from one play can be interpo-
> lated in another to suit the mood of the actors, the audience, and the
> weather. The producer is omnipresent, regulating the movements of
> actors, musicians, and audience. He remains constantly on stage, giv-
> ing the actors their cues, helping children and inexperienced actors,
> and handling props.

The same casual mixing of characters and fragments of plot can be
observed in the other elements of the production. Costumes and prop-
erties are partly symbolic (a bowl of water for the Euphrates River),
partly historical (British officer's jackets for warriors), partly everyday
(sunglasses for villains, automobile hubcaps for shields). Popular songs
and marches are mixed with classical Persian musical modes. Perfor-

mances are adapted to whatever space is available. "None of these practices ever proves distracting to the absorbed audience and actors,"
Chelkowski concludes. "On the contrary, they give each Ta'ziyeh performance special freshness and immediacy."[7]

Whatever the merits of Chelkowski's claim for the Ta'ziyeh as an
"unconscious avant-garde" theater, its unique position as the only
significant Islamic religious cycle and, moreover, its development within
the very distinctive Persian cultural context prevent it from being utilized to make any more general argument about a native avant-garde in
the Middle Eastern theater. When we turn to the more central and modern tradition of Arabic theater in the region, however, we find a number of much more self-conscious experiments in this direction, but
growing, as does the Ta'ziyeh, out of indigenous material and traditions,
not out of a borrowing from European sources.

The dramatist universally recognized as the most important modern
playwright in the Arabic theater and the first to gain a substantial international reputation is Egypt's Tawfiq al-Hakim (1899–1987), the best-
known dramatist of the Arab world. His mature period began with the
play *Ahl al Kahf (The Sleepers in the Cave),* which opened the new Egyptian National Theatre in 1935 and established the modern literary drama
in that country. The range of al-Hakim's more than eighty plays is enormous, including philosophical dramas, plays drawn from history and legend, realistic plays, fantasy and symbolic dramas, and works of science
fiction. Al-Hakim studied law in Paris from 1925 to 1928 and constantly
attended the theater during those years. He remained extremely conscious of and interested in the changing trends in European drama, creating among his many plays works that closely reflect many of the European styles of the 1930s through the 1960s. He was also, however,
extremely conscious of his position and his responsibilities as an Egyptian dramatist. Very much reflecting the tradition of Ibsen and the modern social drama, he recognized the importance of realism for dealing
with the problems of modern society, but when he began searching for
a new dramatic approach that would grow from Egyptian, not European
sources, it was to the avant-garde and experimental theater that he
looked.

Al-Hakim's key play in this respect is, somewhat paradoxically, also
his best known internationally. This is *Ya Tali al-Shajara (The Tree
Climber),* published in 1962. Critics of al-Hakim have almost universally
attributed this drama's striking formal experimentation to the influence
of the French Theater of the Absurd, with which al-Hakim unquestion-

ably became familiar during a sojourn in Paris in 1959.[8] However, such critics ignore the major argument made in al-Hakim's important preface to this play, omitted from all translations into other languages.[9] In this preface al-Hakim reports that indeed he found in Paris such dramatists as Ionesco, Vauthier, and Adamov being hailed as the inventors of a new approach to the drama, but, al-Hakim continues, when he returned to Egypt and began to consider the artistic traditions of his own culture, he realized that here was "the true ground which held in its bosom" the material of this so-called "totally modern art."

> If the defining characteristic of modern art (painting, sculpture, the-ater, etc.) is the expression of reality by unreality, utilizing irrational-ity and illogic in each artistic creation, and relying upon abstraction in order to achieve new effects and impressions, then all this was known to the ancient and popular artists here in our own country ever since antiquity.[10]

Citing the example of the ancient Egyptian artists, who knew of cubism millennia before Picasso and of the tales of the Arabian Nights, which utilized surrealism long before literary Europe discovered this approach, al-Hakim concludes that an artistic spirit opposed to realism emerged in his culture because "in our country the artist of the people, painter or writer, instinctively perceived this deep and rich source of artistic expression long before Western artists discovered it and developed the-ories about it."[11] Later he observes that "our popular art knew all these secrets before any of these schools, without us being aware of what it was doing."[12]

On these grounds, al-Hakim insists that his experimental theater, despite its rejection of realism, should not be placed in the now "well-defined category" of the European avant-garde, because of the consid-erable role played in the development of this theater by "my own nature on the one hand, and on the other my popular Egyptian sources of inspi-ration." He therefore proposes that this work needs a new critical descriptive term, such as "idealized, popular nonrealism."[13]

Although al-Hakim returned regularly to the school of realism, he continued to explore also the nonrealistic and nonrational world of rep-resentation opened to him by Egyptian popular culture, which he con-tinued to see as providing a more stimulating inspiration than the more internationally visible, but for him less compatible, French avant-garde. None of al-Hakim's subsequent experimental drama achieved the success of *Ya Tali al-Shajara,* but he nevertheless produced a substantial body of such work, among which one might cite *Rihlat Qitar* (*A Train Journey,* 1964), which gathers a variety of contemporary Egyptian characters on a strange and clearly metaphorical train, and two works from 1966—the full-length *Masir Sarsar* (*The Fate of a Cockroach*), which satirizes contemporary political action under the traditional guise of a folk allegory, and the one-act *Kull Shay' fi Mahallih* (*Not a Thing Out of Place*), an upside-down, madhouse depiction of life in an Egyptian village.

The success and international visibility of Tewfik al-Hakim inspired a whole generation of significant dramatists in the Middle East and particularly in Egypt, where the political situation in the late 1950s and the 1960s encouraged a remarkable flourishing of theater. The overthrow of the monarchy in 1952 and the emergence of the military government headed by Nasser profoundly altered the course of modern Egyptian and Middle Eastern history. Culture was not high on the agenda of the new regime, although to the extent that it involved a democratization of the arts and a means of spreading information for the government, it did receive certain support, and this was particularly the case with theater. The new Ministry of National Guidance supported three national theater companies, an experimental, and a puppet theater in addition to opera, operetta, ballet, and circus. Al-Hakim was awarded a State Prize for Literature and the Republican Chain, a decoration usually given only to visiting heads of state, and an important new generation of playwrights emerged to take advantage of all this encouragement. With the support of the minister, Dr. Abdel-Qadir Hatem, and of Dr. Sarwat Okasha in particular, drama enjoyed a freedom of expression often denied other areas of the written word.[14] Although this freedom was somewhat surprising given Nasser's general suspicion of the political reliability of the literary establishment, Egypt's growing independence from Western Europe, and particularly from France and England, brought to a head in the Suez crisis of 1956, brought the government and most of its leading dramatists into agreement at least upon the major matter of developing a modern Egyptian theater that would deal with Egyptian concerns and be emancipated, insofar as possible, from the traditional heavy reliance upon the English and French.

Most of the dramatists of this new generation, like al-Hakim, and many of their European and American contemporaries, even while emphasizing Egyptian themes and subjects, tended still to favor the traditional realistic social drama in the tradition of Ibsen and Shaw, as can be seen in Nu'man Ashur's *Il Nas illi Taht* (*The People Downstairs,* 1956), a work similar in tone and influence to John Osborne's *Look Back in Anger* in Britain. A number of the new dramatists, however, also produced more experimental drama, and some of the most important such work showed itself strongly in harmony with the new sense of nationalism and independence from Western Europe by looking for inspiration, as al-Hakim had done in *Ya Tali al-Shajara,* not to the work of the European avant-garde, but to the nonrealistic performance tradition of their own culture.

The outstanding example of this orientation was *al-Farafir* (*The Flipflops,* 1964) by Yusif Idris, the best known of the immediate followers of al-Hakim. Idris, one of the most widely read short-story writers of the Arab world, also produced a significant body of drama. His first three plays, written in the mid-1950s, were dramas of social realism, clearly reflecting the interests of the new era. The first two, both short, dealt with the sufferings of the poor and exploited, while the third, Idris's first full-length play (*Al-Lahza al-Harija, The Critical Moment,* 1957) deals with the effects of the Suez war on a middle-class Egyptian family and a British soldier. During the seven years following this play, Idris devoted himself to short stories and journalism, but during this time he also devoted much thought to the creation of a new kind of Egyptian drama, one that would be truly Egyptian in both subject matter and technique. To this end he developed an approach that he outlined and defended in an influential series of articles entitled "Our Egyptian Theatre" published in 1965 in the leading literary periodical, *al-Katib.*

Actually the program Idris proposed in these articles, both in its motivation and its strategies, was not radically different from that suggested by al-Hakim in his preface to *Ya Tali al-Shajara* three years before, but the far greater visibility of the journal *al-Katib* brought these arguments to the forefront of Egyptian literary discussion and encouraged the idea, still widely held among writers on the modern Egyptian theater, that al-Hakim's drama remained essentially in the tradition of the European avant-garde (in particular, of its most recent manifestation, the theater of the absurd), while Idris opened the way to a distinctly different, Egyptian-based mode of experimental drama.[15] Certainly, Idris's rhetoric was perfectly adapted to the new nationalist and populist spirit of post-Suez Egypt. Hitherto-neglected folk and popular forms of entertainment not only began to receive unprecedented scholarly attention but began to attract the interest of experimental artists. The medieval Arabic oral rhymed narration, the *maqama,* began to attract the attention of modern poets, as did the shadow play tradition, the *Karagoz,* that was closely related to it. The remarkably complex and sophisticated tenth-century shadow plays created by Ibn Daniyal were published for the first time in 1963. A highly developed performance consciousness was clearly apparent in these early works; indeed, the introductory remarks to the first, *Tayf al-Khayal,* provide a significant defense of the power of theatrical embodiment, calling performance "a supreme art that by the very fact of substantiation will supersede that which is mere imagination."[16] Suddenly a native and popular entertainment tradition long predating the modern European-oriented tradition began to come to the attention of scholars and theater artists of that region, with significant influence in the work of both.

Idris's series of articles in *al-Katib* fitted perfectly into this new orientation. He argued that what had been accepted as the Egyptian drama up to the present time, traditional or experimental, successful or not, had been written according to Western models, and that the time had come to develop a drama that was uniquely Egyptian. Like the new government, he advocated a turning away from the traditional European-oriented "high art" to seek inspiration in indigenous local and folk manifestations, such as the *maqama,* the shadow theater, or the village *samir,* a popular festival in which villagers gather to improvise entertainments involving singing, dancing, and impersonation. Idris's campaign to free himself from European traditions led him somewhat paradoxically, but not inconsistently, to develop a strategy exactly parallel to that of an important segment of the European avant-garde, seeking a regeneration of the drama by a sophisticated reworking of popular and folk traditions.

One of the leading Egyptian dramatists of the late 1960s, Rashad Rushdi, utilized the mechanical farce of the shadow theater and folk theater as a basis for the grotesque social conflicts in his *Itfarrag Ya Salam* (*Come to the Show,* 1966) and *Halawat Zaman* (*Past Sweets,* 1967), and the publication of Ibn Daniyal's twelfth-century *babat* encouraged both scholars and playwrights to explore further the modern possibilities of this form. In his study in the late 1960s, *The Art of Comedy from Shadow Plays to al-Rihani,* Ali al-Rai traced a performance tradition from the medieval *maqamat* tales, dramatized by Ibn Daniyal, through the Middle Eastern shadow play tradition, to a popular late-nineteenth-century Syrian performer, George Dakhul, who brought this traditional material into the live popular farce theater of turn-of-the-century Syria and Egypt.[17] Al-Rai's work in turn inspired the Moroccan actor-director and playwright al-Tayyeb al-Siddiqi to go back to one of the *maqamat* utilized by Ibn Daniyal to create a modern experimental political drama played in the style of the puppet theater called *al-Maqama al-Madariyya*. Performed in Damascus in the spring of 1973, it had a great impact and clearly demonstrated the effectiveness of this approach.[18]

The articles in *al-Katib* would probably in themselves have made Idris the leading theater spokesman for the new Egyptian avant-garde, but he solidified this position by the creation of a major new play, his first in seven years, *al-Farafir* (*The Flipflops*, 1964), which brilliantly put his theories into practice and served as a landmark in the modern Egyptian theater. In the extensive prefatory notes to the play ("Some observations about the performance of the text"), Idris not only gave detailed instructions for its staging and interpretation, but related these suggestions directly to the arguments he had developed in his essays in *al-Katib*. Several sections ("Concerning the Character of the Flipflops" and "The Relationship of Flipflops to Others") demonstrate that the Flipflop shares certain characteristics with the licensed fool and the prankster rogue so common in many folk literatures, the foe of all pretension, the skilled acrobat and the witty improviser, charming, irreverent, and irrepressible. Despite the universality of such characters, Idris emphasizes their particular development within the Egyptian tradition, tracing much the same trajectory as that subsequently developed much more fully in the study by Ali al-Rai, from the rogue heroes of the medieval *maqama* and *Karagoz,* through the folk adventures of the Arab witty trickster Juha, to popular early twentieth-century burlesque comedians like Ali al-Kassir and Najib al-Rihani.[19]

Al-Farafir, although highly original in concept and execution, is filled with echoes of this traditional material. The opening dialogue between the *farfur* and his master, discussing tasks he can perform, is modeled directly upon a section of the just-published shadow play by Ibn Daniyal *Agib wa Gharib,*[20] and other traditional shadow play sequences are echoed in subsequent passages. A conflict between rival brides for the master's hand in marriage is carried out in the form of a series of traditional village entertainments: dances, a mock duel with sticks *(tahtib),* and a rhymed *maqama* dialogue.[21]

As this latter sequence suggests, perhaps the most important traditional element in Idris's experimental theater was not the character of the *farfur* itself, but the context in which the *farafir* appeared, the traditional village performance/celebration, the *samir*. The first section of Idris's preface ("The Stage") calls for a presentation in the manner of such a performance, which developed with spectators totally surrounding the action and continually sought to involve these spectators.[22] The *samir* offered to Idris the model of a largely improvised entertainment, with much physicality and mixture of disparate elements and, apparently most important to him, created in a situation where the boundary between audience and performers was extremely fluid. This free movement, Idris argued, created what could be the essence of a particularly Egyptian avant-garde, a state of spiritual elation he called *al-Tamasruh,* in which actor and spectator became fused into one.

After the success of Idris's *al-Farafir* the village *samir,* with its associations with improvisation and the mixing of role-playing and reality, gained considerable popularity among the new wave of Egyptian dramatists. Mahmud Diyab, for example, utilizes it most originally and engagingly in his *Layali al-Hasad (Harvest Nights,* 1967) and his *al-Halafit (Worthless People,* 1969). Traditional song, dance, outdoor games, and improvisations are featured, along with actors slipping in and out of their parts and exchanging places with spectators.

Although the theoretical claims made by Idris for *al-Farafir* are in fact no more radical than those of al-Hakim in the preface to *Ya Tali al-Shajara,* the former's great reputation as a groundbreaking and particularly Egyptian work is not undeserved. Al-Hakim's play brilliantly undercuts traditional structures of logic and dramatic expectation, but Idris more directly engages the operations of the dramatic event itself. His innovations have been compared by various critics to the experiments of Brecht, Pirandello, and the absurdists (and his metatheatrical playfulness seemed to this writer strongly reminiscent of the romantic irony of Tieck), but Idris's claims to the inspiration of native folk traditions seem convincing and, even for those determined to stress European influence on his work, demonstrate that the non–European folk tradition of the Middle East provides at least the potential for an alternative avant-garde inspiration.

The preface to Idris's next play, *al-Mahzala al-Ardiyya (The Farce of the World,* 1966) also begins with an evocation of his articles in *al-Katib,* and this play is even more freewheeling than *al-Farafir* in its mixture of illusion and reality, realistic and symbolic elements, and abrupt changes in focus. The performative and metatheatrical element is less developed than in *al-Farafir,* however, and the particular relationship to the native performance traditions stressed in the earlier work seem less clear here. His subsequent plays, like the later works of al-Hakim, continue to experiment with dramatic form, drawing both from European and Egyptian sources, but it was the two plays *Ya Tali al-Shajara* and *al-Farafir* and the critical writings surrounding them that have provided the center for a modern Egyptian experimental theater drawing upon native rather than European inspiration. Their interest in such popular local folk entertainments as the folktales of the witty prankster, the abstract and grotesque *Karagoz,* or the improvisations of the village *samir* have clearly continued to influence subsequent Egyptian experimental theater.

The cultural preeminence of Egypt in the Arab world in general and in the Middle East in particular during most of the twentieth century guaranteed that the interest of leading Egyptian dramatists like Idris and al-Hakim in developing an avant-garde drama utilizing indigenous material would also lead dramatists in other Arabic countries with a comparatively strong theater tradition to similar experimentation. In Syria, the other Middle Eastern home of the modern Arabic drama, such an interest could be clearly seen in the work of Sadallah Wannus, second only to Tawfiq al-Hakim in terms of his recognition as an Arabic play-wright. Wannus spent the early 1960s in Cairo studying Arabic literature and the years 1966 to 1968 in Paris, where he became extremely interested in Brecht. His early one-act plays, such as *Gutha ala al-Rasif* (*The Corpse on the Sidewalk,* 1964) and *al-Garad* (*The Locusts,* 1965), suggest a blending of al-Hakim's dramas of ideas and the techniques of the Middle Eastern puppet theater. To these elements Wannus added a Brechtian touch (while reworking an Arabic folk animal fable) in a didactic parable *al-Fil ya Malek al-Zaman* (*The Elephant, King of the World,* 1969).

Although most of his plays have illuminating theoretical prefaces, Wannus's most complete statement of his dramatic philosophy appeared in the essay "Bayanat li-masrah arabi gadid" ("A New Arabic Theatre Explained"), which appeared in October 1970 in the Damascus periodical *al-Marifa.* In this influential essay, Wannus took issue with the common assumption that the founders of the modern Arabic drama blindly followed European models, arguing that they in fact judiciously combined elements from those models with techniques and material from native performance traditions and folklore, a strategy to which Wannus strongly urged a return.[23]

During the 1960s and 1970s, when Wannus was establishing himself as a dramatist and critic, the European avant-garde of Brecht and the Absurdists was much in vogue in the Arab world. While Wannus admired the political theater of Brecht, he also argued that neither of these European approaches could be successfully transferred to Syria, where they would be too alien for audiences with a quite different experience of both performance and philosophy.[24] Instead, he looked within the folkloric performance tradition of his own country for elements that would both provide a new experimental basis for his work and at the same time open it more directly to his public. On these grounds he followed al-Hakim in recommending devices like the traditional Arabic storyteller, the *hakawati,* and followed Idris and others in recommending the active participation of audience members in the performance. Thus *Mughamarat ra's al-mamaluk Jabir* (*The Adventure of Mamluk Jabir's Head,* 1969) is built upon the entertainment provided by Amm Mu'nis, a *hakawati* who appears in a modern Arab café and recounts to its patrons, with the aid of several assistants who play multiple roles and carry scenery on and off the stage, the story that gives the play its title. Like al-Hakim, Wannus felt that these traditional modes of blurring the lines between actor and character and performance and audience provided an Arabic base for a politically oriented theater in the style of Brecht, to which Wannus gave the name *masrah al-tasyis,* "theater of politization."[25] In *al-Malek huwa 'l-Malek* (*The King's the King,* 1977) Wannus weaves sequences from traditional farce entertainments and puppet theater into a retelling of a tale from the *1001 Nights,* the entire performance guided and presided over by a pair of *hakawati*-like figures called "leaders of the play," Zahid and Ubayd.

Other major Syrian dramatists during the 1970s followed the lead of Wannus in the development of indigenous material for experimental purposes. The prolific Walid Ikhlasi has created several episodic plays inspired by the *hakawati* and the shadow play traditions. His *al-Sirat* (*The Path,* 1976), for example, creates a moving political parable out of the career of a theater janitor who is pressed into service as a clown and finds a popular but self-destructive career playing routines based on the shadow theater that reinforce the established order. Muhammad Maghut's surrealistic satire *al-Muharridj* (*The Jester,* 1973) fascinatingly combines elements of Arabic and Western theater, opening with the arrival of a troupe of itinerant dancers and entertainers who set up a temporary stage next to a café in the slum quarter of an unidentified Arab city. There they perform a grotesquely distorted version of *Othello* narrated by *Quari al-Tabl* (The Drum-Player), a semiliterate *hakawati.* The part of Othello is played by the jester of the title, who also takes on a number of other roles and performs in the exaggerated style of traditional popular farce, while the Drummer interprets the downfall of Othello as a British plot designed by the imperialist Shakespeare to discredit an Arabic hero.

The attention to such indigenous sources for avant-garde experimentation stimulated in Egypt, Syria, and elsewhere by the dramatic theories and practice of Idris received important support in a small but influential book, *Qalabuna al-Masrahi (Our Theatrical Form),* published by Tawfiq al-Hakim in 1967. In the introduction to this book, al-Hakim modestly but clearly reminded his readers that he also had been a pioneer in the dramatic exploration of native performance traditions. Following the establishment of a tradition of European borrowings and adaptations, he notes, efforts began to be made to develop a more distinctly Egyptian approach to drama by

> trying to link, even if it were by the thinnest of threads, this new art to some of the old artistic manifestations among our common people. It occurred to me as it occurred to others to contribute to such efforts. In the year 1930, while I was working in the countryside, I wrote the play *al-Zammar* [*The Piper*], giving it a countryside title. The protagonist was a *samir* piper in the evenings and worked during the day at a rural health clinic. And he transformed this clinic into a real *samir.* Then later, in the year 1956, I created *al-Safqa* [*The Deal*], which attempted to include within the action of the play folk arts of the countryside such as dances, songs, and stick battles and was set in the open air or in front of a platform.[26] In the year 1962 I made another attempt to relate some of our ancient folk practices to the most recent trends in contemporary art in *Ya Tali al-Shajara* [*The Tree Climber*], the concern of which was, "Is it possible to connect the most recent trends in world art to the course of our own popular and traditional art?"[27]

Later in this essay, al-Hakim suggests another traditional model for modern experimental dramatists; the storyteller, or *sha'ir,*[28] who has been entertaining the public in village squares and coffeehouses since the Middle Ages, accompanying himself on a primitive violin, the *rababa.* Al-Hakim notes that the storyteller was often accompanied by a second performer, the *batal* (meaning hero or protagonist), who would impersonate various roles in the story that were introduced and continually commented upon by the storyteller. Al-Hakim claims this as one of the most ancient forms of folk theater, and he also remarks upon the similarity of the work of the *batal,* a single performer who presented a variety of characters but without seeking to fully embody them, to the theories of Brechtian acting.[29] This was clearly part of the appeal of this traditional form to al-Hakim, who agreed with Brecht that such an approach encouraged the sort of engaged and critical audience that al-Hakim also desired.

Somewhat surprisingly, al-Hakim, although he continued to experiment with dramatic form in a number of plays written after this essay, never attempted to utilize this particular approach. He contented himself with offering a few examples of episodes from Greek and modern theater to suggest how they might effectively be reworked in the storyteller-protagonist manner. Other, younger dramatists took up his suggestion, however, adding an important strain to the tradition of experimentation with folk forms and material. Naguib Surur, an Egyptian actor and director, created in 1963 for the Cairo Pocket Theatre the tragic love story *Yassin wa Bahiya (Yassin and Bahiya)*, which not only by its success proved the validity of al-Hakim's thesis, but provided a striking modern experimental variation on the traditional form when, near the end of the play, the playwright himself enters the action, pushing aside his own *sha'ir* to claim that role for himself, a wandering poet exiled by political oppression from his native village. This merging of folk presentation, of impersonation and reality, and of storytelling and political commentary provides an excellent example of Egyptian experimental theater of the 1960s.

The storyteller, generally called the *hakawati,* has become an important source of inspiration for experimental work in many parts of the Arab world since the late 1960s. Although the theater of Arabic North Africa (the Maghreb) is, strictly speaking, outside the scope of the present study, the *hakawati* has been central to recent experimental work, particularly in Tunisia and Morocco. The popular dramatist and director al-Tayyeb al-Siddiqi presented in the late 1970s a whole series of productions at the *Masrah Annass* (People's Theater) of Casablanca based on the work and careers of famous historical Arabic storytellers and oral poets such as Abderrahman al Majdoub, Badi al-Zamman al-Hamadhani, and Abdul Rahman al-Majdub, and one-character plays based on the *hakawati* tradition indeed became so popular in Morocco that a national festival devoted entirely to them was held in Rabat in 1977.[30]

The wandering *hakawati* is a familiar figure in traditional popular entertainment throughout the Middle East, in Egypt, Syria, Lebanon, Palestine, Jordan, and Iraq, and in each of these countries al-Hakim's attention to the theatrical potential of this figure struck a responsive note. Two of the best-known experimental companies of this region in the late twentieth century took their name from this figure and sought inspiration for their innovative techniques in the tradition of folk entertainment. One of the leading experimental companies of Lebanon in the late 1960s was the Firqat Muhtaraf Bayrout lil-Masrah (Beirut Workshop

Theater Company), founded in 1968 by Roger Assaaf and Nidaal al-Ashqar under the inspiration of Joan Littlewood's Workshop, Joseph Chaikin's Open Theatre, and the Living Theatre of Julian Beck and Judith Malina. Ten years later, in 1979, Roger Assaaf left this company to establish a new group called *Firqat Masrah al-Hakawati* (The Story-teller's Theater Company), which, as its title suggests, was devoted to seeking not European but Arabic models for its performance models. Chief among these was the art of the *hakawati*, which the company developed in a manner which, as al-Hakim had suggested, resulted in an Arabic experimental theater with certain similarities to Brecht. The most successful production of this company was its *Hikaayaat Min Sanat 1936 (Stories from the Year 1936).*

At almost the same time, another major *Hakawati* theater was orga-nized in Palestine by one of the leading modern theater figures in that country, François Abu Salem. Abu Salem was the founder of one of Palestine's first professional companies, Balaleen (Balloons), in 1971, less overtly political than the majority of Palestinian companies of that time (and since) but strongly devoted nevertheless to social causes, collective creation, and the use of folk and popular material. After a split in the group over political and artistic concerns, Abu Salem founded two other short-lived experimental companies in the mid-1970s and then in 1977, a company called Al-Hakawati, which remained the leading theatrical company in Palestine until its demise in 1993. It was reorganized, how-ever, as the first Palestinian national theater, which still bears this name.

Despite its title, this group was less specifically devoted to the story-teller's technique than its Lebanese namesake, but such techniques were among the many nonrealistic and usually folk-based narrative devices used by the company in their collectively improvised productions. Most of the shows were developed from original material, although occasion-ally a foreign text was adapted to their unique style of performance, as in their highly successful 1985 production of excerpts from Dario Fo's *Mis-tero Buffo,* called *Hikayat Assalat Al-Ukhra (Stories of the Heretic's Prayer).*

Probably the best known internationally among recent experimental theater companies is Cairo's El Warsha (The Workshop), which from its beginnings in the fall of 1987 has been dedicated to creating experimen-tal work based on elements of Egyptian folk culture, even when dealing with European texts from such dramatists as Handke, Pinter, and Fo. Hassan El-Geretly, the founder and artistic director of the company, which numbers around twenty members, not only organized training sessions for his actors to work with masters of popular traditional performance arts, but whenever possible, welcomed such masters into the company as fully participating members. Thus Hassan Khannoufa and Ahmed Al-Kumi, famous shadow-puppet artists, began working with the company in 1989 for an Egyptianized version of Jarry's *Ubu* plays drawing heavily upon the aesthetics and practice of this form. Dakhli Seweity, a former national champion of traditional stick fighting and a renowned authority in the ancient tradition of *tahtib,* which includes this martial art and its ritualized twin, stick dancing, has been closely associated with the company from its beginning. Perhaps the most influential of the popular masters associated with the company has been the renowned *sha'ir* Sayyid Al-Dawi, from upper Egypt.

A key work in the development of the company's aesthetic and reputation was the 1993 *Ghazir el-Leil (Tides of Night),* growing directly out of their focus on traditional storytelling. It tells the story of a tragic love affair between a ballad singer and a girl whose parents disapprove of his profession. The performance, itself based on ballad and storytelling devices, but also utilizing stick dancing, folk music, and shadow puppets, was first performed in the European-style Hanagar Theatre in Cairo, but for a revival in the garden of the British Consulate, the company's designer, Tarek Abou El-Fotouh, inspired by the setting of the play during a folk festival, a saint's feast *(Mouled),* conceived the idea of housing it in one of the sorts of temporary tent structures traditionally erected for such festivals. So perfectly suited was this surrounding to the performance that one of El-Fotouh's specially designed tents has been utilized, whenever possible, for all of their subsequent work.

Tides of Night, along with *Layaly El-Warsha,* an accompanying collection of material demonstrating the company's interest in popular forms—stories, sketches, stick fights, shadow and hand puppets, and popular songs—toured to the London International Theatre Festival in June 1997 and to the Kennedy Center in Washington in April 1998, achieving a significant international success. At the same time the group has served as a leader and a model for experimental theater companies throughout the Middle East.

In the fall of 1999, I was fortunate enough to see the most recent production by this distinguished company, *Ghazl-El-Amaar (Spinning Lives),* created in 1998. This storytelling performance was developed out of selections from the thousands of verses of one of the great epic poems of the Middle East, *Al-Sira-al-Hilahyya,* from the eleventh-century

nomadic tribe, the Beni Hilal. The key performer in the production was
the *sha'ir* Sayyid Al-Dawi, a regular member of the company, but also
one of the most famous living storytellers, reportedly the only individual
who can recite the entire *Al-Sira-al-Hilahyya* from memory, accompanying himself, as his predecessors have done for centuries, upon the simple stringed instrument, the *rabab*. Exactly in the manner suggested by
Al-Hakim, Al-Dawi provided the background and continuity, while the
El Warsha company acted out sequences from his ongoing narrative.
According to the director, Al-Dawi's familiarity with the material and
the enormous scope of the original allowed him to take the performance
in different directions every evening, providing a significant improvisatory element to the work.[31] The dancing, mime, and physical skills
of this talented company were extraordinary, but I shall never forget the
astonishing, almost hypnotic power of the *sha'ir* and his simple musical
accompaniment. He was striking physically, extremely tall and thin,
with craggy Bedouin features, but beyond that he exuded a physical
presence and authority that I have rarely experienced in the theater,
even though I could scarcely understand a word of what he was singing.
In him, and in the ongoing experimentation of companies like El Warsha, the visions of Al-Hakim, Idris, and Wannus of a modern Arabic theater that would find a powerful experimental inspiration in the most
ancient indigenous performance sources, is clearly being fulfilled.

Notes

1. The geographical scope of this essay requires some explanation. The theatrical
tradition I am exploring is primarily that of the modern Arab world, which in terms of
theater has been historically dominated by Egypt and Syria. These are the two Arab states
with the most fully developed modern theater tradition, and not coincidentally, are the
two states in which, despite a dominant colonial and postcolonial influence from the
European theater, a modern avant-garde tradition not drawn from European sources has
developed, both in theory and practice. Although obviously it is a significant element of
the Middle Eastern scene, and in modern times one of its most important producers of
theater, I do not discuss the Israeli theater, since its development (aside of course from
the heavy indebtedness to the European stage) has very little in common with the theater of its Arab neighbors, especially in respect to the avant-garde experimentation that
concerns me here. On the other hand, I will devote some attention in the opening of
this essay to the Ta'ziyeh theater of Iran, which is neither Arabic nor, some would argue,
strictly Middle Eastern, because it does provide some important background for the discussion of a modern avant-garde in the Arab Middle Eastern theater.

2. Jonas Barish, *The Anti-Theatrical Prejudice* (Berkeley: University of California
Press, 1981).

3. M. M. Badawi, *Modern Arabic Drama in Egypt* (Cambridge: Cambridge University Press, 1987), 1. Badawi is too careful a scholar to leave matters at that, however. A

few sentences later he makes an important qualification often omitted in the work of less conscientious scholars: "Yet the Arab world did have certain indigenous types of dramatic representation at the time, some even going back to medieval Islam. These traditional types determined to some extent the manner in which the imported form was conceived and subsequently developed."

4. *Festival of Arts Series* (Tehran, 1975); *Performing Arts Journal* 2.1 (1977); *Dialog* 21.6 (Warsaw, 1976).

5. Peter J. Chelkowski, ed., *Ta'ziyeh: Ritual and Drama in Iran* (New York: New York University Press, 1979).

6. Ibid., 1–11.

7. Ibid., 9–10.

8. See, for example, Badawi, *Modern Arabic Drama,* 74.

9. Indeed it has never been translated at all, although there is a French translation of one section of the preface in the collection *Anthologie de la Littérature Arabe Contemporaine: Les Essais,* ed. and trans. Anouar Abdel-Malek (Paris: Editions du Seuil, 1965), 420–25.

10. Tewfik al-Hakim, preface to *Ya tale al-shagarah* (Cairo, 1962), 15 (translation mine).

11. Ibid., 17–18.

12. Ibid., 26.

13. Ibid., 21.

14. Anthony McDermott, *Egypt from Nasser to Mubarak: A Flawed Revolution* (London: Croom Helm, 1988), 231–32.

15. See, for example, Badawi, *Modern Arabic Drama,* 74, 156.

16. Ibrahim Hamadah, ed., *Khayal al-zill* (Cairo, 1963), 144.

17. Ali al-Rai, "Some Aspects of Modern Arabic Drama," in *Studies in Modern Arabic Literature,* ed. R.C. Ostle (Warminster, Eng.: Aris and Phillips, 1975), 173–74.

18. Ibid., 174.

19. Ibid., 132–34.

20. Ibrahim Hamada, *Khayal al-zill,* 188–231.

21. Yusuf Idris, *Al-Farafir* (Cairo, 1966), 177.

22. Yusuf Idris, *Al-Mahzala al-Ardiyya, al-Farafir* (Cairo, 1966), 131.

23. *Al-Marifa* 104 (October 1970), reprinted in *Dar al-Fikr al-Gadid* (Damascus and Beirut, 1988), 30. The same argument, it should be noted, had been developed a few years earlier in *The Art of Comedy from Shadow Plays to al-Rihani* by the theorist and historian Ali al-Rai.

24. For Wannus on Brecht, see Nabil Haffar, *Muhadata ma'a Sa'dallah Wannus* in *at-Tariq* (Beirut, 1986), 2:104. On Wannus and the theater of the absurd see Friederike Pannewick, *Der andere Blick* (Berlin: Klaus Schwarz Verlag, 1993), 12.

25. Sadallah Wannus, preface to *Mugamarat ra's mamluk Gabir* (Beirut, 1980), 41.

26. In the postscript to this play, al-Hakim characterizes the work as "experimental," addressing four ongoing problems of the modern Egyptian theater: language, the physical space, the public, and realism. The use of folk elements and the setting of the play in a village square addressed the last three of these problems, presenting traditional familiar material in an engaging way to a public unused to theater, and suggesting a performance space for communities that had no established theater building. Tawfiq al-Hakim, *Al-Safqa* (Cairo, 1956), 160.

27. Al-Hakim, *Qalabuna al-Masrahi* (Cairo, 1967), 9–10.

28. Al-Hakim uses the usual Egyptian word for storyteller, which can also mean poet or narrator. The more common term in Syria and elsewhere in the Middle East is *hakawati*.

29. Al-Hakim, *Qalabuna al-Masrahi,* 13–14.

30. Abdelkrim Berrechid, "Morocco," in *The World Encyclopedia of Contemporary Theatre,* ed. Don Rubin, vol. 4, *The Arab World* (London: Routledge, 1999), 174.

31. Interview with Hassan El-Geretry, Cairo, September 20, 1999.

Made in Mexico
The Theatrical Avant-Garde and the Formation of a Nation

Adam Versényi

In the annals of Western European theater history Mexico's place in the early-twentieth-century avant-garde is largely relegated to a footnote. Unimportant in and of itself, Mexico is only considered as the location of Antonin Artaud's hallucinogenic experiences under the influence of peyote among the Tarahumara Indians. Those experiences led Artaud to the formation of his own innovative theories regarding the theater. Less commonly known is the existence of the Mexican theatrical avant-garde of the early twentieth century and its place in the creation of a national ethos following the Mexican Revolution.

Where the modernist movement in Latin America provided the impetus for novelists and poets to break free of European forms, the Spanish American theater at the beginning of the twentieth century was still firmly wed to the Spanish tradition epitomized by the works of Jacinto Benavente. Like their counterparts in the League of Revolutionary Writers and Artists, the Mexican theatrical avant-garde of the 1920s and 1930s sought to introduce new forms of theatrical expression that would create a truly Mexican theater capable of joining with the independent spirit fostered by the Revolution. A new nation was being born and needed its own theater. The search for this Mexican theater followed various paths. On the one hand were those groups, like the Grupo de los Siete (1926) and the Comedia Mexicana, which pushed the Mexican theater mired in well-made-play formulas to adopt new perspectives and stylistic methods of treating middle-class themes. On the other hand were those groups, like Teatro de Ulises (1928), Teatro de Orientación, and the Ciclo Post-Romántico, which tried to move away from the Mexican theater's traditional focus upon farce and *costumbrista* (or folkloric) plays. They transposed the stylistic concepts used by European stages to the Mexican context in order to break the stranglehold of romanticism and realism. Perhaps most important, however, were those like Teatro de Ahora, who sought a theater of epic proportions that could capture the scope of the changes to Mexican society instigated by the Revolution.

While the early decades of the twentieth century brought an unprecedented flow of ideas and artistic forms between Europe and Latin America, these years were also a period in which Latin American artists deliberately explored and responded to cultural and aesthetic issues generated by travel within the Americas themselves. A revolution in communications technology including telegraph, radio, film, and print served to break down boundaries between nations and between urban and regional centers. Mexico City became part of a series of important cultural centers in the Americas that included Buenos Aires, Lima, Havana, Santiago de Chile, and New York. The conscious desire to both describe and shape the new international reality led to the creation of new forms of art. Frequently these art forms challenged the traditional relationship between the artist and society. The Latin American avant-garde firmly established its own national, regional, and continental identity, an identity arising out of specific socioeconomic conditions particular to each region. Nelson Osorio has explained this trumpeting of its own independence by the Latin American avant-garde as an expression of hope for political and ideological change in confluence with the anti-oligarchic currents of the period.[1]

Perhaps the greatest inspiration of the era for Latin American avant-garde artists was the Mexican Revolution of 1910 and the subsequent constitution ratified in 1917. In Mexico the growing middle class, the working class, and the peasantry banded together to express their grievances. Miners, urban workers, and peasants saw the revolutionary constitution as an opportunity to win recognition of the right to unionize and strike, minimum wages, an eight-hour workday, and universal male suffrage. The political and educational influence of the Catholic Church was vastly curtailed, the land and subsoil were declared state property, and a significant program of agrarian reform was launched. None of these initiatives took place immediately, generating both labor unrest and strong opposition, such as the Cristero rebellion of the late 1920s by members of the church and the Catholic faithful. Agrarian reform was largely unsuccessful until the administration of Lázaro Cárdenas (1934–40), which also nationalized the oil industry.

This revolutionary fervor was fertile ground for the Mexican avant-garde and its commitment to political and social change leading to political activism. Such a commitment found its expression in the revolutionary content of artworks and in formal experimentation that attempted to give birth to a new world. Art was conceived of as capable of changing one's perceptions of the world and, thereby, changing the world itself. Aesthetic ideology saw art not as a reflection of society but as a participatory agent shaping society. Perhaps the best-known example of this orientation in the Mexican context is the muralist movement with its explicit goal of combining fine art and popular arts and crafts. Impelled by the support of Mexico's minister of education, José Vasconcelos, artists such as Diego Rivera, David Alfaro Siqueiros, and José Clemente Orozco splashed the walls of the new government's edifices with socially committed murals that fused together Renaissance fresco technique, Soviet-style socialist realism, stylistic components and startling images of contemporary Mexican popular culture, and pre-Columbian art. In his "Manifesto to the plastic artists of America," (Barcelona, 1921), Siqueiros called for "a public art, a monumental and heroic art, a human art . . . Pre-Columbian in inspiration and workerist in orientation."[2]

The years immediately following the Revolution saw the Ministry of Education promoting performance forms such as the *teatro de masas* (mass theater) that reoriented elements of religious folk drama toward an understanding of Mexican history, promoting progress informed by the goals of the Revolution and the revolutionary government. The *teatro de masas* plays were gigantic pantomimes utilizing thousands of actors. They rejected colonial notions of history and attempted to resuscitate an Aztec nobility of spirit as the foundation for the nation's new life.[3] While the *teatro de masas* and other kinds of popular performance sought to create new forms, the conscious altering of the contours of the apparatus in the European avant-garde with surrealism and Dada's interest in vaudeville, cabaret, and the circus was largely nonexistent in early-twentieth-century Mexico. This is due to the fact that forms employed by the European theatrical avant-garde to break out of what they saw as stultifying, though compositionally coherent, dramatic performances that were textually based, already had a long tradition in Latin American society and would not have been looked upon as innovative. The first truly Latin American theater performance is, arguably, the Argentine *Juan Moreira* (1884/1886), which began life as a circus performance before giving birth itself to the *teatro guacho*. Today's Mexican cabaret performers such as Jesusa Rodríguez, Astrid Hadad, Paquita del Barrio, Francis, and Tito Vasconcelos are so successful precisely because they continue the long tradition of the satirical revue in Mexico stretching back to at least the nineteenth century. Also dating back to the nineteenth century was the Mexican itinerant circus form called the *carpa*. The *carpas* were groups of itinerant performers who moved their collapsible stages from town to town, setting up in the main square or the middle of a street, and presenting a program of song, skits, and comedy that spoke directly to their mixed-class audience. There was a relaxed, informal atmosphere in these performances in which the audience and the performers engaged each other directly, with audience members giving the performers suggestions, and the performers soliciting the audience for money and cigarettes. The material presented in the *carpas* was highly satirical and frequently political in nature. The *carpa's* central character, the *pelado* (naked one), became the Mexican national clown. A penniless underdog, he brought the popular concerns and spirit ignored by official society into performance.

In the 1920s the new medium of radio and the burgeoning recording industry popularized the Mexican *corrido* as part of mass culture, while melodramatic films, those that underscored patriotic historical themes, and films that dealt with aspects of the life of the growing middle class or reprised contemporary crimes also became common. Rivera, Orozco, Siqueiros, and other members of the League of Revolutionary Writers and Artists searched for ways to create art that was both national and popular, that spoke to the masses and served the goals of the Revolution. The transition to a politically conscious, popularly oriented, and revolutionary theater was less direct in the theater. Three divergent paths created the necessary space for the development of a theater that could be seen as "Made in Mexico." The first stage in that development was the work of two companies, the Grupo de los Siete (Group of Seven) and the Comedia Mexicana (Mexican Stage).

In 1926 the Grupo de los Siete, composed of the playwrights Carlos Noriega Hope (1896–1934), Ricardo Parada León (1902–1972), the Lázaro brothers (1899–1973), Carlos Lozano García (1902–), José Joaquín Gamboa (1878–1931), Víctor Manuel Díez Barroso (1890–1930), and Francisco Monterde (1894–1985), published a manifesto (reproduced in the appendix to this essay) demanding that certain concrete steps be taken to renovate a moribund Mexican theater. The type of theater this manifesto derides was that prevalent in the Mexico of the day. The Mexican theater of the early twentieth century was still entrenched in the actor-manager system of production, where a well-known star produced performances in which he or she played the lead role to great effect against under-rehearsed members of the acting company. The repertoire performed consisted largely of imported farces, French boulevard revues, and Mexican *costumbrista* along with the periodic visit of a Spanish or Italian company on tour, such as that of María Guerrero or Margarita Xirgu, performing classic Spanish and foreign plays. In the midst of these conditions the manifesto by the Grupo de los Siete lacks any particular aesthetic proposition. Rather, it focuses upon a series of practical matters calling for a more diverse repertory, the inclusion of more Mexican playwrights, and audience education. These structural changes in theater production are seen as the answer to the paucity of vibrant, professionally created work on the Mexican stage. The commercially oriented Comedia Mexicana took all these steps at the time, especially in its first five seasons. Between them, the Grupo de los Siete and Comedia Mexicana were responsible for the introduction of theatrical styles as diverse as Pirandello, Maeterlinck, Lenormand, and Chekhov into Mexico, while simultaneously promoting Mexican playwrights. Although the Grupo de los Siete articulated its program of searching for a theatrical method of depicting the post revolutionary urban middle class onstage in a way that departed from the Mexican theater's traditional focus on rural folklore, it was the Comedia Mexicana that brought that program into effect through its well-attended productions and greater longevity as an institution. The practical innovations of the Grupo de los Siete and the Comedia Mexicana laid the groundwork for the second stage in the development of the Mexican theater carried out by groups like Teatro Ulises, Teatro de Orientación, and the Ciclo Post-Romántico.

The Teatro Ulises, founded in 1928, is perhaps the most studied group in Mexican theater history of the early twentieth century, and is frequently cited as the initiator of the Mexican avant-garde. The members of Teatro Ulises were all amateurs, with the exception of Julio Jiménez Rueda, who directed their first program. Between January and July 1928 Jiménez, Salvador Novo, Xavier Villarrutia, and Celestino Gorostiza directed a series of works that were produced by Antonieta Rivas Mercado, who had just returned from a European trip and made her house available for the performances. Each play was performed only twice and, instead of the typical theater program of the day tossed off on ordinary paper, Teatro Ulises handed its patrons a program on "magnificent imported paper, printed in two different colors, 37 by 53 cm in size, folded in fourths with excellent typography and design,"[4] an incredible luxury for the time that marked one's theatergoing experience as different from the moment one entered the theater space. Salvador Novo's speech at the first public performances of the fledgling theater group (reproduced in the appendix to this essay) describes Teatro de Ulises' motivating force and its aesthetic orientation. Novo paints a picture of earnest amateur artists who, finding nothing to interest them on the Mexican stage, turn toward foreign works and theatrical approaches in order to reinvigorate the moribund national scene. By demonstrating in all modesty what can be written for the theater, Teatro Ulises hopes to impel all those involved in the Mexican theater to new heights of quality and expression.

Novo's manifesto responds not only to the commercial production of frivolous and intellectually unchallenging material critiqued by the Grupo de Siete, but more precisely to the kind of "serious" drama produced by Mexican theaters of the period. In the early twentieth century Mexican theater was still thoroughly enmeshed with the Spanish tradition of José Echegaray, Jacinto Benavente, and the brothers Álvarez Quintero. Echegaray (1832–1916) was the first playwright to win the Nobel Prize for Literature. While he wrote some effective social drama, the vast majority of his plays are neoromantic works brimming over with excess passions. Benavente (1866–1954), who also won the Nobel Prize in 1922, was the favorite of major theater companies throughout Spain and Latin America for more than forty years. Several of his plays were produced on Broadway and in the West End as well. Noted for his creation of complex female characters, his popularity as a playwright is most often attributed to the rarified atmosphere of his plays in which characters of privilege speak elegant dialogue. Serafín Álvarez Quintero (1871–1938) and Joaquín Álvarez Quintero (1873–1944), known as the "golden brothers," packed audiences into Spanish theaters for almost fifty years to see their stylized, quasi-episodic renditions of Andalusian life and customs. Eschewing in-depth investigation of the hardships of rural social reality, the Álvarez Quintero brothers falsely represented Spanish rural life as solely pretty and sweet. These are the plays Salvador Novo in his speech (see appendix) mentions as he describes strolling through Mexico City's streets, experiencing "the daily deception of not finding a single theater where there was anything worth watching." By presenting "foreign works the local impresarios don't dare bring to their own theaters because they understand they would lose business," Teatro Ulises sought to educate Mexican audiences and producers of the range of work and styles being created internationally. In doing so they hoped to break through the stranglehold of socially irrelevant material produced on the Mexican stage, expand stylistic diversity, and create a space for Mexican authors to produce their work.

While Teatro Ulises was the first serious attempt to present the European avant-garde theater on the Mexican stage, its brief existence (the group performed a total of six productions with a limited range) makes one question how large an impact Teatro Ulises alone could have had upon the Mexican theater. With the exception of O'Neill's *Welded,* its entire repertory was selected from the sort of poetic theater written by Lenormand, Cocteau, Vildrac, and Dunsany, precisely the sort of work that Gorostiza, Villarrutia, and Novo themselves would later produce. During the same period others, such as the Mexican director Alfredo Gómez de la Vega (1897–1958), produced plays by Valle-Inclán, Grau, Nicodemi, D'Annunzio, Pirandello, Andreyev, Antonelli, and Pagnol. Teatro de Orientación produced Romains, Chekhov, Gogol, and Giraudoux. The Ciclo Post-Romántico weighed in with productions of Kaiser, Toller, Ibsen, Strindberg, Pirandello, and Dostoyevsky's *The Brothers Karamazov* in an adaptation by Jacques Copeau and Jean Croué; and Julio Bracho, under the influence of Max Reinhardt's gigantic productions at the Deutsches Theater and the Salzburg festival, directed a huge production of O'Neill's *Lazarus Laughed* involving hundreds of actors and students. All of these groups and individual theater artists contributed to broadening the perspective of both the Mexican audience and its theater practitioners by exposing them to new forms of writing, acting, and direction. This largely structural impact, however, did little to create a Mexican form of the avant-garde. The culmination of the development of a truly Mexican early-twentieth-century dramaturgy, the creation of an avant-garde theater made in Mexico, forms the third and final stage of the trajectory that has been traced here. These other individual and Mexican theater groups turned to the theater as a vehicle for expressing political and social themes that not only dealt with the events of the Revolution, but also looked at middle-class and proletarian problems from a leftist perspective. One of the playwrights involved in this trend was Elena Alvarez.

Alvarez's *Dos dramas revolucionarios* (*Two Revolutionary Dramas,* 1926) are, more than plays, brief dramatic sketches dealing with class perceptions of poverty. In the first, *Muerta de hambre (Dying of Hunger),* a woman and her child are discovered lying on the ground in front of a church. The woman's breasts are exposed and her legs show a good bit of thigh. Both she and her child are in need of a good scrubbing. The piece consists of five scenes in which everyone that passes, including two pious women, two foppish young men, two dirty old men, two ostentatious bourgeois women, and a priest all comment, with greater and lesser degrees of lasciviousness, on the woman's condition. Each of them castigates the disrespect she displays for the church by lying drunk before its doors. Some of the men go so far as to abuse her, the two young men stepping on her breasts to see whether they will express milk or *pulque* (a strong alcoholic drink popular with the lower classes), the priest kicking her to get her to move.

It is only in the final scene, with the appearance of a common "man of the people," that the woman receives any help. He determines she is not drunk but faint from hunger, and gives her something to eat. He also upbraids the priest, telling him that he is just like everyone who is rich— they have so much to eat, they cannot conceive of anyone dying of hunger. The man's final words are, "Jesus Christ would not have driven a woman dying of hunger from the doors of his temple."[5]

Alvarez's writing is a simple, direct example of a didactic theater. Its view of society is crystal clear. Although the dialogue occasionally descends to the level of political cant, Alvarez's characters are always interesting. There is nothing trite or stereotypical about the people she creates, and it is especially fascinating to see the way their ghoulishness is used to depict society's structural biases. More importantly, *Muerta de hambre* presents a greater sophistication in the revolutionary attitude toward the church. While clearly anticlerical, the play's final statement makes a distinction between the institutional church and Christ's teachings. The hypocritical behavior and social biases of the characters in *Muerta de hambre* are shown to be the very instruments by which large segments of the population are marginalized in direct contrast to religious doctrine.

In 1930 a Spanish translation of Erwin Piscator's *The Political Theatre* was published in Madrid. Soon distributed in Mexico, Piscator's theories caught the imagination of two young playwrights, Juan Bustillo Oro (1904–1989) and Mauricio Magdaleno (1906–1986), who founded Teatro de Ahora (Now Theater) in 1932. This company lasted only a brief time, but had a profound effect upon subsequent Mexican theater with its attempt to find a Mexican equivalent of Piscator's approach. The Teatro de Ahora performed several works by the two founders, and their own adaptation of Ben Jonson's *Volpone* called *Tiburón* (*Shark,* 1932).

During his childhood Bustillo Oro's father was the administrator of the Teatro Colón, an important Mexico City theater of the time. Until he was fifteen, when the Teatro Colón was converted into a movie house, Bustillo Oro had free rein of the theater, educating himself about acting and directing in what he later called "this fantasy palace." In addition to attending every production at the Colón, Bustillo Oro also spent many hours playing with puppets. Despite the fact that he later studied law and became involved in politics, these early experiences contributed to what he would accomplish with Teatro de Ahora. Teatro de Ahora came into being when Bustillo Oro met another young law student, Mauricio Magdaleno, and together they decided to "radically distance ourselves from the kind of theater being done and try to create theater with a social conscience. One that was antibourgeois, revolutionary. We named it Teatro de Ahora. A nonconformist teacher, Don Narciso Bassols, became our godfather in the Ministry of Education and gave us the use of the Hidalgo theatre where it stood in disrepair in the Regina neighborhood."[6]

While the Teatro de Ahora's first productions failed to garner a huge audience, Bustillo Oro and Magdaleno intended to launch another series of productions that never came to fruition. They described what they had already accomplished and their future plans in a manifesto printed in the *Revista de Revistas* (reproduced in the appendix). Teatro de Ahora's manifesto stakes out its opposition to what it sees as the pervasive influence of sentimental, commercial, and foreign works that only anesthetize an audience whose sensibilities are already dulled by Hollywood films and commercial radio. In contrast Teatro de Ahora proposes to create theater that will contribute to the social transformation of Mexico.

Bustillo Oro was the author of two plays, *Justicia, S.A. (Justice, Inc.)* and *Masas (Masses)*, whose productions planned for Teatro de Ahora's second program were never realized, as well as a play called *Los que vuelven (Those Who Return)*, which Guillermo Schmidhuber has called the first Chicano play in Mexican dramatic literature.[7] In *Los que vuelven* a poor Mexican family emigrates to the United States to escape hunger and the violent upheavals of the Revolution, only to encounter the economic hardships of the Great Depression. The parents evade deportation and go north to search for their son, who has lost his hand in a factory accident, and see their daughter, now married to an Irish laborer with U.S. citizenship. When they arrive, their son-in-law, fearing that feeding them will mean the death of his wife and the child she carries, turns them in to the immigration authorities, and they are deported back to Mexico. During the journey the mother dies and the father, seeing a one-handed corpse at the bottom of a heap of bodies near the border, turns upon the soldiers accompanying him, fighting to reclaim the body. In the confusion he is shot dead and then his body is thrown upon the pile to be burned with all of the other corpses. While the play contains a number of melodramatic elements that diminish its overall power, Bustillo Oro writes in a realistic and popular style previously unseen in the Mexican theater.

Both *Masas* and *Justicia, S.A.* are significantly more mature works. In *Masas* Bustillo Oro dramatizes the revolutionary movement in an unnamed Latin American country that leads to the fall of one dictator and the creation of another. The play revolves around the interactions of three main characters: Porfirio Neri, the idealistic leader of the Socialist Party, who, after the triumph of the revolution is corrupted by power; Máximo Forcada, a union leader who refuses to compromise his ideals regardless of the personal or political cost; and Luisa Neri, Porfirio's sister and Forcada's husband, who takes up her husband's work after her brother has him assassinated as a threat to the revolutionary government in power. Bustillo Oro's characters are all well developed, with Luisa presenting us with the kind of strong, vital woman absent from the Mexican theater of the period. What truly distinguishes the play, however, is Bustillo Oro's incorporation of a number of techniques taken from Piscator's epic theater and adapted to the Mexican stage.

Masas places us in the center of its revolutionary atmosphere through the use of film projections of massive political rallies and workers on strike, and creates an effective aural score for the text through the strategic placement of loudspeakers in the audience that periodically assail us with taped radio news broadcasts and the voices of the masses that form an early-twentieth-century version of a Greek chorus. The stage itself is huge, with enormous banners of different colors used to mark the constantly evolving political situation. Each of the three acts ends with a massive tableau of some sort in which we see gigantic projections of the shadows of the two revolutionary leaders embracing at the beginning of the play, or hear machine-gun fire unleashed upon the protesting multitudes as Neri seeks to consolidate his power after assassinating his old ally and brother-in-law. Characteristically, Piscator's approach to production was such that the theater overwhelmed the dramatic text until it became one small portion of the total event. In *Masas* the means of production is called for *in* the text itself, placing new demands upon the theatrical apparatus used by the Mexican stage. Dramaturgically Bustillo Oro calls for a use of the apparatus that Piscator created directorially. This is perhaps most evident in the play's epilogue, where, as Neri gives an address to Congress, the theater becomes filled with groups of supportive congressional deputies and groups of striking workers denouncing Neri, all interspersed through the audience and in the balconies. As Neri gives his address, the shouts of the people participating in a Strike of Hunger and Death can be heard closing in from all sides: from behind the stage itself, out in the theater's lobby, in its corridors. Behind Neri at the podium a screen is revealed upon which is projected the image of the striking workers, all wearing skull masks. Machine-gun fire erupts from all directions, leaving an empty street on the screen. Gradually, the striking demonstrators approach in the distance while closer to us soldiers erect a machine gun. We then see a parade of men carrying skulls in their hands. Suddenly they raise the skulls in their right hands. Dissolve to an army on parade, dissolve to a multitude of people filling the plaza, dissolve to machines, and dissolve to the upraised hands of the marchers against hunger. That image is suddenly replaced by the image of everyone wearing skull masks, then of the same faces without the masks. While we hear machine-gun fire from all directions, once again the individual faces dissolve into an enormous human skull, which, in turn, is replaced by the words "The End" on the screen as the play comes to conclusion. What distinguishes Bustillo Oro's approach to this type of theater from the European forms that inspire him is the vibrancy of the colors employed and the muscularity of the images created. His utilization of Piscator's techniques in *Masas* creates a theatrical equivalent of the Mexican muralists call for art that was simultaneously "public, heroic, and human."[8]

Bustillo Oro tries to alter the theatrical apparatus dramaturgically in *Justicia, S.A.* as well. *Justicia, S.A.* deals with an idealistic lawyer named Santos Galvez and his socially ambitious wife Luz, whose constant carping about their financial situation has led him to accept a position as a judge in a provincial industrial center. While Santos Galvez justifies his decision to himself by envisioning his judicial role as the impartial arbiter of the law, he soon finds his conception of the law sorely tested. Even before he and his wife have unpacked on the night of their arrival Santos Galvez receives a visit from the local industrialist Hilario Salgado. Salgado comes armed with two fully prepared judgments for Santos Galvez to sign. One condemns three leaders of the union at Salgado's factory to death on trumped-up charges of having raped a young woman, while the other exonerates Salgado's son of having raped another girl. In order to save his position and please his wife Santos

Galvez, rather than resign in protest as his predecessor did, signs the judgments and spends the rest of the play plagued by his own conscience and a series of apparitions. The play moves back and forth between realistic marital squabbles and confrontations with Salgado, and a surrealistic and expressionistic plane composed of shadow projections, film sequences, puppets, and the lamentations and accusations of an invisible chorus. On this plane of the action we see Santos Galvez commit the crimes himself for which he has falsely sentenced others; or, in another magnificent scene, the judge becomes a factory worker in the Justice Incorporated Company, where he operates a machine lubricated by human flesh and blood that creates gold coins. In the hands of Bustillo Oro techniques reminiscent of European surrealism and expressionism are combined with Mexican iconography surrounding the Day of the Dead to create an original theatrical form that is socially oriented in its critique of a corrupt judicial system yet is presented to its audience employing images from Mexican popular culture.

Mauricio Magdaleno also focuses on social ills in his plays, but Magdaleno presents those ills as a result of the damage caused to the indigenous character by foreign exploitation of Mexican resources. Magdaleno's best play is entitled *Trópico* and deals with the story of Cecil Chester Bond, who has come to Mexico from New York as president of the American Tropical Gum Company.[9] He is accompanied by another U.S. citizen, Ben Sunter, who spouts biblical chapter and verse, calls himself a good Quaker, and is scandalized by the Indians' habits and their belief in more than the one true God. The North Americans, aided by compliant Mexicans, proceed to take over. Chico Díaz, a rich landowner, essentially forces his daughter Rosarito to become Bond's lover. When Marcelino Contreras, the man Rosarito has loved since they were children, returns and discovers the new situation, he rebels and gathers an Indian army that attacks and destroys the American Tropical Gum Company's installations.

In the meantime, Bond, alcoholic and suffering from malaria, has become more and more incoherent. At the beginning of the play an old Indian predicts that the jungle will destroy the company. Bond now claims that his fever is the jungle, the jungle in Rosarito's skin, blood, and kisses, a jungle he wants to consume. At the same time Magdaleno makes it clear that it is the jungle that drives the rebel Marcelino, turning him hard and cruel. When Marcelino is captured, Rosarito finds herself torn between the two men and prevails upon Bond to release him.

In the play's final scene Sunter has sent for Bond's daughter, Alma, to try and convince Bond to return to the United States. She arrives with two friends, Gloria, a movie star, and, George N. Atkinson, her director. They plan to use the jungle to shoot a few scenes for their latest movie, but Atkinson quickly realizes that what is happening around him would make an incredible movie and starts to film clips for an epic entitled *Trópico*. Atkinson films Bond sitting on the floor, playing cards and rolling cigarettes Indian style with his Indian servant, while Alma tries to convince him to return with her, and Sunter fulminates against the voluptuous nature and vice-ridden life of the tropics. Marcelino, humiliated by his earlier release, returns for vengeance and takes Bond, Sunter, and Chico Díaz captive. Rosarito now pleads with him to spare Bond and her father as she reveals that she carries Bond's child. Marcelino frees them all, pushes Rosarito away in disgust, and sets the factory on fire. As the red light of the blazing factory fills the sky another Mexican collaborator, Juan de Dios, appears. A pompous lawyer with pretensions to high culture, Juan de Dios is covered in ditch reeds and moss from head to foot and moves "like a vegetable form." He says that, fearing for his life, he disguised himself as an innocent vegetable. As this vegetable figure crosses the stage the North Americans run screaming for their planes, and Bond plunges into the jungle (as if into a tunnel, Magdaleno tells us) crying out for Rosarito. His cries echo all over the stage, "a jeering singsong, ending in something that could be a bird's cry or a cackle of laughter."[10] Magdaleno's Mexicans greet the North Americans as representatives of a new kind of divine order that will bring economic wealth and civilized well-being. The final scene, with its complex layering of "civilized" and "primitive" cultures, greed, lust, revenge, freedom, death, and new birth—is a phoenix born from the ashes of the blazing factory?—picks up the muralists' challenge of combining modern popular culture with indigenous culture in yet another theatrical form.

Unable to control the course of events on his own, Sunter, the pietistic representative of gringo religion, sends for Bond's daughter, Alma, whose name in Spanish means "soul." Her "soul"-ful presence as a member of the next generation and, consequently, a force for renovation and renewal, is intended to provide Sunter with an ally in his battle against the tropical forces that are consuming her father. This "soul," however, brings Gloria and Atkinson with her. These two characters are members of the "civilized" world that the Mexicans aspire to, but their profession is one that deals exclusively in temporary and illusory images of life. Confronted with the vitality of the tropics, Atkinson abandons his original, comparably empty, plans in an attempt to capture the density that surrounds him. He films the "inferior" tropics consuming the "superior" representatives of North American civilization.

The tropical presence is shown to touch all of the characters involved and, in doing so, to invert the conceptions of wealth and civilization upon which the majority of the characters have based their actions. Bond was originally the dynamic force whose Tropical Gum Company was to be the medium by which the primitive tropical culture would "bond" with its superior northern culture. By the end of the play he is the one who has "bonded" with the "primitive" culture he came to replace. The tropics are a fever that has entered his bloodstream in the form of his love for Rosarito, and she now carries his child, a seed he has planted that binds him to the jungle. Magdaleno shows us how completely Bond has been integrated into the tropical milieu by his actions in the final scene. As Alma and Sunter, the representatives of the culture he has abandoned, attempt to convince him to return to the United States, Bond assumes the actions and attitudes of not only an Indian, but an Indian servant to the white gringos. Sitting on the floor, he is now physically beneath all those who surround him, and is taught Indian techniques by a man who was once subservient to him. The master-servant relationship has been completely inverted but, since the Indian servant's previous willingness to perform servile tasks for the gringo has invalidated him as a true representative of indigenous culture, Bond has bound himself to another illusion of culture, one that will ultimately flicker and die like one of Atkinson's movies.

In contrast to Bond and the Indian servant, Magdaleno gives us Marcelino, the modern equivalent of the Aztec warrior Cuauhtémoc, who valiantly fought Cortés after Moctezuma's death. Marcelino forms his indigenous army and, like Cuauhtémoc before him, sets forth to drive out the foreign invaders. Unlike his Aztec ancestor, Marcelino succeeds in breaking the grip on power held by the modern conquistadores. In doing so, he is shown to be both a strong, capable military commander and a magnanimous leader. He frees his North American captives in the same way that Cortés refused, initially, to put Cuauhtémoc to death, but in doing so Marcelino has paid a much higher price than Cortés ever did, for he has lost Rosarito. By becoming Bond's lover and carrying his child, Rosarito has become a modern Malinche, Cortés' Aztec concubine and interpreter who supplied him with the linguistic key to conquest and gave birth to the first mestizo child, thereby becoming a symbol of the foreign rape of Mexico.

While Magdaleno gives us Marcelino as the indigenous warrior whose decisive torching of the factory will wipe out the North American presence, he also gives us the image of Juan de Dios, the lawyer who believed in the superiority of the foreign culture, as "a vegetable form." This Mexican who attempted to deny his link to the tropics is depicted as literally consumed by them. As the North Americans escape by using the technology he so admired, Juan de Dios is returned to an earlier point on the evolutionary chain, becoming a part of that jungle undergrowth into which Bond himself disappears. The spiraling references to death and rebirth are shown through the depictions of Alma, Rosarito, the fire, and Juan de Dios's (John of God's) reincarnation as a part of the jungle. The entire play shows us the resurrection of the indigenous and tropical sensibility that reasserts its power over the territory the North Americans see as an extension of their empire.

John Nomland comments that Magdaleno attempts to create true tragedies, but his work is marred by his propensity for introducing a beautiful young woman whose sexual attractiveness provides the play's catalyst. He criticizes this aspect of Magdaleno's work as falling back upon an outmoded Mexican tradition and observes that Bustillo Oro manages to break free of such traditional plotting to create something entirely new. While I would not disagree with Nomland's analysis, it seems to me that he misses the point. Magdaleno has taken the traditional bourgeois plotting and turned it on its head, expanding the Mexican societal codes to push them to new levels, and stretching the boundaries of Mexican dramaturgy to introduce new techniques, thereby introducing new visions of the world to the Mexican theater.

In 1933, the same year that Bustillo Oro and Magdaleno's plays were published, another volume of plays appeared titled *Tres obras del teatro revolucionario (Three Revolutionary Plays)* by Germán List Arzubide (1898–1998). Two of the plays included, *Las sombras (The Shadows)* and *El último juicio (The Last Judgment),* the one a depiction of Mexico City's working poor, the other a one-act play in which the world's workers unite to put God on trial for their suffering, are not well realized. The third play, however, is a small masterpiece. Entitled *El nuevo diluvio (The New Flood),* it is a satiric view of the Revolution. After the flood Noah has set himself up as an ark builder, providing luxurious arks complete with various floors and attached garages for the animals that can afford them. Noah mistreats his workers, all sheep, so that he can suck as much money as possible from the pigs, monkeys, elephants, and other animals that are his customers. The only animal who expresses any dissatisfaction with this arrangement is the rebellious Coyote, who warns Noah that for food, clothing, and shelter the animals will rebel. "There will be another flood, but it will be ours. It already advances like an enormous wave from the east. Remember Noah, I am the one preaching now, construct your ark and tremble, soon it will rain fire and blood."[11]

When the wolves and sheep, led by Coyote, finally do rebel, all the other animals go running to Noah for protection. Following the advice of his brutal foreman, the Dog, Noah has been building his arks with inferior materials to cut costs. As the approaching revolutionaries advance singing *The Internationale* the other animals rush aboard a newly constructed ark, trampling the Dog to death in the process. Too weak to hold their weight, the ark collapses, killing them all.

The decision to place the play in this sort of fantasy world is an excellent one. It saves the play from becoming merely a didactic tract. The play clearly has a message to teach and presents it forcefully, but the animal characterizations allow List Arzubide much greater freedom for satirical touches. In this fashion the Pig is a banker, the Cow a suffragette, the Rat a philosopher, the Vulture a priest, the Tiger a general, the sheep workers, and so on. The humor employed lightens the political thrust, actually making it much more effective through the creation of a kind of grotesque fairy tale or bizarre children's story world that delights and makes us more disposed to hear the play's thesis.

Beyond Teatro de Ahora and playwrights inspired by its example, the only other early-twentieth-century theater company to espouse popular values was the Teatro de las Artes (Theater of the Arts) founded by the Japanese director Seki Sano. Seki Sano arrived in Mexico in 1939 after having worked as Meyerhold's assistant in the Soviet Union and having spent a brief time in New York City. In Mexico he joined with the U.S. ballerina Waldeen to found a theater school based on Stanislavskian and Meyerholdian aesthetics. Calling themselves "A theatre of the people for the people,"[12] Teatro de las Artes produced an eclectic mixture of a number of ballets, dramatizations of novels, and Mexican and foreign plays of a progressive nature. In 1942 they asserted (see appendix) that Teatro de las Artes was born to provide the people with a weapon for self-improvement through the creation of a genuinely popular theater.

In addition, Teatro de las Artes founded an itinerant theater group called Teatro de la "V," shorthand for Caravana Cultural y Artística

"Victoria." The Teatro de la "V" performed under the motto "Art in Service of the Democracies" and was formed to support the allied cause in the Second World War by presenting antifascist pieces utilizing marionettes, song, and radio throughout the country. Due to scant Mexican interest in the war, the Teatro de la "V" quickly folded. Seki Sano left Teatro de las Artes in 1948 to form the Teatro de la Reforma with another North American, Luz Alba, and the Mexican actor Alberto Galán. Teatro de la Reforma, however, displayed little interest in political themes, concentrating instead on the same sort of aesthetic of introducing foreign works to Mexico seen in the work of Teatro Ulises or Teatro de Orientación. The poetic orientation of these theater groups, however, lacks any indication of the postrevolutionary context in Mexico and does little to advance a specifically Mexican dramaturgy or advocate for social innovation. In the theatrical avant-garde of the 1920s and 1930s in Mexico only Teatro de Ahora and a few others sought, fitfully, to create theater infused with the aesthetic innovations of the European avant-garde but truly Mexican in orientation and expression. Bustillo Oro and Magdaleno with their work in Teatro de Ahora were the first Mexican theater artists whose experimental efforts attempted to incorporate world theatrical innovation into the Mexican theater, rather than simply superimpose European theatrical innovation on the Mexican stage. While their efforts and those of a few others during the second and third decades of the twentieth century were only fragmentary in nature, they laid the foundation for the subsequent development of Mexican dramaturgy and theatrical technique into one of the most vibrant theatrical cultures of the twentieth century.

Appendix

Manifesto of the Grupo de Los Siete, 1926

WE WANT TO CONSIGN TO THE SHELF FOREVER the antiquated repertory of plays that, in today's world, are inane and ridiculous and can no longer be endured;

WE WANT TO EXPEL FROM THE THEATERS those merchants who live their lives apart from art; the silly comedians who foment deplorable tastes in the public; the so-called "artistic" directors, who are neither artists nor directors but who are, in large part, responsible for the fact that the artistic criteria exercised by the public are lowered every day; the venal impresarios who, with the presentation of the most imbecilic works have found a comfortable way to enrich themselves, while excusing their actions by claiming that no cultured theater audience exists today in Mexico that merits attention. Now is the time to show them their mistake by refusing to attend their productions, by refusing to be fooled;

WE WANT THOSE WHO DESIRE TO LAUGH to go to the circus rather than farces lacking common sense or wit, since the circus with its clowns is without a doubt funnier and less grotesque than those farces. (No one should assume that we are enemies of good fun; but neither do we believe that comedy on stage must be, perforce, coarse and vulgar);

WE WANT INSTEAD TO LEND effective support to those companies and actors undertaking artistic work or, at least, those laboring with good intentions;

WE WANT THE AUDIENCE TO DISCARD the passive attitude it has exercised until now and applaud or whistle, resolutely, because warm applause and noisy whistles when merited, are more useful to authors and their interpreters and speak more loudly in favor of the spectators' dignity;

WE WANT TO IMMEDIATELY PUT AN END to this dirty, clumsy parody of a form called French revues that even the inhabitants of Mexico tolerate and that have invaded everyplace from the best theaters to the humblest huts because, in spite of the fact that lyric writers want to produce work of a different type, the mercantilism of the producers imposes the revue upon us;

WE WANT IT TO BE KNOWN that authors exist throughout the Republic whose work can be presented alongside the best of those from other countries, not only the Grupo de los Siete or the Unión de Autores Dramáticos, but also a great number of Mexican authors who have picked up something of the national spirit and who are put off by the disdain of the producers and many actors and actresses who insist upon imagining that Mexican playwrights' brains aren't of the same quality as those of foreign authors;

WE WANT THE PUBLIC NOT TO insist on attending productions at ridiculous prices that make it impossible to costume actors properly or provide adequate scenery, but, at the same time, when they do pay that they demand good performers, correct pronunciation, and modern work, all well rehearsed.

WE, THE GRUPO DE LOS SIETE, INSIST that we are not pursuing any self-interested goal. All we want is for the Mexican public to receive the productions its culture merits. We insist that we will no longer suffer the ironic comments of those incapable of producing anything themselves, those who possess no other weapon than mockery when confronted by sincere effort of any kind.

"A los nuestros y a los otros," *Universal Ilustrado* 457 (1926), in Magaña Esquivel, *Medio siglo de teatro mexicano, 1900–1961* (Mexico City: Instituto Nacional de Bellas Artes, 1964), 60–61.

Remarks by Salvador Novo at the Opening of Teatro de Ulises, 1928

The first principle upon which Teatro de Ulises was founded was that of leisure. Today no one should doubt the sudden utility of leisure. This organizing group of leisure persons contained a painter, Agustín Lazo, whose paintings nobody liked. A philosophy student, Samuel Rosas, whom Professor Caso didn't care for. A poet and essayist, Gilberto Owen, who produced strange things, and a young critic named Xavier Villarrutia who disliked everything. On long afternoons, having nothing Mexican to read, they talked about foreign books. That was how they got the idea of publishing a little magazine of criticism and curiosity. Later, it having become night, they started down the route all of us have followed many times that takes you through Bolívar Street, from the Teatro Lírico to the Teatro Iris, casting a melancholy glance at the Teatro Fábregas, continuing on to the Teatro Principal, and, now lacking the strength to reach the Teatro Arbeu, finally passing by the Teatro Ideal. Nothing to see. The daily deception of not finding a single theater where there was anything worth watching. This was where they got the idea to form a small private theater, in the same way that, lacking a good concert hall or cabaret, each of us buys a record from time to time to play on our Victrola.

As I said before, and want to make clear above all, this primitive group of leisure persons that first began the journal *Ulises* and then formed a theater group, never thought about bringing the private dramatic games with which they occupied themselves in their frequent leisure moments to the public stage. I have always held that one should say the right things. This is a matter of self-respect, since to praise a thing first and then afterward do it diminishes one's dignity, as well as runs the risk of unfavorable comments regarding those who preach well yet act so poorly. This just goes to show how enviable it is to be a legislator. The natural thing for us to have done would have been to form numerous nuclei of intelligent and adaptable enthusiasts with good breeding. These patient and studious people would submit themselves without objection to the strict discipline of a wise and enthusiastic dictator who would supervise everything from the noise of the rising curtain to the smallest hand gesture; from the slightest pause in the dialogue to a made-up forehead. Someone who would assign parts to so many people in such a way that no one would have to perform the miracle of fitting themselves into a part that they weren't born for simply because there was no one else available to do it. Although they have no connection to us, many groups with the highest ideals would work quickly to perform the desired miracle.

In place of all that we have had to content ourselves with the ten, when all present, people in Teatro Ulises who, lacking any professional aspirations or ambitions, have accepted the task of collaborating on plays that will, perforce, come from a reduced group of those with a limited number of characters and possibilities. Not a great deal has offered itself to us. With great pleasure would we do *Lazarus Laughed* or *Strange Interlude, Anna Christie* or *The Hairy Ape,* by the O'Neill who gave us *Welded.*

What we are trying to do is inform the Mexican audience of foreign works the local impresarios don't dare bring to their own theaters because they understand that they would lose business. Ulises undertakes this journey, leaving the affection of its few' loyal friends at home, and ventures out into public with all of this significance. We want to see if it is correct that people won't go to see O'Neill because they are satisfied with Linares Rivas. All of us have renounced the petty vanity of our literary names in order to dress ourselves, for one night, in the slightly grotesque mask of an actor, someone who pretends for money. And we want, by the force of our efforts, to enter into terrain that is not now nor will ever be ours, in order to make clear that our sole objective is to make what we have consented to produce known. Forget that we are Villarrutia, Señora Rivas, or myself, as you see us called Orfeo, Miguel Cape, or Eleonora. As they say, we've gone to the blackboard to demonstrate Newton's binomial theorem. May the professor and the impresario, if we have convinced them, permit us to return to our desks and continue observing, so that they can call upon those who make this their living and push things forward. If that happens it will be our greatest reward.

May 1928

Salvador Novo, "Words on Opening Night," in Magaña Esquivel, *Medio siglo de teatro mexicano, 1900–1961* (Mexico City: Instituto Nacional de Bellas Artes, 1964), 60–61.

Manifesto of the Teatro de Ahora, 1932

Soon we will renew our attempt. The labor we began February 12 and which closed its first cycle on March 12 has not ended for our audience nor accomplished our objectives.

The Teatro de Ahora's second cycle will soon begin: possibly next week or the following. . . . But, before talking about what we are after with this new attempt, let us summarize what we have accomplished both for ourselves and for others.

Keeping in mind the extremely modest resources upon which we were able to draw as we began this journey, we must affirm that we did not scrimp an iota of our will and inventiveness in carrying out our task. Nevertheless, we knew what we were about and had no illusions. We knew, for example, that the most we could aspire to was to point out a firm path for theatrical production in Mexico. This is true, above all, in times like ours when it is necessary to pay attention to the historical role furnished to the writer—and even more so to the playwright. We knew, as well, that people in Mexico don't go to the theater, and those that do go sneer at everything made in Mexico. This is even more the case when it is a question of shows like those the Teatro de Ahora has offered in which the mawkishness of the flappers isn't flattered, in which no cheap syrups are provided to sweeten the digestion, and in which not the least concession is made to the taste of the average citizen, anesthetized by film and radio. This has been one of Teatro de Ahora's major sins: we have banished those sweet themes that fill a very elevated percentage of our daily lives through the influence of the movies—Yankee movies in particular. We would have been something more than deluded if we had had the idea that we could accomplish a complete victory in this atmosphere flattened by the dense, egoistic social temperature of the day. One in which an economic system weakens before caving in upon itself. But it is exactly in moments like these that useful art should make itself felt, in defiance of those who still believe that the role of art should be reduced to soothing men's ears, and that theater without amorous conflict isn't theater.

We have tried to realize the first test of a theater that is substantially ours. To the tariff of nationality can be added the absence of mawkishness and its intransigent attitude when faced with the social reality of these days. We must create a disastrous economic balance sheet, at least if we understand things using the criteria of the impresario of Spanish farces or the Yankee movies. Romantically, it would be worthwhile repeating that we plow the wind and sow the sea. But realistic common sense—and that is the way we have always been disposed to take the course of events—tells us that the earth sucks up the seeds and returns them one day, although that day comes late. As much as we would like it to be so, circumstances haven't sufficiently matured to make our social commitment felt by force. For the rest, we don't care about the value assigned to this work, except in regard to its contribution to the social transformation of our country. For us, who have never seen these days solely as an adventure, there is a concrete goal upon which we will harp as frequently as necessary until everyone who now covers their ears shall hear us. Teatro de Ahora, the first skirmish to free up space for a defined theater in Mexico, whose value—rich or poor—we deliver into the hands of the people.

Revista de Revistas, April 1932, 9–10.

Seki Sano and Waldeen on Teatro de las Artes

Free from "mercantilism," from "degenerate professionalism," from the "star system" and from any other defect that has prevented, until today, the healthy development of a genuinely popular theatre in our country. It will be a weapon in the hands of the people, so that they can improve themselves.

The Teatro de las Artes fights the principle of "art for art's sake"; it is essentially: theatre by the people, for the people.

The Teatro de las Artes is a realistic theatre, free from trivial naturalism or realism, as well as from a formalism distant from the people.

People of Mexico! This is your theatre; it represents your aspirations for progress! Give it your encouragement, support it!

Seki Sano and Waldeen, "Theatre of the People for the People," *El Teatro de las Artes* (Mexico City: Partido de la Revolucion Mexicana, 1942), 1.

Notes

1. See Nelson Osorio, ed., *Manifestos, proclamas y polémicos de la vanguardia literaria hispanoamericana* (Caracas: Biblioteca Ayacucho, 1988).

2. David Alfaro Siqueiros, "Manifesto to the Plastic Arts of America (Barcelona, 1921), in *Encyclopedia of Contemporary Latin American and Caribbean Culture,* ed. Daniel Balderston, Mike Gonzalez, and Ana M. López (London: Routledge, 2000), 3.

3. See Adam Versényi, "The Mexican Revolution: Religion, Politics, and The-

ater," in *Crucibles of Crisis: Performing Social Change,* ed. Janelle Reinelt (Ann Arbor: University of Michigan Press, 1996).

4. Mendoza López, *Primeros renovadores del Teatro en Mexico,* qtd. in Guillermo Schmidhuber, *El teatro mexicano en cierne, 1922–1938* (New York: Lang, 1992), 90.

5. Elena Alvarez, *Dos dramas revolucionarios* (Mexico City: Ediciones de la Liga de Escritores Revolucionarios, 1926), 46.

6. Bustillo Oro, *Vida cinematográfica* (Mexico City: Cineteca Nacional, 1984), 82.

7. Juan Bustillo Oro, *Tres dramas mexicanos: Los que vuelven, Masas, Justicia, S.A.* (Madrid: Editorial Cenit), 1933.

8. Siqueiros, "Manifesto," 3.

9. The play is in Maurico Magdaleno, *Teatro revolucionario mexicano* (Madrid: Editorial Cenit), 1933.

10. John B. Nomland, *Teatro mexicano contemporáneo (1900–1950)* (Mexico City: Instituto Nacional de Bellas Artes, Departamento de Literatura, 1967), 280–81.

11. Germán List Arzubide, *Tres obras del teatro revolucionario* (Mexico City: Ediciones Integrales, 1933), 64.

12. Seki Sano and Waldeen, "Theatre of the People for the People," in *El Teatro de las Artes* (Mexico City: Partido de la Revolucion Mexicana, 1942), 1.

Aesthetics, Politics, and *Vanguardias* in Twentieth-Century Argentinean Theater

Jean Graham-Jones

International criticism of Latin American theater production has frequently tended toward either the imposition of foreign theoretical and practical paradigms or the impulse to read all Latin American theater as "political." The former tendency may have sprung from Latin American theater's deceptive familiarity: "perhaps the single most important obstacle, to the reception of Latin American theater outside the geographical or academic area of study, is not so much that this theater seems different, but that it looks oddly the same, that is, recognizable."[1] International "political" readings of contemporary Latin American theater may have been encouraged by the focus of early contributions to the field; the lack of other studies easily left those unfamiliar with Latin American theater's diversity with a limited view of the region's production.[2] Yet another obstacle to outside reception of Latin American theater production has been what Román de la Campa describes as "the nonsynchronous development of peripherally modern and postcolonial societies,"[3] such nonsynchronicity calling into question the appropriateness of such exclusionary (and possibly foreign) categories as the modern and the postmodern.[4]

The potential dangers posed by such critical tendencies are intensified when dealing with theater in Buenos Aires. With its importance as a port city and long history of immigration, Buenos Aires is generally regarded as the most "European" of Latin American cultural centers. When that heritage is coupled with Argentina's history of political repression, a critical conflation of the foreign and the political may be understandable. I argue, nevertheless, that both tendencies overlook the rich complexities of twentieth-century performance in Buenos Aires. The city's (and, by extension, the nation's) theater constitutes a fascinating and problematic example of cultural self-identification and construction.

Argentina's twentieth-century theatrical avant-gardes or *vanguardias* provide several arresting cases in point.[5] In 1930s Argentina one could speak of two avant-gardes: the politically committed "Boedo" social realists and the apolitical "Florida" Europeanists.[6] Each had its own journal (*Claridad* and *Martín Fierro,* respectively) and even its own figurehead (Roberto Arlt in the former group, Jorge Luis Borges in the latter). Nonetheless, critical studies of Arlt's politically committed and very Argentinean theater frequently point to European influences (particularly that of Luigi Pirandello) to explain the Buenos Aires writer's experimental metadramatics.[7] The discussion of national or international cultural "origins" becomes even more convoluted when one argues, as some critics have done, that both avant-gardes were in some way reconciled in Argentina's independent theater movement.[8]

The debate over national/transnational aesthetic and conceptual influences has continued. There is a long-standing discussion regarding the "origins" of Argentina's theatrical grotesque *(grotesco criollo);* and the experimental dramatists that began writing in the 1950s and 1960s (the best known being Griselda Gambaro and Eduardo Pavlovsky) continue to resist having their early plays dismissed as "absurdist," citing instead the early-twentieth-century local model of the *grotesco criollo* or preferring to conceptualize their work on their own terms.[9]

In this essay, I focus on the two periods most closely associated with the Buenos Aires theatrical avant-garde: the 1930s and the 1960s. I trace the multiple and at times apparently contrary *vanguardias* by self-consciously privileging the local and the national tendencies prevailing in both periods but always against the backdrop of ongoing national/transnational debates. By way of the examples selected, I draw particular attention to local theatrical intersections of politics, aesthetics, and experimentation, in keeping not only with the "avant-garde's" traditional association with experimental aestheticism and self-conscious "antiart" but also with its earliest denotation as a visionary and militant front line.[10] All merit being taken into account when one considers the concept of the avant-garde in Argentina. My "larger" reading of the Argentinean theatrical *vanguardias* takes into account local, multiple nonsynchronicity to demonstrate how the Argentinean avant-garde resists critical reduction to imitative or political theater. Such a demonstration also encourages us to reconsider any easy definition of what constitutes avant-garde theatrical practice. In this sense, my reconsideration of Argentinean *vanguardias* seeks to restore the multiplicity inherent in the term avant-garde.

Vanguardias of the 1930s: From the *Grotesco Criollo* to *Teatro Independiente*

At the beginning of the twentieth century, audiences in Buenos Aires enjoyed both the naturalistic bourgeois theater associated with the region's first great playwright, Florencio Sánchez, and the more "popular" one-act *sainete criollo,* in place since before the century's turn.[11] Indeed, the first decade of the century became known as the "golden age" of theater in the Río de la Plata region.[12] After Sánchez's death in 1910, both forms deteriorated, as David William Foster notes: "[N]ational dramatists were content to emphasize the local-color motifs of nineteenth-century theater or to romanticize the sociohistory of the immigrant."[13] This serious decline in theatrical innovation and quality (if not in quantity) would not be arrested until the 1920s with the development of another local one-act form, the *grotesco criollo.*

Foster has characterized the *grotesco criollo* as the isolated exception to the overcommercialization of Argentinean theater in the 1920s, stating overtly that "one cannot speak of a coherent theatrical movement during this period."[14] In his historical overview of the period's theater, he postpones until 1930 the "crystalization of attempts to rejuvenate national theater of a creative or original intent."[15] I prefer to locate the beginnings of theatrical avant-garde in 1930s Buenos Aires within the earlier *grotesco criollo.* The *grotesco criollo* evolved out of the *sainete criollo* but diverged from its predecessor in very important ways. Although both forms centered on the problems encountered by (mostly) European immigrants to the port city of Buenos Aires, the *sainete*'s melodrama turned tragic in the *grotesco*'s extreme situations, which often ended in the martyrdom of the nonadaptive individual protagonist when confronted by a society in constant change. Whereas the *sainete*'s action focused on the shared public space of the *conventillo*'s patio[16] and the collective experience of cultural encounter and miscommunication, the *grotesco* operated within the interior spaces of private dwellings to reveal the illusory nature of immigrant expectations and to examine the resulting individual failure and frustration. New plays required a new acting style, and performers developed a unique way of unmasking the externalized performances of immigrant life so typical of the *sainete.*[17]

The *grotesco,* as Claudia Kaiser-Lenoir notes, revealed the clash between reality and the protagonist's distorted illusions brought on by his dreams of "hacer la América."[18] Eduardo Romano underscores the relationship between middle-class expectations and *grotesco* frustrations: "the tragicomedy of the *grotesco* protagonist reveals the alienated nucleus of the petty bourgeoisie with its expectations of power."[19] The *grotesco* thus functioned as a reflection of middle-class pessimism, and, as Romano has noted, the box-office success of the *grotesco criollo* was directly affected by the changing fortunes of the Argentinean middle class.[20] Indeed, following its initial success during the 1920s and 1930s, the form's popularity would decline as middle-class optimism grew.[21]

It is thus not difficult to see how the 1920s *grotesco criollo,* with its ties to middle-class expectations and (mis)fortunes and with its innovations with text and performance, directly influenced what is today regarded as the first Argentinean avant-garde wave. With 1929's "crash" and the Great Depression, the myth of the *sainete criollo*'s "American dream" was definitely shattered, overtaken by "the reality of dependency."[22] The year 1930 also saw Argentina's first military coup of the twentieth century. In fact, the Argentinean 1930s were so notorious for their political corruption and repression, their nationalistic xenophobia, and their anti-Semitism that the period became popularly known as the "Infamous Decade."

It was in this environment that Buenos Aires's influential Independent Theater *(Teatro Independiente)* movement was born. It responded to a growing mediocrity in the city's commercial theater, which found itself under the absolute control of producers. Yet even with the commercial theater's privileging of the box office, audiences were waning. At the height of its 1920s popularity, the *grotesco criollo* was attracting some seven million spectators annually; by 1935, attendance had dropped by half, and many of the neighborhood theaters had closed.[23] The Independent Theater movement sought to rejuvenate the Argentine stage through "theater in service to art," in the words of the movement's leader, Leónidas Barletta, a theatrical producer, director, and member of the Boedo group. Founded in 1930, Barletta's Teatro del Pueblo (People's Theater) staged plays by new local authors as well as the latest European and North American plays and Spanish-language "classics." Functioning until Barletta's death in 1975, the Teatro del Pueblo staged more than three hundred plays and attracted more than two million spectators.[24] The group's name was both an homage to the French writer Romain Rolland's concept of the theater as a living art and a statement of Barletta's own commitment to having his theater reach as many Argentines as possible. The Teatro del Pueblo was collectively run by its members, whose names never appeared on the handbills. Not only did the Teatro del Pueblo perform for largely middle-class audiences (albeit at reduced ticket prices), but the troupe also traveled to working-class suburbs in its brightly painted "Carro de Tespis" (Thespis's Cart). Barletta's actors and technicians learned their trades on the job; they performed all the duties required to collectively run the theater. The theater's eternally precarious budget forced the company to create sets and costumes out of the cheapest (often recycled) materials available, an inventive economizing strategy-cum-aesthetic that would be adopted by most of the other independent theaters. The Teatro del Pueblo was also the first Argentinean theater to introduce postperformance discussions, a Buenos Aires tradition that continues to this day. Barletta led these encounters, which he called "polemical theater" in deference to the lively discussions that ensued and his conviction that the spectator was an active participant in the theatrical event. Many theater groups followed suit as Teatro Independiente became the driving theatrical force in Argentinean theater of the mid–twentieth century.

In 1932, Barletta convinced fellow Boedo member and established novelist and journalist Roberto Arlt to write for the Teatro del Pueblo. Arlt would write eight plays, five of which premiered in Barletta's theater before the author's death in 1942.[25] Arlt's dramatic works share the obsessions of his narrative texts (of which his 1929 novel, *Los siete locos* [*The Seven Madmen*], is perhaps the best known): the creation of a new, modern world through the fusion of quotidian reality with grotesque dreams, illusions, and fantasies, and the tragic plight of the proletariat or petit bourgeois "loser" in this new world. His plays stage these same obsessions in innovative ways. In his introduction to *Saverio el cruel,* George Woodyard terms the Argentinean writer "the link that connects the renowned Golden Decade in the Argentinean theater with the contemporary period" and further notes that Arlt is "the author that most represents the innovation and *vanguardia* during the interwar [period]."[26]

Saverio el cruel dramatically illustrates the politics and theatrical experimentation taking place in 1930s Buenos Aires. Building upon the local and international traditions of the *grotesco criollo* and metadramatics, *Saverio* created a sociopolitical critique that cut across all sectors, from the upper class's insatiable desires for absolute control to the working class's dreams of power that terrifyingly approximate Argentina's growing fascism.

The three-act play centers these class power struggles on its two antagonists, Susana and Saverio. The play opens in the middle of a rehearsal: Susana and Pedro, with their cousin Juan, are preparing a pastoral farce to be presented for their other friends, all the bored children of Argentina's landed elite. They anxiously await the arrival of Saverio, a butter salesman and object of their nasty and ultimately fatal practical joke. When he finally arrives, Saverio echoes the typical *grotesco* protagonist: "physically, he's a failure. Twisted tie, faded red shirt, the expression of a dog seeking sympathy."[27] The group asks Saverio to play the role of the terrible Colonel, enemy of Susana's Queen Bragatiana, and in order to do this, they convince Saverio that Susana has gone mad and that the only way to rehabilitate her is by accompanying her in the farce, a staged acting-out of her madness. Saverio, flattered and concerned, accepts the role. Act 2 begins with Saverio rehearsing alone in his modest boarding room, "uniformed in the style of a fantastical colonel from some ridiculous second-rate Central American republic."[28] Saverio literally loses himself in his role and, in an apparent dream-state, negotiates with a British arms dealer before being interrupted by Susana's cohorts, who patronizingly admire his costume and critique his performance. Their superior attitude quickly turns fearful when a guillotine is brought to Saverio's room, and they run away as Saverio scorns: "What miserable riffraff. . . . There's nothing to be done, they just don't have the aristocratic sense of butchery. But it doesn't matter, my dear sirs. We'll organize the terror."[29] Loudspeakers broadcast news of the "dictator" Saverio's plans, cut off by the maid Simona, who has come to make Saverio's bed.

By the end of act 2 three dramatic worlds have been introduced: the "real world" of the play, the inset play of the rehearsed farce, and Saverio's delirium of power—a dream within a farce within a play whose tragic essence is made explicit when all three worlds converge in act 3. The final action takes place on the farce's stage: "a deep-red salon. Doors to each side. Upstage on a carpeted platform, a throne. A few lit candles. Open windows. A backdrop with a crescent-shaped form against some trees. The invited guests wander around, chatting, dressed in eighteenth-century costumes."[30] The play nears its climax when Saverio modifies the farce, revealing that Susana's sister Julia has told him of the practical joke. Susana asks the guests to leave the two of them alone so she can apologize. Susana tries to seduce Saverio, saying that he is as "crazy" as she, and, speaking the farce's text, proposes an alliance: "I'm the splendid sweetheart your heart was waiting for."[31] By now, Saverio has already confessed his initial seduction:

When you all invited me to participate in the farce, since my nature was still virginally free of splendid dreams, the farce transformed my sensibility into a violent reality that hour by hour modified the architecture of my life . . . I who had dreamed about being the equal of a Hitler, a Mussolini, I now understand that all these scenes have only served to fool an imbecile.[32]

When Saverio rejects Susana, she shoots him twice. As the others rush in, the play ends with a dying Saverio saying, "It wasn't a joke. She was crazy."[33]

Saverio el cruel's complex metadramatics confound assurances regarding the action's catalyst, Susana's madness. Just as it is not always clear where the farce begins and ends, it is never entirely clear if or when Susana is playing the roles of Queen Bragatiana or her own madness, and the dilemma is rarely resolved didascalically. It is Saverio who declares that Susana is mad, but he too has experienced delusions of grandeur, as a "director of peoples." Susana and Saverio's disappearances into their roles can be read as a parody of naturalistic acting and Freudian dream analysis, with which Arlt was very familiar. But each character also functions metonymically as representative of the respective class and its aspirations. The 1936 play premiered just four years after the military regime of General José F. Uriburu had ended and during a period in which the conservative elite consistently sought to maintain power over the middle class through fraudulent elections and military rule. Spanish-influenced *hispanidad* was on the rise and brought with it nativistic and nationalistic xenophobia and virulent anti-Semitism. Susana stands in for the Argentinean elite, rich, spoiled, and apparently dispossessed of some of its power. Saverio clearly represents the disenfranchised classes. Both characters dream of power, and in this way *Saverio el cruel* stages a struggle between two socioeconomic classes with a common delirium. Susana and Saverio struggle for control of the dream and ultimately the farce. For Susana, the inset play is a nostalgic fantasy in which a displaced aristocrat regains her lost throne; for Saverio, it is transformed into a fascistic delirium supported by a populist ideology.[34] Each antagonist faces an intraclass opponent (for Saverio, the maid Simona; for Susana, her sister Julia) who questions the fantasy by providing a counterdiscourse but not an alternative. Susana finally offers Saverio an arrangement very similar to that entered into by Argentine conservatives and the military in 1930. When Saverio rejects the offer, Susana kills him.

His class martyrdom notwithstanding, Saverio moves from patient to agent and thus becomes the protagonist of his own tragedy, flawed for having dreamed the borrowed dream of power. Both Susana and Saverio are held responsible for the tragedy; hence Arlt's play is a cautionary tale for elite and disenfranchised alike. By the 1930s the earlier *grotesco criollo* had been opened up to cross and blur class lines, even as it focused on the tragic protagonist's unmasking. Arlt made complex use of metadramatic structures to blur the lines between farce, tragedy, and oneiric fantasy but also to erase the lines separating sanity and madness, representation and reality. The Teatro del Pueblo spectators must surely have asked themselves, in which of these worlds do we live? *Saverio el cruel* masterfully blended aesthetic experimentation with social, political, and historical analysis to critique 1930s Argentina, its vicious power struggles, and all too real delusions of authoritarian grandeur.

It may be hard today to consider as "avant-garde" the Independent Theater movement, with its idealization of a pure "art theater," its rejection of local commercialization and Europeanized experimentation for its own sake, its desire to replace naturalistic acting with "realistic" performance, and its project of raising mass theatrical consciousness and increasing spectator competency.[35] However, I argue that it was precisely its anticommercial mix of theatrical forms, its project of activating the spectator and training the actor, and its efforts to bring together the Argentinean playwright, actor, designer, and spectator that qualified the Independent Theater for consideration as *vanguardista*. The movement worked "to mold a new theatrical consciousness in Argentina through a new respect for theater as high art in the service of society and as a cultural manifestation that can appeal to a broad spectrum of the populace, not just to an elite leisure class."[36] In the face of great economic and political adversity, the Independent Theater movement combined a deeply proletarian and democratic commitment with nonnaturalistic performance and staging strategies to probe Argentina's national identity. The Independent Theater movement spread to such countries as Uruguay, Chile, Bolivia, Paraguay, and Peru. In Argentina, the movement built the foundation for a vital Buenos Aires noncommercial theater scene that continues to this day.

What can the "avant-garde" beginnings of the South American Independent Theater movement contribute to a larger reconsideration of the avant-garde? According to David Graver, prior to 1930 the European avant-garde movements once again began to "incorporate pronounced sociopolitical programs that draw connections between art and life and challenge the hegemony of the dominant culture."[37] Such avant-garde

experimentation declined in the 1930s, and when it reappeared after
World War II, "it [was] a comfortable part of bourgeois cultural institutions."[38] In its initial years Barletta's Teatro del Pueblo bore comparison
with its European contemporaries, but even as growing fascism in
Europe would suppress experimentation, the Teatro del Pueblo, born
during Argentina's "infamous decade," became an artistic focal point for
critiquing Argentina's own growing fascination with fascism. In Teatro
del Pueblo's combination of sociopolitical criticism, innovative theatrical aesthetics, and redefinition of the spectator, we can see the beginnings of not only Argentina's later "realistic" theater but also future
experiments in popular, engaged performance. As such, 1930s independent theater in Argentina blurs the lines separating realism and aestheticism, art and politics, forcing us to rethink the categories of avant-garde
theatrical production created by their European contemporaries.

Experimentation, Realism, and Sociopolitics Meet *Vanguardia* in the 1960s

As stated earlier, much of the Independent Theater's work, given its
"social-realist roots"[39] and goal of making the theater an indispensable
element of national cultural life, reflected a more "realistic" (albeit nonnaturalistic) aesthetic of streamlined acting styles, carefully designed and
executed sets, lights and costumes, and a direct relationship with the
audience. The *Nuevo Teatro* (New Theater) movement carried on the
Independent Theater's project of staging socially committed local and
foreign plays. By the late 1950s, the Buenos Aires theater scene was
dominated by a more critical realism, introduced in 1949 with *El puente
(The Bridge)* by Carlos Gorostiza and followed by works from the
period's leading playwrights, such as Agustín Cuzzani, Andrés Lizarraga,
and especially Osvaldo Dragún. During the 1960s, with Argentina once
again under military dictatorship, the so-called *realistas* became increasingly "reflective."[40] Authors such as Ricardo Halac, Roberto Cossa,
Carlos Somigliana, Germán Rozenmacher, and Ricardo Talesnik wrote
plays that exposed and reflected upon Argentinean middle-class obsession with personal prestige and financial success and the failed and frustrated but complicitous individual, much like their contemporary, the
U.S. playwright Arthur Miller.[41] These Argentinean playwrights quickly
became known as the "sixties generation."

It would oversimplify matters to claim that the Independent Theater exerted such a narrow albeit obviously important influence. The movement's above-described experimentation with theatrical production, together with innovations such as those already noted in Roberto Arlt's plays, also opened up possibilities for more abstract experimentation. Nevertheless, by 1960 two ostensibly mutually exclusive paths led away from the Earlier *Teatro Independiente* movement. In many critical histories they were dichotomized as simply *realismo* versus *vanguardismo*.

Such terminology poses immediate problems of categorization. Néstor Tirri notes three theatrical "orientations" in the 1960s: the aforementioned realist-naturalist, the avant-garde, and the experimental.[42] He deems plays by such local dramatists as Eduardo Pavlovsky, Griselda Gambaro, and Alberto Adellach to be *vanguardista* in the European "absurdist" mode. "Experimental" for Tirri denotes the "faddish, esthetic frivolities"[43] usually associated with the productions taking place at Buenos Aires's Di Tella Institute. I perceive no such easy division between what Tirri compartmentalizes as "avant-garde" and "experimental." On the contrary, many of these productions converged in several important, historically decisive ways and beg a clarification regarding the term *vanguardia* as it was used in the 1960s. Other commentators of the period use *vanguardia* in a wider-reaching manner than does Tirri. In 1985 Argentinean playwright and actor Eduardo Pavlovsky described his early 1960s, supposedly *vanguardista* theater as "exasperated realism," a theater that sought out new languages and fused the symbolic with the real.[44] Ana Longoni and Mariano Mestman employ the term *vanguardismo* to speak of the period's visual arts, taking avant-garde to be that which is understood as both rupture and advancement.[45]

Another issue raised by Tirri's use of the term is his reduction of Argentinean *vanguardia* to the European theater of the absurd. Although Pavlovsky has asserted that all avant-garde theater points back to Beckett, he also claims that Beckett and Ionesco are models that (primarily foreign) scholars have imposed on Argentinean avant-garde theater. In a 1985 article, Pavlovsky states he did not read Ionesco before writing his 1962 *La espera trágica (The Tragic Wait),* much as Griselda Gambaro maintains not to have seen Beckett before writing her first "absurdist" play, the 1965 *El desatino (The Blunder).*[46] I return to my earlier use of the plural term *vanguardias* as a means of encompassing much of the period's local cultural production. The broader usage allows me to examine the many interactions between the various theater practitioners and performers and avoid unnecessary divisions such as those established by

Tirri. It will also enable me to make connections between the two Argentina's *vanguardista* moments, the 1930s and the 1960s, in order to arrive at a more meaningful definition of the avant-garde.

Buenos Aires in the 1960s enjoyed multiple active avant-garde theater and performance scenes. As one participant remembered, "During that period, you defined, you acted, and you argued: happenings, conceptual art, oral street literature, experimental theater."[47] From 1958 to 1970, the downtown Torcuato Di Tella Institute was the symbolic center of *vanguardista* music, visual arts, film, theater, and performance. Playwrights such as Griselda Gambaro premiered early works in the downtown institute, while in another part of the city, Eduardo Pavlovsky wrote and performed in his early "absurdist" plays. There were bars, workshops, and even communal living-performance spaces where intellectuals, visual artists, actors, and musicians congregated to stage exhibits, create events, and exchange and debate ideas.[48]

In 1960, Eduardo Pavlovsky and Julio Tahier formed the group Yenesí, Buenos Aires's "first institution dedicated to the systematic staging of foreign and Argentine *teatro de vanguardia*."[49] Pavlovsky called the group's work "total theater" or "theater toward a total reality."[50] In addition to producing plays by such European absurdists as Ionesco and Arrabal (as well as the shorter and more traditional plays of Chekhov, Pirandello, O'Casey, and Dürrenmatt), Yenesí premiered Pavlovsky's own earliest plays, including *Somos (We Are)* and *La espera trágica (The Tragic Wait)* in 1962, *Un acto rápido (A Quick Act)* in 1965, and *Robot* in 1996 before the group dissolved.[51]

Pavlovsky's early plays have only a few characters, who either remain unidentified or are identified by gender, relationship, or profession (e.g., Bricklayer, Someone, Wife, Lover). These characters are usually engaged in frustrated attempts at intercommunication. In performance, the taped recordings and projected images caused spectators to question whether or not they had just witnessed a character's staged thoughts or an exercise in psychodrama (an interpretation further reinforced by the playwright's own work as psychiatrist specializing in group therapy). It might be tempting to dismiss Pavlovsky's 1960s work, as Schanzer does, as lacking "an idea and an ideology,"[52] but I concur with Dubatti, who notes that "Pavlovsky's avant-garde theater is profoundly bound to Argentine society. His absurdist methods construct scenic metaphors of profound opacity and broad polysemy, but always within the frame of the *situated* character, *contextualized* with local sociohistorical references."[53]

Other "absurdist" playwrights of the period also saw their work dismissed as mere copies of European experimentation, or as apoliticized drafts for their later, more "important" plays. Griselda Gambaro not only had her early plays categorized in both ways, but she was further condemned locally for having premiered her early work in the Di Tella Institute.[54] The Di Tella was criticized by avant-gardists and realists alike: The former argued that the institute could not be considered *vanguardista* given its strong ties to foreign (especially U.S.) art galleries, museums, and foundations and its hegemonic promotion of Argentine experimentation to the growing international market. The *realistas* found such Di Tella events as their world-renowned Happenings frivolous and irresponsible. Most of the Di Tella's theatrical activity took place in the Centro de Experimentación Audiovisual (Center for Audiovisual Experimentation), or CEA, one of the institute's three centers. The CEA produced plays,[55] dance-theater performances, cabarets, musical parodies, experimental group performances, and international happenings and experiences. Its theater practitioners brought experiences ranging from participating in the local Teatro Nuevo movement to working abroad with the Living Theatre.

Of the many experimental "actors" groups performing in the Di Tella (and elsewhere in Buenos Aires),[56] Teatro Grupo Lobo (Wolf Theater Group) is perhaps most "emblematic" of the period.[57] Between 1967 and 1971, its eleven members staged a number of "experiences," beginning with *Tiempo lobo (Wolf Time)* in the Di Tella, which one critic described as "a sadomasochistic spectacle that attempted to break spectators out of their habitual passivity. They were caressed, threatened, and attacked in such a rigorously controlled manner that there was little space left for spontaneity or improvisation."[58] Lobo continued to develop as a group, collaborating with other groups, directors, and musicians. Member Martha Serrano described their process as follows:

> In a socially repressive and theatrically paralyzed environment, a group of young people from diverse theater backgrounds came together in search of their own form of expression. Starting with traditional techniques (Stanislavsky, song, mime, etc.), they arrived at the discovery of languages that produced a rupture with the original codes, breaking down the barriers between these [various] languages in the need to find new forms of spatial exploration and communication between the performers and the audience. The new structural concept and the capacity for risk produced moments of interaction

with the audience, taking them to an active participation that modified the performance space itself. This produced a work in constant construction, a whirlpool of visual and auditive images.[59]

Lobo's *Tiempo de fregar* (*Time to Rub,* 1969) was created in collaboration with CEA director Roberto Villanueva. There was no script, only a collaborative process of creation followed by a series of public rehearsals in which audience reaction and interaction was sought out. Art critic Udo Kultermann provides a brief description of the *Tiempo de fregar* "experience": "As the spectators enter the theater the players dance with them, in a dance that progresses in intensity as the evening goes on until erotic contact is made. . . . [A]uthenticity of experience replaces theater art."[60] The production was invited to the Nancy Festival that year but could not obtain the required funding; however, in 1970 the group would travel to Brazil, where they collaborated with the Living Theatre, before dissolving in 1971.

The Di Tella was also the notorious home of Buenos Aires's mid-1960s "happenings."[61] Its best-known *happenista,* Marta Minujín, had already staged events in Europe and other Latin American countries, including 1964's happening in a soccer stadium in Montevideo, Uruguay, which she filled with muscular men, motorcyclists, and young couples wrapped in tape while spectators were pelted from the air (Minujín controlling everything from a helicopter) with live chickens and bags of flour. "La Menesunda," from 1965, had people going up and down stairs through a maze of neon and television sets, whose images merged the participants' faces with those of people on the street outside the Di Tella. According to Minujín's own description of the event, "they went down inside a woman's cranium, where they were covered in makeup and given massages and made up. This was a little head that turned with a single door; when the door came by, you entered. It was a swamp; it was a round piece with gigantic intestines. It was the inside of a television set."[62] In 1966 she organized "Simultaneity in Simultaneity," a transnational happening that tied in local activities with events in New York and Berlin, organized respectively by key "happenists" Allan Kaprow and Wolf Vostell. She would go on to stage events all over the world. Minujín's work was informed by McLuhan's concerns about mass media and individual reception, and rarely did her spectator-as-participant events not possess a darker edge about the effects of mass consumption on the individual.

In the midsixties Griselda Gambaro staged her first plays at the Di

Tella's CEA, beginning with *The Blunder.* The 1965 production of the short two-act play was directed by Jorge Petraglia, who had worked in the New Theater and nine years earlier (in 1956) had staged Argentina's first production of *Waiting for Godot.* In *The Blunder,* just as in Gambaro's *Los siameses (The Siamese Twins)* (which Petraglia premiered at the CEA in 1966),[63] domestic violence is inseparable from social violence.[64]

In *The Blunder,* Alfonso wakes up one morning to find his foot caught in a black metal trap, which he found in a dumpster the night before and brought home as a present for his mother. Alfonso remains trapped as he and the "artifact" deteriorate together. Each opportunity to free him is postponed as Alfonso's mother, his friend Luis, and his wife Lily ignore his needs and take advantage of his confinement. The one person willing to help him, a young man, is distracted or not allowed to do so until finally, as everyone celebrates Lily's pregnancy (the absent Lily—an American blonde whose zaftig looks have been distorted by Alfonso's imagination—having taken up with Luis), he is able to break the rotten trap. It is too late; Alfonso has died without regaining his freedom. Like the protagonists of Gambaro's other plays of the period (and not unlike the 1920s *grotesco* tragic protagonist or Arlt's proletariat or petit bourgeois losers), Alfonso unconsciously participates in his own victimization. He seems unwilling to do more than ask for help in surmounting the small day-to-day obstacles (such as emptying the bedpan or being carried home from a park after being abandoned overnight by his own mother and friend) and is apparently incapable of focusing on the larger situation of his imprisonment.

Years later Diana Taylor noted that "the round metal trap engulfing Alfonso's foot is not an 'absurdist' image but the sign of a new womb/weapon that gives birth to a new life/death."[65] However, at the time of the play's premiere, not everyone could reconcile *The Blunder*'s avant-garde aesthetics with its social commentary. When *The Blunder* was awarded the theater journal *Teatro XX*'s 1965 prize for best play by a contemporary Argentinean playwright, the two opposing jury members resigned from the journal.[66] Three years later, another *realista* playwright, Ricardo Halac, published a violent critique of Gambaro's theater in which he argued that only brutally "realistic," and not "absurdist" theater, could effect social and political change.[67]

Even this cursory overview of Gambaro's early play and the Di Tella's other "experiences" demonstrates that sociopolitical critique and aesthetic experimentation were not so easily separated. Nor were the lines as neatly drawn in daily theatrical practice, despite assessments of the period that divided the two in an ideological debate between politically committed realism and apolitical, absurdist experimentation. Many of the same actors that performed in "realistic" plays also participated in experimental efforts. For example, Norman Briski acted in plays by such *realistas* as Dragún and Gorostiza; he also created, directed, and performed in Di Tella productions; and by the late 1960s he was creating sociodramatic experiments throughout Argentina as cofounder of one of the country's most politicized and polemical experimental troupes, Grupo Teatro Popular Octubre (October Popular Theater Group).

The socioaesthetic blurrings of the 1960s Argentinean *vanguardias* helped foster the 1970s generation of "political" playwrights.[68] Open militancy and social uproar in the late 1960s had led to the creation of a theme new to the Argentinean theater—parricide—and early 1970s plays such as Ricardo Monti's *Una noche con el señor Magnus e hijos (An Evening with Mr. Magnus and Sons)* (1970) and Guillermo Gentile's *Hablemos a calzón quitado (Let's Talk Frankly)* (1969) overtly staged the (real or symbolic) father's death at the hands of his children. This was, however, a new kind of politicized theatricalism. Early 1970s plays mixed genres, metaphors, and structures to foreground the theatrical event itself. Behavior was self-consciously ritualized in internal performances that not only emphasized familial ceremonies but also the power relations between the dominator and the dominated.[69]

By the 1970s, a powerful aesthetico-political shift had already taken place in Buenos Aires theater, coinciding with Argentina's brief return to democracy that would be cut short by 1976's military coup. With Argentina's return to democracy (and Peronism), "group theater" activities escalated. A 1970s participant, Enrique Dacal, recalls:

> We barely had time to do urgent, awkward, and necessary group theater. A theater that went beyond politics and understandable subversion. A theater that managed to take away the fear from before and give one courage for what was to follow. A theater between two horrors that would mean the death or exile for many theater practitioners. The rest of the 1970s gave shelter to a theater of survival.[70]

Collaborative experiments became commonplace, and by the early 1970s *creaciones colectivas* were the norm for many student and nonprofessional groups. Well-known leftist intellectuals who had not written for the theater before began to create plays.[71] In the 1970s, Gambaro's theater shifted in focus from the complicitous victim's experience to "the drama of disappearance, obsessed with the 'missing': the missing people, the absent values, the nonexistent judicial and moral frameworks, the unfathomable reasoning, the grotesque national and international indifference toward the situation."[72] Pavlovsky's plays became more overtly "revolutionary."[73] By the mid-1970s too, even the "sixties generation's" reflective realism had been transformed into a more hybrid "critical realism."[74] In 1976, Halac premiered *Segundo tiempo (Second Half),* in which a married couple's inner fears and desires are acted out onstage, intercutting the play's more "realistic" structure, and Roberto Cossa's 1977 *La nona (The Granny)* (staged during the darkest period of the 1976–83 military dictatorship) transformed the *grotesco criollo* into a savage allegory of the filicidal destruction of the Argentine middle class at the hands of a repressive order.

Buenos Aires's 1970s "political" theater and performance successfully built upon multiple local, supposedly antithetical, models of realism and avant-garde. This fusion of avant-garde and realist aesthetics and thematics taking place in the late 1960s and early 1970s laid the groundwork for the theater of resistance in the late 1970s. Once again, the case was being made for seeing the Argentinean *vanguardias* as something more than the sum of their "avant-garde" parts.

Conclusion

A final cautionary tale regarding the difficulties inherent in international recognition and appreciation of local Buenos Aires avant-garde innovation brings us back to my opening observations regarding multiple Latin American *vanguardias.* In 1968 U.S. performance theorist and practitioner Richard Schechner spent six weeks traveling throughout Latin America with theater producer and critic Joanne Pottlitzer. In a subsequent interview with Pottlitzer, Schechner stated that "Latin American theatre doesn't reflect the terrific changes their society is going through. Their styles are basically nineteenth-century." He went on to criticize Latin American theatre's "preoccupation with North American forms at the expense of their own" and considered Buenos Aires to be the most bizarre illustration:

> [O]ne company was doing [Jean Claude Van-Itallie's] *America Hurrah* and another [Megan Terry's] *Viet Rock,* at the same time the government was being very repressive. Another avant-garde theatre was doing something by Beckett. Nothing seemed to touch the real life of the theatre people, let alone other people.[75]

Schechner suggested that Buenos Aires intellectuals might be weaned "from the breast of North American culture" by doing a "Peronistic" play: "It would take real balls to do a Peronistic play."[76]

In the early 1980s, John King leapt to Buenos Aires's defense by noting that "Schechner's observations demonstrate a lack of perception regarding the political restrictions on theatre of this period."[77] King rightly pointed out that two years after Schechner's trip, the U.S. critic would have been able to see a "Peronistic" play, *El avión negro*—the first collaborative attempt of the "sixties generation" playwrights to create a hybridic 1970s-style "political" theater. Nevertheless, for King, Schechner's comments highlighted Buenos Aires theater's "accomplishments, virtues, and limitations,"[78] and he supported Schechner's statement by citing the Di Tella's mixed-quality achievements, the experimental promise of several groups, and the losses of other promising artists.

A more pluralistic reading of Buenos Aires's avant-garde as multiple, locally produced *vanguardias* offers an alternative to Schechner's neo-colonialist comments and King's arbitrary limitations on what constitutes "theater." Buenos Aires in the 1960s was a complex site of theatrical production, in which various and supposedly opposed trends were already cross-pollinating. The sociopolitical realism already present in the supposedly "absurdist" 1960s plays suddenly became more visible in the 1970s. Briski's late 1960s sociodramatic "experiments" with Octubre, instead of being dismissed as nontheater, could just as easily have been read as a *vanguardista* combination of "real-world" realism with formal experimentation. The Di Tella and other groups' theater "experiences" received praise years later, from Buenos Aires theater director Alberto Ure, for having transformed local actor training by making "theater show up as a life experience for the actor, not offering answers but rather posing questions in encounters with the audience."[79] Even these few counterreadings clearly demonstrate the limitations of Schechner's statement that "Nothing seemed to touch the real life of the theatre people, let alone other people."

Throughout the twentieth century, Buenos Aires theater production eluded any easy division between politics and aesthetics, or between their supposed counterparts of realism and avant-garde. In this essay, I have examined two periods often known as the first and second avant-garde waves in order to trace the multiple and at times apparently antithetical *vanguardias* and demonstrate the nearly always productive tensions between these avant-gardes and other prevailing theatrical trends, national and transnational. Rather than focusing on local origins and outside influences, I have noted that, in each instance, Buenos Aires *vanguardias* were shaped by local forms and in turn shaped others. By positioning these avant-gardes at the intersection of local sociopolitics, aethetics, and experimentation, their transformation of Buenos Aires (and Argentinean) theater becomes obvious, as do their roles in local cultural self-identification and construction. Furthermore, Buenos Aires's multiple *vanguardias* not only resist previously imposed critical reduction; they also remind us of the hybridic potential inherent in any and all cultural production labeled as "avant-garde."

Notes

1. Diana Taylor, "Transculturating Transculturation," *Performing Arts Journal* 13.2 (1991): 96.

2. Examples of such early critical "political" collections include Leon Lyday and George Woodyard's *Dramatists in Revolt: The New Latin American Theatre* (Austin: University of Texas Press, 1976), and Gerardo Luzuriaga's *Popular Theatre for Social Change in Latin America: Essays in Spanish and English* (Los Angeles: UCLA Latin American Center Publications, 1978). Although these pioneering works were and continue to be enormously valuable contributions to the field, the lack of other studies left the outside spectator or reader unfamiliar with Latin American theater's diversity.

3. Román de la Campa, *Latin Americanism* (Minneapolis: University of Minnesota Press, 1990), 83.

4. From the mid–twentieth century onward, Latin American theorists have been developing theories that focus on the continent's "in-between" state. For further reading, see the writings of Fernando Ortiz, *Contrapunteo cubano del tabaco y el azúcar* (Caracas: Biblioteca Ayacucho, 1978); Angel Rama, *Transculturación narrative en América Latina* (Montevideo: Fundación Angel Rama, 1989); Néstor García Canclini, *Hybrid Cultures: Strategies for Entering and Leaving Modernity,* trans. Christopher L. Chiappari and Silvia L. López (Minneapolis: University of Minnesota Press, 1995); Román de la Campa and John Beverley, *Subalternity and Representation: Arguments in Cultural Theory* (Durham: Duke University Press, 1999); and Walter Mignolo, *Local Histories/Global Designs: Coloniality, Subaltern Knowledges, and Border Thinking* (Princeton: Princeton University Press, 2000). In "Transculturating Politics, Realism, and Experimentation in 1960s Buenos Aires Theatre," *Theatre Survey* 43 (2002): 5–19, I set forth my own "hybridic" reading of the period's theatrical production.

5. Rather than employ the other roughly equivalent term, *vanguardismo* (literally, "avant-gardism"), I will use the term *vanguardia* in conformance with Argentinean usage. Furthermore, and in response to John Beverley and José Oviedo's contention that "the not quite identical Spanish equivalent of modernism is *vanguardismo*" (introduction to *The Postmodernism Debate in Latin America,* ed. Beverley, Oviedo, and Michael Aronna [Durham: Duke University Press, 1995]), I find that the term *vanguardias* frees me from limiting my discussion to early-twentieth-century *vanguardista* movements. Argentinean uses of the term *vanguardias* come much closer in meaning to the so-called historical avant-garde spanning the first seventy years of the twentieth century. The term often appears in plural form, and these multiple *vanguardias* suggest multiple phenomena,

movements, and aesthetics. Thus, to avoid confusion with *vanguardismo*'s use as the translation of the historically specific term modernism, I adopt the term *vanguardia* as it is used in Argentina and simply translate it as avant-garde.

6. As the theater director and Boedo member Leónidas Barletta, wrote, "those of *Martín Fierro* [Florida] wanted a revolution for art, those of *Claridad* [Boedo] wanted art for the revolution" (qtd. in Raúl Larra, *Leónidas Barletta, el hombre de la campana* [Buenos Aires: Conducta, 1978], 47). Unless otherwise noted, all translations from Spanish are mine.

7. Pirandello's *Six Characters in Search of an Author* premiered in Buenos Aires in 1922. Many of the Italian playwright's plays were staged in Buenos Aires in the late 1920s and in Sicilian dialect. Pirandello himself visited Argentina on several occasions during this period. While Pirandello undeniably enjoyed a strong presence on the 1920s–30s Buenos Aires theater scene, the development and success of the local *grotesco criollo* and later avant-garde performance should not be attributed exclusively to such European influences, as this essay intends to demonstrate.

8. I would further note that 1930s Argentinean theatrical avant-garde has been far less studied than have been the narrative works of Borges or even Arlt. Román de la Campa (in noting how Latin American literary specialists have ignored Borges's contemporaries, the Cuban anthropologist Fernando Ortiz and the Peruvian essayist José Mariátegui) has asserted that "[t]he 1930s evidences a Latin American epistemological avant-garde that has been overshadowed by its literary counterpart" (79). I wonder if 1930s experimental theater also constitutes part of de la Campa's overshadowed "epistemological avant-garde."

9. The Argentinean playwright Osvaldo Dragún's dramatic concept of *animalización* (animalization) comes immediately to mind. Dragún saw his concept, developed in the 1960s and 1970s, as an extension of the early-twentieth-century *grotesco criollo:* "I take *grotesco* to mean that which is deformed, and the grotesque in the theater, what's deformed in society. What's deformed in society is what's unnatural about society. So, the unnatural produces a deformity that, deep down, is nothing more than animalization. It is man projected onto the reality of animals and things." "Osvaldo Dragún: Teatro, creación y realidad latinoamericana," interview in *Teatro: Hoy se comen al flaco. Al violador,* ed. Miguel Angel Giella, Meter Roster, and Leandro Urbina (Ottawa: Girol Books, 1981), 14–15.

10. In my use here of the term *vanguardia,* I restore to the aestheticized and antiart notions of the avant-garde the political valence present in its "fierce opposition to the underpinnings of bourgeois society and its institutions" (James Harding, introduction to *Contours of the Theatrical Avant-Garde: Performance and Textuality,* ed. Harding [Ann Arbor: University of Michigan Press, 2000], 10), what Laurence Senelick calls "Art as a disruptive 'fifth column'" ("Text and Violence: Performance Practices of the Modernist Avant-Garde," in Harding, 16), and what comes close to David Graver's characterization (in *The Aesthetics of Disturbance: Anti-Art in Avant-Garde Drama* [Ann Arbor: University of Michigan Press, 1995]) of the earliest nineteenth-century European avant-garde art:

> Avant-garde artists act as an advance guard for the "army" of adherents to a particular revolutionary political program. They scout the enemy territory (the current sociopolitical milieu) with their vivid analyses of contemporary life and prepare it for

invasion by disseminating rousing slogans and sparking hopes for a better future. They are an elite corps manning an exposed position in the fight for a better world. Although they are confirmed enemies of the current sociopolitical power structure, they define themselves in terms of their allegiance to a political cause and a vision of the future rather than solely in terms of their discontent with the status quo. (3)

11. Derived from nineteenth-century Spanish *sainetes* and *zarzuelas,* the local *sainete criollo* staged the (sometimes violent) encounters of the *criollo* and immigrant cultures in Babelian melodramas that often included music (frequently the *sainete criollo*'s musical companion, the tango). One of the *sainete criollo*'s most celebrated practitioners, Alberto Vacarezza, described a typical plot: "A *conventillo* [multifamily dwelling] patio/an Italian super/a leathery Spaniard/a broad, a smooth talker/two thugs with knives/flirtatious words, a love affair/obstacles, jealousies, arguments/a duel, a knifing/uproar, shooting/ help, cops . . . curtain" (qtd. in David Viñas, *Grotesco, immigración y fracaso: Armando Discépolo* [Buenos Aires: Corregidor, 1997], 16–17). For a book-length study of the genre, see Silvia Pellarolo, *Sainete criollo/Democracia/Representación. El caso de Nemesio Trejo* (Buenos Aires: Corregidor, 1997).

12. The first decade of the twentieth century is most closely identified with Florencio Sánchez (1875–1910), who produced at least sixteen plays before his untimely death. Most of Sánchez's plays take place in urban spaces, but he is best known today for a trilogy of rural "gaucho" tragedies: *M'hijo el dotor (My Son the Doc,* 1903), *La gringa (The Immigrant's Daughter,* 1904), and *Barranca abajo (Down the Ravine,* 1905). Sánchez's was a naturalistic theater of thesis plays about the conflicts between the established *criollo* populace and the new European immigrants. Despite the author's anarchist, bohemian, and socially critical tendencies, his plays effectively consolidated the realist bourgeois theater as the region's dominant theatrical model.

13. David William Foster, *The Argentine "Teatro Independiente," 1930–1955* (York, S.C.: Spanish Literature Publishing Co., 1986), viii.

14. Ibid., vii.

15. Ibid., viii.

16. The *conventillo* was a multifamily dwelling typically located in the southern suburbs of Buenos Aires and occupied by newly arrived immigrants.

17. The Argentinean *grotesco criollo* is intimately linked to the theater of writer, director, and producer Armando Discépolo (1887–1971). The author of more than thirty plays of various genres, Discépolo was the first Argentinean to call his plays "grotescos," beginning with the 1923 *Mateo* and ending his writing career with 1934's three-act *Relojero (Watchmaker).* See Osvaldo Pelletieri's study that accompanies Discépolo's collected works, *Obra dramática de Armando Discépolo,* 2 vols. (Buenos Aires: Editorial Universitaria de Buenos Aires, 1987–90) as well as excellent analyses of the *grotesco criollo* by David Viñas, *Grotesco, immigración y fracaso,* and by Eva Claudia Kaiser-Lenoir, *El grotesco criollo: Estilo teatral de una época* (Havana: Casa de las Américas, 1977). Actors such as Luis Arata developed an intense acting style to complement the *grotesco criollo*'s ferocious unmasking of failed immigrant dreams.

18. Kaiser-Lenoir, *El grotesco criollo.*

19. Eduardo Romano, "Grotesco y clases medias en la escena argentina," *Hispanoamérica* 15.44 (1986): 31.

20. Ibid., 34.

21. It is not surprising that the *grotesco* reappeared (as the *neogrotesco*) in the late 1960s amid growing pessimism and economic decline.

22. Viñas, *Grotesco, inmigración y fracaso,* 54.

23. Romano, "Grotesco y clases medias," 32.

24. Larra, *Leónidas Barletta,* 93.

25. The eight plays are *300 millones* (*300 Million,* 1932), *Prueba de honor* (*Proof of Honor,* 1932), *Saverio el cruel* (*Saverio the Cruel,* 1936), *El fabricante de fantasmas* (*The Maker of Ghosts,* 1936), *La isla desierta* (*The Desert Island,* 1937), *Africa* (1938), *La fiesta del hierro* (*The Feast Day of Steel,* 1940), and *El desierto entra a la ciudad* (*The Desert Comes to the City,* 1942). Arlt also published several dramatic "sketches" *(bocetos): Separación feroz* (*Ferocious Separation,* 1938), *La juerga de los polichinelas* (*The Punchinellos Go on a Spree,* 1939), *Un hombre sensible* (*A Sensitive Man,* 1939), and *Escenas de un grotesco* (*Scenes from a "Grotesco,"* 1934), the last deemed to be a "prefiguration of *Saverio el cruel*" by Fernando Moreno Turner, "La Fábrica de Mentiras. A propósito de una 'bulería' de Roberto Arlt," in *Seminario sobre Roberto Arlt,* ed. Alain Sicard (Pitiers: Centre de Recherches Latino-Américaines, 1978), 114.

26. George Woodyard, "Roberto Arlt," in *3 dramaturgos rioplatenses. Antología del teatro hispanoamericano del siglo XX,* ed. Woodyard, Frank Dauster, and Leon Lyday (Ottawa: Girol Books, 1983), 87.

27. Further proof of *Saverio*'s origins in *grotesco* can be found in the aforementioned Arlt sketch, *Escenas de un grotesco* (published in 1934), which clearly contains the germ of the later play. Roberto Arlt, *Saverio el cruel* in *Obra completa,* vol. 3 (Buenos Aires: Planeta, 1991), 294.

28. Ibid., 307.

29. Ibid., 318.

30. Ibid., 321.

31. Ibid., 320.

32. Ibid., 328–29.

33. Ibid., 332.

34. Eduardo Romano notes the similarities between *Saverio el cruel* and the *grotesco:* Arlt's play "demonstrates, nakedly, the true face of the petit bourgeoisie, always fascinated with the social sectors above it and disposed to deny its connected inferiors, thus its predisposition to accepting dictatorial political solutions" ("Grotesco y clases medias," 34).

35. In a 1941 article, Robert Arlt answered the question of theater as "independent of what?": "Independent of a relationship that the commercial author establishes premeditatedly with the primary preferences of the best-fed indices of inferior spectators. . . . The more faithfully the independent author tries to express his theatrical reality, the farther he positions himself from the commercial theater" (*La Hora,* reproduced in Foster, *Argentine Teatro Independiente,* 139).

36. Foster, *Argentine Teatro Independiente,* ix.

37. Graver, *The Aesthetics of Disturbance,* 6.

38. Ibid., 11.

39. Foster, *Argentine Teatro Independiente,* 52.

40. For more detailed accounts of 1960s Argentinean *realismo,* see Néstor Tirri, *Real-*

ismo y teatro argentino (Buenos Aires: Ediciones La Bastilla, 1973); the essays collected in Osvaldo Pellettieri's *Teatro argentino de los '60, continuidad y ruptura* (Buenos Aires: Corregidor, 1989); and Graham-Jones, "Transculturating Politics."

41. Tirri claims that Miller "is the foreign playwright to whom Argentine dramatists with a concentrated production between 1960 and 1970 have most decidedly related and are most indebted" (*Realismo y teatro argentino,* 17).

42. Ibid., 11.

43. Ibid., 12.

44. Eduardo Pavlovsky, "La vanguardia teatral en la Argentina," *Teatro* 5.23 (1985): 36.

45. Ana Longoni and Mariano Mestman, *Del Di Tella a "Tucumán Arde": Vanguardia artística y política en el '68 argentino* (Buenos Aires: Ediciones El Cielo Por Asalto, 2000), 18.

46. Griselda Gambaro, *El desatino. Teatro 4* (Buenos Aires: Ediciones de la Flor, 1990), 59–106.

47. Enrique Dacal, "Apuntes finiseculares para la historia del teatro de Grupos en la Argentina," *Diógenes. Anuario crítico del teatro latinoamericano* (1991), 34.

48. The entire area around the institute's "crazy block" was filled with activity. Even the United States Information Service's Lincoln Library was directly across from the Di Tella. I thank David William Foster for reminding me of the Lincoln's presence and its earlier, more open role in the 1960s.

49. Gerardo Ferández, "Del peronismo a la dictadura military," in *Escenarios de dos mundos,* ed. M. Pérez Coterillo, 4 vols. (Madrid: Centro de Documentación Teatral), 1:142.

50. Quoted in Jorge Dubatti, "Estudio preliminar," in *Teatro complete I,* by Eduardo Pavlovsky (Buenos Aires: ATUEL, 1997), 7–44. For information on Pavlovsky's theories of theater and politics, see the extensive interviews collected in Dubatti, *La ética del cuerpo* (Buenos Aires: ATUEL, 2001).

51. Eduardo Pavlovsky, *Teatro de vanguardia (Somos, La espera trágica, Un acto rápida, El robot* and *Alquien)* (Buenos Aires: Ediciones Cuadernos de Siroco, 1966).

52. George O. Schanzer, "El teatro vanguardista de Eduardo Pavlovsky," *Latin American Theatre Review* 13.1 (1979): 9.

53. Dubatti, "Estudio preliminar," 13.

54. For a detailed history of the institute, including interviews with key participants, see John King, *El Di Tella y el desarrollo cultural argentine en la década del sesenta* (Buenos Aires: Ediciones de Arte Gaglianone, 1985). For accounts of the Di Tella's many events, see Enrique Oteiza, "El Di Tella y la vanguardia artística de la década del 60," in Pellettieri, *Teatro argentino de los '60,* 59–71; Oscar Masotto et al., *Happenings* (Buenos Aires: Jorge Alvarez, 1967); Jorge Romero Brest, *Arte visual en el Di Tella* (Buenos Aires: Emecé, 1992); Liliana B. López, "El 'happening' y el Instituto Di Tella," in *De Eugene O'Neill al "Happening": teatro norteamericano y teatro argentino 1930–1990,* ed. Osvaldo Pellettieri and George Woodyard (Buenos Aires: Galerna, 1996), 71–81; and Longoni and Mestman, *Del Di Tella.*

55. In addition to plays by such local writers as Gambaro and Norman Briski, the CEA produced experimental versions of international plays, including Osborne's *Luther,* Genet's *Death Watch,* Shakespeare's *Timon of Athens,* Jarry's *Ubu in Chains,* and Tirso's *The Joker of Seville.*

56. Other groups active in the late 1960s and early 1970s included Teatro de la Tribu (Theater of the Tribe), Yezidas, Once al Sur, Orestiada, and Nosotros.

57. Dacal, "Apuntes finiseculares," 33.

58. King, *El Di Tella,* 146.

59. Quoted in Dacal, "Apuntes finiseculares," 33.

60. Udo Kultermann, *Art and Life,* trans. John William Gabriel (New York: Praeger, 1971), 106. Lobo is the only Argentinean theater group included in Kultermann's discussion, placed among better-known groups such as the Living Theater, La Mama, the Performance Group, and the Open Theater. A photo of *Tiempo de Fregar* is also reproduced.

61. In 1971 Kultermann lists seven cities as centers for happenings: New York, Paris, Vienna, Düsseldorf, Tokyo, London, and Buenos Aires (43–44).

62. Quoted in King, *El Di Tella,* 246.

63. Griselda Gambaro, *Los siameses. Teatro 4.* (Buenos Aires: Ediciones de la Flor, 1990), 108–55.

64. As Diana Taylor notes, all of Gambaro's 1960s plays (including the period's best known, *El campo* [*The Camp,* 1967]) "dramatize the progressive decomposition of social and judicial structures designed to keep violence contained and thus under control" ("Violent Displays," in *Information for Foreigners,* by Griselda Gambaro, trans. and ed. Marguerite Feitlowitz [Evanston, Ill.: Northwestern University Press, 1992], 161–75).

65. Diana Taylor, *Theatre of Crisis: Drama and Politics in Latin America* (Lexington: University Press of Kentucky, 1991), 97.

66. The two resignation letters were published in the next issue of *Teatro XX,* together with editor-in-chief Kive Staiff's response and a negative review by Ernesto Schóó of *realista* Roberto Cossa's latest play, *Los días de Julián Bisbal (The Days of Julián Bisbal).*

67. Ricardo Halac, "Pesquisa en torno de un cadaver que respire," *Argentores* 1 (1969): 10–22.

68. The impressive number of Argentine "political" plays staged in the early 1970s prohibits the inclusion of a complete list here, but even a partial title survey will give the reader some idea of the theater being created: *¿Qué clase de lucha es la lucha de clases? (What Class of Struggle is the Class Struggle?)* by Beatriz Mosquera; *Cháu Papá (Bye, Dad)* by Alberto Adellach; *Chúmbale (Sic 'em)* by Oscar Viale; *Soldados y soldaditos (Soldiers and Little Tin Soldiers)* by Aída Bortnik; and *Historia tendenciosa de la clase media argentina . . . (Tendentious History of the Argentine Middle Class . . .)* by Ricardo Monti.

69. The 1970s playwrights clearly saw themselves as distinct from their "*vanguardista*" predecessors. The playwright Ricardo Monti makes this clear in his "Requiem for the Avant-Garde" as he follows the trend in equating *vanguardismo* with absurdism:

> But what happens with the new generation of playwrights? They've awakened to a world shaken up, in which entire peoples more and more actively seek out, without turning up their noses to violence, the right to determine their [own] lives. The themes they feel forced to confront are absolutely different from those of the fifties avant-garde. . . . The point of divergence appears to be the following: Man is history's object, he suffers from it. Man is history's subject, he creates it. (qtd. in Tirri, *Realismo y teatro argentino,* 203–4)

70. Dacal, "Apuntes finiseculares," 24.

71. Such was the case of David Viñas, who won 1972's municipal prize for his politico-historical play *Lisandro,* which ran for three years.

72. Taylor, *Theatre of Crisis,* 98.

73. Dubatti, "Estudio preliminar," 14.

74. The earliest "critical realist" attempt was the *El avión negro* of 1970, a series of sketches about Perón's Argentine return, written collaboratively by Cossa, Somigliana, Talesnik, and Rozenmacher.

75. Joanne Pottlitzer, "Conformists in the Heart: An Interview with Richard Schechner," *Drama Review* 14.2 (1970): 40.

76. Ibid.

77. King, *El Di Tella,* 148.

78. Ibid.

79. Alberto Ure, "El ensayo teatral, camp crítico (I)," *Cuadernos de investigación teatral de San Martín* 1.1 (1991): 176. It merits noting that the word Ure employs, *ensayo,* means both rehearsal and essay. Both semes remit to the idea of probing, testing, trying out, and Ure incorporates the larger paratheatrical idea of exploration in his discussion of the theatrical rehearsal process.

From "Vanguard" to "Avant-Garde"?
Questioning the Progressive Bengali Theater of Kolkata

Sudipto Chatterjee

> [S]ocial-chauvinism (Socialism in words, chauvinism in deeds) is the utter betrayal of Socialism, complete desertion to the side of the bourgeoisie; . . . this split in the working-class movement is bound up with the objective conditions of imperialism.
> —V. I. Lenin, *Imperialism, the Highest Stage of Capitalism*

Premise

The term *avant-garde* will not generally show up in any parlance, or even casual conversations, on Bengali theater in Kolkata.[1] Most labels and definitive terms coming out of Euro-American art movements in the twentieth century (for example, surrealism, impressionism, or minimalism), more often than not, arrive with their specific histories when culled up in Bengali intellectual/academic discourse. The only exception to this rule are broader terms like *realism* or *absurdism* that have a wider acceptance in defining specific kinds of plays and production styles in Bengali theater. Consequently, the term *avant-garde* comes only with specific references to the art movements in Europe or (less so) America in the early twentieth century and then again in the 1960s, never as a neutral term that could be used independently of its particular historical extraction.

However, if we try to dissociate the term *avant-garde* from its historical lineage, in our attempt to define it in terms of the general characteristics of the phenomenon itself, we can extrapolate (in accord with the larger purpose of this volume) a more formalistic meaning. Gary Garrels describes the avant-garde usefully as "the engine of thrust and forward motion that aids art in its progression from one stage to another."[2] If this general definition is kept in mind, it is possible (nay, necessary; unless we are willing to let the term rust in disuse!) to look at the history of the postindependence (meaning after India's independence from British rule in 1947) "progressive" Bengali theater of Kolkata and identify certain specific moments when the definition and function of theater in this society were called into question and, consequently, the art itself was redefined in terms of both form and content, message as well as medium in the "forward motion . . . [of] its progression from one stage to another." Specifically, at this introductory stage of the essay, I would like to draw readers' attention to the words *progressive* and then, its noun form, *progression*. These words lie at the heart of a lexicographically contained reading of the term *avant-garde*. "Progressive," the adjective, as a derivative of the noun *progression*—advancement, forward movement—suggests "liberation" from all that is moribund and immovable, as a movement that strikes at the heart of institutionalized and/or passively and unquestioningly accepted forms and norms of artistic practice. However, the status of being *moribund* and *immovable* is in itself a derivative, an arrival in time, a function of a history where an impulse loses the name of action, through co-option, overuse, or general exhaustion in relation to itself, and is emptied of the very meaning that once propelled it. In other words, the term *avant-garde* is relative to a certain cyclicality of historical progression and is confined by the same history in its own mires. By attempting to situate it outside the immediate exigencies of its Euro-American historical context, we can free up the expression and help it become impervious to the burden of time. Thereby, we open it up to describe or read more phenomena than its historical specificities allow it to within the Western paradigm—and, thus, turn it into a more useful analytical tool that can be applied to different cultures.

But that, by itself, cannot be a worthy purpose. One may very well object to this exercise: why, to what extent, and more importantly, to what end do we need to "rescue" the term from its own history and apply it to phenomena beyond its specific cultural contexts (in this case, the Euro-American)? One could, plausibly, carry on ad nauseam about this, but it should suit our purposes to say that when a term is borrowed arbitrarily from (and in emulation of) one cultural or historical context and applied disregardfully to a different site, it carries with it a code of hegemony, a discourse of cultural domination that accompanies the reading itself. Thus when *avant-garde* is used as a frame of reference to define a moment in Bengali theater history, it may very well implicate a comparison with the way the term is associated with Euro-American theater history, thus turning the reading of the history of Bengali theater into a subset of its Euro-American counterpart, obstructing a reading in this theater's own terms. But when treated neutrally and without any attendant historical baggage, not only is the term freed up, it may also liberate certain normative, uncritical ways of viewing or reading "other" cultural phenomena and, in turn, free the very modes of cultural hegemony that such transpositions could perpetuate.

No doubt, this is a perilous undertaking, but it is also one that needs to be taken if we are to reckon with "a vitally diverse cultural expression [that] is now emerging, even under economic duress, from various regions, countries, and groupings of people"[3]—not only the "emerging" and the contemporary, but also "other" histories. Such a reinvestment of the term *avant-garde,* which rips it out of its own history by displacing it from the source culture(s) and then placing it in another (read "an *other*") context, might bring the term closer to its lexicographic denotation and push us toward (the possibility, at least, of) a more egalitarian reading of cultures, a more evenhanded consideration of difference and other-ness, moving as we into a new century. This becomes a politically significant "act" particularly in the postcolonial moment, when postcoloniality itself needs to be interrogated and redefined against the ongoing ravages of neocolonialism and new imbalance of political power and mounting hegemony that is beginning to dominate the world in ways more visible than ever before. *Avant-garde,* after all, essentially implies the challenge of the iconoclast against all modes of languishment and stagnation, co-option as well as domination.

All of the above may appear somewhat simplistic, because no term with any historical ancestry can be dehistoricized fully: the baggage may well be taken off the conveyor belt (of historicity), but cannot be fully redeemed, even if the identification tags have been carefully removed or the contents emptied. Traces of the contents—a scent, a scratch left inside the bag by something that was in there once, the memory of what was inside—will continue to linger. So, of what effective use is this apparent neutralization of the avant-garde as a term? There is one usefulness that has not crossed our path as yet. When consciously taken out of the Euro-American historical context and purposefully (mis)placed in a different cultural-historical site, the neutralization of the term is not merely a wishful thought but rather a conscious analytical approach where the reference to the historical lineage of the term is used as a caveat for us to be vigilantly aware of the difference between the two histories that the same term is being used for. In other words, to reinvest or reinscribe *avant-garde* with a different functionality at an

"other" cultural site is not about rubbing out its prior points of historical reference (because, as we have seen, that is impossible), but rather to
write over it with a critical awareness of the difference and the new historical relationship by means of which this exercise will revitalize the
term.

It is with this view that the present essay looks at the rise and decline
of the "progressive" Bengali theater of Kolkata, attempting to identify its
moments of "avant-garde" thrusts and impulses since 1947, the year the
British formally ended their rule over India. While this essay cannot take
everything into account, it does posit a few vital questions about the
developmental and formal nature of the Kolkata-based Bengali theater
even while staying within the framework of a historical narrative. And,
in so doing, one might hope to open the possibility of art (the art of the
thespian, in our case) being an agency of interrogation that exposes and
makes foul the operation of hegemony, of all categories of domination—political, cultural, historical, social, aesthetic.

Is the notion of the "avant-garde" a cultural universal? Can it be a
free-floating signifier, signaling beyond the flames of history? If there is
a question that burns behind this essay, it is that.

The Indian Peoples' Theatre Association: Vanguard or Avant-garde?

The trajectory of India's independence more or less coincides with the
Indian Peoples' Theatre Association (IPTA) movement, which has had
a tremendous impact on theater in West Bengal. It was from this movement that an alternate "leftist" theater formed in the late 1940s. This
new, leftist theater eventually went on to challenge the seventy-year-old
commercial Western-style public theater of Calcutta, now known as
Kolkata. The public theater was a product of colonial hybridity that had
emerged in the last half of the nineteenth century, a hybridity marked by
an active interaction between colonial British modes of performance
(the theater that the British in India had brought from England to the
colony) and the available indigenous forms of folk performance.[4] While
taking on the appurtenances of realistic stagecraft and adopting the tenets
of acting from the British theaters, the new Western-style Bengali theater looked for its subjects in the myths and legends of its "Indian" heritage. That is not to say that this theater altogether rejected the performative elements of the available native forms, but rather that the
assimilation was negotiated through the creation of a third hybrid entity

that was neither wholly native, nor European. It had a character of its own, right from the beginning, going side by side with the hybrid formation of the mixed population of colonial Kolkata, where commerce and employment opportunities were forcing caste and religious distinctions to break down among the natives toward the creation of a civil society that had to define itself anew.

In (and through) this process, Western-style Bengali theater was initially launched as a site of pleasure for the urban rich Bengali intelligentsia—the bābus.[5] From the 1870s, however, bābu theater gradually moved to the more democratic forum of the ticketed theater. Very soon, it had a corps of professional actors, and the whole setup turned into a profit-oriented commercial enterprise. The Bengali public theater blossomed in the last quarter of the nineteenth century through the first three decades of the twentieth century, even as it became more and more dominated by commercial concerns. Profiteering had always been a goal of this owner-dominated theater, but by the 1930s, it had affected its creative possibilities. The same theater that had responded to nationalist political causes in the late nineteenth and early twentieth century, with a certain (albeit problematic) perception of political concern, was now rendered generally impotent and feeble. It had lost contact with the political reality of the country, being dissociated from the same indigenous roots that had midwifed it into existence. It had little impact on the sociocultural life of Bengal between the wars, as India's movement toward independence from colonial rule gained momentum.

However, it would not be wholly truthful to assert that the Indian Peoples' Theatre Association came into being as a consequence of the public theater's inability to respond to the political situation. The IPTA movement came as a direct outcome of the political agenda of the Communist Party of India. In fact, as Malini Bhattacharya has persuasively argued, the IPTA movement was never really conceived of as a movement before it had spontaneously surfaced through the activities of several, often local, left-oriented cultural groups that worked to spread the gospel of Communist ideology in the context of the Indian independence movement. The British Government had banned the Communist Party of India, paralyzing it. In its dire need to resurface, the party decided not to participate in the 1942 Quit India movement led by Gandhi, and found political articulation in an agenda that overtly placated an antifascist position over an anti-British standpoint. This strategy allowed the party to (somewhat) inoculate itself against the wrath of the Raj. It was also in absolute synch with the internationalist perspective of

the Communist movement worldwide. Until the division of the Communist Party into pro-democratic (which committed themselves to
working through the election-based democratic system of governance,
as proposed by the Indian constitution) and antidemocratic factions
(which continued to pursue the cause of creating a socialist system) in
the 1960s, the party configured itself largely as a Soviet-style party. The
negotiations regarding how and whether the party would or would not
participate in the postindependence political system of the new democratic Indian nation came much later. But what remains clear is that during the early forties the party chose to subscribe to the antifascist, instead
of supporting the anticolonial, agenda that other nationalist parties,
mainly the Indian National Congress, had adopted.[6] What enhanced the
efficacy of this standpoint further was Japan's aggression toward the
British Indian empire. The Japanese air forces had bombed Chittagong,
a far eastern district of undivided Bengal. This incident alone granted
immediate political relevancy to the Communist Party's antifascist
agenda—the fascists had literally touched the Indian landmass. But
underneath the explicit antifascist agenda lay anti-imperialist, antifeudal,
and anticapitalist antecedents. And as a potent backdrop, the party zoned
in on the terrible famine of 1942 that rocked Bengal and other parts of
India, caused not by natural causes, but almost entirely by black-market-
ing entrepreneurs and the British empire's need to bankroll the war at
the colony's expense.

The IPTA movement clearly worked from two dimensions—cen-
trifugally and centripetally. On the one hand, traveling performing
troupes sponsored directly or indirectly by the party went from urban
centers into the villages to rally mass support and organize peoples'
movements; on the other, local (often) rural troupes came forward on
their own in support of the cause. The effects of this cultural
trafficking—between the urban and the rural, the intelligentsia and the
peasant/workers moving toward each other—strengthened the movement. There were spontaneous and reciprocal exchanges of form and
content. Many religious and ritual forms of performance—musical performance genres and folk theater forms—were being reconstituted and
reinscribed to respond to the political cause. At the same time, specific
urban performative devices—the realism of the proscenium stage and its
technological attributes like lights, sets, makeup, and special effects—
were being read and transcribed into hitherto unvisited spaces. A different kind of hybridity was beginning to surface, one that simultaneously
engaged performativity as well as ideology. This was particularly evident

first in the spontaneous and exponential dissemination of "folk" songs with antifascist/imperialist themes, and through the efficacy of some agit-prop[7] plays produced by urban performers whose forms and performative norms were absorbed by peasants or workers, who themselves started to compose and perform their own plays. While the express purpose of the agit-prop style was clearly tied in with the agenda of the party, the performative styles and the specificities of content were not entirely based on received European or Soviet models. Particular exigencies of the situations being addressed, often very local, were taken into account to make the performances relevant to the audiences being wooed, but then there were also items that portrayed larger causes and events that related to ideology at the broadest level. Also, while there were smaller performances—musicals, tableaus, and skits—that did not need much in terms of productional paraphernalia, there were longer plays that had high production values and could not do without elaborate arrangements pertinent to proscenium stage–style performance. In this regard, the two plays that stand as prime examples were *Jabānbandi (The Statement)* and *Nabānna (The Harvest),* written by Bijan Bhattacharya, codirected with Sombhu Mitra, and produced in 1944.

Much later, in 1978, while reflecting on what *Nabānna* had contributed to Bengali theater, Sombhu Mitra wrote:

> We were then thinking of new plays, new [styles of] performance. For models we could only think of Western plays, images of their stagecraft. But this country (meaning India) has its own sensibility, too. But we could find no congruence between that and our contemporary theater, our acting styles. Some people started asking why we weren't doing revivals of anything that was "rural," while others started setting sloganistic, unliterary writings to rural melodies in their attempts to create a bridge [between urban and rural]. It was at that agitated juncture—when we were all banging our heads over what one meant by language, by culture, by form, by content—Bijan came up with his [plays] as the first step out.[8]

What Mitra calls "the first step out" was a stride toward a possibility, a plausible ground for negotiations between classes and cultures, (yet) an(other) option to create a new theatrical hybrid that could go beyond the city-bound public theaters (and this time with a political purposefulness hitherto unseen in Bengali theater) with an eye to indigenous needs and practices, straddling the urban and the rural, the native and the eign. This endeavor, however, was not a smooth-sailing project all the way. Despite the familiar rural milieu that the plays operated within, the alien devices of urban realism and the technical brilliance of proscenium-style stagecraft were problematic for the target rural audiences, who were used to stylized, nonrealistic folk performance. While the style of urban realism, deeply informed by the late-nineteenth- and twentieth-century European tradition, did not always communicate to rural audiences (there were instances in which audiences would request explanatory commentaries in the middle of a performance), the technical appurtenances needed for the successful execution of these productions often made it difficult for them to travel. On a certain level, these were plays written for the people that at times the people themselves did not understand. Malini Bhattacharya makes the point succinctly:

> [T]he theme of *Nabānna* had greater possibilities, and its realism, which lay in suggesting the exact visual and linguistic details of peasant life, was certainly a breakthrough. But the means of bringing such realism closer to the cultural forms familiar to the rural audiences remained unexplored. The experiment remained limited to the proscenium stage.[9]

They were productions that for their values were not always portable enough to travel and be performed in technically ill-equipped rural spaces and facilities. Yet, the program-book published on the occasion of the play's premiere had declared in no uncertain terms,

> [IPTA's] task is, on the one hand, to awaken an almost waning culture, and, on the other, give it new life by pulling it into the expansive domain of the masses. Civilization and culture will be enriched in a new way by this public mode of communication.[10]

But that was not to be. In its first run, *Nabānna* was performed only fourteen or fifteen times. But the play died untimely not merely for its unportability. There was also the lack of continued patronage from the party and the refusal of the public theaters of Kolkata to give it a commercial run.

The Communist Party had other things in mind while *Nabānna* cried for support. With a wish to capitalize on the momentum the activities of the IPTA had gained, the party spawned a Central Squad in 1945, made up of many nonparty artists (IPTA being the party's democratic front), to create performances that would rule from the top and serve up models for the local squads. However, the same issue of production values that had affected *Nabānna*—stagecraft, performance technology, and sophistication of urban performative expression—interfered. Although it resulted in the creation of a number of fine pieces by artists who were to become stalwarts in the decades immediately following[11]—for example, the brothers Uday and Ravi Shankar—it also stole from the movement its spontaneous character, the sparkling immediacy of a performance that emerges under the impact of a certain urgency from within a group of people. This investment in the Central Squad also drew the party away from supporting productions like *Nabānna*.

The (Resistible) Rise of the Group Theatre

Consequently, in the 1950s many of the leading theater directors and playwrights, such as Sombhu Mitra and Bijan Bhattacharya—and later Utpal Dutt (Bengali Datta) and Ajitesh Banerjee, along with others—broke away from the party-mandated agenda of the IPTA and formed groups of their own, which led to the formation of the largely Kolkata-based Group Theatre movement. This exodus of the artists who led the IPTA stemmed from a debate that riled the ranks of the association right from the beginning—a dichotomy that was always there in the heart of the conflicting centrifugal and centripetal traffic of the movement itself. The tenuous concord between the rural and urban performance modes was short-lived and worked while there was political urgency that affected both the middle-class intelligentsia and the subaltern classes. But the success of the "plead-and-bargain" policy of the Indian National Congress in securing India's political independence from British rule, and the Communist Party's failure to capitalize on the mass appeal and grassroots support it had started to garner in the early 1940s and to prevent the partition of Bengal in 1947, damaged the IPTA movement, its Bengali wing at least, irrevocably. Although attempts were made to revive it in the new West Bengal, the movement could never again scale the heights it had reached in the 1940s. The theater artists who could revive the movement were now decidedly concentrating on the Group Theatre movement. They had left the IPTA with the realization that individual will, what Rustom Bharucha has called the "self-consciousness of the modern artist,"[12] and the concomitant importance of free

artistic experimentation in theater were inherently opposed to performing along party mandates. Theater needed to be politically responsible
but not politically customized by party agendas. Moreover,

> [t]hese inner dissensions led to the breakdown of the [IPTA] move-
> ment, which coincided with the end of the second World War and
> the imminence of India's independence. The common enemies of
> fascism and imperialism could no longer serve as rallying points for a
> collective solidarity.[13]

However, most of these theater groups, although now freed from
party control and not directly dependent on its patronage, continued to
be heavily political, supporting the leftist cause from the outside. Erstwhile IPTA stalwarts thus jump-started the Group Theatre movement,
not only as performers and directors, but also as organizers and producers in a desperate effort to create a viable alternative to the commercial
public theaters of Kolkata—an "avant-garde." These groups, from the
early 1950s onwards, continued to produce some of the best theater to
be seen in India up until the 1970s. It was in their hands that Chekhov,
Ibsen, Pirandello, Brecht, and other masters of the Western theater
found a voice for the first time in an Indian context.

There is a contradiction here that needs to be reckoned with. A large
number of the plays that came out of the Group Theatre movement
were written by European playwrights. Why did these intellectuals and
practitioners choose to stage Western plays? Is this evidence of a continuing colonized mode of thinking? Dregs and traces of the British Raj
and Europhilia? Or is there an "avant-garde" impulse here, staging these
plays to strike a blow against the commercial theater? While surface evidence weighs heavily toward identifying this as a Eurocentric propensity, one can also see in it an effort to be "internationalist" in the same
mode in which the Communist Party and its factions were operating at
that time. The emphasis was not so much in inscribing the stage with
revivals of all things indigenous, thereby serving a nationalist agenda, but
to create a permeable thoroughfare where classics from Europe (historically the most "understood" and familiar of foreign cultures for the
Indian intelligentsia) could be brought into an Indian fold largely
through adaptations and, at times, direct translations, when adaptation
would not work. One can note in this choice of plays among the urban
Bengali theater makers an anxiety about (often expressing itself as a resistance to) defining one's own culture in terms of a singular point of orig-

ination. The effort was not merely to make theater "Indian," but rather
to broaden the scope of "Indian" theater by infusing it with importations
from the outside; to create a new "Indian" theater that would at one and
the same stroke be an internationalist theater, an intercultural enterprise
that celebrated hybridity and spoke to a society that dealt with both East
and West at every level of sociocultural engagement and interaction.
This has been a steady trait of Bengali progressive theater from the earliest days of the Group Theatre movement, even through the 1970s and
1980s, when most of Indian theater was engaged in what has been
labeled the "Theatre of Roots." While the nationwide Theatre of Roots
movement sought to fashion a national identity in the reinscription of
indigenous forms of theater under the modernist light, Bengali theater,
with a few exceptions, functioned in isolation and continued to work
within the scope of hybrid formations that brought East and West
together. The Bengali Group Theatre has always placed the responsibility of reflecting its own times politically before choosing or inventing
the most appropriate form for it; whether that "form" was indigenous to
the soil or foreign has seldom been an important consideration. Identity,
when sought in Bengali theater, has never been a formalist project, but
rather a derivative undertaking that has been inclusive of India's
encounter with the West as part of its history, where identity and difference have been configured, if not always reconciled peaceably, within
historical exigencies.[14]

We had noticed similar cultural ideals informing the IPTA productions. But with the Group Theatre movement it went a step further.
Not encumbered with the responsibility of being of the itinerant type
(unlike the IPTA troupes), the Group Theatre could revel in imbibing
Western forms and styles of the proscenium stage. The "avant-garde"
they were creating was a reaction not against Western-style theater, but
rather the commercial, apolitical, ideology-less theater of old Kolkata.
Consequently, neither the proscenium stage nor the Western plays being
produced were part of the problem. The point of contention was to create a theater that went beyond entertainment and appealed to the intel-
lect of the audience, weaned them away from commercial fluff, and gave
theater a definite political function of creating awareness. The other
purpose that went side by side with the political goal was to create
worthwhile art in direct opposition to the frivolous entertainment of the
commercial public theaters. It was a reaction against Bengali theater of
yesteryear that had itself turned into an institution. The "avant-garde"
thrust of the Group Theatre was, thus, more about jettisoning bad art

and less about forming/informing cultural identity. The IPTA had laid the foundations for this move; the Group Theatre shaped it.

Heirs of the IPTA, Masters of the Group Theatre

Sombhu Mitra

Among the Group Theatre stalwarts to emerge from the IPTA was Sombhu Mitra (1914–97), who first appeared on the Bengali stage as an actor in the commercial public theater circuit around World War II. After a few years of circulating among various theater companies, he joined the IPTA in 1948, where he emerged also as a director. In 1951, after breaking with the IPTA, Mitra formed his own theater group, Bahurp, where his genius came to fruition. In 1952, Mitra directed a highly successful production of a Bengali adaptation of Ibsen's *An Enemy of the People* (which he revived several times in his career) and then a completely localized *A Doll's House* in 1958. But all the while, Mitra was locating himself between cultures, trying to find his bearings, scuttling between the theatrical masterpieces of the West and a search for an Indian way of doing theater, and disavowing the modes of naturalism as the only form of theatrical expression. He believed that

> [a]cting should attune itself to express naturally the poetry of passions—the language of poetry. It cannot be accomplished through a naturalistic style alone. We must find a way to pass easily from the naturalistic plane to the subjective. Exterior and interior life should rub shoulders with each other and remain organically related.[15]

Between the two Ibsen productions he took on a new challenge— Rabindranath Tagore (1860–1941). No one, until then, had been able to stage Tagore successfully in a public theater. In fact, the Bengali public theater had practically rejected Tagore as "unplayable." Mitra disagreed. In 1956, he directed Bahurp's production of Tagore's symbolic play *Raktakarabī (Red Oleanders),* which dealt with the tyrannical oppression of workers stuck in a "no exit" gold mine, deep in the entrails of the earth, by a King who remains mostly unseen in the play and is present only as a disembodied voice until the very last moment in the play when he breaks out of himself to cast the first stone at his own tyrannical image. With *Raktakarabī* Sombhu Mitra had appeared as a theater visionary—throwing open doors for Bengali theater that had until then

seemed uninfringeable. In the years to come, Mitra successfully produced other plays of Tagore.

Writing much later about his production of *Raktakarabī*, Sombhu
Mitra said something about his mode of operation as a theater artist that
qualifies the universalist and intercultural propensities of the Bengali
Group Theatre movement:

> The language of art is often compared to the language of lovers. It is
> an intimate language, very open, and one that can touch the inner-
> most parts of one's core. Where little is said but more understood.
>
> But for this [to happen] the artist and the audience need to be
> bound each to each in a common melody. And what more cultural
> ground do they need beyond their shared heritage that ties their
> respective melodies to each other? [I]t is this shared heritage that gov-
> erns all our actions; even our ability to see, our feelings—what is also
> known as "worldview." And it is always from this estimation that a
> performance artist manages to communicate his awareness of the con-
> temporary to the audience. Of course, the objective of the artist and
> the entrepreneur are the same in this regard, albeit with very different
> intentions. The results are different, too. And the rest depends on the
> audience. On society. What will they opt for—the diamond or the
> cut glass?[16]

The "common melody" for *Raktakarabī* was not to be found in a stylized mode of acting that was expected to accompany a nonrealistic, symbolic play. Rather, Mitra went for a very realistic style of acting that made
the symbolic world of the play "real" despite its unreality. He made it
"hyper"-real, turning Tagore's metaphoric underworld of the gold mine
into an identifiable reality, thereby reinforcing the deeper reality of the
oppressed human condition that Tagore had rendered in drama.

In 1964, Mitra made a unique move by producing, on consecutive
nights, Sophocles' *Oedipus Rex* (*Rājā Aydipāus* in Bengali) and Tagore's
Rājā (The King of the Dark Chamber), as part of Bahurūpī's festival of
"Plays of Darkness." The brochure for the festival described the project
in the following words: "This festival is about darkness that is so like
light, and light that so resembles darkness." He had made a philosophic
connection between Sophocles and Tagore and brought them under a
common umbrella, in his search for an "honest" theater that committed,
first and foremost, to its own time and functioned as a faithful mirror of

its visage. Mitra's experiment had made it clear that Bengali theater would have to find its voice at every step in hybridity, between forms as various and contradictory as the action-driven Sophoclean tragedy and the contemplative, poetic Tagore. Mitra's "Indian" theater would neither smack of xenophobia nor kowtow uncritically to all things European. While Mitra's reputation as the first successful producer of Tagore's plays was not questioned, the reviewers were not of one mind in their appraisals of his Bengali version of *Oedipus*. Many critics expressed their thankfulness to Mitra for this pioneering attempt at bringing Greek tragedy to the Bengali stage, or waxed eloquent about Mitra's ritualistic staging of the play—the choric chants, the prophecies of Tiresias—which transported the audience back to a primordial sense of morality, the Greek "logos," that governed all humanity. On the other side of the spectrum were many vociferous critics who did not hesitate to call the production an elitist project that was not very different from the commercial theaters in the admission it charged and the hollow rhetoric of spiritualism and divine destiny it served up. This was not, according to many critics, the kind of people's theater the Group Theatre ought to be producing.

Mitra, finding himself stranded between two plays, two cultures, wrote in 1965:

> The ancient heritage of India extends itself so deep into our lives that it is impossible to ignore it. However, an interceding age of darkness cut off that connection. We woke up to modern consciousness, shaken up by the British. It brought about a period of reawakening in our land. Since then there have been some who have managed to combine the two civilizations within their own selves, and they must command our respect. But that happy resolution has not trickled down into our collective inheritance. As a result, we are fated to be in pain, stalled as we are between the polar attractions. However, if we are to find the answer, we must do so in our own individual ways.[17]

But the criticism did stop Mitra from staying his course. Although he later came to denounce his own choice of producing Sophocles and Tagore back to back in the "Plays of Darkness" festival, the event had made (at least) a symbolic statement about the reality of Bengali theater—the postcolonial impasse of its two-pronged cultural allegiance, its hybridity.

Utpal Dutt

It was in the work of Utpal Dutt (1929–93) that the possibility and effect of the political theater IPTA had succeeded in introducing into the world of Bengali theater was truly felt. Though much younger than Mitra, Dutt was prodigiously prolific both as a playwright and director until his last day. Starting out in the English theater of Kolkata, Dutt joined the IPTA in its postindependence phase very briefly (for less than a year) in the early 1950s, but was very easily disenchanted:

> I was shocked by the extreme indiscipline. What theatre needs first of all is discipline—the discipline that would create a total work of art out of the scenic design, lights, acting.[18]

No wonder, Dutt was thrown out on account of being a Trotskyite, but not before he had acted and directed in several productions that included plays by Michael Madhusudan Dutt, Rabindranath Tagore, Girish Chandra Ghosh,[19] and even Shakespeare. Regardless of the volume of work he did for the IPTA in his short stint, there was no way in which Dutt could have executed his grand production schemes in the IPTA agit-prop setup. Having severed his ties with IPTA, Dutt pursued the commercial road, but with a different kind of theater—a repertory theater group that worked as a single unit in production after production, fighting tremendous financial odds, while never compromising on the productions themselves. Dutt often worked with huge sets and intricate designs, working on big budgets. Two of his best-known productions from this phase—*Angār* (*Charcoal,* 1959) and *Kallol* (*Waves,* 1965)—required a proscenium stage to provide the interiors of a coal mine (which floods, killing many), and a whole starboard of a ship, respectively. Although working outside party binds and dependent on commercial success, it was a theater with serious political intent. He declared in no uncertain terms:

> Revolutionary theatre must *preach* revolution; it must not only expose the system but also call for the violent smashing of the state machine.[20]

Toward the end of the 1960s Dutt expressed sympathy with the Maoist (and the banned) faction of the Communist Party, and after arrest and a short period of imprisonment, Dutt directed his talents toward the largely rural but immensely popular folk theater form of *jātrā*,[21] with the express intention of reaching a wider audience. "In the plays I wrote for the *jātrā*," Dutt said later, "I chose a clearly articulated agitational stance that only went to ensure the popularity of these productions."[22] Among his *jātrā* plays there is even a biography of Mao Tse-tung! After a ten-year engagement with *jātrā* and as many as nineteen *jātrā* plays, Dutt returned to the proscenium Group Theatre stage with his new group, the Peoples' Little Theatre (replacing the Little Theatre Group, which was not so "little" anymore and needed to reflect the aspirations of the people in the naming). Dutt's adventurous and innovative production style, his politicization of a generally entertainment-based theater, his attempt at reinvigorating folk forms, the school of acting he started, the number of actors he trained, the innumerable plays he wrote, his successful acting career in both Bengali and Hindi films—seem like the achievements of several individuals. But in Utpal Dutt, they came together as a staggering combination of versatility and talent. Dutt has written more than forty plays and in his heydays in the 1960s and 1970s, was one of the most controversial, yet prolific, directors working in the Bengali theater.[23]

But even while acknowledging Dutt's genius, one has to be critical of his work. And the pressing question in this regard is whether Dutt's theater provided Bengali theater with an "avant-garde" impetus that could transform it from the core. Did his rhetoric about what theater should be, often expressed ostentatiously in pamphlets, articles and interviews, match up with his productions, particularly in the Peoples' Little Theatre phase of the 1970s? According to Rustom Bharucha's conclusion at the time,

> At this stage in Dutt's enormously successful career, when his plays are regularly performed to packed houses, it is necessary to question his reliance on the entertainment provided by the commercial theatre to raise the revolutionary consciousness of the people. While I believe that it is necessary, even essential, for the revolutionary theatre to entertain, it can only do so with any integrity in the process of enlightening an audience. . . . Unfortunately, in most of Dutt's plays, the "learning," if any, is scarcely pleasurable while the "pleasure" provided by the entertainment of his plays clearly dominates the learning process.[24]

And that is where it stood for Dutt for the rest of the 1970s, particularly since the Left Front, led by the Communist Party of India (Marxist), was democratically voted into power in 1977, when Dutt seemed to give up any active pursuance of a revolutionary theater and settle for a rhetorically revolutionary theater that felt satisfied with patronage from the party and government.

Himani Banerjee contextualizes Dutt's work within the framework of the history of the Communist movement in India at large, and Bengal in particular:

> The CPI [Communist Party of India] before the split in 1964, and since then both CPI and CPI(M), have sought to interject a class perspective into a bourgeois democratic politics. They have structured themselves between the two strands of parliamentary democracy and the hope of an eventual communist revolution in the future. . . . Like them and his forerunners, the theorists and practitioners of the IPTA, Utpal Dutt also tries to negotiate between these two political positions. . . . . Utpal Dutt is in this a true heir of the IPTA.[25]

Ajitesh Banerjee

The third person after Mitra and Dutt who rocked the Bengali stage in the 1960s and 1970s was the youngest, Ajitesh Banerjee (1933–83), the founder-director of Nāndīkār. He, too, was a member of the IPTA for a short while, well after the days of *Nabānna,* and a card-holding member of the Communist Party for some time as well. While Mitra and Dutt spread their productional endeavors out between original and adapted plays, Banerjee was more invested in rearticulating masterpieces of the Western theater for the Bengali stage. His specialization was adaptations. In an essay written in English in 1978, just five years before his premature death at the age of fifty, Banerjee explained:

> The speciality [*sic*] of the Bengalees [is] that they live with the unique kind of individuality from the people living in other states of India. The flow of the classical Sanskrit plays is not [to] be found here. The Bengali plays have never taken anything worth mentioning from it. Rather the Bengali Theatre has developed itself from the admixture [of] folk and foreign theatre. Of course, the plays written by Rabindranath Tagore are glittering exceptions, but those are not that popular.[26]

In other words, like Mitra and Dutt before him, Banerjee too was looking to synthesize the cultural materials that were available to him. Like

Utpal Dutt, Banerjee dabbled with the *jātrā* as well, but only in the last few years of his life as a professional actor, not an innovator or a political interventionist. But his stage productions maintained a good bit of distance with the folk form. The one rare exception was his production that he called a "pālā," a word often used as a synonym for *jātrā*. This was a Bengali version of Eric Bentley's English translation of Bertolt Brecht's *Three Penny Opera*. Banerjee called it *Tin Paysār Pālā*.

Mounted in 1969, Banerjee's version turned Brecht's eighteenth-century London into late-nineteenth-century Kolkata, which was at that time one of the largest colonial cities built by the British. Kurt Weill's music, powered with Brecht's express agenda of using it as an agency of sociopolitical criticism, found new life in a musicscape that was a far cry from the normative styles on offer from the contemporary German commercial music industry. Banerjee's music, instead, was drawn from popular forms of Bengali folk music modified by his own creative interventions. The lyrics were molded along lines of popular nineteenth-century pulp doggerel. However, when one listens to Banerjee's versions of the Brecht-Weill songs, one can see a similar process of using the popular forms against themselves to drive home an unanticipated political message that did not necessarily suit the form, but the dexterous renditions made them so. Something similar had happened to the Brecht-Weill numbers too. Banerjee's capering version of "Mack the Knife" becomes:

ceṣṭā karle hāṅgarera dāṁt dekhte pābe,
kintu jakhan Mahin-bābur churiṭā jhalkābe:
    takhan dekhte pābe nā, pābe nā![27]

Roughly translated, it reads:

You can pry open a shark's mouth and see its tooth,
But when Mr. MacHeath flashes his knife in sooth:
    You won't see a thing, not a thing![28]

Banerjee's version of this song, in every verse, has one line less than Brecht's original. The lyrics being set to a brisker pace, Banerjee's version run at a quicker tempo, unlike Weill's drawn out, diatonic, somewhat plaintive rolling melody. The song was an instant hit in Kolkata when the play opened in 1969. And it continues to be sung with the same kind of fondness by today's Bengali theater-lovers. The play was a great popular success. And in this play, like some of Utpal Dutt's ventures earlier and later, Nāndīkār found commercial success as well. *Tin Paysār Pālā* was staged on the commercial stage on a regular basis for four days a week for quite a length of time, unlike most Group Theatre plays that were performed in the repertory style, with no more than three or four shows a month.

But it was the same popularity that raised the ire of scholarly critics, who blamed Banerjee for breaking the sacrosanct Brechtian rules of the epic theater. A critic, going by the initials "A.M.," from *Frontier,* a leading English-language journal, objected to it in the following words:

> Despite the Bengali text more or less following the original libretto, *Tin Paisar Pala* [sic] is more *Beggar's Opera* than *Die Dreigroschenoper.* The divergence is partly the product of attitude. . . . *Die Dreigroschenoper* is set to music in entirety . . . from the first overture to Macheath's final declamation, it is one integrated whole. [Banerjee's version] does not even attempt any such integration.[29]

But beyond the objection of *Tin Paysār Pālā*'s "form" lay a serious critique of its "content":

> Brecht sans social content amounts to nothing, and this is precisely what Ajitesh [Banerjee's] production almost succeeds in accomplishing. The gay abandon in Brecht is a façade for putting across biting social criticism. But in [*Tin Paysār Pālā*], all the endeavor is for embracing the façade.[30]

But there were others who saw what the production did for Bengali theater. Nemai Ghosh has been one of Bengali theater's most diligent chroniclers. In his recent album/memoirs on the Bengali Group Theatre, *Dramatic Moments,* he fondly (though no less observantly) remembers Ajitesh Banerjee's mise-en-scène for the Brecht play in its Bengali version. An exhaustive quotation seems to be in order. Banerjee's play

> broke away from the Bengali mainstream tradition of a theatre that privileged the well articulated use of the voice and facial expression over the expressive manipulation of the body—in its bold physicality, its celebration of the ugly and the vulgar, its shamelessly catchy tunes, its mockery of conventional morality, its critique of the institutions of law and order. In spite of, or maybe because of, the utterly disorga-

nized and cluttered look of the performance, the theatre seemed to inhabit an open space, which could at ease incorporate and/or transform itself into segments of an elaborate and intricate urban underworld, set in Calcutta in the 1870s, the city slang and the costumes and pointed references providing its locus in time. More than the subtitles on slides, or those inscribed on posters carried across the stage by crudely dancing footmen, it was the songs and recitatives and the acting style that played with and stripped down the typicality of the acts associated with cops and robbers, beggars and whores; allowing the audience insights into the mechanism of games and strategies that wove them into a social system—though the system appeared less political than Brecht read it.[31]

Between the academic position and that of the sympathetic admirer stands Banerjee's own account of his early encounter with Brecht, clarifying his beleaguered state of mind rather humorously.

> I had read a few English and Bengali essays on Brecht. They clarified nothing. The distinction between Stanislavsky's theater and Brecht's "epic" theatre (explained by means of a chart with a dividing line, with Stanislavsky on one side and Brecht on the other, like they distinguish between living and dead organisms in school biology textbooks) had not become the least bit coherent to me. On the contrary, I started to get befuddled about what little I knew of the Stanislavsky system without ever visiting Russia. As a matter of fact, I started to believe that since Brecht believed in Marxism, Marxist intellectuals were using their own muscle power in putting big labels on Brecht's methods and elevating him to a place far higher than he truly deserved.[32]

Whatever the case, Banerjee's Brecht had won the approbation of its audience. Brecht had gained access to a Bengali audience through him, or vice versa. Banerjee's version of Brecht, caught in the crossfire between pedantry and popular taste, demonstrates yet again the ambivalent nature of Bengali Group Theatre's articulation of its own schismed identity. With Nāndīkār, Banerjee also adapted/directed a Bengali version of *The Good Person of Szechuan*. Though not as successful as *Tin Paysār Pālā,* this production too had a brief professional run at the Rangan, a commercial theater in North Kolkata.

Banerjee was the first to bring not only Brecht, but also Pirandello and Chekhov to the Bengali stage—Pirandello's *Six Characters in Search of an Author* and *Enrico IV,* and all of Chekhov's one-act farces, *The Cherry Orchard,* and *The Seagull.* Toward the end of his short career he also staged memorable Bengali adaptations (his own) of Tolstoy's *The Power of Darkness* (1977) and Harold Pinter's *Birthday Party* (1982). In these plays, too, more so in the former, Ajitesh Banerjee was yet again tremendously successful in claiming a Bengali ownership over foreign plays. Having seen Banerjee's version of the Tolstoy play (he named it *Pāp-Punya,* literally *Sin and Virtue*) forty-two times as a teenager, I remember being utterly surprised upon learning, after the first performance I saw, that the play was originally written in Russian! Tolstoy's Christian morality tale, through a cultural dislocation, had found transcultural meaning as Nikita's confession of sin lost its Christian significance and became Niti's act of human courage, the moral power one needs to confess one's guilt before an audience, and the relief of unburdening that follows.

Just before his untimely demise at the age of fifty, Ajitesh Banerjee gave Bengali theater the first taste of Peter Weiss and finally, Harold Pinter, through his adaptations of *Marat/Sade* and *The Birthday Party.* While *Marat/Sade* (Banerjee's version was *Ekti Rājnaitik Hatyā, A Political Assassination*) was produced by a local theater school and did not have a long run, the Pinter play (Banerjee's version was *Tetriśtama Janmadibas, The 33rd Birthday*) continued to be performed posthumously. In both productions, Banerjee, once again, displayed his consummate skills of adaptation. Both these plays are ostensibly "unworkable" within a Bengali milieu. But Banerjee somehow found a way. With *Marat/Sade,* he enhanced Weiss's already complex conceit of the play-within-a-play (Sade playing himself with other inmate/actors playing the leaders of the Revolution) by turning Sade's asylum into a contemporary asylum in Kolkata where an inmate with a theatrical bent of mind chooses to direct Weiss's *Marat/Sade* in Bengali. In Banerjee's version the play is interrupted several times by the inmate-actors who want to return from the world of the French Revolution (all too alien for many of them) to their own surroundings. This adaptation of Weiss's already inventive device made the play ring with a contemporaneity that a straight translation (of which there has been at least one) would never have captured. In this production, too, Banerjee wrote songs that continue to be sung fondly in the Bengali theater world. With the Pinter play, however, Banerjee wanted to deal a blow to a complacent audience with a taste of Pinter's absurdism. Here again, Banerjee adapted the characters into Bengali with the dialogue and all other trimmings, but he made no attempt at making Pinter's play any easier. Huge controversies raged over the production, with letters to newspapers and catcalls in the auditoriums, so much so that Banerjee had to come up with a long explanatory note in a special playbill issued after the first few shows. Written under the nom de plume of a supposed audience member who seemingly has understood the play, it was a clever way of trying to get the Bengali audience to appreciate the play without diluting the production itself. However, despite Banerjee's best efforts, reviewers were not conciliated. But Banerjee, even in ruffling the feathers of a snug and smug audience, had not relented from his project and once again had made his point about Bengali theater's concord with world theater.

Group Theatre: Beyond the Triumvirate

The Group Theatre scene changed in the late 1970s and early 1980s. After years of being aligned with the opposition left-wing parties, the Group Theatre movement suddenly found itself close to the seat of political authority when the Communist Party of India came to power with the Marxist-led Left Front government in West Bengal. In short, the Group Theatre movement graduated from being a voice of opposition to being champions of the ruling party in the state legislature. The party courted the theater groups to do propaganda performances during elections, not on ideological grounds alone, but now in exchange of generous funding and favored access to state-owned auditoriums. The late 1980s complicated the situation further when the Left Front government, in response to the demise of the Soviet bloc, decided to "liberalize" its economic policies and volte-faced to the capitalist mode, while paying lip service nonetheless to Marxism. West Bengal's Group Theatre had to respond to that change, too. In a quizzical return to a commercially oriented theater, the Bengali Group Theatre has betrayed its own original cause. Most groups in Kolkata, notwithstanding several exceptions, have now turned to producing "hit" plays that sell tickets: easy-to-consume, predictable, unadventurous plays. There is little, if any, attempt to experiment or even explore newer, thought-provoking styles. The Group Theatre of Kolkata has stopped asking questions. Instead, what is becoming readily apparent is that there is little difference now between what used to be the commercial theater and the Group Theatre. In fact, one could cogently argue today that the Group Theatre has replaced the commercial theater. It has *become* a commercial theater.

Consequently, things that marked the commercial theater— high histrionics, melodrama, razzle-dazzle special effects, et cetera—have now
come to characterize all of Kolkata's Bengali theater as such. The
Kolkata Group Theatre has lost the battle it once waged. And the irony
of it all is that it has lost the battle to itself. The same actors and directors
who had once thought seriously about the social and political service
that the theater could perform are now more interested in financial success and fame, while paying lip service to a utopian socialism that really
does not exist anymore outside the name and insignia of the ruling party.

The reasons behind this are many. For one, there is the climate of
international consumerism, the logic of late capitalism riding the high
tide of the global collapse of Marxism as an alternate ideology. Yet what
makes the situation so very strange is that Kolkata's Group Theatre, very
like the Left Front government (in power now for twenty-two years)
continues, willy-nilly, to give lip service to Marxism. Many older the-
ater-workers now lament the sad passing of the exciting days of the
IPTA and the glorious age of Sombhu Mitra, Utpal Dutt, and Ajitesh
Banerjee. Ajitesh Banerjee died within five years of the Left Front's
coming into power, well before the dismantling of the Marxist regimes
in Russia and Eastern Europe. Sombhu Mitra retired soon after the Left
Front was voted in. But Utpal Dutt, once rejected by the Communist
Party as a Trotskyite and later for being a Maoist, became a champion of
the Left Front regime soon after its coming to power. The radical politics that had so energized and marked his theater through the 1950s,
1960s, and 1970s were watered down in the 1980s and early 1990s (until
his death in 1993) into an almost puerile custodial defense of post-USSR
Marxism. His last plays were *Kruśbiddha Kiubā (Cuba Crucified)* and *Lāl
Durga (The Red Bastion)*. While the first was a desperate defense of Cuba
in the post-cold-war era, the second (the last play Dutt wrote) was a glo-
rifying portrayal of the last days of Nicolae Ceauşescu and his police state
in Romania.

The death of the Bengali Group Theatre, thus, is intrinsically linked
to the demise of ideology. In sharp contrast to its refusal to genuflect
before party agendas in the early 1950s, after the so-called Left Front
government was voted into power, the Group Theatre sought protection and patronage from the very same party it had once chosen to steer
clear of. Sombhu Mitra and Ajitesh Banerjee may have been exceptions
to that pattern, but their careers were truncated respectively by volun-
tary retirement and untimely passing. The other exception is Badal Sircar (b. 1925), who started by writing plays for the proscenium

stage–bound Group Theatre, but realized soon that a true people's theater needed to be free as much from party mandates as the consumer capitalist market. He started out as a town and regional planning engineer and spent several years in Africa. His career as a playwright began in the 1950s, and by the 1960s he was established as a major new playwright. During this phase of his career Sircar wrote his best plays for the proscenium stage—*Ebaṅg Indrajit, Sārā Rāttir, Bāki Itihās, Pāglā Ghoṛā,* and *Jadi Ār Ekbār.* Late in the 1960s, Sircar realized that theater would need to step out of the consumerist catch-22. With his group Shatābdi (est. 1967), Sircar started in the early 1970s what he christened the "Third Theatre" movement in West Bengal—"First" being the commercial public theater, and "Second" group theaters. Sircar's Third Theatre broke away both from the commercial and the Group Theatre by being "free" in form as well as finance. His was a kind of "poor" theater that rejected money as a means of "buying" theater. Sircar's theater could not be bought, it had to be partaken of; it could not be merely witnessed in a dark auditorium, it had to be participated in.

> Content is the heart of Third Theatre; it is not its purpose to discover a style and preach it. But in order to deliver a subject to the audience—with depth, intensity, and effectiveness—one cannot but look for new styles, and experiment. Not to choose a subject for the sake of style, but rather to find the right style for the subject.[33]

In his Third Theatre phase, Badal Sircar has produced plays like *Michil, Bhomā,* and *Spartacus* that have earned their place in Bengali drama. The septuagenarian Sircar celebrates the demise of Bengali proscenium theater and the death of ideology with an ever-vigilant eye to allow theater to do what it is supposed to do—ask questions. It is not the middle-class intelligentsia's vanguardist onus to speak for the subaltern, to be the ventriloquist-actor. Badal Sircar sets a different task for the theater worker:

> It is not the last word of Third Theatre that the educated middle-class person will, in his spare time, make theater and take it to villages and slums—village folks, factory folks, slum dwellers, will themselves create theater out of their own lives, and show it to people like themselves.[34]

Consequently, Sircar's Third Theatre has attempted to find both its audiences and actors within the same community, though not always successfully. Many of his actors, although performing in open spaces, amid the working classes, for the working classes, still hail from the conscientious middle class. Not simply answered and revealing itself as a complex, contradictory set of issues, the question remains: *Can the subaltern perform?* Does Third Theatre really do what Badal Sircar professes? Who determines what the subaltern masses would like to see or perform for themselves? Is not the very act of prophesying that the subaltern will perform for themselves essentially an act of the same vanguardist intervention that so marked the IPTA project—the urban intellectual spelling out an oracle for the subaltern, as a party organ or otherwise?

Sircar's concern about the disparity between a middle-class theater and middle class workers, one the one hand, and the spectators in villages and slums they want to address, on the other, illuminates one of the central questions of the "avant-garde," or at least of that very strong part of the "avant-garde" that committed the practices of a "new art" toward a direct political interaction with a certain community, namely its audience. This question is still, at different levels of understanding, central to the ideals and practices of community-based theater today both inside and outside India, and one of the issues that highlights—through questions, conundrums, and contradictions—how innovative, how "avant-garde" this movement is.

The problem with the "avant-garde" Bengali theater of the 1940s began when it undertook the project of becoming a catalytic agent between the subaltern masses and the intellectual literati. In the IPTA movement at the time of its birth that catalyst seemed to work, but thereafter it claimed for itself a semiotic excess, an overdetermination of political meaning that got caught in its own rhetoric. The rhetorical spin ended with the global crash of Marxist ideology (insofar as it was represented in the rapid dismantling of the Communist bloc of Eastern Europe), and the decay of Socialist politics in West Bengal, as marked particularly by the dissimulation of the current regime. As Himani Banerjee puts it with remarkable lucidity:

> Given the middle class or petty bourgeois nature of representation in Indian Marxism and communism (both of theory and practice), given the anti-democratic nature of vanguardism and centralism espoused by the communist parties in a non-revolutionary and electoral context, and, finally, given the petty bourgeois nature of the nationalism of Indian de-colonization, there is always the danger of revolutionary intentions and projects sliding into counter-revolution.[35]

Consequently, the progressive, political, left-inclined theater of West Bengal has hit a crisis under which it continues to reel. It cannot define itself with the ideological and moral clarity it achieved for many years. Is there a way out? How can Bengali theater survive this ideological catachresis? The questions are numerous and vexing, and the answers without problems do not seem to be forthcoming. The search will need to go on. The case will need to be reopened. The interrogations need to begin over.

Epilogue

December 2002. I am having a conversation with Suman Mukherjee (b. 1966), one of Kolkata's leading younger directors who has come to the forefront with three new productions back-to-back that are causing theater makers to rethink the role of theater in a Bengal bereft of ideological backbone. Suman Mukherjee's group, Chetana (a thirty-year-old group started by Suman's father, Arun Mukherjee), although still operating within the Group Theatre repertory mode,[36] has offset financial losses with the help of grants, subsidies, and corner-cutting and continues to put up plays. Since 1999, Mukherjee has mounted three productions that have moved and shaken Bengali theater out of its self-righteousness: *Tistāpārer Bṛttānta* (*Tales from the Banks of the Tistā,* 2000) based on a Bengali novel by Debesh Roy, *Mephisto* (2002), a translation of Arianne Mnouchkine's stage adaptation of Klaus Mann's novel, and *Samay Asamayer Bṛttānta* (*Tales of Times-Betimes,* 2003) also adapted from a Debesh Roy novel. What Suman has demonstrated in all three productions, particularly in the *bṛttānta* plays, is that regardless of the many limitations of the Group Theatre system, it is still possible, with incisive imagination and creative managerial skills, to mount plays that can make people think beyond the two boxes that have held Bengali theater in thrall—the ideological and the commercial. Mukherjee's productions, in synch with experimental theatrical practices around the world, are rich in their complexities and reveal the politics of class, culture, and creed in a textured staging that makes an audience think. Productionally, too, Mukherjee, along with his first-time designer, (longtime visual artist and architect) Hiran Mitra, has pushed the confines of seriously delimiting proscenium spaces to create images that linger in the mind and speak in unison with the textual voice of the play. In both the *bṛttānta* plays, for example, Mukherjee and Mitra use shipping ropes hung before the cyclorama, top to bottom. But while in *Tistāpārer Bṛttānta* the rope is hung in a huge loop that swings from time to time, symbolizing the bellowing river Tist whose tales are told by the play, in *Samay Asamayer Bṛttānta* it hangs more like a hangman's rope, which the subaltern "subject/object" of the play (I hesitate to say, "protagonist"), Kelu, climbs in contorted Butoh-like movements.

Ruminating on the future of Bengali theater, Suman tells me, "We have to give a very new problematic to the Bengali theater." He feels that with *Samay Asamayer Bṛttānta,* his theater has reached a moment of crisis where it must perforce break away from its own binding history. I ask in this regard, "Is this then an 'avant-garde' that you are looking for?" Mukherjee smiles mildly even as he retorts, "I think the term *avant-garde* means something very different in the [Euro-American] context. It is born [of] a certain historical moment and carries symptoms of changing perspectives about art and society in postwar Europe. If we 'look through' it to [examine] Bengali theater, by the same parameters of European or [the American] 'avant-garde,' we will miss the fundamental problematic. We have to change our lens, exposure, and the initial raw stock. There will be a closure if we try to perceive the term within the same table of contents and glossary. Jean Paul Sartre coined this word in 1948. What were we doing during the forties? We were just out of the rule of our colonial masters. We were facing disasters like communal riots and *deś bhāg* [partition of India and the resultant creation of East Pakistan out of East Bengal]. We have to coin our own definition of avant-garde."[37]

Do we? Is the "avant-garde" not a universal, free-floating signifier then, as we had hoped to denote at the onset of the essay? Bibhas Chakrabarti, a noted senior theater director in Kolkata, a disciple of Ajitesh Banerjee, had told me something similar in an interview: "We do not need the term *avant-garde* because the term does not define the impulses in our theater. At best, we can talk about avant-gardist moments in our theater where newer forms of theater have, in rebellion, replaced the old ones." But I am not entirely convinced that the term *avant-garde* has not made its way into Bengali theater parlance simply because it is useless. Given the long tradition of intellectual familiarity with Euro-American dogma and dicta, I cannot wholly concur with Mukherjee's or Chakrabarti's position that the Bengali intelligentsia have no use for the term. The reason must lie elsewhere.

While I partially acknowledge the view that the term may not have been specifically useful to define a moment or moments in the history of Bengali theater, perhaps it is also true that Bengali theater has been accommodative in spirit and has not truly experienced a crisis that has forced an epistemic and teleological break to happen within its own bounds. Is it possible that the fancy experimentation that "avant-garde" implied, with space and form, never sat well with the general atmosphere of conservatism in which Bengali theater operated, even while it experimented? That the experiments were mostly confined to "content," not so much about "form" and even less about "space"? I say this because, other than the marginal(ized) attempt of Badal Sircar and a few other theater artists who chose to break away from the spatial configuration of the proscenium and the moribund modus operandi of the Group Theatre system, most of the changes seen in Bengali theater have been at the textual level. The changes that we have seen at the productional level have seldom, if at all, crossed the apron of the proscenium arch. Could "space" (or the limitations thereof) then be a frontier that has not been charted fully by Bengali theater and has been its undoing? Add to this the intersecting and complex problems of managing the economics, the farsightedness (or the lack thereof) of envisaging a theatrical space beyond the fourth wall, an audience that would embrace spatial experiments and patronize them (and not jeer at an experimental version of Pinter, say).

One look at the theater scene in other parts of India will give a quick slide-show of how theater makers in other regions of the country have bravely, often with the direct encouragement of an audience, experimented with form and space. That does not seem to be the case with Bengal. While sloganeering Marxist politics—accommodating itself between the uncomfortable nodes of a liberal democracy and nonexistent dreams of a socialist utopia—has always galvanized the content of Bengali theater and has been used to counter its (so-called) entertaining commercial sibling, the conclusion now seems to be set in an unseemly circumstance, where "slogans" and political postulations are commodified, peddling ware as well. The gulling dream collapsed with the Soviet Bloc, and its ruins, too, are being razed to a flat terrain by the dread wheels of neoimperial global capitalism.

This pushes us further toward solidifying a reading of the Kolkata-based Bengali progressive theater following World War II, the postindependence era, as a theater of, by, and for the middle class, which has always preferred and believed in the hollow doggerel of vanguardist "political" theater. The "desire" to connect with the masses has seldom been more genuine than the fantasy of doing so without ever actually acting on it.

The notion of a free-floating, ahistorical "avant-garde," then, is, indeed, worthless. Perhaps, impossible, too. Perhaps the "moment of crisis" that Suman Mukherjee has identified in his own theater is a crisis to be shared by all practitioners of the art in contemporary Kolkata. A breakage must be imminent. The modus operandi of the Group Theatre system is fast proving impossible to work with. The limits of tolerance have been tested. The moment of catachresis looms large. And what shall we call it? Surely, not an/the "avant-garde"!

Notes

1. In 2001, the state government of West Bengal changed the official name of the city of Calcutta to Kolkata. Calcutta was the name the British gave to the city that was known as *Kalikātā* in nineteenth-century formal parlance. *Kolkata* is the colloquial version of *Kalikātā*. I have consistently spelt the name as *Kolkata* in this essay, without the diacritical marks.

The Bengali language, as it is spoken, presents a big problem when it comes to spelling words in the Roman script, since Bengali pronunciation often has very little to do with its system of spelling, which is predominantly Sanskṛt-based. There are several sounds in Sanskṛt that are not pronounced in Bengali but faithfully rendered, nevertheless, in the written form. This causes a great deal of confusion when one has to transliterate Bengali words into Roman script. For the sake of expedience, all names of all individuals in this essay have been spelt the way in which the persons themselves spelt them in public life when writing in English. When not sure of how they wrote their names in English, I have settled for the spellings commonly used for those names in Indian English. All names of plays and other Bengali words have been spelt with the standard international system of diacritical marks used in transliterating words from any Sanskṛt-based South Asian language.

All translations from Bengali sources used in this essay are mine, unless otherwise indicated.

2. Gary Garrels, *Avant Garde,* in the notes section for an exhibition published on the Internet at http://www.guggenheimcollection.org/site/concept_AvantGarde.html (New York: Guggenheim Museum, 2003).

3. Ibid.

4. I am invoking the term *hybridity* here more or less in the way in which Homi K. Bhabha defines it. Bhabha defines the colonial subject's "desire" for mimicry as one for a "reformed, recognizable Other, as a subject of a difference that is almost the same, but not quite" (*The Location of Culture* [London: Routledge, 1994], 126). "Hybridity," according to him,

> unsettles the mimetic and narcissistic demands of colonial power but reimplicates its identifications in strategies of subversion that turn the gaze of the discriminated back upon the eye of the power. For the colonial hybrid is the articulation of the ambivalent space where the rite of power is enacted on the site of desire, making its objects at once disciplinary and disseminatory—or, in my mixed metaphor, a negative transparency.

Bhabha, *Of Mimicry and Man: The Ambivalence of Colonial Discourse*, October, no. 28, Spring, London, 1986, 173.

The Bengali theater of the nineteenth century exemplified Bhabha's "negative transparency"—something that one can *look at* and *look through*, at one and the same time. What I have tried to argue in the rest of this essay is that Bengali theater of the twentieth century, still working under the tense negotiations with the postcolonial legacy, continues to function in the same way, albeit under significantly different conditions and political, historical, social, and cultural exigencies. The mode of negotiations has changed while the act of negotiation continues, as the hybridity moves toward developing its own singular character.

5. The word *bābu* is used in almost all languages in the Indian subcontinent. The etymology of the word, however, is obscure. Most lexicographers have identified it as having originated out of the Saṅskṛt *bipra*, to *bapra* or *bapt*. Some scholars believe that *bābu* came from the Prakrit *bāpu*, having undergone a consonant shift whereby the "p" became a "b." It is suspected that the word became a signifier of social status only in the eighteenth century. Initially signifying the person addressed to be a landowner, by the end of the century it had became an honorific prefix or suffix to denote the economically privileged, i.e., the *jamidār*s. With the passing of time the prefix softened even further to denote educated men even from the middle class. Some historians, however, have conjectured that the word is actually a Bengali corruption of the English *baboon*, which the colonizers used to identify their subjects and to whose pejorative signification the natives had no access. But this last theory is yet to be substantiated with concrete evidence.

6. Muzaffar Ahmed, a leading Marxist thinker and leader from the early days of the Communist Party, wrote as early as in 1927, creating room for a political discourse that probably eluded the Indian nationalists themselves: "[The] Indian nationalist movement itself is dependent on a struggle between classes. The conflicts between feudals and the new bourgeoisie that have caused a flood of revolutions in Europe—indeed, the greatest example of which is the French Revolution—have never taken place in India largely due to the arrival of the British. . . . From this one can conclude that the nationalist movement [in India] cannot simply be a struggle for independence from British rule, but one from feudalism as well." Muzaffar Ahmed, *Śreṇīsaṅgrām* [Class Struggle], 1926, in *Bāṅgālir Sāmyabād Carcā* [The Practice of Communist Thought among Bengalis], ed. Śiprā Sarkār and Anamitra Dāś (Kolkata: Ānanda Publishers, 1998), 86.

7. The term *agit-prop* derives from the short agitational sketches that were performed under the aegis of the Soviet Communist Party's Agitation and Propaganda Department to inspire the Red Army during the Revolution. In 1918, Vsevolod Meyerhold, the constructivist, had severed ties with the conventions of the bourgeois theater when he produced Vladimir Mayakovsky's *Mystery Bouffe* on the streets of Moscow—combining elements of the tent show with revolutionary poetry—to celebrate the anniversary of the October Revolution to an audience of several thousand. What Meyerhold started became an omnipresent activity in the postrevolutionary Soviet Union. Intended to inculcate and promote an awareness of the Revolution (its history and function) among the masses, its many forms (palaces of culture, use of agitation trains and cars, poster campaigns, and the countless agitation centers, or *agitpunkts*) and performed at factory gates, streets, dockyards, playgrounds, barnyards, and other public places,

served as a powerful means of politically educating the population at large. The agit-prop movement was a vibrant element of popular political theater in the Soviet Union of the 1920s and 1930s. It soon spread throughout the West, aided in most instances by local Communist parties. The IPTA had adopted this strategy of mobilizing masses along lines of the Communist Party's ideology on the cultural front through the reinvestment of various indigenous forms of performance. IPTA's "agit-prop" was Soviet-style in intent, but more proselytizing in nature, because, unlike the Soviet Union, India was prerevolutionary, and there agit-prop was a cultural practice meant to help generate the revolution. The revolution failed to arrive, but the approach lived on to midwife a distinctive style of the progressive ideology-based (or, at least, ideology-laced) Bengali Group Theatre.

8. Sombhu Mitra, "On *Nabānna*" (1978), in *Saṅgsṛti,* August 2000, 14–15.

9. Malini Bhattacharya, "The Indian People's Theatre Association: A Preliminary Sketch of the Movement and Organization, 1942–47," *Sangeet Katak* 94 (1989): 19.

10. Sobha Sen, *Smaraṅe Bismaraṅe Nabānna theke Lāl Durga* [In Remembrance and Oblivion: From *Nabānna* to *Lāl Durga*] (Kolkata: MC Sarkr & Sons, 1993).

11. As an interesting aside, it is worth noting, as Sudhi Pradhan, participant-historian of the IPTA, and citing him Rustom Bharucha, have pointed out that ideological or political commitment to the cause of the IPTA or the Communist Party was not the singular reason why young artists joined the movement. "[T]he advent of the IPTA coincided with their most vulnerable, yet most intense discovery of their emergent vocations" (Rustom Bharucha, *In the Name of the Secular: Contemporary Cultural Activism in India* [Delhi: Oxford University Press, 1998], 47). Pradhan confirms that the IPTA, as "the only organization engaged in serious creative activity [at the time of the World War], . . . attracted ambitious artists with hardly any knowledge of Marxism or People's art" (qtd. in Bharucha, 47).

12. Bharucha, *Name of the Secular,* 45.

13. Ibid., 46.

14. This can be, and has been, read by non-Bengali critics of Bengali theater as a kind of Eurocentrism, a certain leaning toward Western aesthetics, and, by extension, seen (somewhat simplistically) as a kind of negation of the nationalist fashioning of an "Indian" identity that is uncontaminated by the West. This line of criticism, in turn, has made a number of major Bengali theater directors resolutely opposed to formal reinvestments of folk forms, leaving them affixed to the conventions of the one-side open proscenium stage at the cost of formal stagnation. This is dealt with in greater detail toward the end of the essay.

15. Sombhu Mitra, *Building from Tagore,* trans. Samik Banerjee, *Drama Review* 15.3 (1972): 204.

16. Sombhu Mitra, *Naṭak Raktakarabí* [Raktakarab: The Production] (Kolkata: MC Sarkār & Sons, 1995), 52–53.

17. Sombhu Mitra, *Sanmārga-Saparyā* [Worshipping the Way of Truth] (Kolkata: MC Sarkār & Sons, 1990).

18. Utpal Dutt, "An Interview with Samik Banerjee," *Contemporary Indian Theatre: Interviews with Playwrights and Directors* (New Delhi: Sangeet Natak Akademi, 1989), 12.

19. While Tagore, by now, is a familiar name to the reader, the names of Michael Madhusudan Dutt (1824–73) and Girish Chandra Ghosh (1844–1912) may not be. Dutt and Ghosh were the two major Bengali playwrights of the nineteenth century. Ghosh

was also a legendary regisseur-director-actor in the late-nineteenth-century commercial theater, while Michael was the first consummate Western-style dramatist in Bengali.

20. Utpal Dutt, "Theatre as a Weapon," *Drama Review* 15.3 (1971): 225.

21. The *jātrā* is a three-sided open indigenous folk theater form with audience members sitting on all three sides. It is performed still (though the style has evolved quite a bit), mainly in the Eastern Indian states of Bengal, Assam, and Orissa. Traditionally, its performance space *(rangabhūmi)* is a square area built under a temporary canopy *(sabhā-maṇḍap)* covering the entire audience-performer area. This is connected by a narrow pathway to the dressing room *(sāj ghar),* which also provides a back wall. The actors use the path to enter the performance space, often with great dramatic flourish. *Jātrā* plays depend heavily on music, songs, and lyrical dialogue. The acting, never meant to be realistic, is often high strung and the plays sentimental. A *jātrā* play could last an entire night.

22. Dutt, "Interview with Samik Banerjee," 16.

23. See Himani Banerjee and Rustom Bharucha, *Rehearsals of Revolution: The Political Theater of Bengal* (Honolulu: University of Hawaii Press, 1983) for more detailed discussions of Utpal Dutt's works.

24. Banerjee and Bharucha, *Rehearsals of Revolution,* 121–22.

25. Himani Banerjee, *The Mirror of Class: Essays on Bengali Theatre* (Kolkata: Papyrus, 1998), 79.

26. Ajitesh Banerjee, *Ajiteś Bandyopādhyāyer Nirbācita Prabandha Saṅgraha* [Collected Essays of Ajitesh Banerjee] (Kolkata: Nāṭyacintā, 1998), 100.

27. Rudraprasad Sengupta and Ajitesh Banerjee, *Naāndīkaar Trayī* [The Nāndikār Triad] (Kolkata: Jatiya Sahitya Parishad, 1972), 109.

28. Compare with John Willet, ed., "The Crimes of Mac the Knife," in *Bertolt Brecht: Poems & Songs from the Plays* (London: Methuen, 1990), 66.

29. A.M., "Brecht in Bengali," in *Saṅgsṛti,* August 2000, 203–4.

30. Ibid., 204.

31. Nemai Ghosh, *Dramatic Moments: Photographs and Memories of Calcutta Theatre from the Sixties to the Nineties* (Kolkata: Seagull Books, 2000), 71–72.

32. Banerjee, *Ajiteś Bandyopādhyāyer Nirbāchita Prabandha Saṅgraha,* 87–88.

33. Badal Sircar, *Tṛtīya Thieṭārer Bāṅglā Darśak* [Bengali Audiences of the Third Theatre] in *S.A.S.: Collected Essays,* ed. Sātya Bhāduri (Kolkata: Naba Grantha Kuir, 1996), 159.

34. Ibid., 160.

35. Banerjee, *The Mirror of Class,* 24.

36. In this system, which has been the modus operandi for group theaters for a while (deriving from the amateur practice), a group rents various spaces a few times a month and moves in and out the same day, building and striking the sets every time. This system is not cost-effective and never has been. Yet this is how group theater has survived in Kolkata for many years. Typically, a group mounting a production in this way puts in its own money (usually borrowed) to raise the production costs and hopes for the production to receive good notices. If it does, the play gets "call" shows where a social or cultural club invites the group to mount the play for a fee. The money made from the fee, in turn, feeds the "hall" shows that the group continues to mount. Casually referred to as the "hall show/call show" system, in this style of operation, the production either stays in repertory or dies, depending on the whims of commerce. It is becoming progressively harder for group theaters to operate in this fashion as the costs of production

have escalated astronomically in recent years and the number of "call" shows are seldom commensurate with the "hall" shows. However, the run system on which the commercial theaters worked (like their Euro-American counterparts) has also proved to be ineffective business strategy. The situation has been further complicated by the rise of middle-class entertainment, the daily TV serials, soaps, and sit-coms. People have less time for theater, in a society where theatergoing has never really been a cultural tradition.

37. Suman Mukherjee, interview by the author, December 2002.

From Liminality to Ideology
The Politics of Embodiment in
Prewar Avant-Garde Theater in Japan

Peter Eckersall

The aim of the avant-garde is nothing less than to bring about a revolution of everyday life by aesthetic means—to transform the modern world. This essay will examine the conditions for Japan's avant-garde theater before World War II. A central theme of my examination will be the experience of embodiment, an active and visceral experience of the flesh in motion that is both essential to the theater experience as a whole and, when the politics of corporeality are brought into play, for example, of special importance in Japan. The avant-garde sensibility was and continues to be a fragile one in the context of Japan's historical landscape, yet one that is ineluctably associated with ideas of cultural exploration, freedom, and above all, resistance to authoritarian forces. In the postwar period this is figured in the rise of a second wave of avant-garde theater tied to the counterculture and student protest movements in the 1960s. In the prewar era, the avant-garde's cultural antagonist was rising militarism (that dystopian strand of the experience of modernity). In the course of their struggle, the avant-garde theater moved from exploring the body as a site of selfhood *(shutaisei)* to transforming itself into a quasi-socialist, social-realist vanguard force that came to reject its own historical formations.

That Japan's experience of modernity is an occurrence of singular intensity is widely acknowledged. The nascent avant-garde sensibility in art and culture that arose in Japan during the 1920s and 1930s followed several decades during which the processes of modernization were absorbed, translated, and refigured. The Meiji Restoration (1868) that saw Japan's reversal of its two-hundred-year-old policy of national isolation *(sakoku)* marked the onset of this period of change that began in earnest in the 1890s and accelerated in the early twentieth century.[1] Newly established institutions and procedures in Japan's governmental, social, cultural, economic, and educational spheres brought about a series of upheavals designed to bring Japan out of feudal decline and transform it into a global force (or at least in the initial impetus, a nation that could resist colonization). Debates about the processes of modernization in Japan constitute a cornerstone of Japanese history in the twentieth century. What scholars have sometimes identified as the "incomplete development of modernity"[2]—a perhaps overly negative description of the intensity and fragmentation of Japan's development—also has led Japan into a fascinating alternative experience of modernity, one that is fractured, contradictory, and contested. This fragmented and transitory experience of modernity has served as a powerful source of material for Japanese avant-garde artists—an ironic complexity when one considers that the avant-garde is the movement that in its wider sense offers the promise of a corrective to modernism's dystopic history.

The avant-garde in Japan is a force of conviction and energy extending beyond its small number of adherents and in counterpoint to dominant forms of cultural production. Although created following direct contact with avant-garde artists in Europe and allied to European cultural experience through its mediation by cosmopolitan elites in Japan, politics and praxis caused the Japanese avant-garde to evolve in dislocation from Europe's cultural revolution. We might productively consider how this sense of distinctive value that alternative cultural expressions hold for Japanese artists became a parallel formation and alternate teleology for avant-garde praxis in general. We might also reflect on how theater changes in reaction to its location and consider ways that the avant-garde was reframed and resituated in Japan.

I will explore these transnational/translational flavors of the avant-garde and its distinctive qualities in Japan by considering three interrelated factors. First, as I've mentioned above, I will highlight the formation of the Japanese avant-garde theater as an experience of embodiment and sensation. To this end, it is striking to note the powerful sense of confidence in cosmopolitan creative visions that were realized in early Japanese avant-garde forms. And while such arts sought to persuade with their epic compositions and ideas—so familiar now to the modern cosmopolitan eye—it was nevertheless Japanese bodies that performed these labors and Japanese audiences that responded to them. Indeed, as will be argued, the rise of avant-garde theater in Japan was centrally connected to ideas of experience. Participation in an expanding and ephemeral phenomenology of modernity in which the body as a site of sensation and knowledge is privileged was a crucial factor in the Japanese approach.

In a second, related point, I note that it was also Japanese power elites and state agencies such as the secret police *(kempitai)* that persecuted and gradually wore down Japan's first-generation avant-garde artists. The rising military-nationalist forces considered the avant-garde decadent and subversive. The avant-garde ran counter to the concept of the *kokutai*—the emperor-centered ideals of national polity. It is therefore pertinent to consider the avant-garde body in contrast to the notion of a body organized by a military-police mentality.

As was noted in a recent controversy about the meaning of the term, *kokutai* was used to describe the essence of prewar Japanese society as "an unbroken imperial line and concept of state as family. The relationship between the emperor and his subjects was likened to that between a father and his children."[3] This ideological and legislative instrument of Japanese imperialism was built from neonationalist readings of history and the belief in an imaginary national essence that all Japanese uniquely embodied. The historian Yoshikuni Igarashi confirms such tangible links between the concept of *kokutai* and embodiment:

[I]deological configurations of nationhood emphasized Japan's organic unity and often resorted to metaphorical representations of the political entity through bodily images. The wartime regime subjected Japanese bodies to rigid regulations: it attempted to create obedient, nationalist bodies by forging ties between nationalist ideology and bodily functions.[4]

Thus, in prewar Japan tram drivers maneuvering their carriages past the imperial palace were reportedly given special dispensation not to be compelled to bow; no one else was allowed to cast their eyes disrespectfully on the imperial vista. The hard-set endurance of the "samurai spirit" was invoked in support of physical activities ranging from school sports to military training exercises. As an expression of national sacrifice people came to physically endure shortages and accept authority almost as a function of identity. Perhaps the embodiment of *kokutai* reached its nadir in the figure of the kamikaze, which was mythologized as a divine, suffering, sacrificial extension of the imperial body politic.

Given such deeply troubled, ultimately destructive events associated with processes of modernization in Japan, we can further consider the degree to which avant-garde performances displayed anxieties and tensions about modernism and power on a wider level. Such apprehensions point to an unresolved sense of crisis in Japanese modernity—not so much an "incompleteness," but rather a dystopian thread in the social and cultural fabric of Japan made visible and above all challenged by the avant-garde. Thus, we might productively consider to what extent the avant-garde was able to resolve ideas of radical selfhood and develop a praxis that could unite art and politics within the physical expression of radical transformation in Japan.

"Aesthetics is born as a discourse of the body";[5] by giving consideration to the politics of embodiment in prewar Japanese theater, I mean to show that the avant-garde was an oppositional vanguard against the logic of capitalism in Japan after the Meiji Restoration and a trenchant critic of Japan's military imperialism. We can read the avant-garde and its various modes of physical expression as sites of resistance to the emergent discourse of national unity, capitalism, and military-imperial control. The avant-garde body can be seen as a countervailing force in Japan's modern experience.

The Historical Context for the Avant-Garde

The unique character of the avant-garde is ineluctably linked to Japanese modernism and modern art. History shows that the avant-garde sensibility and the development of modern arts were immersed in debates arising from modernity's dialectical flows.

Weisenfeld's *Mavo: Japanese Artists and the Avant-Garde, 1905–1931* comprehensively investigates the rise of avant-garde visual arts in prewar Japan.[6] Even so, with some notable exceptions,[7] the prewar avant-garde theater in Japan has not been the subject of extensive study. This is not surprising given the complexity of the issues that arise.

As with wider experiences of modernity in Japan, avant-garde theater evidenced processes of continuity as well as interruptions in the historical order. As countries like Japan expanded their interests in the world, influences from the world at large were "returned," "restored," or "remade" in Japan. On the other hand, Japan's own historical theater culture exhibits aspects of stylization and epic structure that were harbingers of developments in the theatrical avant-garde in general. It is well known, for example, that modern and avant-garde developments in European art during the first part of the twentieth century were often characterized by influences from non-Western cultures, including Japan's. Stephen Barber points to the conflation of creative insights that result from such cultural flows:

> The creative flux between Japan and Europe certainly transmits sensorial insights in both directions and sends inflexible preconceptions and apparent contradictions into a liberating freefall.[8]

The subsequent intertextual and culturally hybrid resonances that seem to emerge from this condition may be read as a manifestation of wider debates over the symbolic order of cultural authority and power in Japan. Such conditions challenge the avant-garde's more simplistic claims to be forever the harbinger of the new, while at the same time, imbuing it with degrees of complexity, subtlety, and cultural specificity that make it a distinctive and powerful agency of change.

Shingeki, or "new theater," is the prototype of modern theater in Japan. Its beginnings as a movement lie with the work of two scholars and Meiji intellectuals, Tsubouchi Shōyō and Osanai Kaoru. Tsubouchi, founder of the Bungei Kyōkai (Literary Association) at Waseda University in 1906, sought to modernize Japanese theater by introducing translations of Shakespeare to Japan.[9] Fundamentally, Tsubouchi believed that the Japanese arts could learn from modern arts elsewhere and wrote widely on questions of theater, literature, and aesthetics. Tsubouchi advocated the development of new modes of critical discourse (*shinshiki hihyō*) steeped in philosophical reflection and comparative methods that might improve Japanese theater and help to create an ideal of high art from Japanese cultural sources.[10] In contrast to Tsubouchi's intercultural reform agenda, Osanai, founder of Jiyu Gekijō (Free Theater) in 1909 at Keio University, advocated the rejection of traditional Japanese theater altogether. According to Osanai, who considered Kabuki and other traditional arts to be outmoded and feudal, Western models of theatrical realism should totally replace traditional theater in Japan. Modern theater appeared new, scientific, and progressive. Osanai was impatient with Japan's historical intransigence. Shingeki appealed to him because it gave rise to a sense of interiority; the complexities of individual agency and selfhood were depicted on the stage.

Meanwhile young shingeki artists faced the immediate challenge of developing a workable infrastructure for the modern theater and an understanding of its dramaturgy that was meaningful for themselves and their audiences. As the eminent shingeki artist Senda Koreya (1904–98)

commented, "you must bear in mind that when modern Japanese theater began, all we had to work with was a group of actors who could
only deliver lines in chanting, Kabuki fashion—even when they performed Naturalistic plays."[11]

Although they fashioned a theater from predominantly European
sources, they did so free of the strict imprint of European cultural history
and with a memory of their long theater history inscribed in the physicality of the actors and the minds of the theater public. In this sense, the
modern theater in Japan was didactically modern and emblematically
other to Japanese theater history. It was contrasted to the traditional theater of Japan, which it also came to politically oppose. The modern theater illuminated Japan's changing social relationships, and it ran counter
to traditional forms; that is, the approved theater of the military regime.
These factors helped shape the social reception of the Japanese avant-
garde. As Senda notes, shingeki came to be roughly divided between
realist and avant-garde—and later still, proletarian—modes of performance, but all three modes were representative of the arts' resistance to
the national identity framework and the status quo.[12]

The avant-garde arose in a context of creative expansion and widespread optimism in Japan, and, by the 1920s, in the context of a new
mass culture, a development long associated in the historical imaginary
with the Taishō era (1912–26). The popular image of *moga* and *mobo*
(modern girls and modern boys) embodying new leisure pursuits such as
strolling the chic and cosmopolitan Ginza shopping district wearing new
fashions was evidence of the rise of an international performative economy of leisure, consumption, entertainment, and bourgeois individualism.[13] What is sometimes called "Taishō democracy" offered limited
political reform when a two-party system emerged and universal manhood suffrage was introduced in 1925. The first regular radio broadcasts
began in the same year, and a national broadcast agency was formed in
the following one. The avant-garde scene contributed to the spirit of
freedom with chic graphic designs and unusual events; its activities were
an important locus for Japan's urban bohemian and intellectual communities.

In reality, the Taishō period was not as progressive as some of its
euphoric cultural images suggested. Adorno's critique[14] of mass culture
as an organizing principle of capitalism and ally of the authoritarian state
was exactly the sense of resistance that many radicals in Japan felt toward
Taishō developments. The socialist movement in Japan was skeptical of
Taishō democracy as a concept. The noted historian of Japan's modern-

ization H. D. Harootunian has argued that the celebration of individualism and the rise of mass society in the context of modern capitalism
were twinned with a war mentality. Accordingly, the Taishō era was
distinguished by a falling in love with "speed and machinery."[15] Meanwhile the agents of industrial capitalism, in partnership with the Japanese
armed forces, were rapidly forging supply lines into Japanese colonial
territories. Thus, for historian Iwamoto Yoshio,[16] a gestating imperialism lurked within the Taishō period of expansion; the seeds for the dis-
membering of the cosmopolitan view already had been sown. In retrospect, it could be argued that the rise of individualism in art and culture
provided a successful point of division around which Japanese society
could be reprogrammed to (in imperial terms) return to a naturalized
state of authoritarianism. In other words, the newfound cosmopolitanism of the avant-garde was crushed by an industrial-military capitalism that practiced cosmopolitanism as imperialism, interculturalism as
the scientific exchange of military research, and embodiment as the
training of soldiers for war.[17]

Shifts in the cultural landscape became increasingly turbulent during
the 1920s as the brief cosmopolitan events of the Taishō era gave way to
nationalist ideology and subsequent outright militarism following the
enthronement of Emperor Hirohito in 1926. The emergent theatrical
avant-garde struggled to take hold and survive in an atmosphere of suspicion, including state attacks on the arts. The Peace Preservation Law
(Chian Iji Hō) of 1925 forbade any activities deemed subversive to the
state. Under the pernicious terms of this law, individuals judged to have
undertaken activities with either the intention or the result of "changing
the *kokutai*" could be imprisoned for up to ten years. So vague was the
wording of the legislation that in reality any activity might be considered
grounds for arrest, certainly including the activities of artists, intellectuals, and dissenters. Thus, the 1920s saw both startling innovations in the
theater and the rise of an ever-increasing authoritarian regime. How
artists responded to these challenges is pivotal to understanding the
transformational agenda of the avant-garde in Japan.

Murayama Tomoyoshi, Mavo, Montage, and the Avant-Garde

The artist Murayama Tomoyoshi (1901–1977) was singularly important
to the emergence of Japan's avant-garde. Murayama broke off his studies in philosophy at Tokyo's elite Imperial University in favor of an artis-

tic career. Visiting Germany in 1922, he became absorbed in the experience of expressionist art. He met with painters, writers, and theater makers and even exhibited his work in the Congress of International Progressive Artists in Dusseldorf.[18] Although he was in Europe for only a brief eleven months, his stay was life-changing, and Murayama "experienced a staggering diversity of artistic activity."[19] He returned to Japan in December 1922 as a full-fledged bohemian, one whose understanding of the avant-garde as a visceral nexus between the creative and the political was formed by his German experience.

This realization led Murayama to immerse himself in the volatile and fragile contemporary Japanese arts scene. Along with painting and graphic arts, he worked extensively in the fields of stage design, playwriting, directing, and performing—including radical modern dance experiments that explored notions of personal subjectivity and free expression. His book *Essays on Proletarian Theater in Japan (Nippon Puroretaria Engeki Ron),* published in 1930,[20] outlined a comprehensive model for theater as a political vanguard. These essays were the first "manifesto" for the theater in Japan to combine the local perspective with a conception of utopian-socialist internationalism. As his writings come to demonstrate, Murayama understood that the avant-garde was a sensibility defined by its very interdependence with the social and political worlds. Murayama was not so much repeating his European experience—given his relatively short stay and lack of cultural expertise, this surely would have been an intense yet fleeting set of impressions; rather, he was trying to discover an avant-garde sensibility that could be lived in Japan. He lived his life pursuing the full range of avant-garde pursuits and practiced the avant-garde doctrine that sought a reconstitution of society and the individual through the creative-political fusion of life and art.

Immediately upon returning to Japan, Murayama joined with fellow artists Masamu Yanase, Kamenosuke Ogata, Shuzo Oura, and Kunio Kadowaki in founding the artist collective Mavo, which became one of the most influential movements in Japan during the 1920s. Mavo aimed not only to reflect and record the world in art but also to use art in ways that might comprehensively change social reality. The Mavo manifesto proclaimed:

We stand at the vanguard and will stand there eternally. We are not bound. We are radical. We revolutionize. We advance. We create.

We ceaselessly affirm and negate. We live in all the meanings of words. Nothing can be compared with us.[21]

We live in all the meanings of words: this intermediary, montage-like statement suggests a striking formulation of avant-garde praxis and a utopian desire. The statement imagines an almost fluid and multidimensional sense of corporeality, interrupting the linear authoritarianism of historical identity formation. The Mavo artists wanted to become harbingers of a radical Japanese selfhood that proposed a fluid yet forceful renegotiation of the self: "We revolutionize. We advance. We create. We ceaselessly affirm and negate" are polemic slogans suggestive of emergent theories of action that exhibit a sense of the performative. The group's absolute commitment to praxis and action as a means of discovering the avant-garde sensibility was emphatic. "Nothing can be compared with us," they wrote. They likened the active pursuit of experimentation and rebellion to an act of theatricality that aimed at the evolution of being. Their theory of embodiment and fulfillment finds an echo in Antonin Artaud's work nearly twenty years later.[22]

Mavo artists wanted their works to be experienced, not observed. They used abstraction, collage, and everyday objects to encourage interactivity and dialogue with the viewer. In their playful designs Mavo artists played a central role in developing various performative acts that might reconstitute the self and construct new possibilities for Japan.

In his 1926 essay "The Study of Construction" ("Kōseiha Kenkyū") Murayama wrote: "Constructivism is cooperative art. It is a kind of social organization. It is the food and drink of the people."[23] This helps to explain Murayama's aesthetic theory of "conscious constructivism" *(ishikiteki kōseishugi)* as a movement connected to the experience of daily life. Japanese cultural reality would be rebuilt through new forms of cooperative organization as aesthetics and politics came to be seen as working in partnership with each other. While this Marxist approach is typical in modern art, the Japanese response was fluid. It did not simply repeat the Soviet ideal that art serves the state, however influential that formulation was among sections of the Left in Japan. Nor at the same time was conscious constructivism immersed in the negative dialectics of Dada. Rather, Murayama's formation embraced facets of both these precedent avenues of praxis but emerged with the reaffirmation that art and society shape each other. This factor points to a distinctive hybridity in the historical avant-garde in Japan, a sense of montage, wherein one system was forged with another. From the composite, new ways of being might emerge. Mavo inferred cultural-political essences differently, with elements of intimacy and distance in perpetual dialogue, as a kind of loose bond. Its sense of being simultaneously situated inside and outside itself in a fashion that would later be associated with Brecht's *Verfremdung* also suggests a parallel development between its own aesthetic and the initial explorations of estrangement as a political aesthetic in eastern Europe.

Of particular relevance to the theater is the constructivist theory of the interrelationship of form and content that according to Murayama must be "intrinsically linked and must not be divided."[24] Conscious constructivism goal was therefore the communication of contemporary experience.[25]

Machine Bodies and Liminal Ones

Mavo artist Okada Tatsuo's *Gate and Moving Ticket-Selling Booth* (*Mon to ken idō kippu uriba*, 1925) is an example of Mavo art extending its reach into the social domain by taking the avant-garde machine into the streets of Tokyo. Okada built a booth that was to be used to sell tickets to art exhibitions. The booth was a surreal construction, looking something like a large gramophone player made from junk parts and found objects. The chaotic collection of bits and pieces that were stuck to the booth as if to perform various unknown functions obscured the presence of a person who sat inside. One eyewitness account reported that "[w]hen visitors approached the machine, the occupant's black hand would suddenly appear and sell them a ticket."[26] The whole machine could be wheeled around and reportedly made appearances at exhibitions and even in neighborhoods where exhibitions were taking place. The booth was an indeterminate and playful blending of art, sculpture, architecture, and performance.

Moving through the city, Okada's ticket booth must have made quite an impression. By introducing the absurd into the everyday and creating moments of confrontation and surprise for the audience, his machine demonstrated a playful collision of art and social as well as spatial reality. One has the impression that the booth was a satirical object in which the spirit of modernity was shown not as a sleek machine, but as an old-fashioned cart. By changing perceptions of everyday life with such interventions artists may have been signaling the enlivening of human sensation and experience. With the ticket-selling booth, the experience of art became momentarily hallucinatory, collective, and participatory; something odd and humorously standing up to conventional social reality.

There is also a sense of the organic about the booth that placed it in a lexicon of urban space and the jumble of the prewar Japanese City. The scale of the work and collection of bits and pieces suggests juxtapositions that fit the historical image of Tokyo as a patchwork of history, familiarity, and folklore. The junk construction doubtless resonated with the shanty buildings that grew up in Tokyo following the citywide turmoil in the aftermath of the Kanto earthquake of 1923.[27] *Gate and Moving Ticket-Selling Booth* was like a piece of old town vaudeville. The black hand was a theatrical effect worthy of *taishu engeki*—a kind of downmarket Kabuki popular among sections of the working class in Japan. While the transformational possibilities of the ticket booth are important to consider, so is its evocation of a less urbanized Japan. In this sense the work recalls an idealized and innocent past. It promotes a kind of chaotic eccentricity that is perhaps erased by the logical mind-set and "progress" of modernity. The old disappears in the name of progress but might be recuperated in the avant-garde.[28]

Meanwhile, in a countercritique of the city, the logic of capitalism and the precision of military dictatorship were depicted in repetitious, machinelike images, monstrous bodies, and expressionistic perception-changing designs for the theater. Murayama's stage design for the Tsukiji Little Theater production of Georg Kaiser's *From Morn 'til Midnight* (1924) points to the capacity of machinery to act as a sign of revolution and a critique of power. Osanai, who directed this famous production, the first of an expressionist play in Japan, described Murayama's set as Japan's first "constructivist stage design."[29]

The design employed a mix of typically German expressionist and Russian constructivist styles of art combined with the montage-like abstraction characteristic of Mavo. Murayama's set featured seemingly massive platforms, performance spaces like components of some industrial form, tilted ramps, and distorted perspective. The impressive scale of the work can be discerned from photographs,[30] which show that the imposing construction filled an already cramped stage at the Tsukiji Little Theater. In one image, three actors sit motionless on a lower level of the set. In their flat expressionist makeup and costume they could be mistaken for puppets or zombies. They are swallowed up by labyrinthine levels of staging. They seem connected to the operation of this constructivist machine; their lack of expression and their physicality and makeup suggests worker alienation, or even the machine's penetration

into their worker bodies. At the same time, they seem to risk disappearing into the set's multiple backdrops and design elements that confuse
perspective and balance.

The design seems to extend beyond the space and attack the audience. The use of montage wherein disparate elements are added to the
scene—symbolic shapes, Japanese and Roman typeface, hard angular
edges and gray tones—helps to convey the expressionist design elements. The machine-like field of view points to the influence of Russian theater director Vsevolod Meyerhold (1874–1940), who was widely
admired in theater circles in Japan at this time.[31]

Japanese expressionism has been interpreted as responding to rising
anxieties in an age of speed and machinery. As Weisenfeld notes, "Mavo
artists addressed mechanization in daily life in ways that reveal their
strong sense of ambivalence. Some Mavo art works thematically and spa-
tially expressed a sense of crisis."[32] Murayama's design for *Morn 'til Midnight* certainly signified such anxieties.

The symbolic relationship of machinery to the avant-garde was a
dialectical one, however, and was understood from a number of differ-
ing perspectives simultaneously. Thus we can observe a contest between
images of the worker as possessed with integrity and dispossessed by
exploitation. In Murayama's designs for the stage, workers' bodies in the
service of revolution fight for presence among alienated machine bodies
colonized by capitalism. Such a contestation of Japanese corporeality in
fact seems to oscillate between the extremes of expressionism on the one
hand and representational mimesis on the other. A sense of Japan's historical anxiety is also visible in these unstable bodies. This is evident in
the contest between an imaginary machine identity wherein Japan's corporeal existence seems fixed and unchangeable and the spectacular,
ever-changing body of modernity.

The reception of abstract and stylized theater may well have pro-
ceeded more comfortably in Japan than in Europe. What Brecht later
came to identify as the gestic nature of the theatrical space, most visible
in the stylization of actors' bodies and design elements, for example, had
precedent in Japan. Thus, in Kabuki theater the actor performs according to stylized and fixed physical conventions. He is often immersed in
a "total" theatrical environment that includes large-scale sets and stage
technologies as well as music and chorus interventions. Unlike the
European modern theater that emerged from the largely impoverished
theatrical aesthetic of the nineteenth century, the Japanese theater was
already comfortable with aesthetic stylization and abstraction—although

it must be stressed, not with the newfound political intent of these modes of expression.

Experimental performance in Japan subsequently followed three parallel although not exclusive paths. The first saw the rise of performance that was predicated on ideas of escape from social conformity, the second on the grotesque body as a metaphor for corruption among Japanese power elites, while the third saw attempts to classify the performing body as proletarian. The remainder of this essay considers each of these paths in turn.

Experiencing the Body

The era saw the appearance of improvised dance experiments that gave expression to the spontaneous experience of the performer. These performances aimed to escape classification, transcend notions of order, and give life to the subjective and inner worlds of the artist. They were liminal and embodied moments of catharsis and pleasure.[33]

In Murayama's *Kitanai Odori* (meaning "dirty-earthy dance")[34] the artist is photographed in his studio in a state of physical release, even ecstasy. His long hair accentuates the androgynous and naked surfaces of his body. The forms of dance seem fluid and unpredictable. These images of sensuality and pleasure run counter to ruling images of masculinity associated with militarist notions of loyalty and sacrifice. As noted above, the Japanese body was imagined in the collective as a manifestation of imperial rites, and it was the sacred mission of Japanese to serve the state without question. *Kitanai Odori* rejects this fascist discourse. It challenges the imperial divinity of the essentialist Japanese body politic with modes of personal exploration, imagination, and a singular experience of identity.

The avant-garde silent film *A Page of Madness* (*Kurutta Ippêji,* 1926), directed by former *onnagata* film actor Kinogasa Teinosuke, is a further testament to the politics of corporeal pleasure in the avant-garde. Set in an asylum, this extraordinary work captures performances of ecstatic, improvised, almost trancelike dance by the "inmates" who are played by leading avant-garde artists of the day. The Japanese cinema scholar Freda Freiberg notes that this masterpiece of the early Japanese cinema is distinguished by

brooding atmosphere, hallucinatory effects and a subjective representation of madness—an interior world more akin to that of German

Expressionist art. In its structure, based more on a loosely associational psychological logic than narrative coherence; and in its use of distorted eye imagery and histrionic performance; the film also prefigures the early surrealist films of Bunuel.[35]

Through these frenetic forms of *butoh*-like intensity, the film expresses a radical transgression of social expectation and norms. In these startling, almost premodern images of ritual excess we not only find a sense of personal liberation expressed, but also the whole basis of social reality may be questioned through the experience of performance. The possibilities and the pleasures of this politics are open-ended; a liminal politics of subjectivity and radical selfhood is prefigured in these bodies that seem to be released from the real world.

A Page of Madness not only enacted cultural, political, and religious taboo; the unbridled nature of the performances worked against the implied political morality of ruling elites. The avant-garde subject was inclined to construct his or her own subjectivity as a marker of selfhood and a mode of alternative social praxis. This challenged fundamentally the Japanese cultural ideal of disregarding personal feelings when in conflict with the demands of the society as a whole—a long-standing ideological practice made extreme in the war era when the individual's sense of self was connected to the state in a corporeal mode of imperial deification.

As these performances opened up spaces in society wherein the nature of identity was questioned, their implied critique of the militarist forces gave rise to powerful countervailing forces of repression in equal measure. The sense of foreboding occasioned by the developing war mentality is particularly visible in the performance of the grotesque in the 1928 avant-garde play *Nero in a Skirt*.

The Grotesque Body as a Sign of War Mentality: Nero in a Skirt

Nero in a Skirt (Sukato o Haita Nero)[36] was written and directed by Murayama and performed by the Shinza (New Troupe) at Tokyo's Asahi Hall in 1928. Written as a puppet play, the text offers insight into the absurd, satirical, perhaps grotesque style of this work in performance. Part homage to Alfred Jarry's *Ubu* plays and part Bunraku (the puppet theater of Japan), *Nero* was set in Russia in 1788.[37] The central protagonist is the Ubu-like character of Catherine the Second, a sixty-year-old, despotic, obese, megalomaniac queen. Three ghostly puppets in the guise of the "skirts of the past, the present, and future" begin the play with a satirical song about Catherine's reign and her "appetites"—gastronomical and sexual. We know from the outset that she is evil and portrayed in the play as a figure of ridicule.

Evoking reference to Japan's advances into Korea and China, the country in the play is at war. The decadent life of Catherine's court is contrasted with the truly awful conditions experienced by her soldiers on the battlefield. A soldier named Lanskoi attracts the attentions of Catherine, who forces him to become her lover. Lanskoi is later sent to the war but so horrible is the experience that he abandons his post and returns to the court. The queen informs him that the punishment for desertion is death and that she must make a public spectacle of Lanskoi to send a message to others who might contemplate escaping the dreadful conditions of battle. Secretly, however, she tells him not to worry, that his execution will be faked, and he will be able to return to the arms of his lover. Lanskoi is thrown into prison and finally executed in a public display of theatrical proportions. Despite her comforting words, the execution is not staged, and Catherine laughs gleefully as Lanskoi's head falls under the sway of the axe.

Catherine is not, however, victorious in the end. The final scene of the play returns to the battlefield. The armies on both sides are by now reduced to very small numbers and everyone is exhausted. Realizing the absurdity of their situation and their misery, the soldiers turn on their commanders and join together as comrades in arms. They tell each other that they are starving and cold and finally decide to commit suicide together. The queen remains, but resistance undermines her power, although the price paid by the soldiers is high. Power is expressed as physical deformity, obesity, and a kind of scatological fecundity. Its emptiness is realized though mass destruction and corruption. Modernity equals war equals genocide.

Nero in a Skirt offers a commentary on the Japanese military and the new emperor. In 1928, when the play was performed, the military were forging links with the imperial house and were expanding their hold on colonial territories in China and Korea. The "skirt" of Nero is possibly a reference to armor designed to protect the ruling forces and repel opposing ones. Furthermore, Murayama wrote the play in an atmosphere of increasing censorship and control. In 1928, the government announced that serious transgressions of the 1925 Peace Preservation Law were now punishable by death.[38]

Murayama wrote at length about the severe censorship laws in force in Japan in *Essays on Proletarian Theater in Japan (Nippon Puroretaria Engeki Ron,* 1991, discussed further below). As he points out, the rules of the censorship code *(keishi chōrei)* were vague and worded in such a manner that they could be applied to a wide range of situations. Murayama cites Section 66, Article 1 of the code, wherein the law states that one could be censored for works deemed to be "pornographic, or of violent intent, works that display criminal methodology, satire of the present administration or foreign policy, things that have a negative effect on education, morals, customs, and public hygiene."[39]

As Murayama points out, this would be absurd if it were not so serious; the censorship code could be interpreted to apply to practically any situation or event. In the theater, a wide range of public officials, from public servants to police, could refuse permits to perform at any time before, and even during, the run of the play. Murayama gives the example of a play being canceled on the grounds that the script called for a character to be "tripped over"; in the mind of the censor the actor "fell." This was ground for the official to rule that the performance had departed from the script and should be stopped.[40]

In depicting the rule of tyranny and malfeasance, *Nero in a Skirt* is a grotesque puppet play with symbolic images of power and calamity. Lurking behind the bloated image of fat Catherine we might discern the imperial household, its rapidly escalating interventions into parliamentary processes, and a deepening sense of ideological dependence on military cliques among the ruling classes in Japan.

Meanwhile, the play challenges the code on almost every level. In a sort of satirical bow to the exclusory articles of the code itself, the play is violent, satirical, scatological, antiauthoritarian, and antirealist in equal measure. It does the opposite of what is intended by the letter of the law, and seems to challenge the authorities to ban it. In *Essays on Proletarian Theater* Murayama wrote of the need to continually resist attempts to control the activities of the artist—of the need for art to refuse the political reality of prewar Japan and for the artist to embody resistance through performance. *Nero in a Skirt* speaks for resistance. However, as social conditions worsened in Japan, radical artists shifted from using metaphor to forging concepts of art as action. The substance of the change was first catalogued in Murayama's *Essays on Proletarian Theater in Japan.*

Essays on Proletarian Theater

These essays are the first and remain the most comprehensive attempt to theorize a Marxist theater culture in the history of Japanese theater. Murayama's theories for a theater of and for the masses completed the transformation of the avant-garde into a socialist force.

The essays note the rise of militarism in Japan and the subsequent rise of surveillance and persecution. Murayama argues that the situation in Japan was reduced to a struggle between the disciplinary forces of capitalism and militarism on the one hand and socialism on the other. He outlines a program for a theater that might best serve the masses and aid the cause of the proletarian revolution. At the same time, he acknowledges how difficult this will be to implement and continually reminds the reader of the difficulties radical-experimental theater faces when in opposition to the authoritarian state.

Among the proposals Murayama makes is a strongly argued case that proletarian theater should not only perform socialist plays but should also give serious attention to building a theatrical movement for the liberation of workers and peasants. He proposes that the movement should present plays set in the actual workplaces of the spectators. If a dispute arises, or a strike action is planned, Murayama proposes that plays should be developed about this and performed during the actual events. Murayama's model here is Piscator, who was an influential figure in Murayama's development as a Marxist theorist for the theater. Muruyama's work here is also harder and more serious than the playful interventions of work like Okada's ticket machine.

The resulting ideological formation of an aesthetics of the everyday became crucially important to the Japanese Left. Harootunian reminds us that the historical quality of the everyday has particular resonance: "everydayness became identified with the 'voiceless' subalterns whose capacity to actualize their aspirations spoke louder than words. It meant, also, that *in acting* they were writing their own history."[41] The avant-garde had already been developing its project through its relations with everyday life (machines, bodies, experiences, subjectivity, etc.); now, that practice underpins the development of the avant-garde as a proletarian force. Given the overruling presence of neonationalist readings of history and identity in the maintenance of Japanese power, attempts to imagine a fairer, more inclusive version of the everyday and to struggle over the interpretation of history came to be a singularly important strategy for the radical arts.

Murayama's proposal for a "documentary theater" included the involvement of professional artists along with troupes made up of workers and peasants. He noted the example set by such groups in regional areas in Japan—in Kyoto, Osaka, Shizuoka, and Kanazawa. In analyzing their potential success, though, Murayama stressed the fact that a lack of funding and the tightening of government censorship undermined such groups. Even worse, in Tokyo, which was at the center of power and afforded easier surveillance, artists were unable to support any such worker theater troupes.

In a later discussion on socialist dramaturgy, Murayama argued that the true proletarian theater must avoid plays that offer only a token support for socialism. Rather, proletarian theater should be easy to understand, must address the problems at hand in a direct manner, and should demonstrate the ultimate wisdom of the socialist model. In this way, the goal of establishing a proletarian realism in the Japanese theater might be achieved. Theater works, moreover, should become instruments of education and debate. Plays should be published in socialist magazines and distributed among workers. Study groups for the education of the masses might also be fruitfully established. Above all, Murayama asserted, everything must be done to fight against the government's general closing down of such theatrical activity and of acts of resistance.

These essays show how the avant-garde in Japan entered a new phase, one that seemed to have cast off its prior estrangement and disembodiment from the cosmopolitan arts. Socialist forces were conspicuous opponents of the emergent fascist powers in Japan and Germany. Proletarian theater was a systemized theater designed to promote the socialist cause and bring about transformation in society and culture. The embrace of social dialectics rather than loosely defined subjectivity brought about a shift in the avant-garde to critiquing the world from the perspective of class and theories of hegemony. As oppositional politics became more urgent and extreme, avant-garde bodies found value in collectivization.

Proletarian Bodies

Murayama's 1929 epic propaganda play, *Chronicle of a Gang (Boryokudan Ki)*, exemplifies this trend. Performed in June 1929 by the Leftist Theater Troupe, it moved away from the expressionist avant-garde style of *Nero*.[42] Set in China during the Opium Wars, the play deals with the themes of revolution and betrayal as young activists try to organize a protest against the combined forces of government, big business, and gangsters. *Chronicle of a Gang* may well be called the chronicle of a revolutionary cell, as it deals with the struggles of young firebrand socialists in their efforts to do their utmost to assist the revolution.

The genre of the play is akin to Epic Theatre and suggests comparison with Brecht and Piscator. In fact, the clarity of the socialist vision here is remarkable, and the play confirms that Japan was a center of proletarian theater. This trend—to write plays with socialist messages and experiment with theater as propaganda—points to a shift in thinking about the possible sites for a radical theater culture in Japan. By the end of the 1920s many theater artists, including Murayama, Senda Koreya and former members of the Tsukiji Little Theater, had moved away from the concept of the avant-garde as subjective or liminal in its abstraction. Instead, they embraced socialism and the radical ideal of art for the masses. *Chronicle of a Gang* and Murayama's collected essays on proletarian theater in Japan are excellent examples of this paradigm shift.

In *Chronicle of a Gang,* two gangsters named Baosan and Debao meet on the banks of a river in Zhengzhou, China. Both are taking new recruits to meet their gang boss, Zhou. At the induction ceremony, all the recruits swear to give their lives for the cause of forming a union with the workers of the national railway. Together with the union, the gang plans to hold a general meeting and rebel against the government. In an aside, though, Debao expresses his doubts about his comrade Baosan, who is a wealthy man and has only recently joined the gang. Zhou explains that Baosan is willing to cooperate and finance their struggle in order to take revenge on the government for murdering his father and confiscating the family property. Zhou assures his comrade that Baosan will be disposed of when he is no longer useful to the cause. However, later on, Zhou is revealed as a double agent who is in league with the authorities. In return for a stock of opium, Zhou agrees to make trouble and undermine the strike action. Meanwhile the revolutionaries steel their resolve, unaware that their plans have been compromised.

When gang leader Zhou and his thugs smash up the union headquarters, the revolutionaries begin to realize the extent of the forces massed against them. They retreat to a nearby inn, where they find themselves surrounded by the police. However, this only serves to strengthen their determination to carry out the general strike and, if necessary, to die for the proletarian cause. Various struggles ensue; some comrades stay true to the revolutionary cause, while others falter.

In the final scene at the railway station, a huge crowd of revolutionary laborers blocks the passage of a train. The laborers face a heavily armed company of military police. Tensions rise until the revolutionaries break the silence, calling on the military to throw down their weapons and join the revolution. The head of the police counters the revolutionaries with an order to get off the tracks because the train is going to depart whether they stand in the way or not. Suddenly, there is murmuring among the revolutionaries, and someone announces that the police have just executed Yeqingshan, a loyal comrade. Someone else announces that the gangsters carried out the execution. Yeqingshan's mother demands revenge for her son's murder, and the revolutionaries rush off excitedly to seek out the gangsters to attack.

Meanwhile, the police chief orders his men to fire on the retreating revolutionaries. After a volley of shots the comrades are mowed down. There is a moment of silence, after which a voice is heard announcing that while the revolutionaries may have lost the battle, they will inevitably win the war. In giving their lives for the revolutionary cause, they will set an example to others who in turn might succeed in overthrowing the military clique, defeating imperialism, and setting up a government controlled by the working classes.

Of course, this is a propaganda play. But it is also a reading of the shifting sands of revolutionary activity in Japan, and also, perhaps, a parody of the situation for artists, some of whom were government spies. Murayama was one of many artists whose political views led to his imprisonment. Meanwhile, other artist–activists recanted their socialist principles *(tenkō)*. The socialist terrain was clearly a slippery one and full of intrigues, counterrevolutionaries, dispirited factions and euphoric ones. Released from his first jail sentence in 1935, Senda notes that at the time, "You could get out by just telling them that, although you would not change your beliefs . . . you would sever your ties with the Party. I came out and found that the central committee of the Party had been completely destroyed."[43]

When seen in this light, *Chronicle of a Gang* appears to be a moral tale designed to steel the resolve of activists in Japan and celebrate their cause, however hopeless and lost it may have seemed at the time. It is a play alive to the intrigues of socialist power struggles, and one that also passes comment on the unruly bedfellows—the military, big business, and imperial forces—who made up the dominant cliques in Japan before World War II.

In the final analysis, the play is interesting not only for its model construction and political critique but also for its location. The China of *Chronicle of a Gang* is very different from the China of Brecht's *The Decision* (The Measures Taken), and the play is certainly different from the didactic parables for which Brecht provided Asian settings. For Japanese artists, the Asian region is not so distant. Far from being removed from cultural experience, the Chinese location was well known. Indeed, Japanese colonization had turned it into conflictual space. As the play was being written and performed, China was being ceded as Japanese territory. The cultural space in this play, however, remains Chinese; the characters are portrayed as proudly resistant and resilient. The fact of Japanese actors playing the roles of Chinese revolutionaries intersects with historical and contemporary experiences in ways that were unknown to most Europeans. The play addresses a contemporary experience of cultural politics, one that perhaps gives hope to all subjects of the imperial regime who seek to resist its force, but one that is at its core focused on the Japanese experience, referencing not only the period of the war, but also the long history of Japan-China relations.

This points to a more generalized consideration of cultural politics and the avant-garde in Japan. The representation of Western society in Japan does not involve the cultural representation of a mysterious other pursued by the European avant-garde. The European world is familiar and internalized in Japan. The Japanese avant-garde, then, was not really interested in the ineffable otherness of Europe. Rather, it was born in a rising sense of its own cultural history.

Conclusion: Embodiment and the Politics of Action

We have seen in this essay that Japan was a culture of intersections and contested forms long before contemporary notions of globalization made such issues central to cultural studies worldwide. By employing this notion in thinking about the avant-garde, we can interweave questions of transmission and locality with a radical politics of action. In this instance, the struggle to give life to a nascent theatrical avant-garde in early twentieth-century Japan reflected rapidly evolving and fractured experiences of modernity itself. At the same time, the concept of a Japanese avant-garde arose from the intersection of art and culture in a specific sociopolitical and historical context. This observation is important in conceptualizing the historical avant-garde in Japan as one rooted in the everyday experience of Japanese society. Crucially, the representations and cultural products of the Japanese avant-garde were made in

Japan. The avant-garde arts engaged the lived experience of Japanese people in a fundamental sense. One measure of this engagement is the influence exerted by this avant-garde on the second wave of avant-garde art and performance after 1945. Another is the central position it holds in the history of Japanese cultural debates.

In the 1920s and 1930s, however, Japanese avant-garde artists were an oppositional and increasingly marginalized body. The persecution of artists became increasingly common, and activities in the radical theater largely ceased, from the 1930s through the end of World War II in 1945. Discourses of the body in performance reflected the ideological divide in Japanese society at large. Those avant-garde bodies that played out narratives of expressionist desire and utopian solidarity with the Communist Internationale stood against the national polity-body of the *kokutai*. Thus, representative oppositional bodies of Japanese modernity in the late 1920s and 1930s were seen both in liminal performances and in proletarian-realist polemics. Both stood in marked contrast to the growing militarized body politic of young soldiers dedicated to the emperor and to the expansion of imperial Japan. Ultimately, avant-garde performance was not a corrective for the rise of militarism. First the individualistic experiential mode of selfhood expression and then the collective solidarity promised in socialist arts came under attack. Neither, it seems, could maintain a sense of embodiment and experience separate from the rising forces of the *kokutai*.

Nevertheless, even while under the constant threat of erasure, the record of productions and live events, abstract designs, and writings for the theater show that this avant-garde was something new and startling. As Senda writes, "We did everything that was new in the world. It was as if a tidal wave of new artistic trends had broken over Japan."[44] This avant-garde was a force to be reckoned with—a blending of politics and art communicated through the body as a force of discovery and resistance.

Notes

1. The Meiji Restoration is so called because Emperor Meiji was "restored" to his central role of leadership and spiritual guidance in the Japanese polity, thereby taking rule from the *bakufu,* or samurai clans. Many historians note that the Meiji emperor was not in fact an absolute ruler and that reforms such as the Meiji constitution introduced a version of parliamentary rule to Japan. The term *Meiji era* follows the Japanese tradition of marking historical epochs by the posthumous name of the contemporaneously reigning emperor: thus, Meiji era, Taishō era, Showa era, etc.

2. Midori Matsui, "The Places of Marginal Positionality: Legacies of Japanese Anti-

Modernity," in *Consuming Bodies: Sex and Contemporary Japanese Art,* ed. Fran Lloyd (London: Reaktion Books, 2002), 142.

3. Quote from Kyodo News Service, "Ministers Divided over Mori's 'Kokutai' Remark," *Kyodo News Service,* 6 June 2000. Controversy over the meaning of this term continues in Japan. The official view that the meaning of *kokutai* is no longer associated with Japanese imperialism and simply means "national policy framework" was contested as recently as June 2000 when the then prime minister of Japan, Yoshiro Mori, used the term in a talk that attacked the Japanese Communist Party's opposition to the imperial system. In essence Mori seemed to be suggesting that the JCP's opposition to the emperor system was against the *kokutai* (the national polity). Mori had previously described Japan as a "divine nation centred on the emperor." Such thinking closely resembles the prewar understanding of the term *kokutai.*

4. Yoshikuni Igarashi, *Bodies of Memory: Narratives of War in Post-war Japanese Culture 1945–1970* (Princeton: Princeton University Press, 2000), 13.

5. Terry Eagleton, *The Ideology of the Aesthetic* (Oxford: Blackwell, 1990), 13.

6. Gennifer Weisenfeld, *Mavo: Japanese Artists and the Avant-Garde, 1905–1931* (Berkeley: University of California Press, 2002).

7. For example, J. Thomas Rimer, *Toward a Modern Japanese Theatre* (Princeton: Princeton University Press, 1974), and Weisenfeld's chapter on performance in *Mavo.*

8. Stephen Barber, "Tokyo's Urban and Sexual Transformations: Performance Art and Digital Cultures," in Lloyd, *Consuming Bodies,* 177.

9. Waseda University (founded 1882) and Keio University (founded 1858) are two of Japan's most elite universities and were among the first modern universities in Japan.

10. See Shōyō Tsubouchi, "What is Beauty?" in *Modern Japanese Aesthetics: A Reader,* ed. Michele Marra (Honolulu: University of Hawaii Press, 1999), 48–64; and Michael C. Brownstein, "Tsubouchi Shōyō on Chikamatsu and Drama," *Currents in Japanese Culture,* ed. Amy Vladeck Heinrich (New York: Columbia University Press, 1997), 281–82.

11. Koreya Senda, "An Interview," *Concerned Theatre Japan* 1.2 (1970): 55.

12. Ibid., 53–55. Such marked contrasts in arts ideology and praxis were played out in the Tsukiji Little Theater (Tsukiji Shōgekijō) founded by Osanai in 1924 as a theater for playing psychologically realist modern drama. By the late 1920s, however, the Tsukiji Little Theater came under the influence of the socialist and avant-garde schools. Tsukiji was the target of attacks by government authorities and nationalist groups during the 1930s; the institution struggled to remain financially viable while artists were harassed and spied upon. The theater was closed in 1940 when a number of key people were arrested. For further information see Benito Ortolani, *The Japanese Theatre: From Shamanistic Ritual to Contemporary Pluralism* (Princeton: Princeton University Press, 1990), 243–57.

13. Jackie Menzies, ed., *Modern Boy Modern Girl: Modernity in Japanese Art, 1910–1935* (Sydney: Art Gallery of New South Wales, 1998).

14. Theodor Adorno, *The Culture Industry* (London: Routledge, 2001).

15. H. D. Harootunian, "America's Japan/Japan's Japan," in *Japan in the World,* ed. Masao Miyoshi and H. D. Harootunian (Durham: Duke University Press, 1993), 198.

16. Iwamoto Yoshio, "Aspects of the Proletarian Literary Movement in Japan," in *Japan in Crisis: Essays on Taishō Democracy,* ed. Bernard Silberman and H. D. Harootunian (Princeton: Princeton University Press, 1974), 156–82.

17. It was only near the end of the era, however, that artists came to view such com-

plex and dystopic concepts of hegemony in their work. Meanwhile individualism and ideas of agency remained very important to the avant-garde's formation. Relevant here is the sociologist John Clammer's suggestion that "the key to modernity (in Japan) is the transformation of the self: *shutaisei*" (John Clammer, *Difference and Modernity: Social Theory and Contemporary Japanese Society* [London: Kegan Paul, 1995], 84). Clammer translates *shutaisei* as "independence of spirit"—a quality of self-identification, subjectivity, and selfhood that has been widely recognized as an enduring feature of Japanese cultural experience in the twentieth century. Elsewhere I have argued that the qualities of selfhood are central to an understanding of the Japanese avant-garde; that concerns with identity and subjectivity are the means by which the radical theater and culture find a unity of intent and shared outcomes (Peter Eckersall, "Theatre Culture in Japan since the 1960s: Reading the Politics of the Avant-garde," Ph.D. diss., Monash University, Australia, 1998). As a consequence, the political formation of the avant-garde relates to questions of individualism *and* society.

18. William Gardner, "Colonialism and the Avant-garde in Japan: Kitagawa Fuyuhiko's *Mancurian Railway*," *Stanford Humanities Review* 7.1 (1999), 12–21.

19. Weisenfeld, *Mavo,* 37.

20. Tomoyoshi Murayama, *Nippon Puroretaria Engeki Ron* (Tokyo: Yumani Shōbō, 1991).

21. Cited in Weisenfeld, *Mavo,* 66.

22. Antonin Artaud, *The Theatre and its Double,* trans. Victor Corti (London: Calder and Boyars, 1970).

23. Ibid., 163.

24. Ibid., 44.

25. With the sensibility of what might be termed "fragmentary wholeness in mind," we might productively begin to think about Japan's situation as a formation of the postcolonial avant-garde. While scholars have considered this as a possibility in respect of the Japanese scene after World War II (William A. Marotti, "Simulacra and subversion in the Everyday: Asasegawa Genpei's 1000-yen Copy, Critical Art and the State," *Postcolonial Studies* 4.2 [2001]: 211–29; and Alexandra Munroe, *Japanese Art after 1945: Scream against the Sky* [New York: Abrams, 1994]), the precedents for that better-known avant-garde of the 1950s are found here in the complex cultural negotiations of the Mavo generation. Such a model explains how external culture was internalized in Japan, but also circulated through alternate social and cultural pathways and transformed into a force that spoke with its own voice.

26. Cited in Weisenfeld, *Mavo,* 110.

27. Tokyo lies at the edge of the vast Kanto plain, a geographic formation that extends from the ocean to the central spine of mountains on the island of Honshu. The Great Kanto Earthquake of 1923 destroyed large parts of Tokyo. More than 140,000 people were killed in the quake and in the subsequent fires and civil disorder.

28. Terayama Shūji and Kara Juro, two leading figures in the avant-garde theater of the 1960s, often recast this folk-gothic atmosphere as a sublime commentary on 1960s Japan. They came to understand what was only partially clear to Okada's generation; the point that the fantastic and the strange in Japan are as likely to be found in premodern culture as they are in interventionist acts.

29. Cited in Weisenfeld, *Mavo,* 219.

30. See Senda, "An Interview," 51; and Tomoyoshi Murayama, *Murayama Tomoyoshi no Bijitsu no Shigoto* (Tokyo: Miraisha, 1985).

31. In Meyerhold's theater, melodrama and realism were banished in favor of abstraction and stylization. He favored the construction of the actor as a form, a political body in the mise-en-scène. Through his systematic actor training—called biomechanics—and a melding of science, art and politics in his constructivist aesthetic regime, he revolutionized thinking about the avant-garde and its relationship to politics. Such ideas of socialist constructivism and a futurist-expressionist corporeality entered the Japanese theater through expressionism. In joining bodies and stage devices with mechanistic design, Murayama's vision for the theater promised a corporeal revolution. It was a futurist-socialist view of the body that sought to celebrate the glorious energies of work and workers and was predicated on a reconsideration of the functions of art and culture in the mass industrial-capitalist society. As for Blau: "The body and machine are embraced, and embrace each other in the higher synthesis" of politics and art (Herbert Blau, "The Surpassing Body," *Drama Review* 35.2 [1991]: 74); this is the ideological basis of constructivism.

32. Weisenfeld, *Mavo*, 126.

33. In retrospect these free-form dances appear similar in style and were perhaps an important precursor to *butō*—the avant-garde dance developed by Hijikata Tatsumi and Ōno Kazuo in the late 1950s and through the 1960s.

34. See images in Weisenfeld, *Mavo*, 235, 237.

35. Freda Freiberg, "Comprehensive Connections: The Film Industry, the Theatre and the State in the Early Japanese Cinema," 2000, http://www.latrobe.edu.au/screen ingthepast/firstrelease/fr1100/fffr11c.htm.

36. Tomoyoshi Murayama, "Sukato o Haita Nero," in *Gendai Nihon Gikyoku Senshū* 5 (Tokyo: Kaukusui Sha, 1991), 424–44. *Sukato o Haita Nero* was first published in *Engeki Shincho* (New Wave Theater), May 1927.

37. The *Ubu* plays of which *Ubu Roi* is perhaps best known were grotesque satirical works loosely based on *Macbeth* and written for the puppet theater by Jarry in Paris in the 1890s. Jarry's production of *Ubu* famously descended into chaos when on the opening night the audience started a riot in the theater.

38. Herbert Bix, *Hirohito and the Making of Modern Japan* (New York: HarperCollins, 2001), 206.

39. Murayama, "Sukato o Haita Nero," 22.

40. Ibid., 25–26.

41. H. D. Harootunian, "History's Unwanted Surplus: Japan and the Irreducible Remainder of Everyday Life," *Postcolonial Studies* 4.2 (2001): 164; emphasis added.

42. Tomoyoshi Murayama, "Boryokudan Ki," in *Gendai Nihon Gikyoku Senshū 6* (Tokyo: Kaukusui Sha), 191–241. Seki Sano directed the 1929 production. The text was first published in the July 1929 issue of *Senki* (Battle Flag).

43. Senda, "An Interview," 63.

44. Ibid., 53.

Angura
Japan's Nostalgic Avant-Garde

David G. Goodman

The Paradox

Rejection of the past and opposition to tradition are hallmarks of the avant-garde. "By the second decade of [the twentieth] century," Matei Calinescu writes, "avant-garde, as an artistic concept, had become comprehensive enough to designate not one or the other, but *all the new schools* whose aesthetic programs were defined, by and large, by their rejection of the past and by the cult of the new."[1]

There is something paradoxical about the avant-garde in Japan, however. To the extent that it has risen above mere imitation of the West and succeeded as an indigenous phenomenon, the avant-garde in Japan has served as a vehicle to access what Miryam Sas in her study of Japanese surrealist poetry calls "cultural memory."[2] The paradoxical quality of the Japanese avant-garde is that it has achieved its greatest success, not when it aimed at some as yet undefined future utopian goal, but rather when it tried to recapture and rearticulate a lost or otherwise irretrievable past. In a word, Japan's most successful avant-gardes have, paradoxically, been nostalgic.

The critic Karatani Kōjin has described the way this paradox has affected how Japanese avant-garde art is perceived in Japan and abroad:

> Westernization has wrestled with a radical paradox ever since [the Meiji period, 1868–1912]: that which is praised as new and anti-traditionalist appears to be mere mimicry in the West, where, conversely, a return to Japanese traditionalism is viewed as cutting-edge. And we remain trapped in this same predicament today. In fact, most of the

Westernizationists who are currently admired in Japan could not be less valued in the West, while Japanese artists who achieve some recognition abroad are those who have literally returned to traditionalism in some sense; it is this return that makes them appear to be avant-garde.[3]

In this essay, I want to examine Japan's nostalgic avant-garde in the theater, its origins, development, and culmination in the riotous decade of the 1960s.

Kabuki

On April 5, 1872, three of the most prominent young representatives of the Kabuki theater—the theater owner Morita Kanya and the playwrights Kawatake Shinshichi (later known as Mokuami) and Sakurada Jisuke III—were called to the First Ward Office in Tokyo and given the following order: "It goes without saying that promoting good and castigating evil should be the mainstay of the theater, and thus henceforth all that is ridiculous and illogical in the theater should be eschewed."[4]

The radicalism of this demand can hardly be overestimated. In line with the modernizing agenda of the new Meiji government, rationality, historical accuracy, and their concomitant realism were henceforth to govern a theater in which "reality" had never played a significant role. Kabuki was based, not on realism, but on a sense of space and time that derived from Japan's religious cosmology. Kabuki evolved out of and developed the religio-aesthetic performance traditions of *kagura* and *nō* the sine qua non of which was the suspension of the normal rules of existence to enable an encounter with transcendent, supernatural forces. Premodern Japanese theater required a sacred space set apart from the profane world where these forces, preeminently the spirits of the dead, could appear. Actors were, simultaneously, powerful shamans who donned the guise of the gods and "riverbed beggars" *(kawara kojiki),* social pariahs who were ostracized for transgressing the worldly order.

Quotidian time, the linear, continuous, irreversible time of everyday life, was suspended in these sacred spaces. Past and present intermixed and became indistinguishable. The time-bound world of the present interpenetrated with the timeless world of the dead, who traveled freely back and forth across the permeable life-death barrier. Time piled up on itself in *sekai,* the prefabricated worlds of Kabuki scenarios; and events took place simultaneously in the past, present, and future in cycles of eternal return. Among the audience, a degree of connoisseurship was assumed and a rich unspoken dialogue was conducted constantly between audience and actors in what the scholar Hirosue Tamotsu called a "secret ritual" *(higi)*.[5] And this "secret ritual" had a political dimension, for it was subversively countercultural—another reason why the theater had to be isolated in specially licensed quarters, "places of evil" *(akusho)* where it could be contained and regulated.

The demand that Kabuki rationalize itself to conform to empirical history thus had far-reaching implications. It was nothing short of a demand that it abandon its religio-aesthetic foundations and reinvent itself as secular "art," healthy family entertainment presentable to dignitaries foreign and domestic. And this reformation of Kabuki foreshadowed reform movements in other realms as well. "It was only through its connection with the reform of drama," Karatani writes, for example, "that the movement to reform prose fiction, that is, the modern novel, was able to exist."[6] Modernization in Japan, as in the West, was a secularizing movement.

Kabuki did as it was told. It abandoned, or at least concealed, its religio-aesthetic foundations. But unwilling and unable to deny its roots in the Edo past, it did not develop into a modern theater. It chose instead to become a museum, faithfully preserving the forms of a bygone day.

Shingeki before World War II

Modern theater developed in Japan, therefore, not as a creative modification of premodern tradition, but through a rupture with it. When Osanai Kaoru, the leading figure in *shingeki,* the Japanese modern theater movement, wrote the following words in 1926, he could not have been more explicit about his intentions.

> Above all, the enemy we must fight against in our effort to establish the *national* theater we hold as our ideal is the traditional theater, that is, Kabuki drama. . . . We must first wage war on this *tradition.* We must destroy *Kabuki patterns;* we must create completely separately *our own theater art* new and free![7]

If avant-garde movements are characterized by their "rejection of the past and by the cult of the new,"[8] then shingeki certainly qualifies as an avant-garde movement. But it is typical of the Japanese avant-garde that, at the same time Osanai was making these belligerent remarks, he was also making moves to recapture the essence of Kabuki and reincorporate it into Japanese modern theater.

Osanai had left on his first trip to Europe in 1912, a worshipful devotee of European modern theater. In 1909, he had founded one of Japan's two most important modern theater troupes, the Free Theater (Jiyu gekijō), dutifully named after Antoine's Théâtre Libre. In Moscow, Osanai saw the Moscow Art Theater's production of Chekhov's *The Cherry Orchard* directed by Stanislavski. In Paris he saw the Ballets Russes perform Stravinsky's *Petrouchka,* Richard Strauss's *Salome,* Debussy's *L'après-midi d'un faune,* and Borodin's *Prince Igor.* He was exposed, in short, to the leading modernist and avant-garde artists of the day.

Osanai was exhilarated by his experience, but he was also intimidated. He realized in a more visceral way than he had before that the achievements of modern theater in the West were predicated on a coherent Western civilization:

Gordon Craig and Stanislavski, Stanislavski and Delacroix, Delacroix and Kandinsky. I learned that the best minds of Europe, irrespective of nationality and race, are at some point reconciled with one another, and I was deeply impressed. It was as if I had witnessed the pinnacles of tall mountains, soaring into the heavens, communing with one another across immense expanses of space.[9]

This experience started Osanai on a lifelong journey to reaffirm the cultural basis of premodern theater in Japan even as he rebelled against it.

What Osanai had in mind was a hybrid of traditional and modern theater. Shortly after his return from Europe in 1915, he founded the Traditional Drama Study Group (Kogeki kenkyū kai) to study late Edo Kabuki plays as the possible basis for a "new national theater" *(shin kokumingeki)* that would combine aspects of Japanese and Western theater.

Why do we want to study Japan's traditional theater at this late date? It is because we want to know the truly beautiful aspects of the country in which we were born. We want to know the truly excellent aspects of the country in which we were born. In other words, we want to know what makes Japan the country that it is. And knowing these things, we want to set the foundation of a new national theater.[10]

A year later, Osanai helped found the Shingekijō, a modern dance theater, about which he wrote, "In addition to a new theater that is neither
Kabuki nor *shimpa,* [we aim] to create a new kind of dance in the future
Japan that will be neither Western nor Japanese but an entirely new form
of dance."[11] Osanai's dream was eventually realized: Shingekijō gave
birth to Ishii Baku, a pioneering dancer who was one of the most important models for Ohno Kazuo and Hijikata Tatsumi, the founders of
Butoh.

When European trends such as expressionism, Dadaism, and surrealism washed over Japan in succeeding waves after World War I, Osanai
perceived them, among other things, as means to recapture the essence
of premodern tradition without surrendering to Kabuki per se. The
essence of Kabuki was nonsense, Osanai argued, and Western avant-
garde techniques were ways to reinject nonsense in modern theater.[12]
Osanai became enthralled with the theatricalism of Max Reinhart. He
developed a plan (that was never realized) to create a Japanese version of
Nikita Baliev's cabaret theater The Bat in Japan. He was an early and
enthusiastic advocate of expressionism. And his last project before his
untimely death in 1928 at the age of forty-seven was an eclectic adaptation of Chikamatsu Monzaemon's 1715 play *The Battles of Coxinga,* using
techniques learned from Meyerhold (who had himself learned much
from Kabuki) and combining, among other things, Chinese, Indonesian,
and Mongolian theater styles.

In short, from the outset, the Japanese avant-garde theater—at least as
it was conceived by one of its leading advocates—incorporated the paradoxical longing to reaffirm and recapture the very theater tradition it was
denouncing and rejecting. And Western avant-garde techniques were
perceived as means to this end.

Not everyone perceived European avant-gardism in this way. As in
Europe following the success of the Russian Revolution, the avant-
garde in Japan became bound up with political radicalism, and artists like
Senda Koreya and Murayama Tomoyoshi, who had spent time in Germany in the early twenties, cleaved closely to their militant European
models. Mavo, the group that Murayama founded and that Peter Eckersall describes elsewhere in this volume, was the epitome of this politicized European-style avant-garde. In short order, avant-garde artists like
Murayama, who had begun as anarchistic iconoclasts, converted to
Marxism and "went on to spearhead the proletarian arts and theater
movements [and] advocated a shift from individualism *(kojinshugi* or
jigashugi) to collectivism *(shūdanshugi)* in line with communist dogma."[13]

In 1933, Murayama, like many other left-wing artists and intellectuals, was forced to commit *tenkō* (political apostasy), proclaiming Marxism inappropriate to Japan's imperial system.

The last hurrah of radical theater in the prewar period was Kubo Sakae's monumental *Land of Volcanic Ash,* staged in 1938.[14] In 1940, the remaining left-wing troupes were ordered to disband and their leaders, including Senda, Murayama, and Kubo, were arrested and imprisoned. Avant-garde theater in the prewar period was over.

Shingeki after the War

When the war ended, the major figures of the prewar period picked up where they had left off, and the major shingeki troupes rapidly established their hegemony in the modern theater world.

A. Horie-Webber has given a succinct description of the evolution of Mingei (The People's Theater), the largest postwar troupe and the one with which Murayama Tomoyoshi was affiliated. The description provides a good sense of shingeki's growing domination in the first quarter century after the war:

> In 1950, when the present Mingei was formed, it consisted of 12 members: 11 actors and 1 director. By 1960, this small group had expanded into a company of 119 members: 51 actors, 13 directorial members, 16 management workers, plus 39 apprentices, producing 16 plays a year, performing 240 nights. In the next ten years, however, that is by 1970, Gekidan Mingei grew into an organization of 250 members producing 10 plays a year, with performances on 600 nights. To understand the enormous scale of this expansion, we can compare these figures to those of the two leading companies in England, the National Theatre and the Royal Shakespeare Company. In both cases the number of acting members of the companies is kept around forty.[15]

Mingei was connected to the Japanese Communist Party, which, through its affiliated labor unions, organized nationwide audiences for Mingei and other modern theater troupes and made shingeki's rapid expansion possible. The success of this system in the years after the war is indisputable, but it also led to a homogeneous repertory of realist plays. After 1956 and Khrushchev's revelations of Stalin's crimes, and then with increasing clarity in the wake of the failure of JCP-led demonstrations against renewal of the U.S.-Japan Mutual Security Treaty in 1960, this alliance of the major theater companies, the JCP, and the labor unions presented itself to the younger generation of the nascent New Left as distinctly unholy.

One member of this younger generation, Kan Takayuki, then a student at Tokyo University and a member of its Theater Study Society (Tōdai gekiken), described his sense that the shingeki system had become a monolith and that it enforced "realism" as a pernicious orthodoxy.

> The realism . . . that is the orthodox theory of the shingeki movement clearly has as its tacit premise a specific ideology of culture and art (not simply the ideology of socialism or communism but the revolutionary theory descended from the official dogma of the International Communist Movement before the war) that relates and commits one to the historical stage at which the transition from capitalism to socialism (the revolution) has arrived. As such, it is naturally antagonistic to all "avant-garde" tendencies in the arts that might be considered virulent or destructive, and it indicates a theory of art that remains within the frame of Socialist Realism (in its contemporary revisionist guise) that would repress all such tendencies.[16]

Kan and his generation identified shingeki as a particular paradigm that committed its participants to a linear understanding of history with an implicit teleology. Far from being in the vanguard, Kan and his cohorts perceived Japan's orthodox modern theater as conservative, repressive, and antagonistic to all experimentation. It was, in a word, Stalinist.

The critic Tsuno Kaitarō who was a student at Waseda University in 1960 and a member of that university's Theater Study Society (Waseda gekiken), has explained the situation in less political, more theatrical terms:

> Shingeki has become historical; it has become a tradition in its own right. The problem of the younger generation has been to come to terms with this tradition. For us, modern European drama [which shingeki has sought to emulate] is no longer some golden ideal as yet out of reach. It is instead a pernicious, limiting influence. Beneath Shingeki's prosperous exterior there is decadence. It has lost the antithetic élan that characterized its origins. Shingeki no longer maintains the dialectical power to negate and transcend; rather, it has become an institution that itself demands to be transcended.[17]

What were the "avant-garde tendencies" to which Kan Takayuki was referring? What alternative to European modernism was Tsuno proposing? Tsuno explained in the same essay,

> We feel that although Shingeki's break with classical Nō and Kabuki was both justified and inevitable, it nonetheless cut us off from the sources of our traditions and trapped us within the restrictive confines of a static, bourgeois institution. Today we are seeking to reaffirm our tradition, but not as our predecessors did in the years leading up to the war. To them, reaffirming traditional values meant an atavistic and uncritical reinstatement of a fictitious, idealized past. We, on the other hand, are attempting to reaffirm our tradition, even when we find it distasteful, in order to deal directly and critically with it. Our hope is that by harnessing the energy of the Japanese popular imagination we can at once transcend the enervating clichés of modern drama and revolutionize what it means to be Japanese.[18]

Tsuno's ideas are summed up in the characteristic slogan of the 1960s *angura* (underground) theater movement: "use the pre-modern imagination to transcend the modern" [zenkindai no szōryōku o motte kindai o norikoero]. What Tsuno was proposing differed fundamentally from what the prewar Japan Romantic School *(Nihon romanha)* and its contemporary epigones like the novelist Mishima Yukio wanted, which was for Japan to venerate its supposedly timeless but in fact recently invented traditions (e.g., the centrality of the emperor to Japanese culture). Tsuno simply proposed using the premodern paradigm of art and theater to free theatrical creativity from the strictures and prescriptions of modernity. His goal was a future, as yet unrealized, "postmodern" theater.

But the immediate task at hand was unequivocal rejection of the shingeki movement. In terms that recall Osanai Kaoru's rejection of Kabuki, the new avant-garde blasted shingeki:

> Ultimately it is our intention to destroy shingeki as an art, shingeki as a system and in its place present before you a concrete alternative contemporary theater distinct from shingeki. . . . What we lack in money we will make up for with our wits, and where we lack experience we will rely on a new sensitivity and on concrete acts; we will explore modes of expression different from shingeki and give them form; we will explore different production systems from shingeki,

different ways of organizing ourselves, different ways of relating to our audiences, and we will give these form as well.[19]

Or, as the text of the poster carrying Theater Center 68/69's "Permanent Theatre Manifesto" read in 1969,

> We act, sing, and dance, of course. But our theater goes beyond these. We write, print, distribute, make, demonstrate, protest, show, study, teach, draw, paste, and run. Taken together, these are what we call "theatre." Down with bourgeois modernity in the theatre! Don't shut the theatre up behind theatre walls! Don't reduce theatre to a commodity! Stop thinking of theatre as something that already exists! Create theatre! Destroy theatre![20]

Angura

The avant-garde theater of the 1960s, known variously as "the little theater movement" *(shōgekijō undō)* and "the underground" *(angura)*, aimed to destroy shingeki, that is, modern theater, and to replace it with a different kind of contemporary theater that would instantiate the Japanese premodern imagination. A consensus emerged that the most radical and "progressive" avant-garde theater would paradoxically be the one that reclaimed most creatively Japan's premodern theater legacy, which shingeki had abandoned. The avant-garde of the 1960s was, in this sense, "traditionalist." It set about more or less systematically to dismantle the edifice of modern theater and create an alternative in its place that would exhibit the main characteristics of the premodern theater described above. This can be seen especially in the underground troupes' use of space, organization of time, and styles of acting.

Three troupes in particular were central to the underground movement. The Situation Theater (Jōkyō gekijō) was founded in 1963 by Kara Jurō, his wife Ri Reisen, and Maro Akaji (who later founded the Dairakudakan Butoh troupe). Theater Center 68/69, which later came to be known as the Black Tent Theater (BTT), was an eclectic group that brought together graduates of Tokyo and Waseda Universities and the conservatory program of the Actors Theater (Hayūzia). It included Tsuno Kaitarō, Satoh Makoto, Yamamoto Kiyokazu, and Saeki Ryūkō among others. The Waseda Little Theater (Waseda shōgekijō), which subsequently evolved into SCOT (Suzuki Company of Toga) and produced the so-called Suzuki method of actor training, was founded by the director Suzuki Tadashi, playwright Betsuyaku Minoru, and actor Ono Hiroshi in 1966. Terayama Shūji's Tenjō Sajiki, which is usually included in this list, belongs to a slightly different lineage and began as a more classically avant-garde troupe, as I shall explain below.

In August 1967, Kara Jurō pitched his red tent theater in the precincts of the Hanazono Shrine in the heart of the Shinjuku district of Tokyo. Kara and his troupe had been performing street theater in the Ginza and Shinjuku, but with the pitching of his red tent, he challenged the fundamentals of Japanese modern theater by transgressing the boundary between the modern and the premodern, between the secular and the religious, between empty, linear, historical time and ahistorical, supernatural time. Eschewing the profane space of theater buildings, he reclaimed the sacred space of the shrine compound and identified his artistic iconoclasm with the outlaws (tekiya, yakuza) and itinerant performers who had performed there for centuries. In the fullness of this space, Kara and his troupe were no longer Stanislavskian individuals probing their inner emotions. They were, they loudly proclaimed, kawara kojiki, come back to challenge modernity in the very heart of the modern city.

As a student at Meiji University, Kara had worked on Sartre for his graduation project, and his newly founded Situation Theater was named for Sartre's "theater of situations." The company's first production was the French existentialist's Respectful Prostitute with Kara in the role of the Senator. The theory of acting Kara espoused at the time was of "privileged bodies" (tokkenteki nikutai-ron), which derived from the theory of "privileged situations" in Sartre's novel Nausea.[21] For Kara, this was an antinomian notion: actors were those who created privileged situations, rising above social convention to reveal existence itself. Like Osanai, the way back to the premodern imagination for Kara was through European philosophy.[22]

Like Kara, Suzuki Tadashi was working to deconstruct the modern play and refocus the theater on the actor's performance—but he was going about it in a far more methodical, systematic way. Suzuki was one of the founders of the Waseda Little Theater, which had been established in 1966 but which had roots going back to the founders' student days at Waseda University around 1960. During its early years, the troupe produced the plays of Betsuyaku Minoru, innovative works like The Elephant (Zō) and The Little Match Girl (Matchi-uri no shōjo) that used a linguistic simplicity influenced by the works of Beckett and Ionesco to explore the aftermath of the war.[23] But in August 1968, Betsuyaku left the troupe, and in 1969 Suzuki staged *On the Dramatic Passions I.* Starring the phenomenal Shiraishi Kayoko, whose husky voice and overwhelming intensity transfixed the audience, *On the Dramatic Passions I* was a collage of scenes from classic modern plays, both Western and Japanese, that displaced the playwright and refocused the theater on the actor's performance. So successful was this experiment that in 1970 Suzuki repeated it in *On the Dramatic Passions II: The Shiraishi Kayoko Show,* which not only acknowledged Shiraishi's personal contribution to Suzuki's evolving vision but also expanded the purview of the collage technique to encompass works of the premodern Japanese imagination from the grotesque and cruel plays of Tsuruya Namboku to the eerily haunted works of Izumi Kyōka. Suzuki was moving back in time to recapture and reaffirm the actor-centered world of Kabuki.

Kara's and Suzuki's emphasis on the actor did not mean that playwriting had gone completely out of favor. The best play of 1969 as recognized by the Kishida Award for Playwriting was Satoh Makoto's *Nezumi Kōzo: The Rat (Nezumi Kōzo Jirokichi),* which was staged in a tiny basement space in the Roppongi district of central Tokyo.[24]

Nezumi Kōzo radically challenged the ubiquitous linear temporality of modern drama. Instead of the beginning, middle, and end of the well-made modern play, where the action develops smoothly and logically to a climactic resolution, *Nezumi Kōzo* pitted linear time, with its implicit goal orientation, the sense that time is going somewhere, against cyclical time, time as eternal return. The action of the play takes place simultaneously in the early nineteenth century and at the end of World War II. The story concerns a group of five characters who have been brought together by their common wish upon a falling star, which is identified variously as Nezumi Kōzo and the atomic bomb. The five characters, who are desperately poor and dream of a revolution that will radically change their lives, are opposed by three incarnations of changelessness, who morph from one form to another, stymieing the characters' initiatives at every turn and transforming their dream of revolution from a goal attainable within history to a mere point on the revolving wheel of fabulous time. The three tricksters deflect and redefine the aspirations of the five downtrodden souls, until at the end of the play we see them consume their own children and then be consumed themselves by a maelstrom of madness and death.

Festooned with the appurtenances of a Shinto shrine, the tiny basement theater where *Nezumi Kōzo* was performed was transformed into a sacred space. Similarly, the temporal structure of the play reflected the shamanic imagination that is characteristic of Kabuki plays like the classic *Sukeroku,* where the ostensible story of a debonair dandy competing with his rich but ugly and superannuated rival for the affections of a beautiful young courtesan is revealed in the end to actually be an episode in the eternal, metahistorical pursuit by a young warrior named Soga Gorō (who had died five hundred years before) of the evil samurai who slew his father and stole his father's sword.[25] There is a chase very much like this in *Nezumi Kōzo,* where the five characters, scavenging for half-eaten turnips in their historical moment, are shown "in reality" to be engaged in an ongoing, metahistorical pursuit of their nemesis, the Lord of the Dawn, through the backwaters of historical time.

As I have argued at length elsewhere, the 1960s were a period when the gods who had been banished from the modern Japanese stage returned in force.[26] This phenomenon, which is a concomitant of avant-garde nostalgia, can also be seen in the evolution of the dance of Hijikata Tatsumi, founder of Ankoku Butoh ("the dance of darkness"). Hijikata, who was influenced through Ohno Kazuo by Ishii Baku and the German expressionist dancers Harold Kreutzberg and Mary Wigman, had begun performing iconoclastic pieces like *Forbidden Colors* (*Kinjiki,* 1959) conceived in the classically avant-garde mode. In October 1968, however, Hijikata performed the epoch-making *Hijikata Tatsumi and the Japanese: Revolt of the Flesh,* which signaled a new direction. As Kurihara Naoko has noted, "The first part of the title indicates that Hijikata was making a conscious change from an apparently 'Western' focus to work that intensely examined his own body, specifically, a male body that grew up in Tohoku [northeastern Japan]."[27] Much has been written about the sources of Hijikata's inspiration, but the most convincing thesis is Nomura Yukihiro's argument that Hijikata studied and then emulated the images of suffering humanity depicted in medieval Japanese, principally Buddhist, art.[28] Whether he was inspired by Nō, as Shibusawa Tatsuhiko suggested, Kabuki, as was argued by Gunji Masakatsu, or medieval Japanese art, as Nomura argues, it is clear that Hijikata was participating in and contributing to the nostalgic, "traditionalist" movement in the performing arts that was sweeping Japan at the time.[29]

Any list of the most important Japanese troupes of the 1960s has to include Terayama Shūji's Tenjō Sajiki, founded in 1967.[30] As the theater critic Senda Akihiko has written, however, "Tenjō Sajiki occupies a different place in the theater world from the Situation Theater, the Waseda Little Theater, and [Satoh's] Freedom Theater."[31] Senda attributes the difference to the fact that, unlike the other troupes, Tenjō Sajiki had

originated neither in university theater clubs nor in the satellite troupes
of the major shingeki companies. Indeed, four years older than Suzuki,
eight years older than Satoh, and not a student in 1960, Terayama shared
little of the political experience that bound the other theater activists
together.

As an avant-garde artist, Terayama conceived himself in the classic
mold of Dalí, Lautréamont, Breton, Buñuel, Artaud, and Fellini. His
display of enormously fat women and midgets, his taste for surrealist
imagery, his interest in homosexuality as sexual "deviance," his constant
desire to shock the bourgeoisie and betray their expectations with happenings, street theater, and other assaults on "reality" were all inspired
by the classic avant-garde he emulated. While he employed premodern
images and artifacts, he did not share his peers' interest in reclaiming the
premodern imagination as such. The fact that Tenjō Sajiki was a regular
at European theater festivals in the 1970s confirmed for his peers in
Japan, who were striving to distinguish what they were doing from
European models, that Terayama was about something quite different
from themselves. Kara Jurō's charge that Terayama was a "cultural scan-
dalmonger" [bunkateki sukyadarisuto] and "an artistic social striver of
the northeaster variety [Tohōkugata geijutsu shusseshugi]" bears this
out. But Senda Akihiko hit the nail on the head when he labeled Terayama the "eternal avant-garde [eien no zen'ei]."[32] Terayama lacked the
nostalgia and "traditionalism" of his contemporaries and represented a
more classic avant-garde approach.

Conclusion: The End of the Avant-Garde

Angura's revolt against modernism and its reclamation of the premodern
imagination succeeded, radically expanding the possibilities of the theater in Japan. Japanese theater rapidly underwent a thoroughgoing
"angurazation," attracting new audiences and widespread media attention. To accommodate the newly popular theater, the Seibu Department Store chain built the Parco Theater (Parco gekijō; capacity 458) in
1973 in the fashionable Shibuya section of Tokyo. This was followed by
a rush among corporations to build state-of-the-art facilities for the new
theater, including, in the 1970s, the Sunshine Theater (capacity 832)
built in Ikebukuro in 1978, and the Hakuhinkan Theater (capacity 381)
built in Ginza the same year.[33] By 1995, numerous theaters studded
Tokyo and other cities, and on average 4.3 new contemporary theater
productions were being opened in Tokyo every day of the year, serving

an audience of more than 3.3 million people.[34] In the mid-1980s, government spending on the arts rapidly increased, culminating in the construction of a multi-million-dollar New National Theater devoted to modern theater in 1997. Abroad, as Karatani Kōjin suggests, "traditionalists" like Suzuki Tadashi and Butoh troupes descended from Hijikata and from Maro Akaji's Dairakudakan came to be regarded as the most cutting-edge representatives of the Japanese avant-garde.

It is hard to imagine from our present vantage point the bipolar theatrical world that existed in Japan prior to the 1960s, with modern theater opposed to premodern forms. Today, everything is permitted, and the variations and hybrid experiments seem endless. Given the elasticity and catholicity of the current scene, which appears able to tolerate almost anything, it is difficult to imagine how a new iconoclasm could get much traction. Experimentation is everywhere, but angura may well have been the Japanese theater's final avant-garde.

Notes

1. Matei Calinescu, *Five Faces of Modernity* (Durham: Duke University Press, 1987), 117.

2. Miryam Sas, *Fault Lines: Cultural Memory and Japanese Surrealism* (Stanford: Stanford University Press, 1999).

3. Karatani Kōjin, "Japan as Museum: Okakura Tenshin and Ernest Fenollosa," trans. Sabu Kohso, in Alexandra Munroe, *Japanese Art after 1945: Scream against the Sky* (New York: Abrams, 1994), 34.

4. Quoted in Tsuno Kaitarō, *Pesuto to gekijō* [Theater and the Plague] (Tokyo: Shbunsha, 1980), 131.

5. Hirosue Tamotsu, "The Secret Ritual of the Place of Evil," trans. David G. Goodman, *Concerned Theatre Japan*, 2.1–2 (1972): 14–21.

6. Karatani, Kōjin, *Origins of Modern Japanese Literature,* ed. Brett de Bary (Durham: Duke University Press, 1993), 54–55.

7. *Osanai Karou zensh,* vol. 6 (Kyoto: Rinsen shoten, 1975), 459–60.

8. Calinescu, *Five Faces of Modernity,* 117.

9. Soda Hidehiko, *Osanai Kaoru to nijusseiki engeki* (Tokyo: Bensei shuppan, 1999), 119–20.

10. Ibid., 126.

11. Ibid., 112–13.

12. Ibid., 230.

13. Gennifer Weisenfeld, *Mavo: Japanese Artists and the Avant-Garde, 1905–1931* (Berkeley: University of California Press, 2002), 249.

14. Kubo Sakae, *Land of Volcanic Ash,* trans. David G. Goodman (Ithaca: Cornell East Asia Program).

15. A. Horie-Webber, "Modernisation of the Japanese Theatre: The Shingeki Movement," in *Modern Japan: Aspects of History, Literature and Society,* ed. W. G. Beasley (Berkeley: University of California Press, 1975), 148–49.

16. Kan Takayuki, *Sengo engeki: Shingeki wa norikoerareta ka,* Asahi sensho 178 (Tokyo: Asahi shimbunsha, 1981), 86.

17. Tsuno Kaitarō, "The Tradition of Modern Theatre in Japan," trans. David G. Goodman, *Canadian Theatre Review,* Fall 1978, 1.

18. Ibid., 19.

19. "Engeki sentaa ni tsuite" (undated mimeograph), 1. Also quoted in Senda Akihiko, "Kaisetsu," *Gendai Nihon gikyoku taikei,* vol. 8 (Tokyo: San'ichi shobō, 1972), 418–19.

20. David G. Goodman, *Angura: Posters of the Japanese Avant-Garde* (New York: Princeton Architectural Press, 1999), 25.

21. Akihiko Senda, *Nihon no gendai engeki* (Tokyo: Iwanami, 1995), 32–34.

22. Scenes of Kara and his troupe performing in Shinjuku are included as a central part of Oshima Nagisa's 1969 film *Diary of a Shinjuku Thief (Shinjuku dorob nikki).*

23. Both of these plays have been translated into English. See *The Elephant* in David G. Goodman, *After Apocalypse: Four Japanese Plays of Hiroshima and Nagasaki* (Ithaca: Cornell East Asia Program, 1995), 183–248; and Robert Rolf and John Gillespie, *Alternative Japanese Drama* (Honolulu: University of Hawaii Press, 1992).

24. Translated in Goodman, *After Apocalypse,* 251–319.

25. Barbara E. Thornbury, *Sukeroku's Double Identity: The Dramatic Structure of Edo Kabuki* (Ann Arbor: Center for Japanese Studies, University of Michigan, 1982).

26. David G. Goodman, *The Return of the Gods: Japanese Drama and Culture in the 1960s* (Ithaca: Cornell East Asia Program, 2003). This volume was originally published as *Japanese Drama and Culture in the 1960s: The Return of the Gods* (Armonk: M. E. Sharpe, 1988).

27. Naoko Kurihara, "Hijikata Tatsumi: The Words of Butoh," *Drama Review* 34.1 (2000): 20.

28. Yukihiro Nomura, "Hijikata Tatsumi to Nihon bijutsu," *Theatre Arts,* no. 5 (1996), 172–81.

29. Shibusawa and Gunji are quoted in ibid., 174–75.

30. The troupe took its name from *Tenj sajiki no hitobito,* the Japanese title of Marcel Carne's 1945 film classic, *Children of Paradise.*

31. Senda, *Nihon no gendai engeki,* 136.

32. Ibid., 135. Kara's comments are quoted on p. 140.

33. Ikebukuro, like Ginza, is a section of Tokyo.

34. Bunka kagaku kenkyūjo (Institute for the Arts), unpublished data. This number represents the total of 1,584 separate productions of modern theater (excluding commercial plays and musicals) divided by 365. Audience figures are actually the total number of seats available and thus reflect the potential, not the actual, audience. If the other performing arts (excluding music) are included, there were 3,755 productions in Tokyo in 1995 or more than 10 new ones mounted every day of the year, serving an audience of 15,527,951.

Border Crossings
Three Transnationalisms of Fluxus

Hannah Higgins

I have argued elsewhere that Fluxus performance is both an extension and critique of that great movement known as American Abstraction or Abstract Expressionism.[1] To limit it exclusively to either domain, critique *or* extension, is to view it either as an unproblematic extension of formal modernism, *or* as a mere negation—just so much neo-Dada chaos. It stands to reason that, as extension and/or critique, what came to be known as neo-Dadaism differs both by aesthetic and social form. Where one set of modern movements might be identified by their ability to express a national gestalt (German Expressionism, American Painting, Italian Futurism, etc.), the other trajectory is rightly described in opposition to these. The other stream, which might be called the avant-garde and which routinely dips into and out of the other (much as a stream bends around stones), is self-consciously transnational, doing its best to transgress and ignore national boundaries, nationalist gestalts, and the other sundry forms of centrist political and economic organization that characterized the modern era.

Typical of this current, the transnationalism of Fluxus is mentioned repeatedly in artists' statements, and is appropriately understood as an indictment of American hegemony in the postwar period. For this reason many Fluxus artists routinely use the term *internationalism* to describe the reach of American power in the postwar period, while arguing for the "internationalism" of Fluxus as different—or for our purposes transnational from the perspective of the nonhierarchical nature of the relationship. For example, Fluxus artist and resident historian Ken Friedman describes Fluxus in transnational terms while using the word *international* to describe American hegemony: "When it came time for

265

America to stand on its own in the international art world, however, politics, economics, and political economics dictated that Abstract Expressionism be treated a some kind of uniquely American triumph," which was rejected by Fluxus artists.[2] Friedman continues, "It is the other tradition that influenced Fluxus, a tradition that has inevitably been neglected because it is antinationalistic in sentiment and tone and practiced by artists who are not easily used as national flag-bearers."[3]

Similarly, Fluxus artist Dick Higgins (my father), listed international-ism as the first of nine points "common among most Fluxworks."[4] As it was used, a transnational ethos is implied. Describing the earliest mur-murs of Fluxus around the globe in the late 1950s and early 1960s, he wrote:

> In Europe there were, in the beginning . . . Wolf Vostell, Nam June Paik, Emmett Williams and Ben Patterson, among others. In the United States there were, besides myself, Alison Knowles, George Brecht, Robert Watts, and others I have already named; also La Monte Young, Philip Corner, Ay-O and still others. In Japan there were Takehisha Kosugi and Mieko Shiomi, and more. Probably there were about two dozen of us in six countries.[5]

From these two artists' statements a pair of basic facts about Fluxus are surmisable. First, for these and other Fluxus artists, the group was inten-tionally transnational from the outset and, second, this transnationalism functions as a core criterion of Fluxus practice. Put differently, the transnationalism of Fluxus does not merely mark its social dimension, but is inherent in the work as well. In what follows I will describe these two aspects of the transnationalism of Fluxus; first by telling the histori-cal narrative establishing the loose network of Fluxus artists, and then through descriptions of several Fluxus works that are structured accord-ing to a transnational paradigm.

The first part of the story of Fluxus as a transnational artists' group is virtually uncontested. Although it is quite impossible to say exactly when Fluxus began, it is possible to establish a time span during which its experimental formats were established and the social nexus of Fluxus was formed. Experiments in sound art, installation, and performance were occurring simultaneously in Japan, Germany, Eastern Europe, and the United States in the late 1950s and early 1960s. These experiments were being carried out by "Group Ongaku" and others at the Sogetsu Art Center in Tokyo, in the classroom and among the students of composer Karlheinz Stockhausen in Cologne, Germany, and around John Cage in New York.

These cells of activity would become united under the rubric of Fluxus in about 1962 and in large part as a result of the travels of Cage around the world. While it might be argued that demonstrating the centrality of an American composer to Fluxus as a community in the pre-Fluxus days merely reiterates the American centered model for postwar culture, I would counter that Cage's travels were logistically possible because of the internationalism of American culture, but that he utilized this access to promote an agenda of transnationalism. In other words, these travels spun a kind of world wide web, or communication network, through which nonhierarchical creative collaborations were made possible.

A World Wide Web?

In 1958 and 1959 several students of the Musicology Program at Tokyo National University and their friends in Fine Arts and Literature established a collaborative, improvisatory music group. By 1960, this collaboration expanded to include dance and was called "Group Ongaku" and included among its members several artist-composers who would become associated with Fluxus after 1962. These were Takehisha Kosugi, Chieko (Mieko) Shiomi, and Yasunao Tone. In 1961 and 1962 this group gave several important concerts at the Sogetsu Art Center in Tokyo. The center constituted the core of Japan's active avant-garde scene. In 1962 Cage visited the center with (then expatriate) Yoko Ono, while on a six-week tour of Japan. Cage dedicated a work to her and her husband at the time, the established experimental composer and future Fluxus artist, Toshi Ichiyanagi. This work resonated with his own, famous *4'33"* of silence. The piece, *0'00"*, is strikingly minimal: "In a situation provided with maximum amplification (No Feedback), perform a disciplined action."[6] These and other concerts were held and the seeds sown for Japanese Fluxus, especially in terms of establishing the written correspondence and creative exchanges that would evolve into later friendships and collaborations.[7]

European Fluxus likewise evolves an aesthetic independently of Cage, albeit eventually developing lines of communication with other groups in contact with him. Since the early 1950s, German serialist composer Karlheinz Stockhausen had been at the center of vanguard music in Germany. His composition course in Darmstadt, which was attended by American minimalist composer La Monte Young (1950) and Korean artist Nam Jun Paik (1957–58), shared an orbit of experimentation with the Darmstadt Circle of poetry and theater that included (in the late 1950s) American expatriate poet Emmett Williams. From 1958 to 1963 Stockhausen also worked through the electronic music studio of WDR (West German Radio) in Cologne (with Paik), as well as the influential performance atelier of his wife, the painter Mary Bauermeister, also in Cologne.[8] An international array of artists later associated with Fluxus could be found circulating through this remarkable atelier and the greater context of it: the list would include Paik, Benjamin Patterson (United States), Wolf Vostell (Germany), and Williams.

Significantly, Events written by Cage's students in New York were presented in Cologne at this atelier in 1960. These were performed at the Contre Festival (a music Festival de Resistance) against the IGNM (International Society for New Music) in June. This four-day series included, from the circle of students associated with Cage, works by Cage, George Brecht and La Monte Young and, from Darmstadt and Cologne, works by Paik and Patterson.

> [Bauermeister] organized a "Contre-Festival," to be held in Cologne over four days in June. . . . The performances included works by John Cage, Toshi Ichiyanagi, Sylvano Bussotti, George Brecht, La Monte Young and Christian Wolff—performed by David Tudor—as well as two concerts by Nam June Paik. . . . (In October) Merce Cunningham and Carolyn Brown danced to pieces by John Cage, Christian Wolff, Earle Brown, Toshi Ichiyanagi and Bo Nilsson, performed by David Tudor and John Cage. One day later, again in the attic studio, one heard and saw compositions by Cage, La Monte Young and Paik—the interpreters were Cornelius Cardew, Hans G. Helms, David Tudor and Benjamin Patterson.[9]

Based in part on these historic concerts involving several Fluxus artists at the Bauermeister atelier, the atelier has been called a "Proto-Fluxus in Cologne."[10]

The nearby German town of Wuppertal, later home of the first "Fluxus"-titled exhibition at Gallerie Parnass in 1962, was the home of the publisher Kalender/Ebeling und Dietrich, which produced scrolled magazines of experimental music and poetry appropriately called *Kalendarrolle No. 1* and *Kalendarrolle No. 2* in November 1961 and June 1962, respectively. These scrolls brought together an international assortment of artists and associates, among them Paik, Patterson, Swiss artist Diter Rot, Williams, and Young—all of whom would later become associated with Fluxus.

In summary, both before and after this context in flux was in flux as an *us,* it included artists from the United States, almost every European country, and Korea and Japan. What remained was to establish the "us" of Fluxus. The lines of communication as well as the terms of collaboration were enabled in large part by the communications network established by Cage's travels. Even in New York, which was to become one center of Fluxus activity in the 1960s, the community of Fluxus developed around this mild-mannered composer.

In John Cage's historic class Composition of Experimental Music at the New School for Social Research in New York in 1958, many future associates of Fluxus in the United States met for the first time. Cage would borrow concert material from this class for the 1960 Bauermeister concerts named above. Similarly, his uniquely minimal event *0'00"* of the 1962 Sogetsu concert adapts from the explorations of his composition class as well. Fluxus artists in Cage's class included a chemist, George Brecht, a collagist, Al Hansen, a poet and composer, Dick Higgins, and another poet, Jackson Mac Low.

Among the experiments produced in the class was a new performance format called the *Event,* which was invented in the class by George Brecht. The Event figures heavily in the subsequent work of most Fluxus artists around the globe, and while the form of documentation differs by artist, most can be scored in the format shown in George Brecht's collected early Events, *Water Yam* of 1963–65 (fig. 1). These call for the performance of everyday rituals or routines (or absurd versions of these) in such a way that the informational structure of the routine—its experiential character, possible contradictions, or normally ignored elements—are thrown into high relief for the performer or viewer. For example, Brecht's Solo for Violin, Viola, Cello or Contrabass (1962) reads simply "polishing."[11] The performer enters, carefully polishes the instrument and leaves, and in so doing shifts the audience's attention from virtuoso performance to preparation of the instrument. Another Event, by Czech Fluxus artist Milan Knizak, is called *Snowstorm No. 1* (1965) and simply instructs that "Paper gliders are distributed to an idle and waiting audience" (fig. 2).[12] What results is a snowstorm of quietly gliding paper airplanes as the audience returns them . . . back and forth and back and forth and so on. The exchange of sheets is experientially beautiful, like the caring gesture toward the instrument as tended to by

Brecht. Both works therefore illustrate the implied attentiveness to the everyday world around the performer demanded by the Event format, which clearly evolves out of Cage's theory of "silent" music as a means of "waking up to the very life we're living."[13]

Collaborations ensued in and around the Cage class. These included the New York Audio Visual Group, which was established by Hansen and Higgins early in 1959. This group held regular Sunday morning performance-meetings at the Epitome Coffee Shop on Bleeker Street in Manhattan. Meetings consisted of collaborations and demonstrations with many artists who would become associates of Fluxus, including fellow student Jackson Mac Low. Relatedly, in 1961, Jackson Mac Low and La Monte Young took over the East Coast issue of a California-based publication called *Beatitude* (renaming it *Beatitude East*), which was released in 1961 as a collection of Events and like-minded experimental musical notations called *An Anthology*. Like the *Kalendarrolle* of Wuppertal, of the twenty-four composers (from Europe, Japan, and the United States) in *An Anthology,* over half would become associated with the rubric *Fluxus* a year later.

An earlier Cage class (1957) had included composer La Monte Young, who introduced the erstwhile organizer of Fluxus and Lithuanian graphic designer, George Maciunas, to the artists of *An Anthology* late in 1960 or early in 1961. That year Maciunas opened a gallery at 925 Madison with his friend Almus Salcius. Albeit originally intended as a site for selling ancient instruments and abstract art, after meeting the artists loosely associated with the Cage class, the program was changed. In 1961 the AG gallery hosted a series of performance evenings of experimental music in order to support a proposed Fluxus Magazine—the first time the name *Fluxus* appears in print.[14] Also in 1961, Japanese expatriate artist Yoko Ono hosted a performance series in her loft with the help of Young.

In summary, as Fluxus slowly evolved into a group, artists, poets, and composers from across the globe took up the highly elastic Event format and corresponding experimental attitude, adapting it to their poetry, dance, daily life, and musical traditions. What resulted was a truly global, avant-garde group. Perhaps it was inevitable that these artists would make transnationalism an explicit or implicit topic in their work. In any case, there are two forms of what might be called "Flux geography" within Fluxus. The first form is representational; the artists addressed an international array of Fluxus artists and made special or altered maps charting (real or imagined) creative exchanges with them. The second

Fig. 1. George Brecht, *Water Yam*. The two exampled, center right, have collaged covers made by Brecht, ca. 1965.

Fig. 2. Milan Knizak, *Snowstorm No. 1* (1965)

form is a bit more ambiguous, although it too reflects the transnationalism of Fluxus. The artists wrote Events for each other as dedications. These dedications routinely address geographic, cultural, and linguistic distances between the artists.

Fluxus Geographers

Border crossings figure heavily in the works of Fluxus artists from virtually every continent and throughout its forty years of activity. In every case, however, a unique Fluxus geography is implied. It is flexible geography of altered state-lines, moving continents, mobile artists, and otherwise fluxing boundaries predicated on an elastic web of personal relationships held together by common interests, free-form socializing, and written correspondence with artists around the globe.

The artists' specific applications of this geographic flux betray the wide range of intentions that typify almost every aspect of Fluxus as a group. There are no fixed outcomes, no agreed-upon manifestos, and no explicit political doctrines dictating the behavior. Rather, the fluxing boundaries have implications that range from the militant to the fine-arts cultural, to the merely social and the experiential in what Fluxus scholar Owen Smith has called "a non-hierarchical density of experience. In this way Fluxus does not refer to a style or even a procedure as such but to the presence of a totality of social activities."[15] Reflecting these social activities, one type of Flux geography suggests the movement of people or information around the globe as it is currently mapped.

In the following 1975 letter to Japanese Fluxus artist Mieko Shiomi, for example, Maciunas uses the transnational community of Fluxus artists to spar with the attorney general of New York, whose office was harassing owners of several artists' co-op housing projects organized by Maciunas and called Fluxhouse Inc.

Dear Mieko,
Could you mail me in an envelope a blank postcard. . . . I will write a message and then send it to you to mail it to the Attorney General in N.Y. It will look like I am in Japan. I will do this from all over the world. Absolutely confuse him. Thanks a lot,[16] George

This simple use of the mail makes a person virtually invisible: the artist is everywhere and therefore nowhere to be found. This project was called "Flux Combat" and its object was the meddling bureaucracy of New

York City, which had a difficult time categorizing (for taxation and regulation) artists' use of industrial space for domestic and studio life. With other Fluxus artists and friends Maciunas had established Fluxhouse Inc. as a cooperative housing scheme that would enable artists to purchase renovated industrial space at cost.[17] When the bureaucracy threatened the project, he sent these subversive requests around the world.

More typical are proposals for circumnavigations of the world published by Maciunas in 1975–76. These would take the form of caravans in "Rover type" trucks, a sailing trip on an eighty-five-foot schooner or, most famously, "a very extensive sailing not just around, but throughout the world" in a converted mine sweeper.[18] These circumnavigations proposed that groups of ten to twelve artists serving various crew functions would travel around the world visiting some hundred various historic (if unrecognized) sites. The last is the most compelling; in contrast to gazing over vast distances through the windows of a plane, through the windows of a truck, or over the side of a boat, the artists would be confined to a vary small space, presumably talking, making Fluxus projects, and occasionally exiting for a visit somewhere. Days might be spent in the unclaimed space of "international waters," while artists from this truly transnational avant-garde group would prowl the dark, deep waters of the world's oceans and least populated regions. What's more, beneath the ocean and in the remotest parts of the world, borders are unmarked and therefore freely passed over. Remarkably, each proposal included equipment lists, technical diagrams of each vessel, proposed itineraries and detailed site maps of many proposed stops.

The most famous Fluxus maps are probably Mieko Shiomi's "Spatial Poems." The first, "Spatial Poem No. 1" (1965), details sixty-nine word locations collected between March and May 1965 (indicated by printed flags) on a hand-drawn map of the world (fig. 3). "Spatial Poem No. 2" (1966) details the directions people were facing around the world at 10:00 P.M. (Greenwich time) on October 15, 1965, and "Spatial Poem No. 3" (1972), a puzzle-calendar. In these Spatial Poems, a moment and action are placed in relative space on a global scale, but at a shared moment in time. The function of time is crucial here as it marks the shared experience, the transposition, of artists the world over. As a written work displaying words and locations across the space of the page, it is most obviously a poem. However, at the moment when the words were found, there was a poem too: imagined but not knowable by the participants since what came before or after one's choice was unknowable. Like Maciunas's Flux Combat postcards, Shiomi's simultaneously ephemeral (as performance) and concrete (as poem) work necessitated correspondence across not one or two, but perhaps forty different national boundaries. The spatial poem is only conceivable, much less realizable, from within the context of a group of artists routinely carrying out transnational, creative exchange.

It comes as no surprise that several Fluxus artists reconfigured maps, historic and contemporary, in manners that reflect this principle of national fluidity. Within Fluxus even the comparatively traditional medium of painting expresses the principle of fluid borders and exchanges; Dick Higgins painted a series of maps overlaid with arrows that sweep across geographical, political, and historic boundaries as well (fig. 4). The arrows derive from Higgins's early experiments with choreography, which he called Graphis works, in the late 1950s. In the Graphis works, performers responded to moving lights, later expressed as lines and arrows as directional and gestural instructions. In the paintings, these choreographic lines suggest the movement of human forms (friends?) freely around the globe: the human body as weather pattern. He called the arrows "wind."[19] Insofar as the map is true to its source, the map paintings are like Maciunas's detailed maps for circumnavigation as well as Shiomi's for the Spatial Poems.

However, another form of Flux geography transforms the maps and their content—altering distances and geographical relationships through assemblage, collage, and scale manipulation. For example, Robert Watts's limited edition Fluxkit *Fluxatalas* (1972), would consist of a box containing about fifty stones from "specific and well described locations (country, town vicinity, which beach or shore, which sea, lake or river) . . . from various parts of the world. (So far we have pebbles from Azores, Minorca, Cycladic Islands, Cape Hateras, end of Long Island, Manhattan . . .)" (fig. 5).[20] Maciunas's label for the edition shows an altered map. This atlas of stones suggests an alternate world geography conceived from the standpoint of mobile, natural artifacts brought together through the collective efforts of this transnational artists' group.

The work harkens back to cabinets of curiosities, those seventeenth-century containers for natural wonders garnered from around the world. Instead of natural wonders that mark each place for its specificity, however, we find simple stones, remarkable for their similarities more than for their differences. What's more, the list of places is idiosyncratic, reflecting the happenstance locations of friends rather than demonstrating the farthest reaches of human travel in the era before commercial tourism.

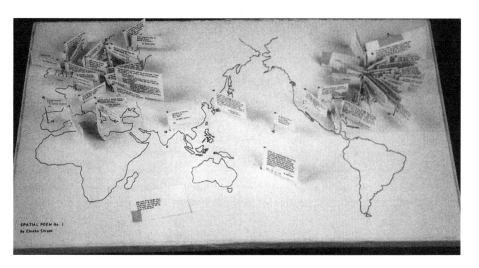

Fig. 3. Mieko Shiomi, "Spatial Poem No. 1" (1965)

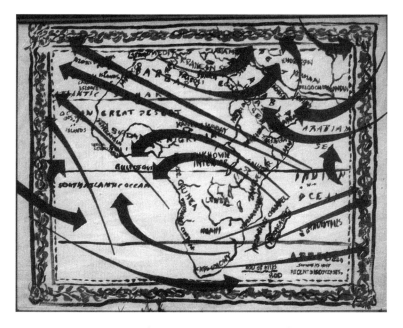

Fig. 4. Dick Higgins, Map Painting, no date

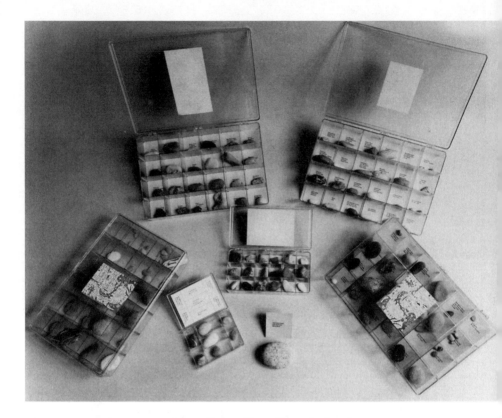

Fig. 5. Robert Watts, *Fluxatalas* (1972)

In a similar vein, French Fluxus poet Robert Filliou described an imaginary, new discipline of geography within his projected, utopian university the PoiPoiDrome—"Geography—streets and roads a man has trod on printed on his shoe soles."[21] This lighthearted take on the subject also suggests the social, as opposed to universal, dimensions of space. There would be identical tracts of paths traversed with friends, and anomalous patterns where the walker trod alone. One imagines two friends comparing soles (souls?).

The second form of transnationalism as practice might be said to take its lead from the social side of Fluxus. In this second form, where Events are written by one artist and dedicated to another, the transnationalism of Fluxus is reflected not literally (as a map), but indirectly, as a cultural by-product of a group routinely engaged in transnational exchange, like Shiomi's spatial poems. The practice is commonplace among Fluxus artists living near each other; however, for the purpose of this argument the list is limited to dedications that cross national boundaries.

For reasons I have been unable to ascertain, a disproportionate number of these dedications involve Korean Fluxus artist Nam June Paik. Higgins included a dedicated Event to Paik in his "Danger Music" series, which places the performer in physical or psychological danger. *Danger Music Number Nine* (For Nam June Paik) of February 1962 reads: "Volunteer to have your spine removed."[22] Paik responded with *Danger Music for Dick Higgins,* "Creep into the VAGINA of a living WHALE."[23]

While in Europe organizing the first Fluxus-titled festivals, Lithuanian expatriate George Maciunas wrote *Twelve Piano Compositions for Nam June Paik* (1962), which American Emmett Williams (who has spent most of his life living in Germany) expanded in another (thirteenth) *Composition to Paik.* Maciunas's series extrapolates from two Brecht Events, the Solo for Violin and his famous Piano Piece (1962) instructing "a vase of flowers on (to) a piano."[24] Maciunas's dedicated compositions for Paik are therefore simultaneously adapted from Brecht—a double homage.

> Composition No. 1 Let piano movers carry piano onto the stage.
> Composition No. 2 Tune the piano.
> Composition No. 3 Paint with orange paint patterns over the piano.
> Composition No. 4 Using a straight stick the length of the keyboard sound all keys together.
> Composition No. 5 Place a dog or cat (or both) inside the piano and play Chopin.
> Composition No. 6 Stretch the three highest strings with a tuning key until they break.
> Composition No. 7 Place one piano on top of another (one can be smaller).
> Composition No. 8 Place piano upside down and *put a vase with flowers* over the sound box.
> Composition No. 9 Draw a picture of a piano so that the audience can see the picture.
> Composition No. 10 Write a sign reading: piano composition no. 10 and show the audience the sign.
> Composition No. 11 Wash the piano, wax and *polish it* well.
> Composition No. 12 Let piano movers carry the piano out of the stage.[25]

Williams responds with *Piano Concert for Paik No. 2* (1965), which involves a Fluxus ensemble or orchestra in the coercion of a pianist:

> Orchestra members seat themselves and wait for the pianist. The pianist enters, bows and walks to the piano. Upon reaching the piano, he jumps from the stage and runs to the exit. Orchestra members run after him, catch him and drag him back to the piano. The pianist must try his best to keep away from the piano. When the pianist is finally returned to the piano, the lights are turned off.[26]

Three years later, Williams made another dedication, this time to the composer who introduced these artists to Maciunas in 1961. *For La Monte Young* (1962) reads, "Performer asks if La Monte Young is in the audience."[27] The piece has a situational humor. The audience invariably looks around for someone by that name to stand up, assuming he is somehow necessary to the performance. Young was not in Europe during the first blossoming of Fluxus Festivals in 1962, although he had already played a crucial role in early Fluxus; perhaps Williams was invoking him, or the irony of his absence during this clearly historic moment.

Paik, on the other hand was part of what Williams has rightly called the "'permanent cadre' of seven traveling performers" during the European tour.[28] Sometime later, in about 1965, Japanese Fluxus artist Takehisha Kosugi would write *South No. 2 (to Nam June Paik)* for his Korean comrade. The text pokes gentle humor at Paik's strong Korean accent, while it simultaneously invites the audience to study the translingual sound (of an English word spoken by an émigré Korean) for an almost unendurable duration:

> Pronounce "SOUTH" during a duration of more than 15 minutes. Pause for breath is permitted but transition from pronunciation of one letter to another should be smooth and slow.[29]

In addition to this long list of dedications to Paik, dedications across European boundaries were also common. For example, George Brecht, then expatriate American living in Niece, wrote *For a Drummer (For Eric)* (1966). The dedication refers to Danish Fluxus artist and onetime student at the Conservatory of Music in Copenhagen, Eric Andersen:

> Drum on something you have never drummed on before.
> Drum with something you have never drummed with before.[30]

One imagines all forms of musicalization—bodies, food, instruments, and so on.

A year later, Swedish Fluxus artist Bengt af Klintberg wrote *Number 4 (Danger Music for Henning Christiansen)* for the Danish Fluxus by that name (famous for painting things a lurid, bright green). The score simultaneously refers to Higgins's "Danger Music" scores in the title and content; "Climb up into a tree. Saw off the branch you sit on."[31] Dick Higgins had also written for this artist in *Danger Music Number Thirty-Three (For Henning Christiansen)* (May 1963), "Have a ball show."[32]

Altogether, these dedicated Events, like the objects discussed before them, demonstrate techniques through which Fluxus artists have made work that demonstrates, or explicitly illustrates, creative exchange with each other across national and cultural boundaries. These are not mere diagrams of the origins of artists, or traveling shows that introduce work around the globe, but actually demonstrate the putting-into-practice of the principle of transnationalism that is central to Fluxus. This is especially true of the use of distant friends to expand the contents of a work, as in the work of Mieko (Chieko) Shiomi. All of these works are, however, *simultaneously* interdisciplinary and transnational in character. These two aspects of its identity cannot be considered separately, especially since there is much work in Fluxus that brings these two principles together. Put differently, the concept of intermedia, to which most Fluxus work belongs, is part and parcel of its transnationalism.

Transnational Intermedia

Walter Ong provides terminology for sensory experience, which I take to be the fundamental subject matter of Events and Fluxkits, as a multinational experience, wherein social contexts shift while the idea of the sensorium (or sensing ability of human beings) remains constant. In "The Shifting Sensorium" he describes culturally unique relationships between the perceptual systems of each society:

> These relationships must not be taken merely abstractly but in connection with variations in cultures. In this connection, it is useful to think of cultures in terms of the organization of the sensorium. By the sensorium we mean the entire sensory apparatus as an operational complex. The differences in cultures which we have just suggested can be thought of as differences in the sensorium, the organization of which is in part determined by culture at the same time as it makes culture.[33]

In other words, the global context of Fluxus Events and objects suggest acculturated readings of the primary information present in them all, even though at all locations the physiological dimension of the Event is shared.

This idea—that the global sensorium suggests a transnational context for primary experience—resonates with a historic essay published by Dick Higgins in 1965 in the *Something Else Newsletter*. In the essay "Intermedia," Higgins (the founder of the press) revived a term used by Samuel Taylor Coleridge in 1812.[34] Higgins used the term *intermedia* to describe artwork that made use of structural continuities between the arts: poetry that was both read and seen as form (visual poetry), poetry that was both read and heard as sound (sound poetry), theater with musical structures inherent to it (Happenings), and all manner of other arts in between.

Significantly, he viewed this structure as having a social dimension. Working against strict categorization in the arts, intermedia would be an alternative to specialization in the arts, as well as to the national pride taken in this or that specialized art form. In other words, for Higgins intermedia work is a historic necessity, functioning in his own time as a foil for specialization of the arts, as well as the overdetermination of painting as *the* art of his time, the late 1950s—an era routinely associated with a near hegemonic dominance of American art.

> The concept of the separation of media arose in the Renaissance. The idea that a painting could be made of paint on canvas or that a sculpture should not be painted seems characteristic of the kind of social thought—categorizing and dividing society. . . which we call the feudal conception of the Great Chain of Being. However the social problems that categorize our time, as opposed to the political ones, no longer allow a compartmentalized approach.[35]

Higgins continues, "I would like to suggest that the use of intermedia is more or less universal throughout the fine arts, since continuity rather than categorization is the hallmark of our new mentality."[36]

Thirty years later, these intermedia relationships were given graphic form as the schematic "Intermedia Diagram" of 1995 (fig. 6). The hovering bubbles of the diagram (whose sizes are indeterminate) imaginarily expand, contract, pass over and through each other in a visualization of the fluidity inherent in the intermedia dynamic vis-à-vis the arts, but also

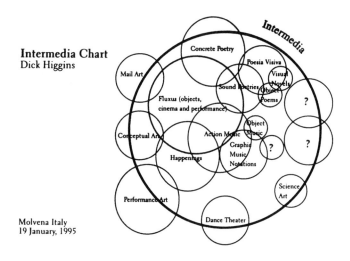

Fig. 6. Dick Higgins, "Intermedia Diagram" (1995)

suggest fluidity of locations, or artists in geographic space. Note his use of the Italian term "Poesie Visiva."

More specifically, the transnationalism of Fluxus artists practicing their work in relationship to each other does not mean that the work has the same meaning everywhere. The same works mean different things as they cross boundaries. To wit, imagine Paik performing Kosugi's *South No. 2* in New York, Japan, or Korea.[37] Similarly, Mieko (Chieko) Shiomi's *Disappearing Music for Face* (1964) is an Event with the following score: "Change gradually from a smile to no smile"[38] (fig. 7). The perceptual system used for these fine motor movements is called proprioception and involves awareness and movement of the body internally. Despite routine efforts to make the transformation as smooth as possible, the movement is always uneven. For muscles (attached to joints), "receptors discharge at a given rate for a given angle . . . and that rate changes when the angle changes."[39] It is impossible to release a smile slowly and smoothly. This is its shared, physiological dimension for performers, as well as audiences watching the piece. In fact, it is the physiology of direct, unmediated experience that all Events have in common.

From the interpretive perspective (of myself: a Western, white, mid-

Fig. 7. Mieko Shiomi's *Disappearing Music for Face* (1964)

dle-class female), however, the piece has an oddly emotional candor, for the disappearing smile seems to project a shift of mood that I commonly associate with melodrama. However, I can also imagine it performed by Shiomi in Japan, where the interpretive attachments to the piece would work differently. It might suggest a vulgar (Western?) display of teeth unbecoming to a woman in public. Moreover, in a locale with poor dental hygiene, the work might also read as a display of teeth betraying specific class, cultural, or racial associations. This latter dimension was explored by George Maciunas in a set of Fluxpost (smiles), 1978—a sheet of stamps consisting of forty-two different smiles by people of many races and means (some with all teeth, others without, and all manner of smiles in between).

    The same sort of interpretive range exists for virtually every Event as it passes through contexts, even though there is a physiological basis for the smile that is shared by the performer and audience alike. This may explain the technological simplicity of the Event format itself. It certainly explains some of why Fluxus has been interpreted in a multitude of ways at the different locations where it is found. In all, the Event belongs to Ong's global sensorium. The Event's basis in everyday life locates it in the sensate categories shared by all human beings. That these have different cultural frameworks throughout the world goes without saying. Nevertheless, some aspect of their informational structures, their ontology, remains constant in space and time. The maps of Fluxus artists reflect this shared community established by the coordination of primary sensations and the cultural productions that have brought them to pass.

In conclusion, it might be argued that Fluxus Events and kits, the paintings and correspondences of the artists, represent just so much crazy knowledge (i.e., without order), or a mere pataphysics (the science of exceptions). While no single chronological or political framework is common to all Fluxus work, it can be said with some accuracy that communitarian feeling in the form of actions and exchanges against political, geographic, and culturally mediated norms is endemic to Fluxus. Insofar as this work is un-systematic, it is real or natural—part of an ever-changing domain of human engagement with the environment. This movement, or flux, is expressed in the structures of art and transnational exchange inherent to Fluxus. In the words of Plotinus, III.4.6 "Even before reason there is the inward movement which reaches out to its own." Reaching out to its own, flux extends to flux.us in whatever form.

Notes

1. Hannah Higgins, *Fluxus Experience* (Berkeley and Los Angeles: University of California Press, 2002).

2. Ken Friedman, "Fluxus and Company," in *The Fluxus Reader*, ed. Ken Friedman (West Sussex, Eng.: Academy Editions, 1998), 242. This essay originally appeared with the exhibition *Fluxus and Company* at Emily Harvey Gallery, New York, 1989.

3. Ibid.

4. Dick Higgins, "Fluxus Theory and Reception," in Friedman, *The Fluxus Reader*, 224. This essay was written in Berlin in March 1982 and revised in April 1985. It was published in "Fluxus Theory and Reception," in *Fluxus Research,* special issue of Lund Art Press, vol. 2, no. 2 (1991). The version printed here also appeared in Dick Higgins, *Modernism Since Postmodernism* (San Diego: San Diego State University Press, 1997). The nine points are (1) internationalism, (2) experimentalism and iconoclasm, (3) intermedia, (4) minimalism or concentration, (5) an attempted resolution of the art/life dichotomy, (6) implicativeness, (7) play or gags, (8) ephemerality, and (9) specificity.

5. Ibid.

6. This is described in detail in David Revill, *The Roaring Silence* (New York: Arcade Publishing, 1992), 203.

7. The centrality of the center in establishing transnational relationships to the

United States and Europe is described in some detail in Alexandra Monroe, "Circle: Modernism and Tradition," in *Japanese Art after 1945: Scream against the Sky* (New York: Abrams, 1994), 128.

8. For details on this period, see Robert von Zahn, "'Refusierte Gesänge,' Musik im Atelier Bauermeister," in *Intermedial, Kontrovers, Experimentell: Das Atelier Mary Bauermeister in Köln 1960–62* (Cologne: Emons Verlag, 1993).

9. Wilfried Dörstel, Rainer Steinberg, and Robert von Zahn, "The Bauermeister Studio: Proto-Fluxus in Cologne, 1960–62," in *Fluxus Virus*, ed. Ken Friedman (Cologne: Gallerie Schüppenhauer, 1992), 56.

10. Ibid.

11. George Brecht, Solo for Violin, Viola, Cello or Contrabass (1962), in *Fluxus Performance Workbook*, ed. Ken Friedman, special issue of *El Djarida* (1980): 16. Many, if not most, early Events are reprinted as scores in this workbook.

12. Milan Knizak, "Snowstorm No. 1" (1965), in Friedman, *Fluxus Performance Workbook*, 29.

13. Michael Kirby and Richard Schechner, "An Interview with John Cage," in *Tulane Drama Review (TDR)* 10.2 (1965): 58.

14. A copy of this program can be found at the Gilbert and Lila Silvermann Collection Archive, New York.

15. Owen Smith, *Fluxus: The History of an Attitude* (San Diego: San Diego State University Press, 1998), 11.

16. Postcard in Gilbert and Lila Silverman Fluxus Collection Archive, New York, dated to 1975. This was part of Maciunas's Flux Combat against Lawrence A Ravitz, the Attorney General of New York City.

17. During the years 1967–68, the collective purchased eight buildings in what is now known as SoHo.

18. These three proposals are held at the Gilbert and Lila Silverman Fluxus Collection Archive and are reprinted in *Fluxus, etc., Addenda 1*, ed. Jon Hendricks (New York: Ink &, 1983), 246–82, quotation, 260.

19. Artists' statement, "About the Map Paintings," 1991, copies in the Dick Higgins Collection, Northwestern University.

20. This list comes from Maciunas's call for contributions in *Fluxnewsletter*, April 1973.

21. Robert Filliou, *Teaching and Learning as Performance Arts* (Cologne: Koening Verlag, 1970), 196.

22. Friedman, *Fluxus Performance Workbook*, 23.

23. Hannah Higgins and Jeff Abel, eds., *A Dick Higgins Sampler* (Chicago: Columbia College Center for Book and Paper Arts, 2001), 9. This score was also published in John Cage, *Notations* (New York: Something Else Press, 1969), unpaginated alphabetical listing.

24. Friedman, *Fluxus Performance Workbook*, 15.

25. Ibid., 40.

26. Ibid, 57.

27. Ibid., 57.

28. Emmett Williams, *My Life in Flux—and Vice Versa* (London: Thames and Hudson, 1992), 30.

29. Friedman, *Fluxus Performance Workbook*, 36.

30. Ibid., 17.

31. Ibid., 28.

32. Ibid., 24.

33. Walter Ong, "The Shifting Sensorium," in *The Varieties of Sensory Experience,* ed. David Howes (Toronto: University of Toronto Press, 1991), 28.

34. Cited in Dick Higgins, "Intermedia," *Something Else Newsletter* (1965), reprinted in *Horizons: The Poetics and Theory of the Intermedia* (Carbondale: Southern Illinois University Press, 1983). For Coleridge's use of the term, see *The Collected Works of Samuel Taylor Coleridge,* Vol. 5: *Lectures 1808–1819: On Literature,* edited by R. A. Foakes (Princeton: Princeton University Press, 1987), "Lecture 3: On Spenser."

35. Ibid.

36. Ibid., 22.

37. I have gone into some depth about this mechanism in "Fluxing Across the Sensory," the exhibition *Fluxus* at Villa Croce in Genoa, Italy.

38. Friedman, *Fluxus Performance Workbook,* 49.

39. James Jerome Gibson, *The Senses Considered as Perceptual Systems* (Boston: Houghton Mifflin, 1966), 110.

Contributors

Marvin Carlson is the Sidney E. Cohn Professor of Theatre and Comparative Literature at the Graduate Center of the City University of New York. He is the author of over one hundred articles in the areas of theater history, theater theory, and dramatic literature and the founding editor of *Western European Stages*. His work has been translated into thirteen languages. His most recent book, *The Haunted Stage* (2001), received the Joseph Calloway Prize. In 2005 he was awarded an honorary doctorate from the University of Athens.

Sudipto Chatterjee is Assistant Professor in the Department of Theater, Dance, and Performance Studies at the University of California, Berkeley. His book *The Colonial Stage(d): Woman, Nation, and Hybridity in 19th Century Bengali Theatre* is soon to be published by Seagull. He is also writing a book on Indian popular theater that will be published by Routledge. In addition, he is a playwright, director, performer, and filmmaker working both in Bengali and English. His most recent work is *Man of the Heart*, a bilingual solo-performance piece. He also has completed a documentary on *pandvani*, a traditional solo-performance genre in Central India. He is a member of the University of California Multi-campus Research Group in International Performance and Culture.

John Conteh-Morgan teaches French and Francophone African American and African Studies at Ohio State University and is editor of *Research in African Literatures*. His publications include *African Drama and Performance* (coedited with Tejumola Olaniyan, 2004), *Theatre and Drama in Francophone Africa* (1994), and translations of Paulin Hountondji's *The Struggle for Meaning: Reflections on Philosophy, Culture, and Democracy in Africa* (2002) and Louis Sala-Molins's *Dark Side of the Light: Slavery and the French Enlightenment* (2006). He is a contributor to *The Cambridge Guide to Theatre* (1995) and a contributing advisory editor for *The Oxford Encyclopedia of Theatre and Performance* (2003).

Peter Eckersall is Senior Lecturer in Theatre Studies at the University of Melbourne. His research interests include Japanese theater and culture and experimental performance movements. He is dramaturg for the contemporary performance group Not Yet It's Difficult. He has published widely on Japanese theater and is coeditor of *Alternatives: Debating Theatre Culture in an Age of Con-fusion* (2004).

Harry J. Elam, Jr., is Olive H. Palmer Professor in the Humanities and Chair of the Stanford Drama Department. He is the author of *Taking It to the Streets: The Social Protest Theater of Luis Valdez and Amiri Baraka* (1997) and *The Past as Present in the Drama of August Wilson* (2004) and coeditor of four books: *African American Performance and Theater History: A Critical Reader* (2001); *Colored Contradictions: An Anthology of Contemporary African American Drama* (1996); *The Fire This Time: African-American Plays for the Twenty-first Century* (2004); and *Black Cultural Traffic: Crossroads in Performance and Popular Culture* (2005). His articles have appeared in *American Drama, Modern Drama, Theatre Journal,* and *Text and Performance Quarterly* as well as in several critical anthologies. Professor Elam is also a past editor of *Theatre Journal* and is on the editorial boards of *Atlantic Studies, Journal of American Drama and Theatre,* and *Modern Drama.*

Joachim Fiebach is Professor Emeritus of Theatre Studies at the Humboldt-Universität zu Berlin. His current research deals with historical, comparative studies in cultural performance and theatricality. His books include *Von Craig bis Brecht* (1975, 1991), *Kunstprozesse in Afrika: Literatur im Umbruch* (1979), *Die Toten als die Macht der Lebenden: Zur Theorie und Geschichte von Theater in Afrika* (1986), *Inseln der Unordnung: Fünf Versuche zu Heiner Müllers Theatertexten* (1990), and *Keine Hoffnung Keine Verzweiflung: Versuche zur Theatralitaet und Theaterkunst* (1998). He is also the coeditor, with Antje Budde, of *Herrschaft des Symbolischen: Bewegungsformen gesellschaftlicher Theatralität Europa-Asien-Afrika* (2002) and editor of *Manifeste Europäischen Theaters: Grotowski bis Schleef* (2003).

David G. Goodman teaches Japanese literature at the University of Illinois at Urbana-Champaign. From 1969 to 1973 in Tokyo, he edited and published *Concerned Theatre Japan,* Japan's only English-language theater magazine, which is now available online. His books on modern Japanese theater include *After Apocalypse: Four Japanese Plays of Hiroshima and Nagasaki* (1994), *The Return of the Gods: Japanese Drama and Culture in the 1960s* (1988), and *Angura: Posters of the Japanese Avant-Garde* (1999). His CD-ROM, *Concerned Theatre Japan: The Graphic Art of Japanese Theatre, 1960 to 1980,* won a New York Art Directors Club Silver Medal in 1999.

Jean Graham-Jones is Associate Professor of Theatre at the City University of New York. Her recent publications include *Exorcising History: Argentine Theater under Dictatorship* (2000) and *Reason Obscured: Nine Plays by Ricardo Monti* (ed. and trans., 2004). She is currently the editor of *Theatre Journal*.

James M. Harding is Associate Professor of English at the University of Mary Washington. He is coeditor (with Cindy Rosenthal) of *Re-Staging the Sixties: Radical Theaters and Their Legacies* (2006) and editor of *Contours of the Theatrical Avant-Garde: Performance and Textuality* (2000). He is a former editor of *Theatre Survey* and is the author of *Adorno and a Writing of the Ruins: Essays on Anglo-American Literature and Culture* (1997).

Hannah Higgins lectures internationally on Fluxus, the avant-garde, interdisciplinary art movements, and material culture. She received her Ph.D. in art history from the University of Chicago in 1994 and is Associate Professor in the art history department at the University of Illinois at Chicago. She is the author of many journal articles and book chapters and of the book *Fluxus Experience* (2002). She is currently writing *Life of the Grid,* to be published by MIT Press. She is the daughter of Fluxus artists Dick Higgins and Alison Knowles.

John Rouse is Associate Professor at the University of California, San Diego. He is the author of *Brecht and the West-German Theatre: The Practice and Politics of Interpretation* (1989) and numerous articles on German theater, Robert Wilson, and other topics. He is one of the editors of *TheatreForum* and a past editor of *Theatre Journal.* He is a member of the University of California Multicampus Research Group in International Performance and Culture.

Adam Versényi is a scholar, critic, and translator of Latin American theater. His books include *The Theater of Sabina Berman: The Agony of Ecstasy and Other Plays* (2003), *Dictionary of Literary Biography: Latin American Dramatists* (ed.) (2005), and *Theatre in Latin America: Religion, Politics, and Culture from Cortes to the 1980s* (1993). He is Professor of Dramaturgy and Chair of the Curriculum in International and Area Studies at the University of North Carolina at Chapel Hill and dramaturg for PlayMakers Repertory Company.

Index

Academics: American academy, 92
Acting: actor, 106, 147; actor training, 51; *al-Tamasruh,* 135; Brechtian acting, 138; pantomime, 147
Adamov, Arthur, 10, 130
Ade, Sonny, 86
Adedeji, Joel, 77, 79
Adellach, Alberto, 177
Adorno, Theodor, 14, 230
Aesthetics, 228, 229; aesthetic categories, 6; aestheticism, 93; and Americas, 146; and decadence, 92; European, 146; experimental, 169; and ideology, 147; Latin American, 146; Meyerholdian, 160; minimalism, 192; non-European, 34; nonillusionism, 114; non-Western, 42; radical aesthetics, 10, 92, 102; Stanislavskian, 160; Western, 42. *See also under* avant-garde
Africa, 11, 34, 44; and African elite, 100; Arabic North Africa, 139; art in, 44; avant-garde's interest in, 70; Bambara, 86; Benin, 70; Eastern Africa, 80, 81; European influence in, 81; Francophone Africa, 35, 94; Guinea, 75; African identities, 81; Ivory Coast, 96; Kenya, 80; and *Mambo Leo,* 82; and mombasa, 80; Morocco, 139; and pan-Africanism, 116; and African performance, 10, 68, 71, 80; and African poetry, 18; separatist churches of, 95; South Africa, 96; Sundiata, 75; Swahili, 75, 80, 81; Tanganyika, 82; theatrical cultures, 111; Tunisia, 139; University College Dar es Salaam, 82, 83; Univer-

sity of Eastern Africa, 82; Zulu, 83. *See also under* colonialism; Congo; Lega; Niger Delta; Nigeria; Sub-Sahara; Tanzania; Yoruba
Alba, Luz, 161
Albee, Edward, 51
Alexander the Great, 128
Al-Ashqar, Nidaal, 140
Al-Dawi, Sayyid, 142; *Ghazir el-Leil (Tides of Night),* 141
Al-Hamadhani, Badi Al-Zamman, 139
Al-Hakim, Tawfiq, 10, 137, 139, 142; *Ahl al Kahf (The Sleepers in the Cave),* 129; *al-Safqa (The Deal),* 138; *al-Zammar (The Piper),* 138; on Egyptian experimental theater, 130; *Kull Shay' fi Mahallih (Not a Thing Out of Place),* 131; *Masir Sarsar (The Fate of a Cockroach),* 131; *Qalabuna al-Masrahi (Our Theatrical Form),* 138; *Rihlat Qitar (A Train Journey),* 131; *Ya Tali al-Shajara (The Tree Climber),* 129, 131, 132, 135, 138
Al-Kassir, Ali, 134
Al-Katib, 132, 134
Al-Kumi, Ahmed, 141
Al-Majdoub, Abdul Rahman, 139
Al-Majdoub, Abderrahman, 139
Al-Naqqash, Marun, 126; *al Baknil,* 126
Al-Rai, Ali, *The Art of Comedy from Shadow Plays to al-Rihani,* 133, 134
Al-Rihani, Najib, 134
Al-Siddiqi, al-Tayyeb, 133; and *Masrah Annass (People's Theater),* 139